enVisionmath2.0

Volume 1 Topics 1–7

Authors

Randall I. Charles
Professor Emeritus
Department of Mathematics
San Jose State University
San Jose, California

Jennifer Bay-Williams
Professor of Mathematics Education
College of Education and Human Development
University of Louisville
Louisville, Kentucky

Robert Q. Berry, III
Associate Professor of Mathematics Education
Department of Curriculum, Instruction and Special Education
University of Virginia
Charlottesville, Virginia

Janet H. Caldwell
Professor of Mathematics
Rowan University
Glassboro, New Jersey

Zachary Champagne
Assistant in Research
Florida Center for Research in Science, Technology, Engineering, and Mathematics (FCR-STEM)
Jacksonville, Florida

Juanita Copley
Professor Emerita, College of Education
University of Houston
Houston, Texas

Warren Crown
Professor Emeritus of Mathematics Education
Graduate School of Education
Rutgers University
New Brunswick, New Jersey

Francis (Skip) Fennell
L. Stanley Bowlsbey Professor of Education and Graduate and Professional Studies
McDaniel College
Westminster, Maryland

Karen Karp
Professor of Mathematics Education
Department of Early Childhood and Elementary Education
University of Louisville
Louisville, Kentucky

Stuart J. Murphy
Visual Learning Specialist
Boston, Massachusetts

Jane F. Schielack
Professor of Mathematics
Associate Dean for Assessment and Pre K-12 Education, College of Science
Texas A&M University
College Station, Texas

Jennifer M. Suh
Associate Professor for Mathematics Education
George Mason University
Fairfax, Virginia

Jonathan A. Wray
Mathematics Instructional Facilitator
Howard County Public Schools
Ellicott City, Maryland

Mathematicians

Roger Howe
Professor of Mathematics
Yale University
New Haven, Connecticut

Gary Lippman
Professor of Mathematics and Computer Science
California State University, East Bay
Hayward, California

ELL Consultants

Janice R. Corona
Independent Education Consultant
Dallas, Texas

Jim Cummins
Professor
The University of Toronto
Toronto, Canada

Savvas Learning Company LLC, 15 East Midland Avenue, Paramus, NJ 07652

ISBN-13: 978-0-328-89111-5
ISBN-10: 0-328-89111-8

11 2022

Digital Resources

You'll be using these digital resources throughout the year!

Go to SavvasRealize.com

MP

Math Processes Animations to play anytime

Solve

Solve & Share problems plus math tools

Learn

Visual Learning Animation Plus with animation, interaction, and math tools

Glossary

Animated Glossary in English and Spanish

Practice Buddy

Online Personalized Practice for each lesson

Tools

Math Tools to help you understand

Assessment

Quick Check for each lesson

Help

Another Look Homework Video for extra help

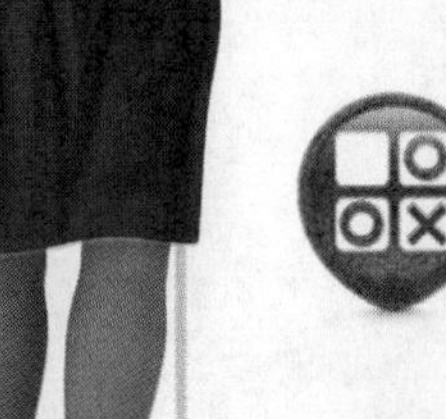

Games

Math Games to help you learn

eText

Student Edition online

ACTIVe-book

Student Edition online for showing your work

SAVVAS realize™ Everything you need for math anytime, anywhere

Hi, we're here to help you.
Let's have a great year!

Contents

Digital Resources at SavvasRealize.com

And remember, your eText is available at SavvasRealize.com!

TOPICS

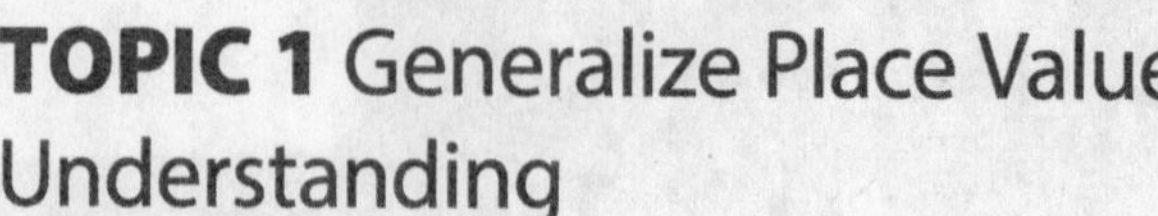

TOPIC 1 Generalize Place Value Understanding

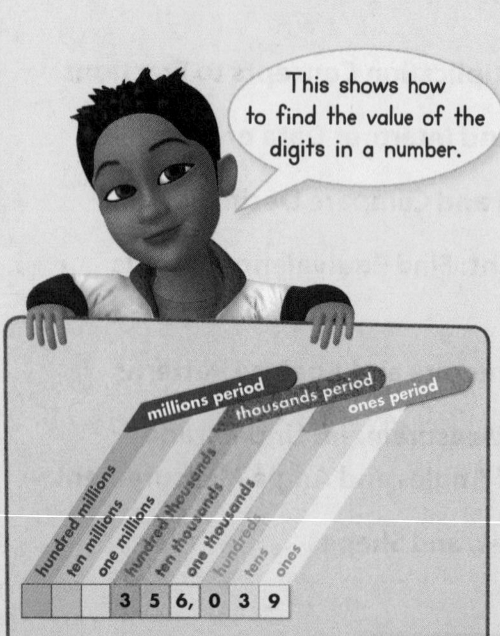

TOPIC 2 Fluently Add and Subtract Multi-Digit Whole Numbers

This shows one way to add whole numbers.

$$\begin{array}{r} \scriptstyle 1\ 1 \\ 9{,}263 \\ +\ 7{,}951 \\ \hline 17{,}214 \end{array}$$

TOPIC 3 Use Strategies and Properties to Multiply by 1-Digit Numbers

*Lesson exclusively for Indiana at the end of this volume

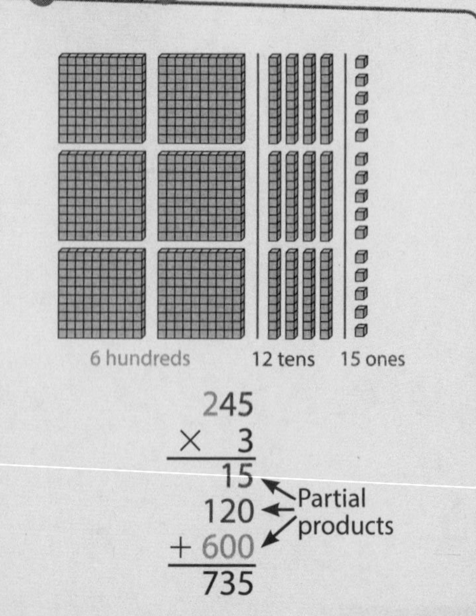

TOPIC 4 Use Strategies and Properties to Multiply by 2-Digit Numbers

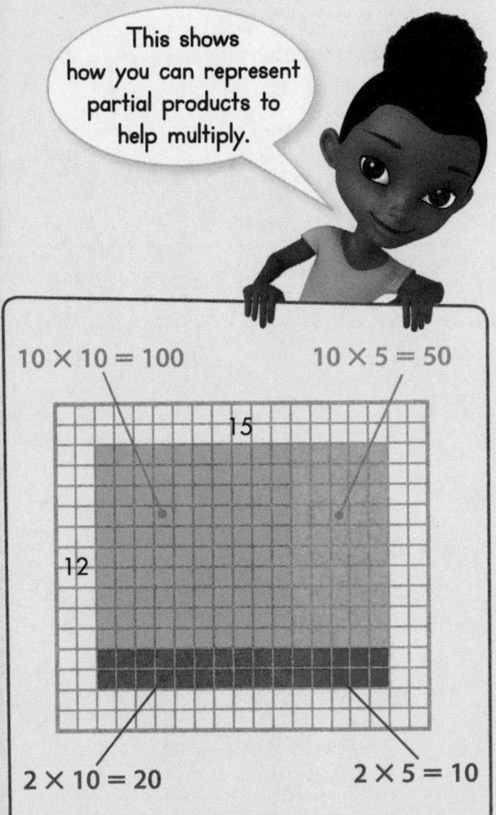

This shows how place value can help you divide.
13 R3
4)55
− 4
15
− 12
3

TOPIC 5 Use Strategies and Properties to Divide by 1-Digit Numbers

TOPIC 6 Use Operations with Whole Numbers to Solve Problems

This shows how you can represent a comparison situation.
42
3
n times as many

TOPIC 7 Factors and Multiples

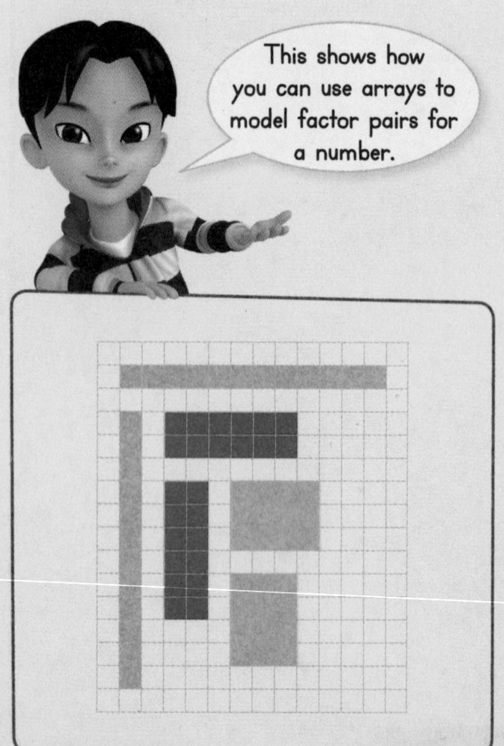

This shows how you can use arrays to model factor pairs for a number.

KEY

- Critical Content
- Important Content
- Additional Content

Grade 4 Indiana Standards

Indiana Mathematics Standards

NUMBER SENSE

4.NS.1 Read and write whole numbers up to 1,000,000. Use words, models, standard form and expanded form to represent and show equivalent forms of whole numbers up to 1,000,000.

4.NS.2 Compare two whole numbers up to 1,000,000 using $>$, $=$, and $<$ symbols.

4.NS.3 Express whole numbers as fractions and recognize fractions that are equivalent to whole numbers. Name and write mixed numbers using objects or pictures. Name and write mixed numbers as improper fractions using objects or pictures.

4.NS.4 Explain why a fraction, $\frac{a}{b}$, is equivalent to a fraction, $\frac{(n \times a)}{(n \times b)}$, by using visual fraction models, with attention to how the number and size of the parts differ even though the two fractions themselves are the same size. Use this principle to recognize and generate equivalent fractions. [In grade 4, limit denominators of fractions to 2, 3, 4, 5, 6, 8, 10, 25, 100.]

4.NS.5 Compare two fractions with different numerators and different denominators (e.g., by creating common denominators or numerators, or by comparing to a benchmark, such as 0, $\frac{1}{2}$, and 1). Recognize comparisons are valid only when the two fractions refer to the same whole. Record the results of comparisons with symbols $>$, $=$, or $<$, and justify the conclusions (e.g., by using a visual fraction model).

4.NS.6 Write tenths and hundredths in decimal and fraction notations. Use words, models, standard form and expanded form to represent decimal numbers to hundredths. Know the fraction and decimal equivalents for halves and fourths (e.g., $\frac{1}{2} = 0.5 = 0.50$, $\frac{7}{4} = 1\frac{3}{4} = 1.75$).

4.NS.7 Compare two decimals to hundredths by reasoning about their size based on the same whole. Record the results of comparisons with the symbols $>$, $=$, or $<$, and justify the conclusions (e.g., by using a visual model).

4.NS.8 Find all factor pairs for a whole number in the range 1–100. Recognize that a whole number is a multiple of each of its factors. Determine whether a given whole number in the range 1–100 is a multiple of a given one-digit number.

4.NS.9 Use place value understanding to round multi-digit whole numbers to any given place value.

Dear Families,

The standards on the following pages describe the math that students will learn this year.

Critical Content Important Content Additional Content

Indiana Mathematics Standards

COMPUTATION

4.C.1 Add and subtract multi-digit whole numbers fluently using a standard algorithmic approach.

4.C.2 Multiply a whole number of up to four digits by a one-digit whole number and multiply two two-digit numbers, using strategies based on place value and the properties of operations. Describe the strategy and explain the reasoning.

4.C.3 Find whole-number quotients and remainders with up to four-digit dividends and one-digit divisors, using strategies based on place value, the properties of operations, and/or the relationship between multiplication and division. Describe the strategy and explain the reasoning.

4.C.4 Multiply fluently within 100.

4.C.5 Add and subtract fractions with common denominators. Decompose a fraction into a sum of fractions with common denominators. Understand addition and subtraction of fractions as combining and separating parts referring to the same whole.

4.C.6 Add and subtract mixed numbers with common denominators (e.g. by replacing each mixed number with an equivalent fraction and/or by using properties of operations and the relationship between addition and subtraction).

4.C.7 Show how the order in which two numbers are multiplied (commutative property) and how numbers are grouped in multiplication (associative property) will not change the product. Use these properties to show that numbers can by multiplied in any order. Understand and use the distributive property.

ALGEBRAIC THINKING

4.AT.1 Solve real-world problems involving addition and subtraction of multi-digit whole numbers (e.g., by using drawings and equations with a symbol for the unknown number to represent the problem).

4.AT.2 Recognize and apply the relationships between addition and multiplication, between subtraction and division, and the inverse relationship between multiplication and division to solve real-world and other mathematical problems.

4.AT.3 Interpret a multiplication equation as a comparison (e.g., interpret $35 = 5 \times 7$ as a statement that 35 is 5 times as many as 7, and 7 times as many as 5). Represent verbal statements of multiplicative comparisons as multiplication equations.

4.AT.4 Solve real-world problems with whole numbers involving multiplicative comparison (e.g., by using drawings and equations with a symbol for the unknown number to represent the problem), distinguishing multiplicative comparison from additive comparison. [In grade 4, division problems should not include a remainder.]

4.AT.5 Solve real-world problems involving addition and subtraction of fractions referring to the same whole and having common denominators (e.g., by using visual fraction models and equations to represent the problem).

4.AT.6 Understand that an equation, such as $y = 3x + 5$, is a rule to describe a relationship between two variables and can be used to find a second number when a first number is given. Generate a number pattern that follows a given rule.

GEOMETRY

4.G.1 Identify, describe, and draw parallelograms, rhombuses, and trapezoids using appropriate tools (e.g., ruler, straightedge and technology).

4.G.2 Recognize and draw lines of symmetry in two-dimensional figures. Identify figures that have lines of symmetry.

4.G.3 Recognize angles as geometric shapes that are formed wherever two rays share a common endpoint.

4.G.4 Identify, describe, and draw rays, angles (right, acute, obtuse), and perpendicular and parallel lines using appropriate tools (e.g., ruler, straightedge and technology). Identify these in two-dimensional figures.

4.G.5 Classify triangles and quadrilaterals based on the presence or absence of parallel or perpendicular lines, or the presence or absence of angles (right, acute, obtuse).

Indiana Mathematics Standards

MEASUREMENT

4.M.1 Measure length to the nearest quarter-inch, eighth-inch, and millimeter.

4.M.2 Know relative sizes of measurement units within one system of units, including km, m, cm; kg, g; lb, oz; l, ml; hr, min, sec. Express measurements in a larger unit in terms of a smaller unit within a single system of measurement. Record measurement equivalents in a two- column table.

4.M.3 Use the four operations (addition, subtraction, multiplication and division) to solve real-world problems involving distances, intervals of time, volumes, masses of objects, and money. Include addition and subtraction problems involving simple fractions and problems that require expressing measurements given in a larger unit in terms of a smaller unit.

4.M.4 Apply the area and perimeter formulas for rectangles to solve real-world problems and other mathematical problems. Recognize area as additive and find the area of complex shapes composed of rectangles by decomposing them into non-overlapping rectangles and adding the areas of the non-overlapping parts; apply this technique to solve real-world problems and other mathematical problems.

4.M.5 Understand that an angle is measured with reference to a circle, with its center at the common endpoint of the rays, by considering the fraction of the circular arc between the points where the two rays intersect the circle. Understand an angle that turns through $\frac{1}{360}$ of a circle is called a "one-degree angle," and can be used to measure other angles. Understand an angle that turns through n one-degree angles is said to have an angle measure of n degrees.

4.M.6 Measure angles in whole-number degrees using appropriate tools. Sketch angles of specified measure.

Indiana Mathematics Standards

DATA ANALYSIS

4.DA.1 Formulate questions that can be addressed with data. Use observations, surveys, and experiments to collect, represent, and interpret the data using tables (including frequency tables), line plots, and bar graphs.

4.DA.2 Make a line plot to display a data set of measurements in fractions of a unit ($\frac{1}{2}$, $\frac{1}{4}$, $\frac{1}{8}$). Solve problems involving addition and subtraction of fractions by using data displayed in line plots.

4.DA.3 Interpret data displayed in a circle graph.

Process Standards for Mathematics

PS.1 MAKE SENSE OF PROBLEMS AND PERSEVERE IN SOLVING THEM.

Mathematically proficient students start by explaining to themselves the meaning of a problem and looking for entry points to its solution. They analyze givens, constraints, relationships, and goals. They make conjectures about the form and meaning of the solution and plan a solution pathway, rather than simply jumping into a solution attempt. They consider analogous problems and try special cases and simpler forms of the original problem in order to gain insight into its solution. They monitor and evaluate their progress and change course if necessary. Mathematically proficient students check their answers to problems using a different method, and they continually ask themselves, "Does this make sense?" and "Is my answer reasonable?" They understand the approaches of others to solving complex problems and identify correspondences between different approaches. Mathematically proficient students understand how mathematical ideas interconnect and build on one another to produce a coherent whole.

PS.2 REASON ABSTRACTLY AND QUANTITATIVELY.

Mathematically proficient students make sense of quantities and their relationships in problem situations. They bring two complementary abilities to bear on problems involving quantitative relationships: the ability to decontextualize—to abstract a given situation and represent it symbolically and manipulate the representing symbols as if they have a life of their own, without necessarily attending to their referents—and the ability to contextualize, to pause as needed during the manipulation process in order to probe into the referents for the symbols involved. Quantitative reasoning entails habits of creating a coherent representation of the problem at hand; considering the units involved; attending to the meaning of quantities, not just how to compute them; and knowing and flexibly using different properties of operations and objects.

PS.3 CONSTRUCT VIABLE ARGUMENTS AND CRITIQUE THE REASONING OF OTHERS.

Mathematically proficient students understand and use stated assumptions, definitions, and previously established results in constructing arguments. They make conjectures and build a logical progression of statements to explore the truth of their conjectures. They analyze situations by breaking them into cases and recognize and use counterexamples. They organize their mathematical thinking, justify their conclusions and communicate them to others, and respond to the arguments of others. They reason inductively about data, making plausible arguments that take into account the context from which the data arose. Mathematically proficient students are also able to compare the effectiveness of two plausible arguments, distinguish correct logic or reasoning from that which is flawed, and—if there is a flaw in an argument—explain what it is. They justify whether a given statement is true always, sometimes, or never. Mathematically proficient students participate and collaborate in a mathematics community. They listen to or read the arguments of others, decide whether they make sense, and ask useful questions to clarify or improve the arguments.

PS.4 MODEL WITH MATHEMATICS.

Mathematically proficient students apply the mathematics they know to solve problems arising in everyday life, society, and the workplace using a variety of appropriate strategies. They create and use a variety of representations to solve problems and to organize and communicate mathematical ideas. Mathematically proficient students apply what they know and are comfortable making assumptions and approximations to simplify a complicated situation, realizing that these may need revision later. They are able to identify important quantities in a practical situation and map their relationships using such tools as diagrams, two-way tables, graphs, flowcharts and formulas. They analyze those relationships mathematically to draw conclusions. They routinely interpret their mathematical results in the context of the situation and reflect on whether the results make sense, possibly improving the model if it has not served its purpose.

PS.5 USE APPROPRIATE TOOLS STRATEGICALLY.

Mathematically proficient students consider the available tools when solving a mathematical problem. These tools might include pencil and paper, models, a ruler, a protractor, a calculator, a spreadsheet, a computer algebra system, a statistical package,

Process Standards for Mathematics

or dynamic geometry software. Mathematically proficient students are sufficiently familiar with tools appropriate for their grade or course to make sound decisions about when each of these tools might be helpful, recognizing both the insight to be gained and their limitations. Mathematically proficient students identify relevant external mathematical resources, such as digital content, and use them to pose or solve problems. They use technological tools to explore and deepen their understanding of concepts and to support the development of learning mathematics. They use technology to contribute to concept development, simulation, representation, reasoning, communication and problem solving.

PS.6 ATTEND TO PRECISION.

Mathematically proficient students communicate precisely to others. They use clear definitions, including correct mathematical language, in discussion with others and in their own reasoning. They state the meaning of the symbols they choose, including using the equal sign consistently and appropriately. They express solutions clearly and logically by using the appropriate mathematical terms and notation. They specify units of measure and label axes to clarify the correspondence with quantities in a problem. They calculate accurately and efficiently and check the validity of their results in the context of the problem. They express numerical answers with a degree of precision appropriate for the problem context.

PS.7 LOOK FOR AND MAKE USE OF STRUCTURE.

Mathematically proficient students look closely to discern a pattern or structure. They step back for an overview and shift perspective. They recognize and use properties of operations and equality. They organize and classify geometric shapes based on their attributes. They see expressions, equations, and geometric figures as single objects or as being composed of several objects.

PS.8 LOOK FOR AND EXPRESS REGULARITY IN REPEATED REASONING.

Mathematically proficient students notice if calculations are repeated and look for general methods and shortcuts. They notice regularity in mathematical problems and their work to create a rule or formula. Mathematically proficient students maintain oversight of the process, while attending to the details as they solve a problem. They continually evaluate the reasonableness of their intermediate results.

Problem Solving Handbook

Math processes are ways we think about and do math.

Math processes will help you solve problems.

Problem Solving Handbook

Math Processes

1 Make sense of problems and persevere in solving them.

2 Reason abstractly and quantitatively.

3 Construct viable arguments and critique the reasoning of others.

4 Model with mathematics.

5 Use appropriate tools strategically.

6 Attend to precision.

7 Look for and make use of structure.

8 Look for and express regularity in repeated reasoning.

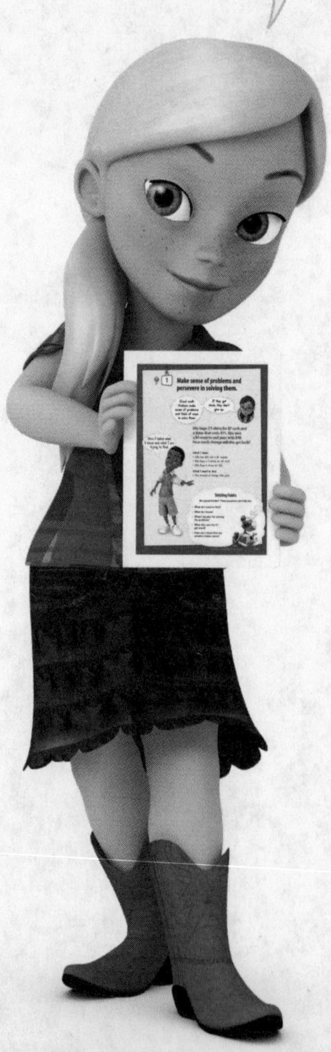

There are good Thinking Habits for each of these math processes.

Make sense of problems and persevere in solving them.

Good math thinkers make sense of problems and think of ways to solve them.

If they get stuck, they don't give up.

Mia buys 2 T-shirts for $7 each and a dress that costs $15. She uses a $4 coupon and pays with $40. How much change will Mia get back?

Here I listed what I know and what I am trying to find.

What I Know:

- Mia has $40 and a $4 coupon.
- Mia buys 2 T-shirts for $7 each.
- Mia buys a dress for $15.

What I need to find:

- The amount of change Mia gets.

Thinking Habits

Be a good thinker! These questions can help you.

- What do I need to find?
- What do I know?
- What's my plan for solving the problem?
- What else can I try if I get stuck?
- How can I check that my solution makes sense?

MP
2

Reason abstractly and quantitatively.

Good math thinkers know how to think about words and numbers to solve problems.

I drew a bar diagram that shows how things in the problem are related.

Sam buys a box of 6 thank you cards that costs $12. How much does each thank you card cost?

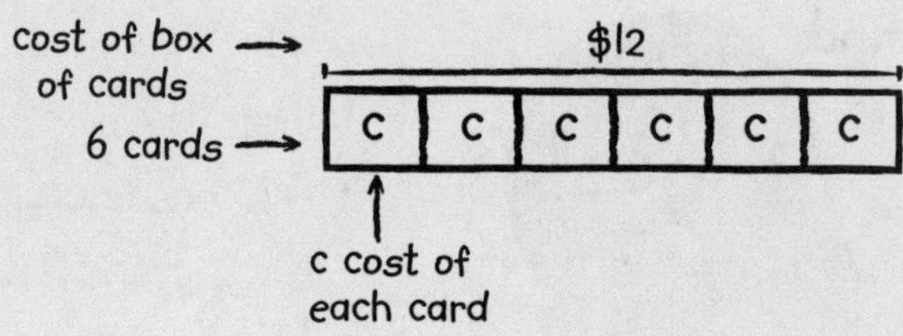
cost of box of cards
$12
6 cards
c c c c c c
c cost of each card

$12 ÷ 6 = c

Each card costs $2.

Thinking Habits

Be a good thinker! These questions can help you.

- What do the numbers and symbols in the problem mean?
- How are the numbers or quantities related?
- How can I represent a word problem using pictures, numbers, or equations?

Construct viable arguments and critique the reasoning of others.

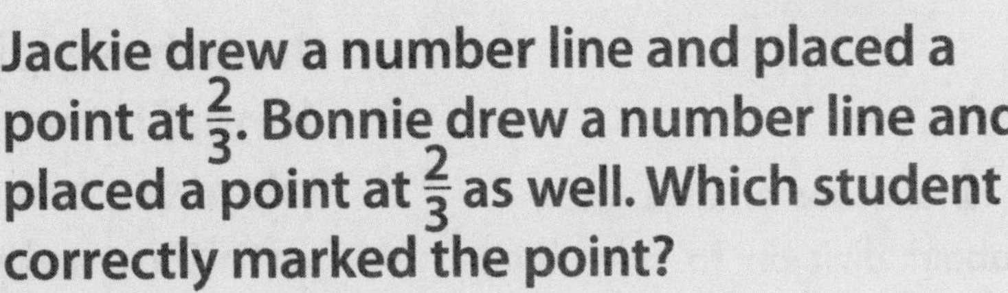

Good math thinkers use math to explain why they are right. They can talk about the math that others do, too.

I wrote a clear argument with words, numbers, and symbols.

Jackie drew a number line and placed a point at $\frac{2}{3}$. Bonnie drew a number line and placed a point at $\frac{2}{3}$ as well. Which student correctly marked the point?

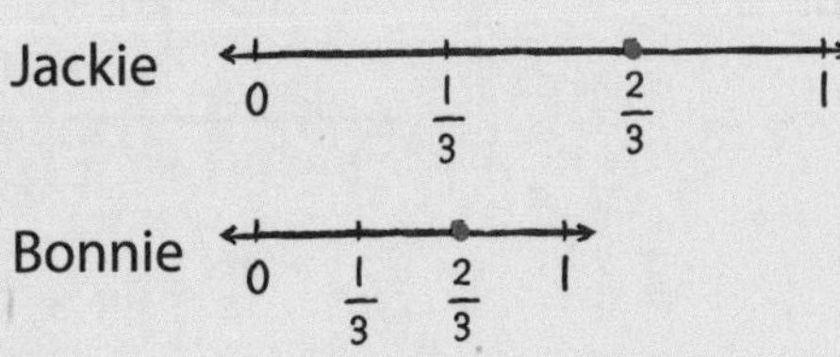

$\frac{2}{3}$ is correctly marked on both number lines. The two number lines are different lengths, but both show three equal parts.

Thinking Habits

Be a good thinker! These questions can help you.

- How can I use numbers, objects, drawings, or actions to justify my argument?
- Am I using numbers and symbols correctly?
- Is my explanation clear and complete?
- What questions can I ask to understand other people's thinking?
- Are there mistakes in other people's thinking?
- Can I improve other people's thinking?

Model with mathematics.

Good math thinkers choose and apply math they know to show and solve problems from everyday life.

I can use what I know about division to solve this problem. I can draw a picture to help.

Josie has a piece of twine that is 45 feet long. She wants to use the twine to tie up plants in her garden. If Josie cuts the twine into 9 equal pieces, how long is each piece?

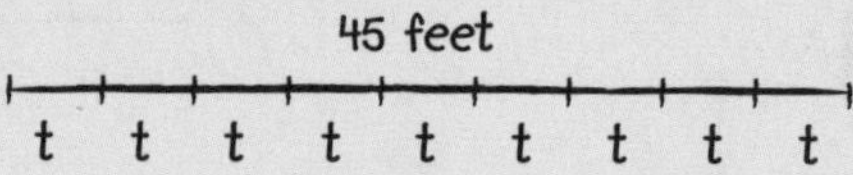

$45 \div 9 = t$

Each piece of twine is 5 feet long.

Thinking Habits

Be a good thinker! These questions can help you.

- How can I use math I know to help solve this problem?
- How can I use pictures, objects, or an equation to represent the problem?
- How can I use numbers, words, and symbols to solve the problem?

Use appropriate tools strategically.

Good math thinkers know how to pick the right tools to solve math problems.

I decided to use counters because I could make an array to solve the problem.

Hank has $13 in his wallet. He earns $15 more for mowing a lawn. He would like to download movies that cost $7 each. How many movies can Hank download? Choose a tool to represent and solve the problem.

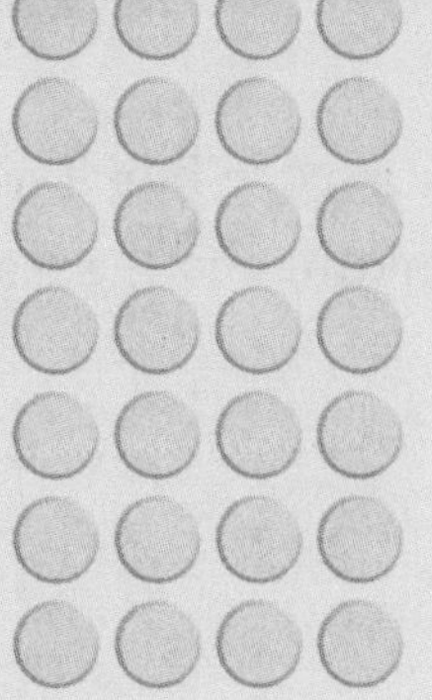

$13 + $15 = $28
$28 ÷ $7 = 4
Hank can download 4 movies.

Thinking Habits

Be a good thinker! These questions can help you.

- Which tools can I use?
- Why should I use this tool to help me solve the problem?
- Is there a different tool I could use?
- Am I using the tool appropriately?

Attend to precision.

Good math thinkers are careful about what they write and say, so their ideas about math are clear.

I was precise with my work and the way that I wrote my solution.

Write three clues to describe a square.

Clue 1: I have 4 right angles.

Clue 2: I have four sides that are the same length.

Clue 3: I have 2 sets of sides that are parallel.

A square has 4 right angles, 4 sides with the same length, and 2 sets of parallel sides.

Thinking Habits

Be a good thinker! These questions can help you.

- Am I using numbers, units, and symbols appropriately?
- Am I using the correct definitions?
- Am I calculating accurately?
- Is my answer clear?

Look for and make use of structure.

Good math thinkers look for relationships in math to help solve problems.

I used what I know about basic facts to solve the problem.

Use <, >, or = to compare the expressions without calculating.

$3 \times 6 \bigcirc 3 \times 9$

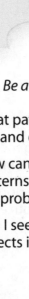

Thinking Habits

Be a good thinker! These questions can help you.

- What patterns can I see and describe?
- How can I use the patterns to solve the problem?
- Can I see expressions and objects in different ways?

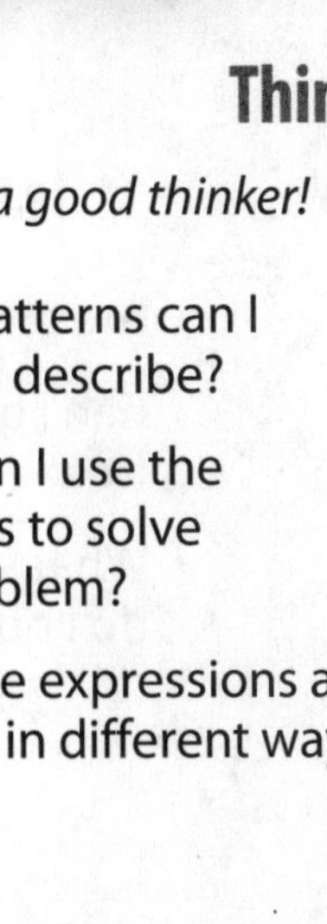

MP
8

Look for and express regularity in repeated reasoning.

Good math thinkers look for things that repeat, and they make generalizations.

I used reasoning to generalize about calculations.

Cathy has arranged some shells in two different ways. One array has 2 rows with 6 shells in each row. The other array has 6 rows with 2 shells in each row. Do both arrays have the same number of shells? Explain.

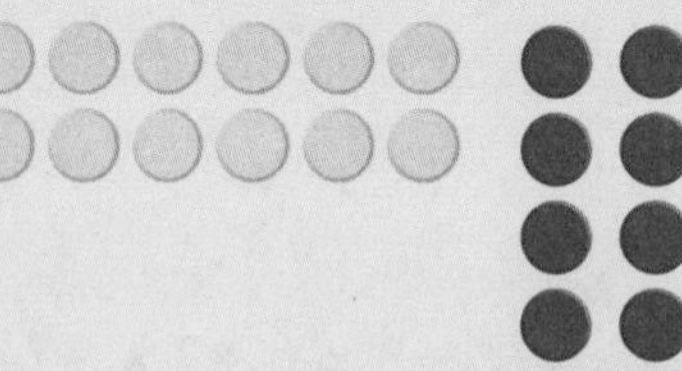

Yes, both arrays have the same number of counters. The arrays are the same except that the number of shells in the rows and columns are reversed.

Thinking Habits

Be a good thinker! These questions can help you.

- Are any calculations repeated?
- Can I generalize from examples?
- What shortcuts do I notice?

Problem Solving Handbook

Problem Solving Guide

These questions can help you solve problems.

Make Sense of the Problem

Reason Abstractly and Quantitatively

- What do I need to find?
- What given information can I use?
- How are the quantities related?

Think About Similar Problems

- Have I solved problems like this before?

Persevere in Solving the Problem

Model with Math

- How can I use the math I know?
- How can I represent the problem?
- Is there a pattern or structure I can use?

Use Appropriate Tools Strategically

- What math tools could I use?
- How can I use those tools strategically?

Some Ways to Represent Problems

- Draw a Picture
- Make a Bar Diagram
- Make a Table or Graph
- Write an Equation

Some Math Tools

- Objects
- Grid Paper
- Rulers
- Technology
- Paper and Pencil

Check the Answer

Make Sense of the Answer

- Is my answer reasonable?

Check for Precision

- Did I check my work?
- Is my answer clear?
- Did I construct a viable argument?
- Did I generalize correctly?

Problem Solving Handbook

Problem Solving Recording Sheet

This sheet helps you organize your work.

Name Carlos

Teaching Tool 1

Problem Solving Recording Sheet

Problem
Lynda wants to buy a bike that costs $80. Her father will help by paying for $20. She will earn the rest by walking dogs. She earns $6 for each dog she walks. How many dogs does Lynda need to walk in order to have enough money for the bike?

MAKE SENSE OF THE PROBLEM

Need to Find
Number of dogs to walk

Given
Earns $6 per walk
Bike costs $80
Dad's part is $20

PERSEVERE IN SOLVING THE PROBLEM

Some Ways to Represent Problems

- ☐ Draw a Picture
- ☑ Make a Bar Diagram
- ☐ Make a Table or Graph
- ☑ Write an Equation

Some Math Tools

- ☐ Objects
- ☐ Grid Paper
- ☐ Rulers
- ☐ Technology
- ☑ Paper and Pencil

Solution and Answer

$80
$20 | d dollars
Dad's money | Lynda's money

$20 + d = 80$
Lynda must earn $60.

Money earned → $60
Dogs walked → $6 d

$60 ÷ $6 = 10
Lynda must walk 10 dogs.

CHECK THE ANSWER

I used operations that undo each other to check my work.
10 × $6 = $60 $60 + $20 = $80
My answer is reasonable.

T1

Problem Solving Handbook

Bar Diagrams

You can draw a **bar diagram** to show how the quantities in a problem are related. Then you can write an equation to solve the problem.

Add To

Draw this **bar diagram** for situations that involve *adding* to a quantity.

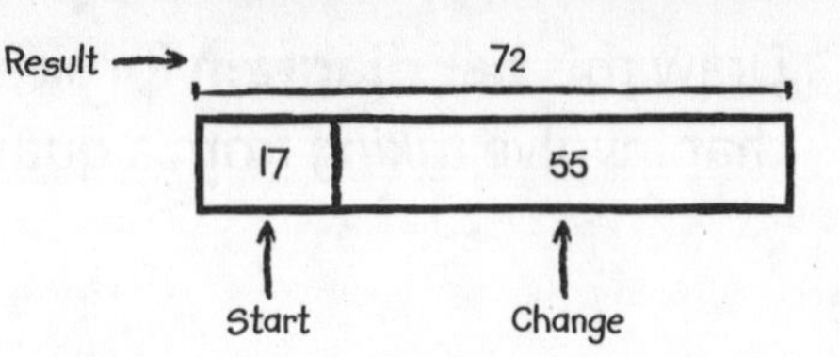

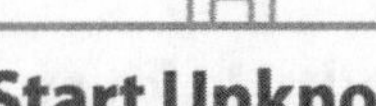

Change Unknown

Monica bought the used desk below at a yard sale. She also bought a sofa. Monica spent a total of $153. How much did she spend on the sofa?

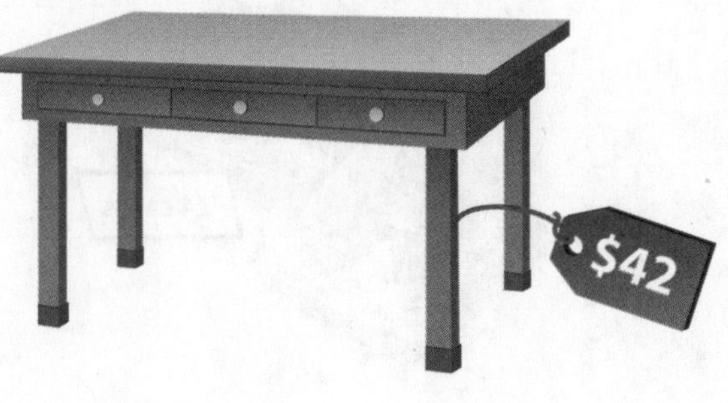

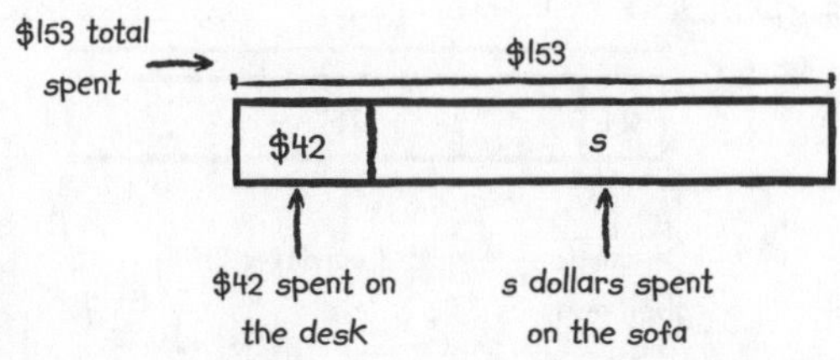

$\$42 + s = \$153$

Monica spent $111 on the sofa.

Start Unknown

Avery had some colored pencils. Then his brother gave him the pencils shown below. After that, Avery had 98 pencils. How many colored pencils did Avery start with?

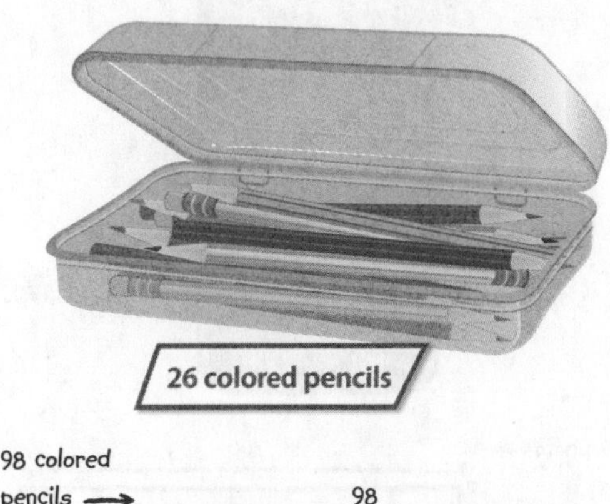

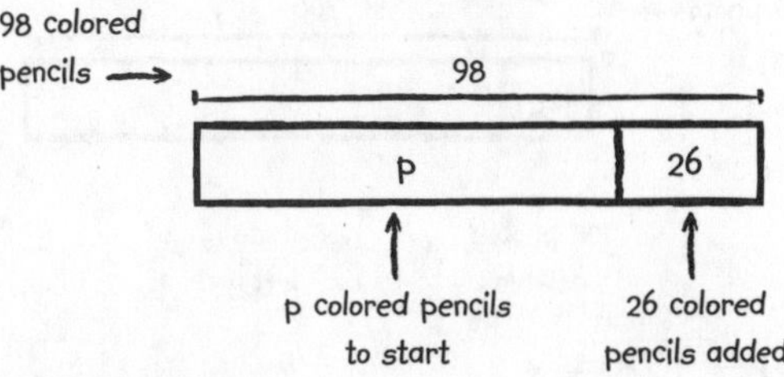

$p + 26 = 98$

Avery started with 72 colored pencils.

Problem Solving Handbook

Bar Diagrams

You can use bar diagrams to make sense of addition and subtraction problems.

Take From

Draw this **bar diagram** for situations that involve *taking* from a quantity.

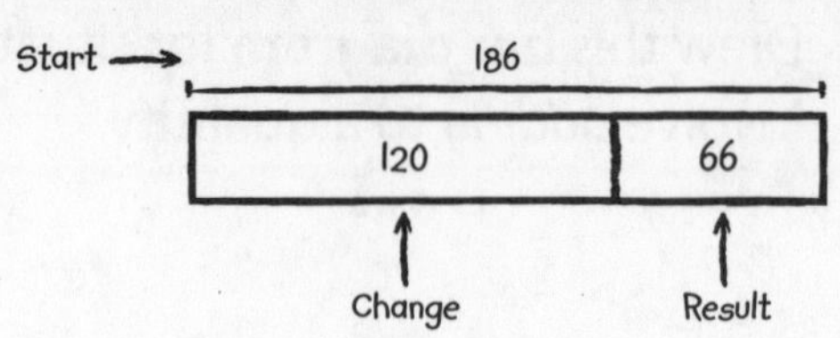

Result Unknown

The number of photos on Jenna's phone is shown below. She deleted 128 photos. How many are left?

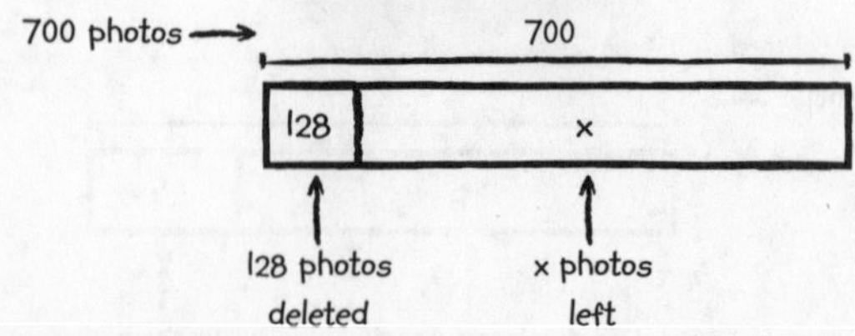

$700 - 128 = x$

Jenna has 572 photos left on her phone.

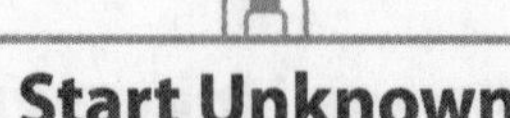

Start Unknown

Alex had a collection of baseball cards. Then he gave the cards below to his brother. Now Alex has 251 cards. How many cards did Alex have before he gave cards to his brother?

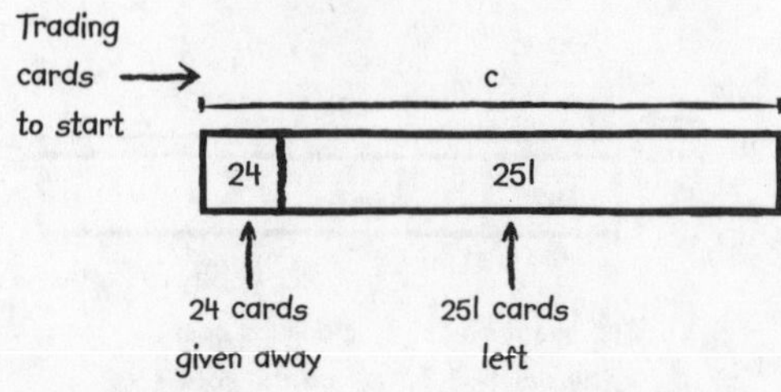

$c - 24 = 251$

Alex had 275 baseball cards before he gave the cards to his brother.

The **bar diagrams** on this page can help you make sense of more addition and subtraction situations.

Put Together/Take Apart

Draw this **bar diagram** for situations that involve *putting together* or *taking apart* quantities.

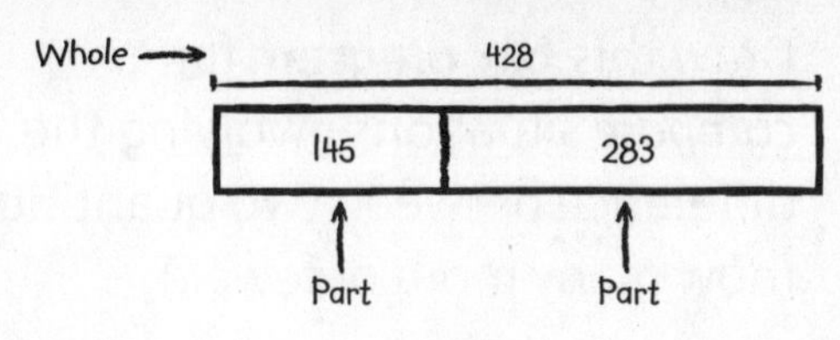

Whole Unknown

Tanner drove from his home to Providence, Rhode Island, and back over two days. Each way was 27 miles. How far did Tanner drive?

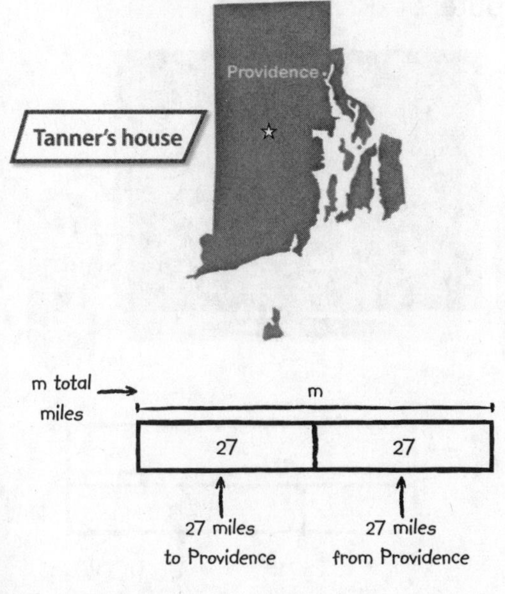

$27 + 27 = m$

Tanner drove a total of 54 miles.

Part Unknown

Mrs. Addy's class collected a total of 128 cans on Tuesday and Wednesday. How many cans were collected on Wednesday?

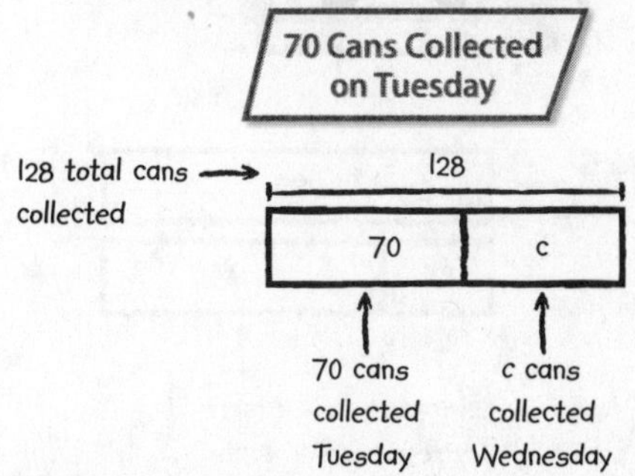

$70 + c = 128$ or $128 - 70 = c$

Mrs. Addy's class collected 58 cans on Wednesday.

Problem Solving Handbook

Bar Diagrams

Compare: Addition and Subtraction

Draw this **bar diagram** for *compare* situations involving the difference between two quantities (how many more or fewer.)

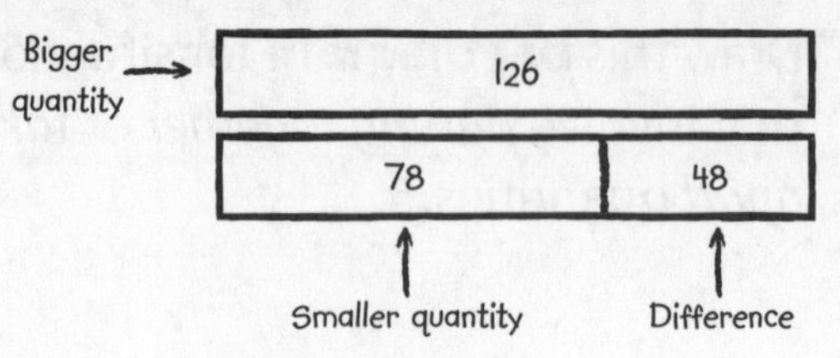

Difference Unknown

Perri read the entire book shown below. Jay read 221 facts in the book. How many more facts did Perri read than Jay?

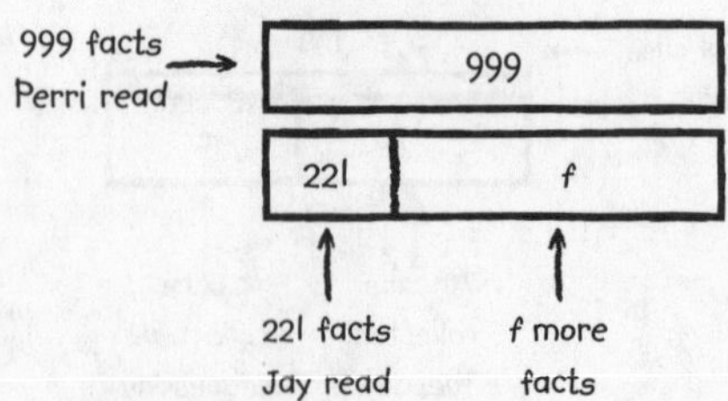

$221 + f = 999$ or $999 - 221 = f$

Perri read 778 more facts than Jay.

Smaller Unknown

Stanley has 234 fewer songs on his computer than Joanne. Joanne has 362 songs on her computer. How many songs does Stanley have on his computer?

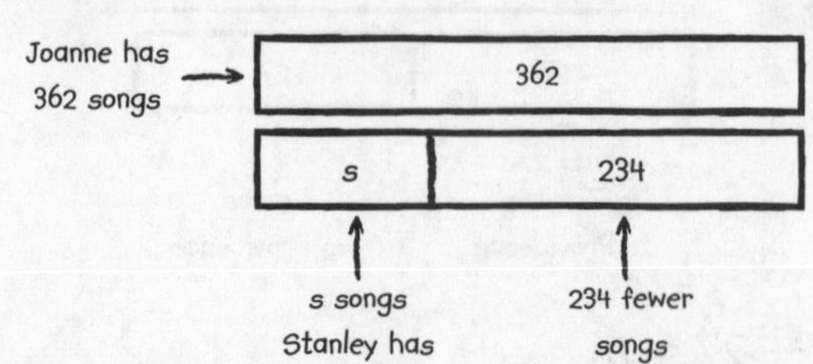

$362 - s = 234$ or $s + 234 = 362$

Stanley has 128 songs on his computer.

The **bar diagrams** on this page can help you solve problems involving multiplication and division.

Equal Groups: Multiplication and Division

Draw this **bar diagram** for situations that involve *equal groups.*

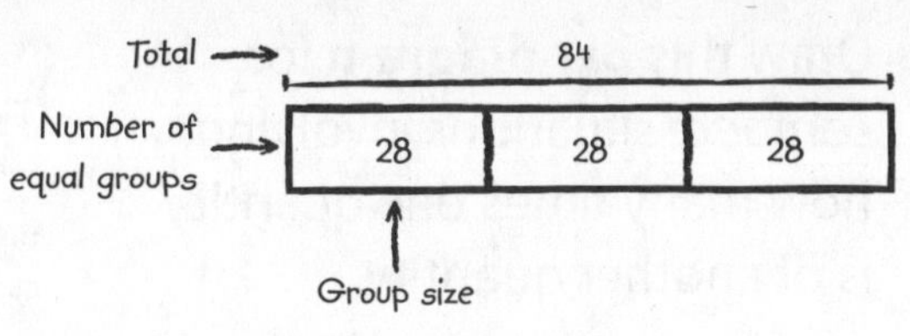

Number of Groups Unknown

Malik spent $27 riding the train this week. How many times did Malik ride the train?

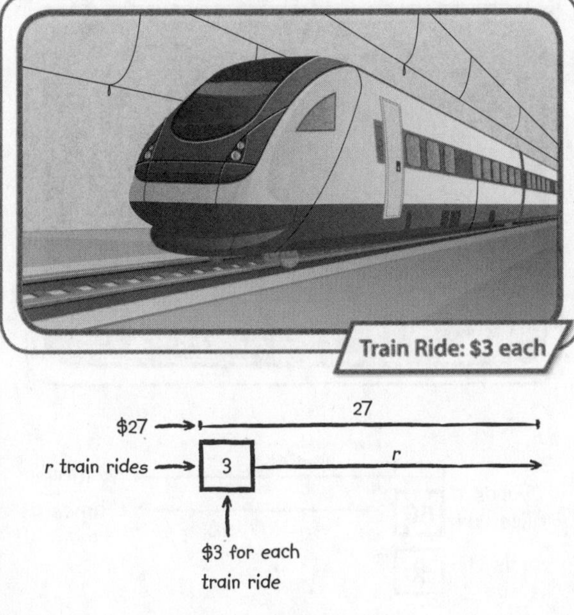

$r \times 3 = 27$ or $27 \div 3 = r$

Malik rode the train 9 times.

Group Size Unknown

If 36 cookies are packaged equally in the boxes below, how many cookies will be in each box?

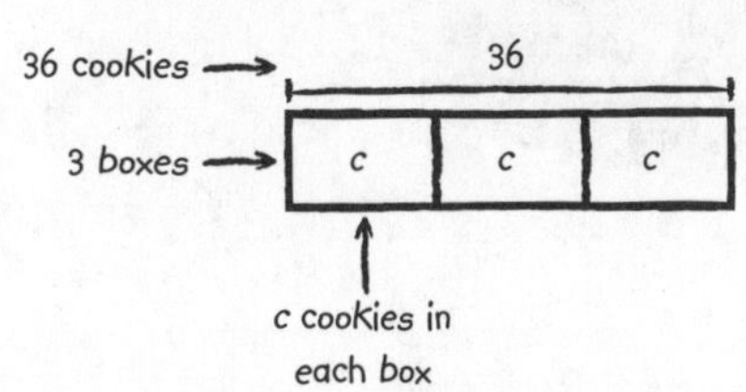

$3 \times c = 36$ or $36 \div 3 = c$

Each box will have 12 cookies.

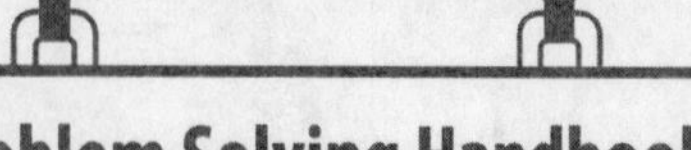

Problem Solving Handbook

Bar Diagrams

Bar diagrams can be used to show how quantities that are being compared are related.

Compare: Multiplication and Division

Draw this **bar diagram** for *compare* situations involving how many times one quantity is of another quantity.

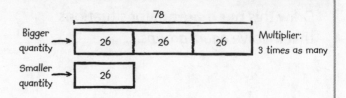

78

Bigger quantity → 26 | 26 | 26 — Multiplier: 3 times as many

Smaller quantity → 26

Bigger Unknown

On Saturday, a deli sold 8 times as many sandwiches as wraps. They sold 14 wraps. How many sandwiches did they sell?

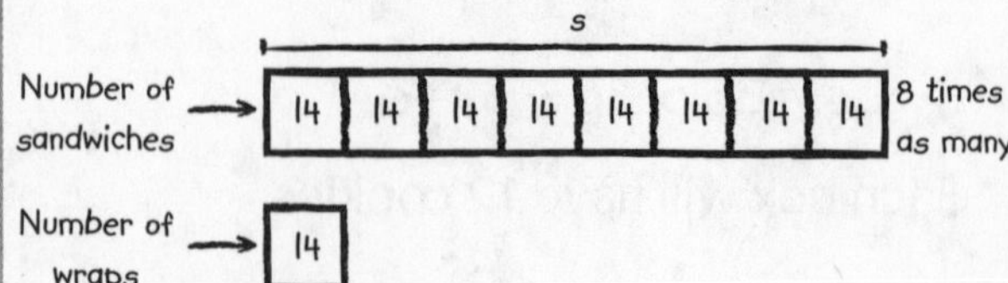

$14 \times 8 = s$

They sold 112 sandwiches.

Multiplier Unknown

Alice ran 300 yards. Uri ran 50 yards. The distance Alice ran is how many times the distance Uri ran?

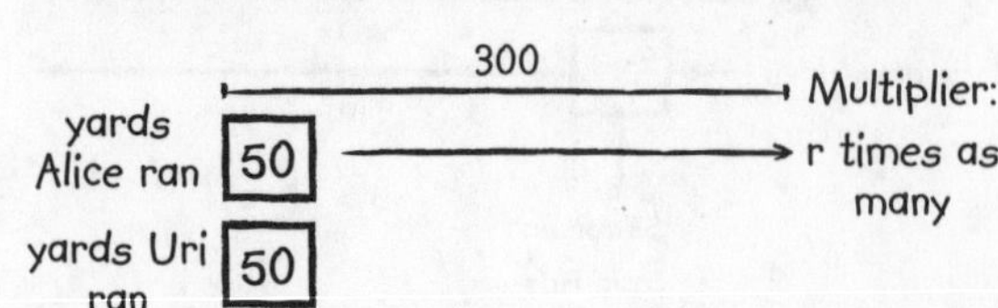

$r \times 50 = 300$ or $300 \div 50 = r$

Alice ran 6 times the distance Uri ran.

TOPIC 1

Generalize Place Value Understanding

Essential Questions: How are greater numbers written? How can whole numbers be compared? How are place values related?

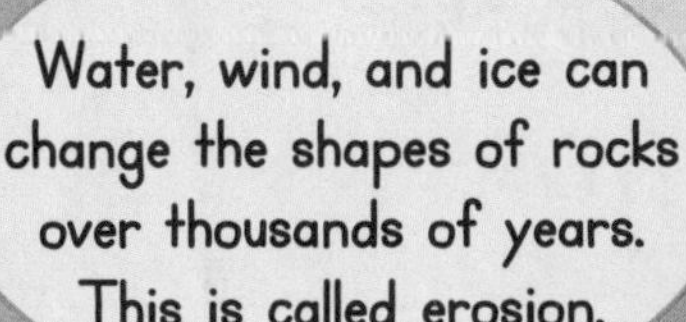

Water, wind, and ice can change the shapes of rocks over thousands of years. This is called erosion.
Kannesteinen rock in Norway got its shape from the sea that surrounds it.
Mountains, caves, and some islands are kinds of rock formations. Here is a project about caves and greater numbers.

Math and Science Project: Caves

Do Research Use the Internet or other sources to find the depths in feet of the 5 deepest caves in the world.

Journal: Write a Report Include what you found. Also in your report:

- Make a place-value chart that includes the five depths.
- Write each depth in expanded form.
- Use "greater than" or "less than" to compare the depths of two of the caves.

Name ____________________

Review What You Know

Vocabulary

Choose the best term from the box. Write it on the blank.

- expanded form
- place value
- number line
- rounding
- number name
- whole number

1. The numbers 0, 1, 2, 3, 4, and so on are called __________.
2. A number written using only words is written using a __________.
3. Replacing a number with a number that tells about how many or how much is called __________.
4. __________ is the value given to the place of a digit in a number.

Comparing Numbers

Compare each set of numbers using >, <, or =.

5. 201 ◯ 21
6. 313 ◯ 313
7. 289 ◯ 290
8. 7 ◯ 70
9. 725 ◯ 726
10. 82 ◯ 82
11. 614 ◯ 641
12. 618 ◯ 618
13. 978 ◯ 987

Place Value

Tell if the underlined digit is in the ones, tens, hundreds, or thousands place.

14. <u>9</u>,482
15. 8,0<u>0</u>0
16. 1,5<u>0</u>6
17. <u>8</u>,005
18. 5,<u>1</u>00
19. <u>2</u>,731

In this topic, you will learn more about place value.

Rounding

20. **Construct Arguments** Use the number line to describe how to round 450 to the nearest hundred.

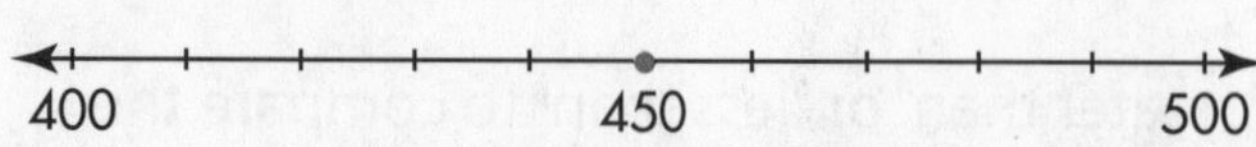

A-Z Glossary

My Word Cards

Use the examples for each word on the front of the card to help complete the definitions on the back.

3,946

↑

hundreds

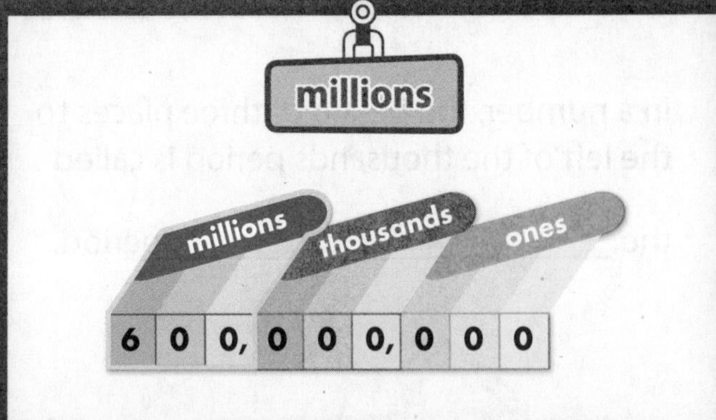

expanded form

2,000 + 400 + 70 + 6

2,476

greater than symbol (>)

$10 > 5$

10 is greater than 5

$5 < 10$

5 is less than 10

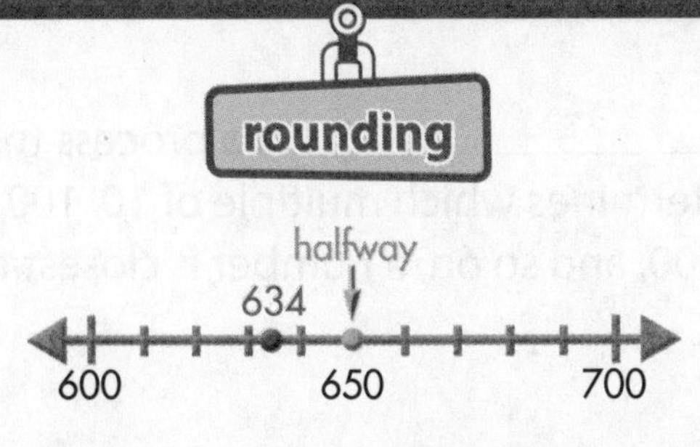

Is 634 closer to 600 or 700?

There are more toys in the larger box than the smaller box.

My Word Cards

Complete each definition. Extend learning by writing your own definitions.

In a number, the period of three places to the left of the thousands period is called the ________________ period.

________________ is the position of a digit in a number that tells the value of the digit.

A number written as the sum of the values of its digits is written in ________________.

In a number, a ________________ is a group of three digits, separated by commas, starting from the right.

In a number sentence, a symbol that points toward a lesser number or expression is called a ________________ ________________.

In a number sentence, a symbol that points away from a greater number or expression is called a ________________ ________________.

A ________________ is a statement that is believed to be true but has not been proven.

________________ is a process that determines which multiple of 10, 100, 1,000, and so on, a number is closest to.

Name ________________________________ Solve

Solve & Share

A singer sells 46,902 copies of her album in one week. In one year, she sells 729,664 copies. Write these numbers using number names.

Lesson 1-1
Numbers Through One Million

I can ...
read and write numbers through one million in expanded form, with numerals, and using number names.

Content Standard 4.NS.1
Process Standards PS.2, PS.3, PS.5, PS.6, PS.7

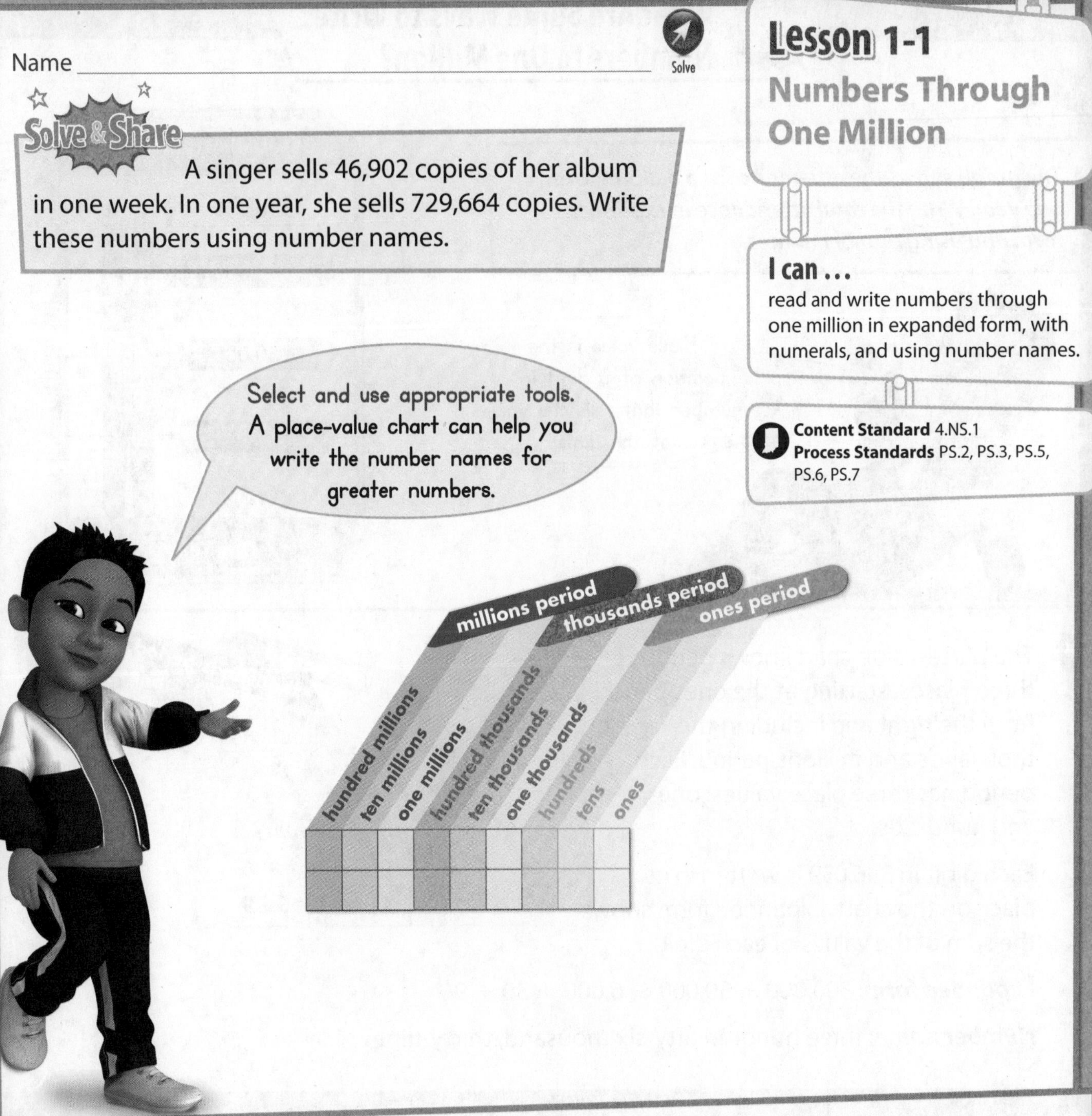

Look Back! Be Precise Look at the number names you wrote. What do the number names have in common? What do you notice about the labels for each of the periods?

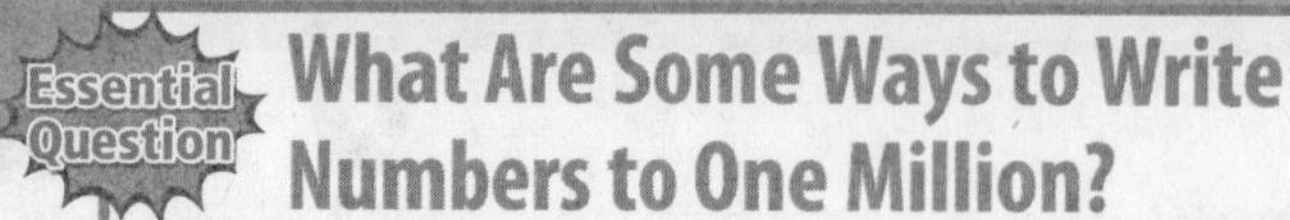

What Are Some Ways to Write Numbers to One Million?

A

The graph shows the attendance at a ballpark over one year. Write the total attendance in expanded form and using number names.

Place value is the position of a digit in a number that tells the value of the digit.

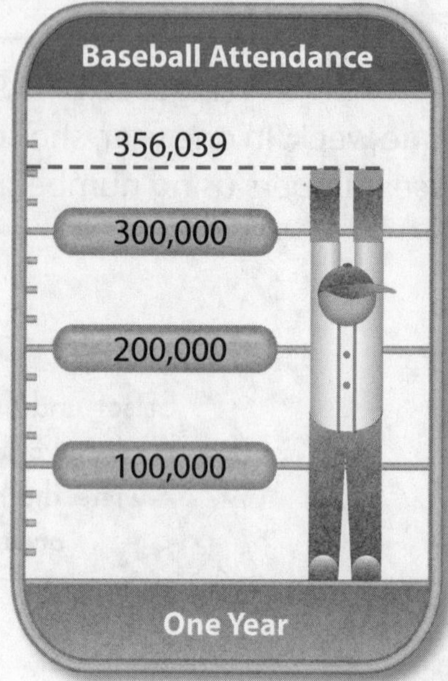

B

The place-value chart shows periods of three places, starting at the ones period from the right and including the thousands and millions period. Each period has three place values: ones, tens, and hundreds.

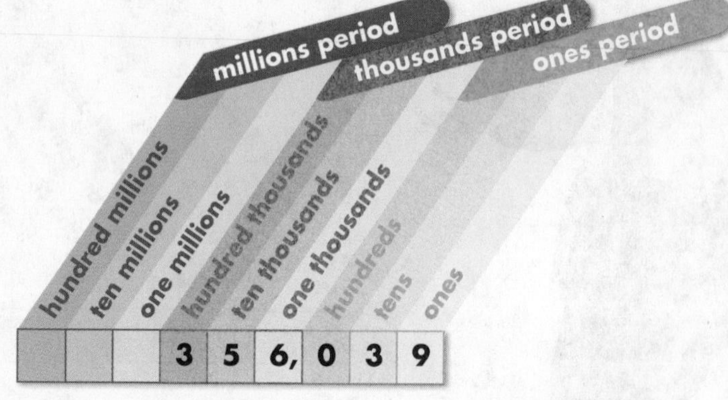

Each digit in 356,039 is written in its place on the chart. Expanded form shows the sum of the values of each digit.

Expanded form: 300,000 + 50,000 + 6,000 + 30 + 9

Number name: three hundred fifty-six thousand, thirty-nine

Convince Me! **Look for Relationships** What pattern exists in the three places in each period?

Name ______________________

Practice Buddy Tools Assessment

Guided Practice*

Do You Understand?

1. Use number names and numerals to write 900,000 + 60,000 + 3,000 + 100 + 4.

2. **Reasoning** What is the greatest number that has one comma when written with numerals and with number names?

Do You Know How?

3. Write 7,320 in expanded form.

4. Write 55,426 using number names.

5. In a recent year, 284,604 fans attended the hockey playoffs in Chicago. What digit is in the thousands place in 284,604?

You can use a place-value chart to help write numbers.

Independent Practice

6. Write the number using number names. Record the number in the place-value chart.
300,000 + 10,000 + 6,000 + 20 + 9

For **7–9**, write each number in expanded form.

7. 7,622

8. 294,160

9. 43,702

For **10–12**, write the number names.

10. 1,688

11. 331,872

12. 44,444

*For another example, see Set A on page 37.

Problem Solving

13. **Use Appropriate Tools** Letitia wrote one thousand, two hundred four in a place-value chart. What mistake did she make?

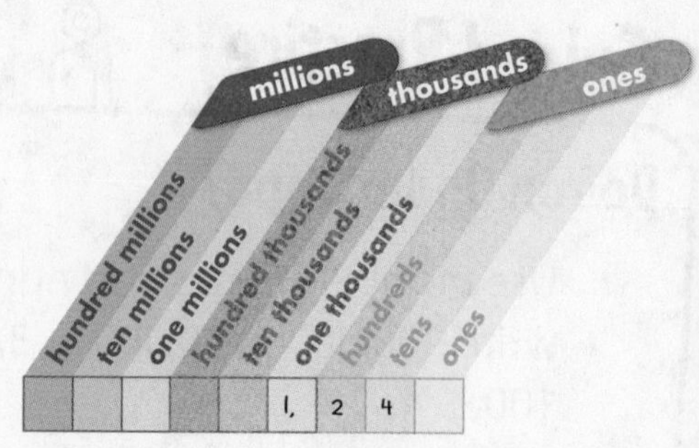

14. **Reasoning** In 2016, the world's oldest tree was 5,066 years old. Write the number that is one hundred more using number names.

15. Jessica wants to buy a new team jacket that costs $35. If Jessica saves $5 a week for 4 weeks and $4 a week for 3 weeks, will she have enough money to buy the team jacket? Explain.

16. **Vocabulary** Drew wrote the following sentences: "A period is a group of any 3 three digits in a number." Do you agree with Drew? If not, how would you correct him?

17. **Higher Order Thinking** Two numbers have the same digit in the millions period, the same digits in the thousands period, and the same digits in the ones period. Do these two numbers have the same value? Explain.

Assessment ISTEP+ Ready

18. Wallace writes the number 72,204 in a place-value chart. Select the places that will be filled on the chart.

- ☐ ones
- ☐ tens
- ☐ thousands
- ☐ ten thousands
- ☐ hundred thousands

19. Krista wrote 6,014 in expanded form. Select all the values Krista wrote.

- ☐ 6,000
- ☐ 100
- ☐ 14
- ☐ 10
- ☐ 4

Name ______________________

Homework & Practice 1-1

Numbers Through One Million

Another Look!

A place-value chart can help you read greater numbers. This chart has three periods: millions, thousands, and ones.

According to a recent census, the city of Boston was home to 625,087 people. Each digit of 625,087 is written in its place on the chart.

You can write the number in expanded form and using its number name.

600,000 + 20,000 + 5,000 + 80 + 7

six hundred twenty-five thousand, eighty-seven

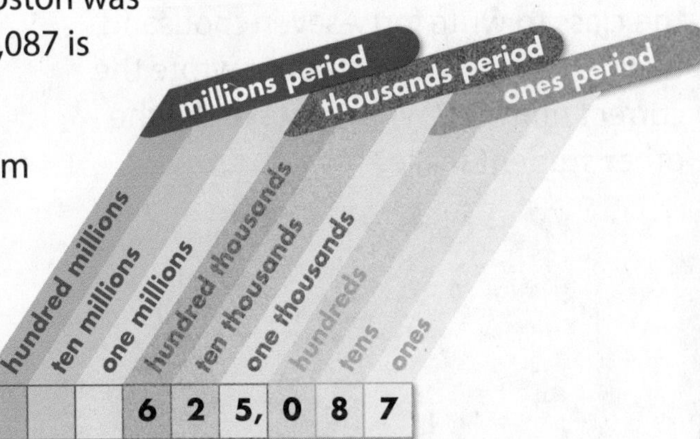

1. Write six hundred twelve thousand, three hundred in the place-value chart. Then write the number in expanded form.

2. Write forty-one thousand, two hundred eleven in the place-value chart. Then write the number in expanded form.

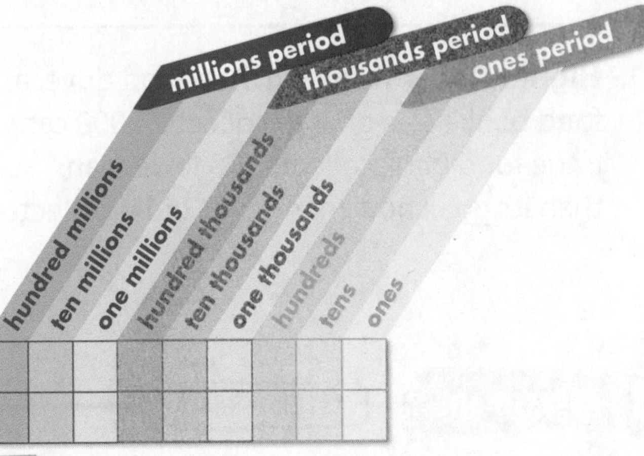

For **3–5**, write each number in expanded form.

3. 500,000

4. 64,672

5. 327

For **6–8**, write the number names.

6. 92,318

7. 428,737

8. 8,216

9. Jackson has 5 boxes of 3 golf balls. Elsa gives Jackson 2 more boxes of 3 golf balls. How many golf balls does Jackson have now?

10. Thirty-five thousand, four hundred seventeen people attended a county fair. Write this number using numerals.

11. Construct Arguments The teacher asks the class to write forty-seven thousand, twenty-seven. Which student wrote the correct number? What mistake did the other student make?

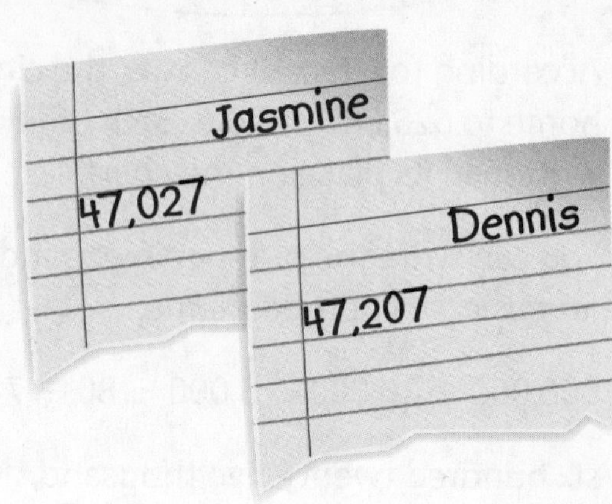

12. Higher Order Thinking At a food drive, a food bank has a goal to collect 24,000 cans. If the food bank collects 100 fewer cans than its goal, how many cans did it collect?

Think about which place values have to change.

Assessment — ISTEP+ Ready

13. A comic book store has 26,298 comics in stock. Select all the places in 26,298 that have the digit 2.

- ☐ ones
- ☐ tens
- ☐ hundreds
- ☐ thousands
- ☐ ten thousands

14. Mike wrote 209,604 in expanded form. Select all the values Mike wrote.

- ☐ 200,000
- ☐ 9,000
- ☐ 900
- ☐ 60
- ☐ 4

Name ______________________________

What is the relationship between the value of the first 5 and the value of the second 5 in 5,500? ***Solve this problem any way you choose.***

Lesson 1-2
Place Value Relationships

I can ...
recognize that a digit in one place has ten times the value of the same digit in the place to its right.

Content Standard Extends 4.NS.1
Process Standards PS.2, PS.3, PS.8

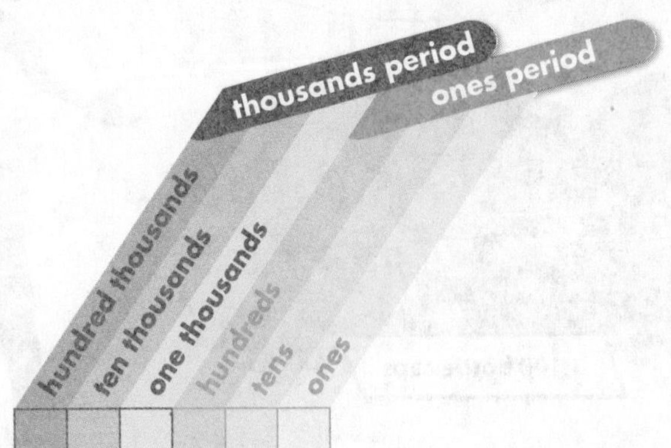

Use reasoning. You can use place value to analyze the relationship between the digits in the problem.

Look Back! Reasoning Describe two ways 5,000 and 500 are related.

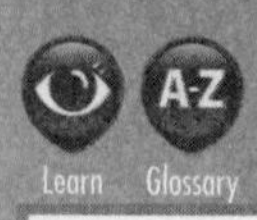

How Are the Digits in a Multi-Digit Number Related to Each Other?

A

Kiana collected 1,100 bottle caps. What is the relationship between the values of the digit 1 in each place?

A place-value chart can help you examine the relationships between digits in a number.

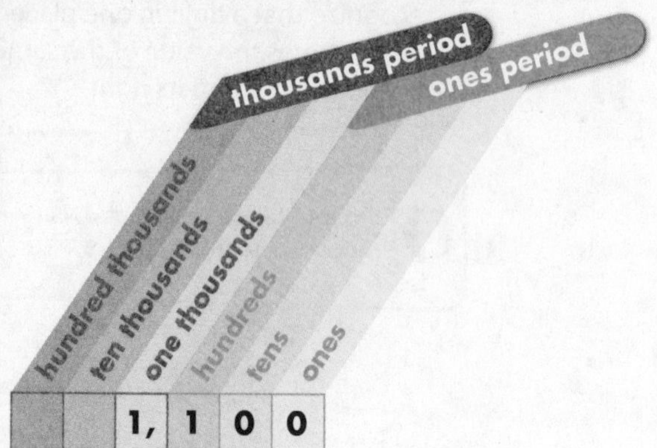

B 1,100

The first 1 is in the thousands place. Its value is 1,000.

The second 1 is in the hundreds place. Its value is 100.

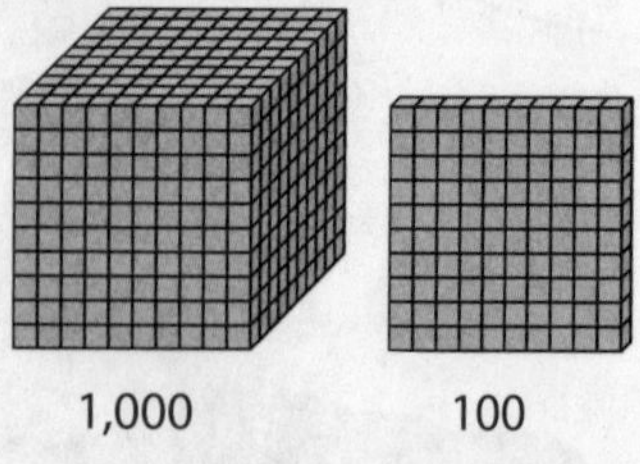

C How is 1,000 related to 100?

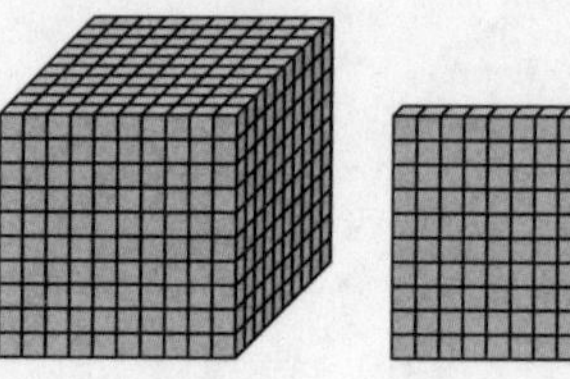

10 hundreds are equal to 1 thousand.

When two digits next to each other in a number are the same, the value of the digit on the left is always ten times as great as the digit on the right.

Convince Me! **Generalize** Is the value of the first 4 ten times as great as the value of the second 4 in 4,043? Explain. What can you generalize about the value of digits that are two places apart in a number?

Name ______________________________

Another Example!

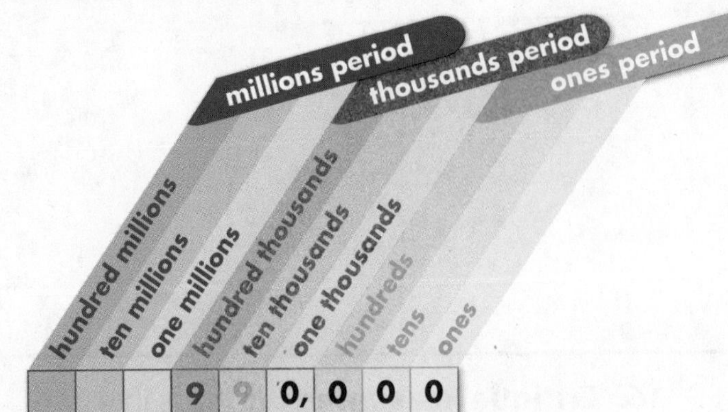

The first 9 is in the hundred-thousands place. Its value is 900,000.

The second 9 is in the ten-thousands place. Its value is 90,000.

The value of the first 9 is ten times as great as the value of the second 9.

Guided Practice*

Do You Understand?

1. **Reasoning** Is the value of the first 5 ten times as great as the value of the second 5 in 5,045? Explain.

2. **Construct Arguments** Is the value of the 2 in 23,406 ten times as great as the value of the 3? Explain.

Do You Know How?

For **3–4**, name the values of the given digits in each number. What is the relationship between the values of the given digits?

3. the 7s in 7,700

4. the 4s in 440,200

Independent Practice

For **5–12**, name the values of the given digits in each number.

5. the 2s in 6,228
6. the 5s in 55,714
7. the 4s in 14,423
8. the 8s in 880,000
9. the 9s in 19,409
10. the 7s in 7,772
11. the 3s in 31,239
12. the 6s in 926,361

*For another example, see Set B on page 37.

Problem Solving

13. Construct Arguments What can you say about the 3s in 43,335?

14. Critique Reasoning Mia says in 5,555, all the digits have the same value. Is Mia correct? Explain.

15. Number Sense In 1934, there was an extreme drought in the Great Plains. In the number 1,934, is the value of the 9 in the hundreds place ten times the value of the 3 in the tens place? Explain.

16. Critique Reasoning Vin says in 4,346, one 4 is 10 times as great as the other 4. Is Vin correct? Explain.

17. Describe 2 ways to find the area of the shaded rectangle.

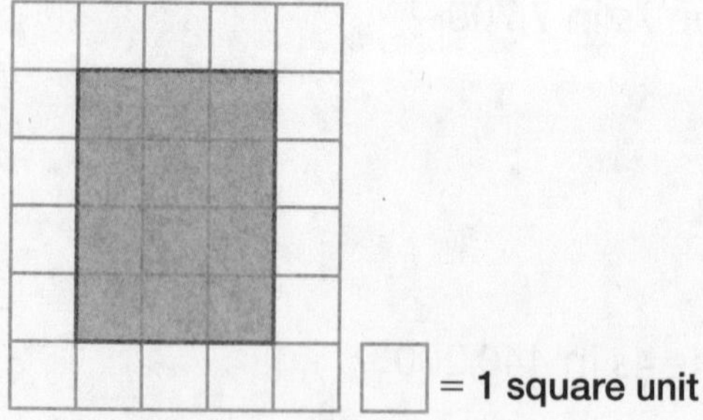

18. Higher Order Thinking In 448,244, how is the relationship between the first pair of 4s the same as the relationship between the second pair of 4s?

Assessment — ISTEP+ Ready

19. Which group of numbers shows the values of the 4s in 44,492?

Ⓐ 40,000; 4,000; 400

Ⓑ 40,000; 400; 40

Ⓒ 4,000; 400; 4

Ⓓ 400; 40; 4

20. In which number is the value of the red digit ten times as great as the value of the green digit?

Ⓐ 335,531

Ⓑ 335,531

Ⓒ 335,531

Ⓓ 335,531

Name ___________________________

Homework & Practice 1-2

Place Value Relationships

Another Look!

In 3,300, what is the relationship between the value of the digit 3 in each place?

3,300

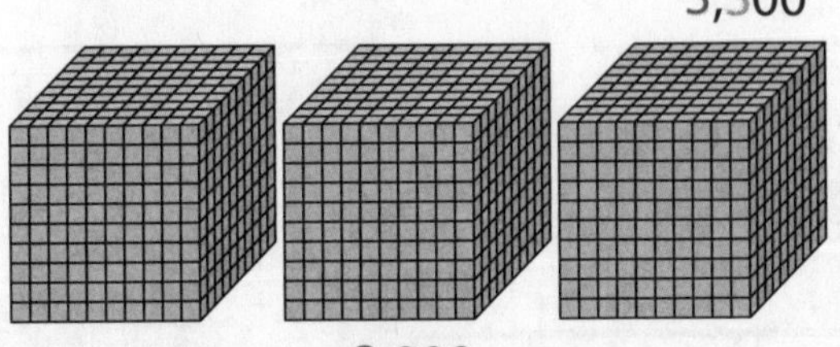

3,000 | 300

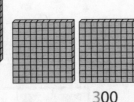

The first 3 is in the thousands place. Its value is 3,000.

The second 3 is in the hundreds place. Its value is 300.

When two digits next to each other in a number are the same, the digit on the left is always 10 times as great as the digit on the right.

Since 3,000 is ten times as great as 300, the first 3 has a value 10 times as great as the second 3.

1. Write the value of the digit in the hundreds place and the value of the digit in the tens place in 440. What is the relationship between the value of the digit in each place?

440

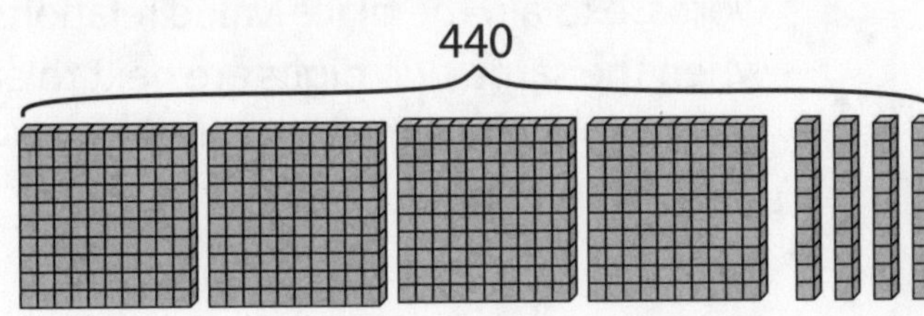

____ ____

The ____ in the hundreds place has a value ____ times as great as the ____ in the ____ place.

For **2–3**, write the values of the given digits.

2. the 4s in 4,400

3. the 8s in 88,000

For **4–5**, describe the relationship between the values of the given digits.

4. the 6s in 6,600

5. the 4s in 44,000

6. What is the relationship between the 6s in 660,472?

7. Name the value of each 2 in 222,222.

For **8–9**, use the graph at the right.

8. Who sold the most cups of lemonade? Who sold the fewest?

9. Algebra How many cups of lemonade were sold in all? Write and solve an equation.

10. Reasoning Is the relationship between the 7s in 7,742 and the 7s in 7,785 different in any way? Explain.

11. Higher Order Thinking In your own words, explain the place-value relationship when the same two digits are next to each other in a multi-digit number.

12. Which of the following shows the values of the 5s in 15,573?

Ⓐ 500 and 5

Ⓑ 500 and 50

Ⓒ 5,000 and 50

Ⓓ 5,000 and 500

13. In which number is the value of the red digit ten times as great as the value of the green digit?

Ⓐ 622,126

Ⓑ 622,126

Ⓒ 622,126

Ⓓ 622,126

Name ______________________________

Lesson 1-3
Compare Whole Numbers

I can ...
use place value to compare numbers and record my comparisons using <, =, or >.

Content Standard 4.NS.2
Process Standards PS.1, PS.2, PS.3, PS.4

Solve & Share

A robotic submarine can dive to a depth of 26,000 feet. Which oceans can the submarine explore all the way to the bottom? ***Solve this problem any way you choose.***

You can model with math. Use what you know about place value to help solve the problem.

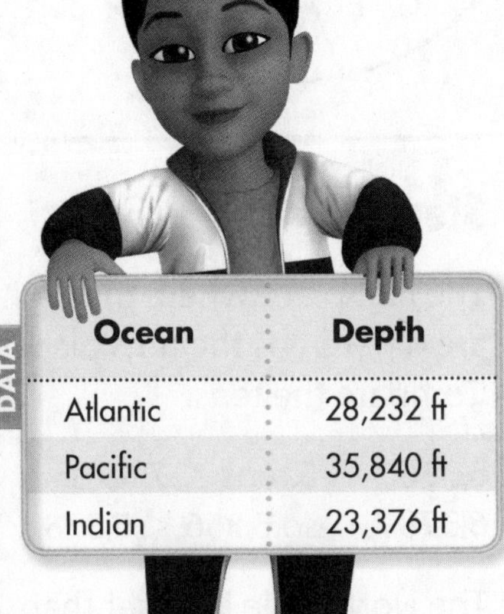

DATA

Ocean	Depth
Atlantic	28,232 ft
Pacific	35,840 ft
Indian	23,376 ft

Look Back! Construct Arguments Which of the oceans listed is the shallowest? Explain.

How Do You Compare Numbers?

A

Earth is not perfectly round. The North Pole is 6,356 kilometers from Earth's center. The equator is 6,378 kilometers from the center. Which is closer to Earth's center, the North Pole or the equator?

The symbol > means "is greater than", and the symbol < means "is less than".

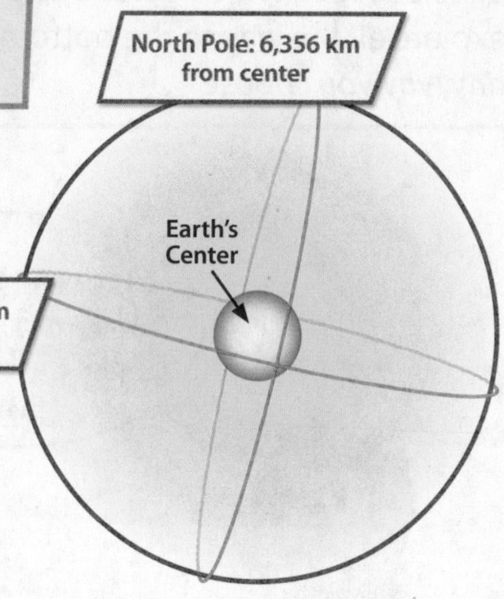

B

Step 1

Write the numbers, lining up places. Begin at the left and compare.

6,356
6,378

The thousands digit is the same in both numbers.

C

Step 2

Look at the next digit, compare the hundreds.

6,356
6,378

The hundreds digit is also the same in both numbers.

D

Step 3

The first place where the digits are different is the tens place. Compare the tens.

6,356
6,378

5 tens < 7 tens,
so 6,356 < 6,378.

The North Pole is closer than the equator to Earth's center.

Convince Me! Reasoning Is a whole number with 4 digits always greater than or less than a whole number with 3 digits? Explain.

Name ______________________________

Practice Buddy Tools Assessment

☆ Guided Practice*

Do You Understand?

1. **Reasoning** Which place do you use to compare the numbers 60,618 and 60,647?

2. Morocco has a total area of 442,300 square kilometers. Uzbekistan has a total area of 447,400 square kilometers. Use >, <, or = to compare the two areas.

Do You Know How?

For **3–7**, complete by writing >, =, or < in each ◯.

3. 2,643 ◯ 2,643

4. 62,519 ◯ 64,582

5. 218,701 ◯ 118,692

6. 32,467 ◯ 32,467

7. 19,219 ◯ 1,921

Independent Practice

For **8–13**, complete by writing >, =, or < in each ◯.

8. 22,873 ◯ 22,774

9. 912,706 ◯ 912,706

10. 22,240 ◯ 2,224

11. 999,999 ◯ 1,000,000

12. 68,425 ◯ 78,425

13. 57,219 ◯ 6,274

For **14–18**, write which place to use when comparing the numbers.

14. 394,284
328,234

15. 6,716
6,714

16. 32,916
32,819

17. 12,217
11,246

18. 812,497
736,881

Remember to compare each place value, starting on the left!

*For another example, see Set C on page 37.

Problem Solving

For **19–20**, use the table at the right.

Sales at Danny's Books	
Fiction	48,143
Fantasy	42,843
Biography	41,834
Science	41,843
Humor	14,843

19. Which genres at Danny's Books did **NOT** sell better than Science?

20. Which genres at Danny's Books sold better than Biography?

21. Celia bought 3 bags of 4 hamburger buns and 3 bags of 8 hot dog buns. How many hamburger and hot dog buns did Celia buy?

22. **Make Sense and Persevere** Write three numbers for which you would use the hundreds place to compare to 35,712.

23. **Math and Science** The Illinoian Stage began about 300,000 years ago. The Wolstonian Stage began about 352,000 years ago. Compare 300,000 to 352,000.

24. **Model with Math** An orchard in Maine has 5,287 apple trees. An orchard in Vermont has 5,729 trees. Use $<$, $>$, or $=$ to write a comparison between the number of trees in each orchard.

25. In 2010, the population of Alaska was 710,231. Write this number in expanded form, and write the number name.

26. **Higher Order Thinking** Explain how you know 437,160 is greater than 43,716.

ISTEP+ Ready

27. Draw a line to show the place value you would use to compare.

4,264 and 5,269	ones
12,764 and 12,674	ten thousands
998 and 997	hundreds
138,725 and 128,715	thousands

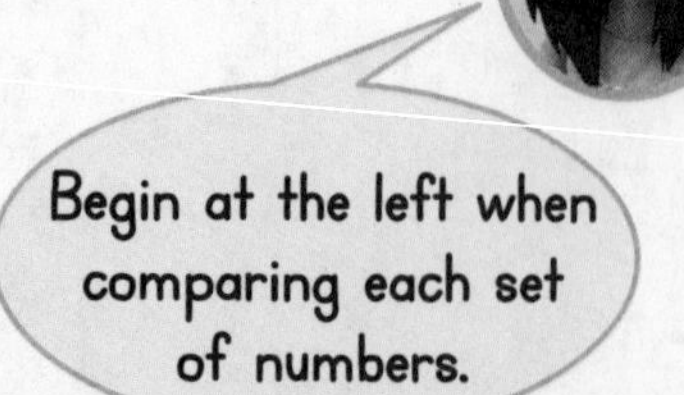

Begin at the left when comparing each set of numbers.

Name ______________________________

Homework & Practice 1-3

Compare Whole Numbers

Another Look!

Which distance is greater: the moon's distance from Earth on February 7 or its distance from Earth on March 5?

Which place value can you use to compare the numbers?

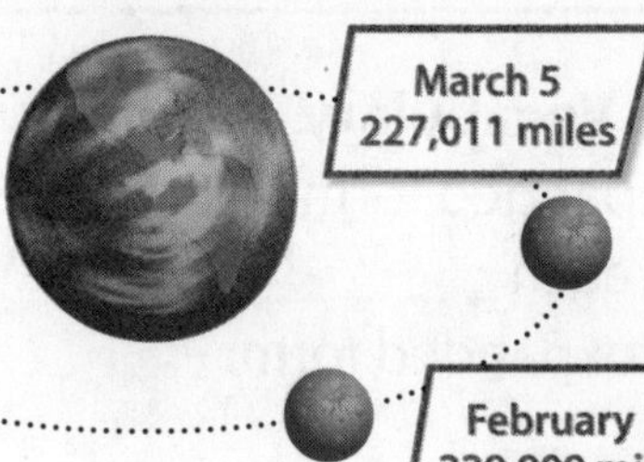

Write the numbers, lining up the places. Begin at the left and compare.

229,909
227,011

The hundred thousands digit is the same in both numbers.

Continue comparing the digits from left to right.

229,909
227,011

The ten thousands digit is the same in both numbers.

The first place where the digits are different is the thousands place.

229,909
227,011

Compare.
9 thousands > 7 thousands, so 229,909 > 227,011

The moon's distance from Earth is greater on February 7.

For **1–9**, complete by writing >, =, or < in each ◯.

1. 854,376 ◯ 845,763
2. 52,789 ◯ 52,876
3. 944,321 ◯ 940,123
4. 59,536 ◯ 59,536
5. 3,125 ◯ 4,125
6. 418,218 ◯ 41,821
7. 72,746 ◯ 7,756
8. 634,674 ◯ 635,647
9. 1,000,000 ◯ 1,000,000

For **10–15**, write which place to use when comparing the numbers.

10. 3,176
3,472

11. 899,451
756,451

12. 28,119
28,124

13. 94,283
96,281

14. 1,983
1,982

15. 490,165
390,264

16. **Model with Math** Use $<$ or $>$ to write a comparison between 2 of the city populations shown in the table.

City Populations

DATA	
Hauserberg	129,616
Devinsville	128,741
Mandel Village	129,788

17. **Vocabulary** A number written in expanded form is written as the sum of each ______________. Write 39,005 in expanded form.

18. According to the 2010 census, the state with the fewest people is Wyoming, with a population of 563,626. Write the number that is ten thousand greater than 563,626.

19. **Higher Order Thinking** Celia writes the addition problems shown. She says she can tell which sum will be greater without adding. How does Celia know?

20. Find the sums. Write a comparison using $>$, $<$, or $=$.

21. Draw a line to show the place value you would use to compare.

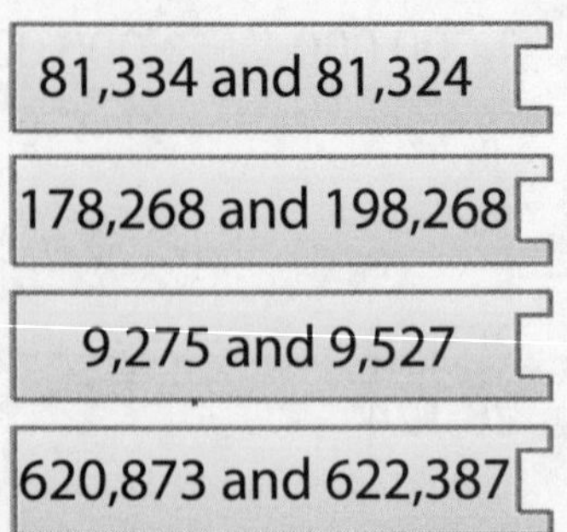

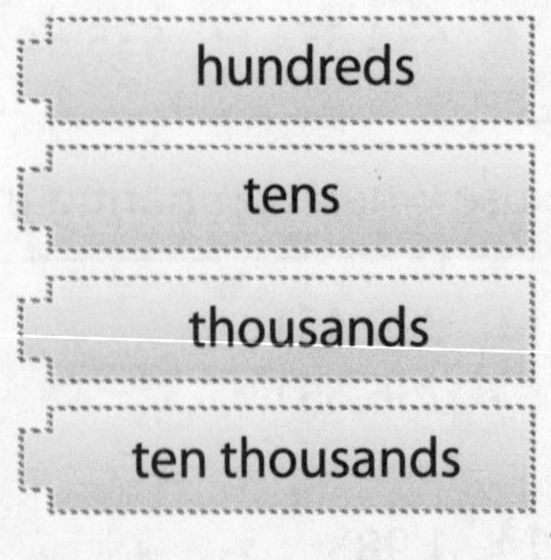

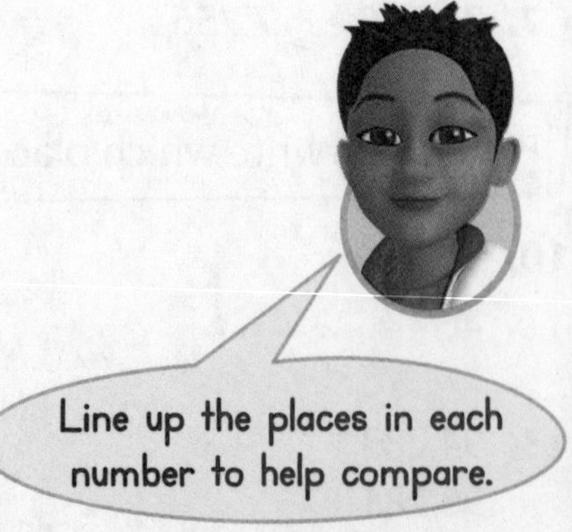

Line up the places in each number to help compare.

Name ______________________________________

Solve

Lesson 1-4
Round Whole Numbers

I can ...
use place value to round numbers.

Content Standard 4.NS.9
Process Standards PS.2, PS.3, PS.5

Solve & Share

List 7 numbers that round to 300. Use a variety of numbers. ***Solve this problem any way you choose.***

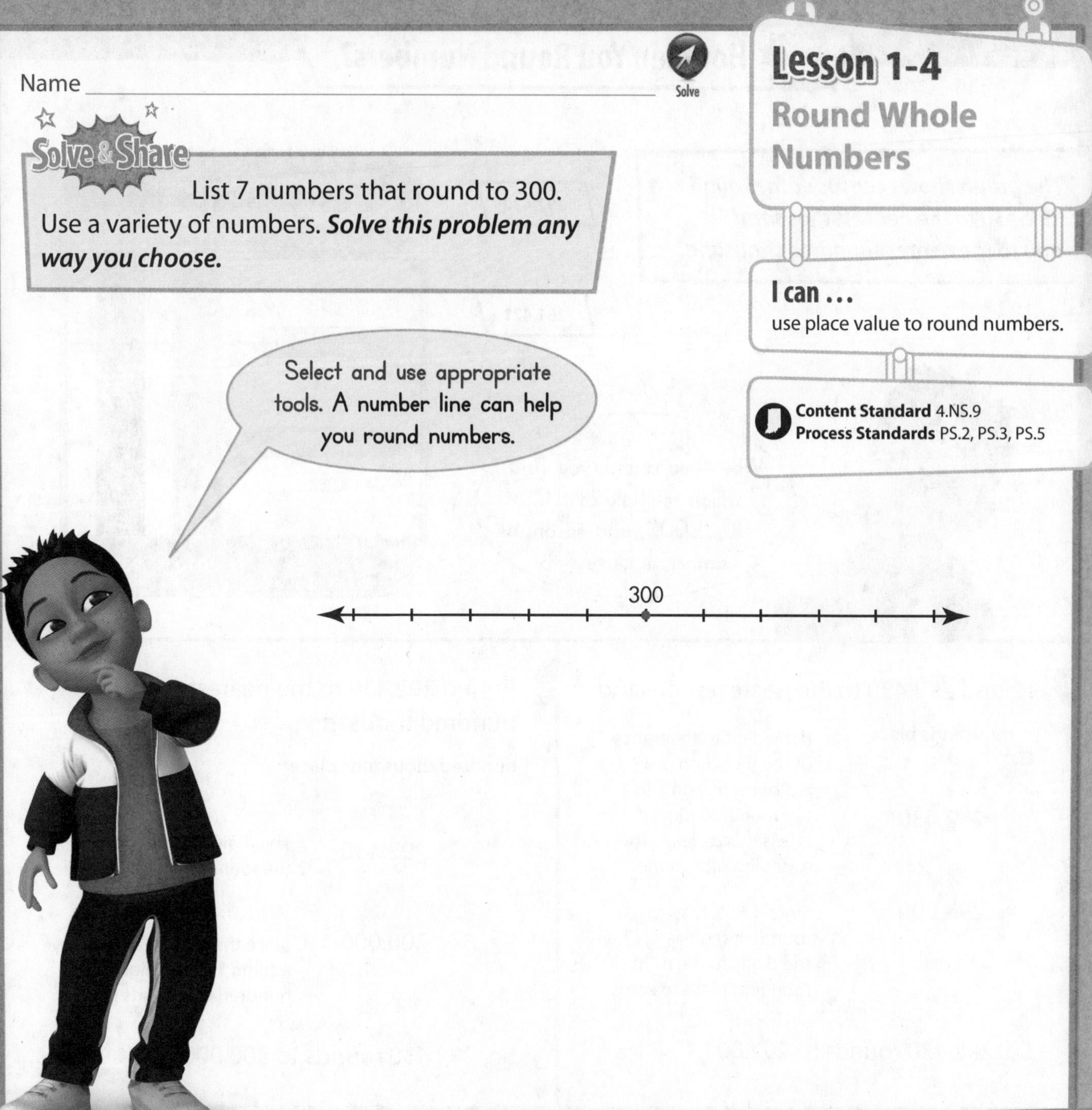

Select and use appropriate tools. A number line can help you round numbers.
300

Look Back! Reasoning What do you notice about the digits in the tens place of the numbers in your list?

Learn Glossary

Essential Question

How Can You Round Numbers?

A

The graph shows census data. Round 292,430 to the nearest thousand and to the nearest hundred thousand.

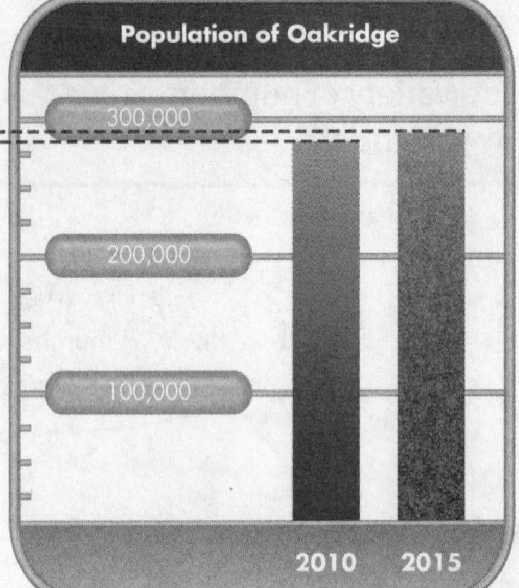

When you round, you find which multiple of 10, 100, 1,000, and so on, a number is closest to.

B

Round 292,430 to the nearest thousand:

thousands place

↓

29<u>2</u>,430

If the digit to the right of the rounding place is 5 or more, add 1 to the rounding digit. If it is less than 5, leave the rounding digit alone.

292,000

Since 4 < 5, leave the rounding digit as is. Change the digits to the right of the rounding place to zeros.

So, 292,430 rounds to 292,000.

C

Round 292,430 to the nearest hundred thousand:

hundred thousands place

↓

<u>2</u>92,430

The digit to the right of the rounding place is 9.

<u>3</u>00,000

Since the digit is 9, round by adding 1 to the digit in the hundred thousands place.

So, 292,430 rounds to 300,000.

Convince Me! **Critique Reasoning** Ellie says, "When I round these three numbers, I get the same number for two of them." Anthony says, "Hmmm, when I round these numbers, I get the same number for all three." Who is correct? Explain.

Three Numbers		
1,483	1,250	1,454

Name ______________________________

Guided Practice*

Do You Understand?

1. **Construct Arguments** Explain how to round a number when 7 is the digit to the right of the rounding place.

2. A city's population is 421,906. Round 421,906 to the nearest hundred thousand and to the nearest thousand.

Do You Know How?

For **3–8**, round each number to the place of the underlined digit.

3. $12\underline{8},955$ **4.** $85,6\underline{3}9$

5. $\underline{9},924$ **6.** $1\underline{9}4,524$

7. $\underline{1}60,656$ **8.** $\underline{1}49,590$

Independent Practice

For **9–32**, round each number to the place of the underlined digit.

9. $4\underline{9}3,295$ **10.** $\underline{3}9,230$ **11.** $\underline{2}77,292$ **12.** $54,\underline{8}46$

13. $4,0\underline{2}8$ **14.** $\underline{6}38,365$ **15.** $45\underline{3},280$ **16.** $17,\underline{9}09$

17. $\underline{9}56,000$ **18.** $5\underline{5},460$ **19.** $3\underline{2}1,679$ **20.** $417,5\underline{4}7$

21. $1\underline{1}7,821$ **22.** $\underline{7}5,254$ **23.** $9\underline{4}9,999$ **24.** $66\underline{6},821$

25. $\underline{2},420$ **26.** $\underline{9}00,985$ **27.** $\underline{9},511$ **28.** $73,0\underline{6}5$

29. $6,3\underline{2}1$ **30.** $29,\underline{9}98$ **31.** $6\underline{1},217$ **32.** $\underline{7}9,945$

For another example, see Set D on page 38.

Problem Solving

33. For each zoo in the table, round the attendance to the nearest hundred thousand.

Zoo Attendance	
Zoo D	234,679
Zoo E	872,544
Zoo F	350,952

34. **Number Sense** Write four numbers that round to 700,000 when rounded to the nearest hundred thousand.

35. A forest ranger correctly rounded the number of visitors to a park to be 120,000 visitors. Write a number that could be the actual number of visitors if he rounded to the nearest ten thousand.

36. Amy counted the number of boys and girls at a party. She recorded the results in the tally chart below.

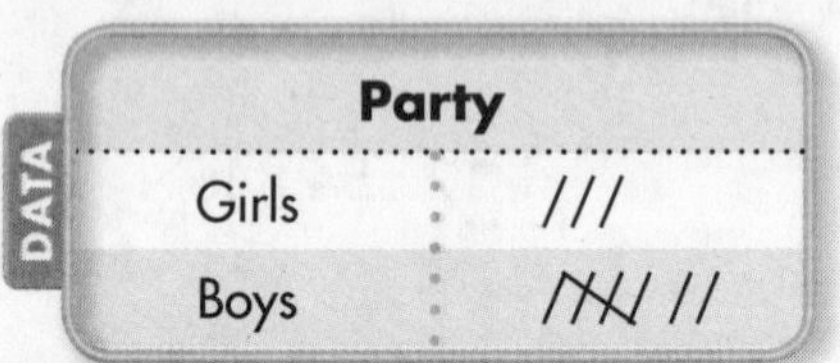

Party	
Girls	///
Boys	~~////~~ //

How many more boys than girls were at the party?

37. **Higher Order Thinking** Liz attended class every day since she started school as a kindergartner. She said she has been in school for about 1,000 days. What numbers could be the actual number of school days if Liz rounded to the nearest ten?

38. Siobhan rounds 99,498 to the nearest thousand and gets 100,000.

Part A

What mistake did Siobhan make?

Part B

Is it possible for a 5-digit number to be rounded to a 6-digit number? Explain.

Name ______________________

Homework & Practice 1-4
Round Whole Numbers

Another Look!

The graph shows census data for three U.S. cities. Round each number to the nearest ten thousand.

To round numbers, look at the digit in the place to the right of the place value the number is rounding to.

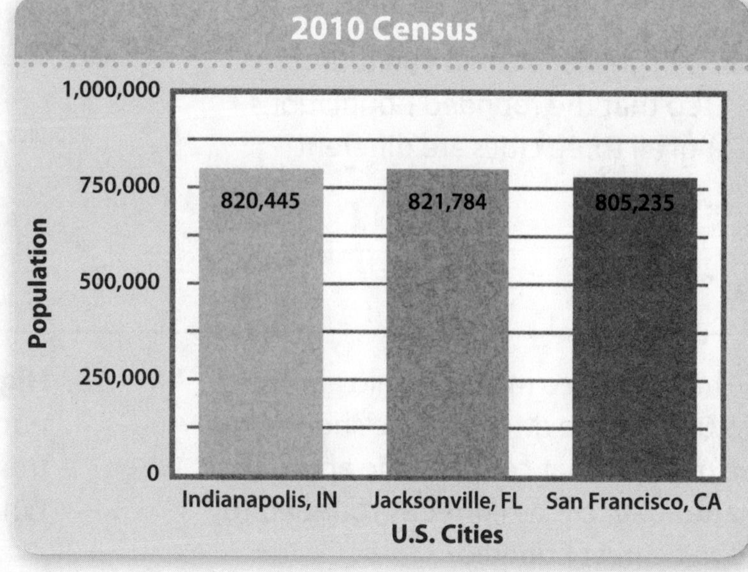

ten thousands
↓

8<u>2</u>0,445 820,000	When the digit to the right is 0, change the rest of the digits to the right to 0.
8<u>2</u>1,784 820,000	When the digit to the right is 1, 2, 3, or 4, change it and all the digits to the right to 0.
8<u>0</u>5,235 810,000	When the digit to the right is 5 or greater, add one to the digit in the rounding place and change all the digits to the right to 0.

For **1–12**, round each number to the place of the underlined digit.

1. <u>1</u>60,656 **2.** <u>1</u>49,590 **3.** 117,<u>8</u>21 **4.** <u>7</u>5,254

5. 2,4<u>2</u>0 **6.** 900,9<u>8</u>5 **7.** <u>4</u>40,591 **8.** 2<u>0</u>5,000

9. 5<u>8</u>,365 **10.** 1,<u>8</u>76 **11.** 61,<u>2</u>29 **12.** <u>7</u>,849

13. Math and Science Use the data in the graph at the right.

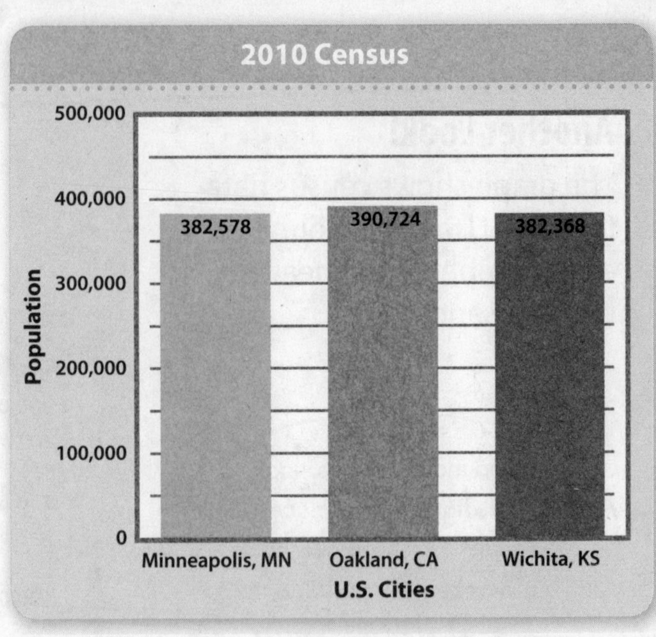

a. Which place could you round to so that the rounded populations of all three cities are the same?

b. Which place could you round to so that the rounded populations of all three cities are different?

14. The box office manager said about 5,000 people attended the show. Write a number that could be the actual attendance if he correctly rounded to the nearest hundred.

15. Higher Order Thinking A 5-digit number has the digits 0, 5, 7, 9, and 0. To the nearest thousand, it rounds to 80,000. What is the number? Explain.

16. Aisha thinks 1,275 rounded to the nearest hundred is 1,200 because "2 is less than 5."

Part A

What might be Aisha's misunderstanding about rounding?

Part B

Help Aisha correct her mistake by explaining rounding to the nearest hundred.

Name ______________________________

Solve & Share

The land areas of three states are shown in the table. Mickey said Alaska is about 10 times greater than Georgia. Explain why Mickey is or is not correct. Construct a math argument to support your answer.

DATA

State	Land Area (in square miles)
Alaska	570,641
Georgia	57,513
Hawaii	6,423

Problem Solving

Lesson 1-5

Construct Arguments

I can ...

construct arguments using what I know about place-value relationships.

Process Standards PS.3 Also PS.1, PS.2, PS.6
Content Standard 4.NS.2

Thinking Habits

Be a good thinker!
These questions can help you.

- How can I use numbers, objects, drawings, or actions to justify my argument?
- Am I using numbers and symbols correctly?
- Is my explanation clear and complete?

Look Back! Construct Arguments Mary said Georgia's land area is about 10 times greater than Hawaii's land area. Is Mary correct? Construct a math argument to support your answer.

How Can You Construct Arguments?

A

The table shows the retail sales per person in three states. Bella says Arizona had more retail sales per person than Massachusetts.

DATA

State	Retail Sales per Person
Arizona	$13,637
Iowa	$13,172
Massachusetts	$13,533

How can you construct a math argument that supports Bella's conjecture?

I will use what I know about place value to compare numbers.

A conjecture is a statement that is believed to be true but has not been proven.

B

How can I construct an argument?

I can

- give an explanation that is clear and complete.
- use numbers and symbols correctly in my explanation.
- use numbers, objects, drawings, or actions to justify my argument.
- use a counterexample in my argument.

C

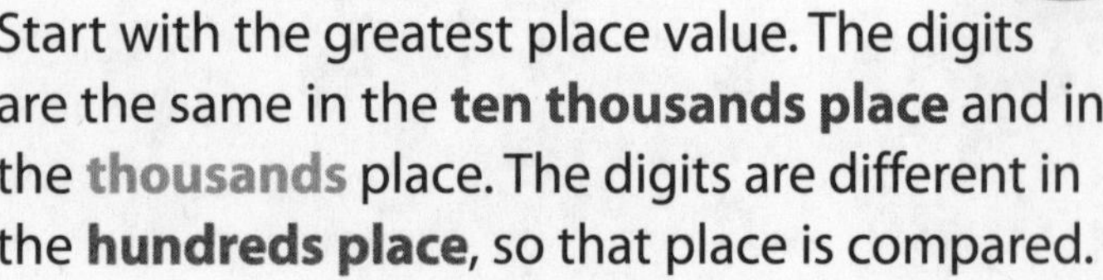

Bella's statement makes sense.

Start with the greatest place value. The digits are the same in the **ten thousands place** and in the **thousands** place. The digits are different in the **hundreds place**, so that place is compared.

$13,637
$13,533

600 > 500

So, $13,637 > $13,533.

Bella is correct. Arizona had more retail sales per person than Massachusetts.

Convince Me! **Construct Arguments** Gayle said Arizona had more retail sales than Massachusetts because 7 > 3, so $13,637 > $13,533. Construct an argument to explain whether or not Gayle is correct.

Name ____________________

Practice Buddy Tools Assessment

Guided Practice*

Construct Arguments

Use the table on the previous page. Jorge said Massachusetts has more retail sales per person than Iowa.

When you construct arguments, you justify your conclusions.

1. What numbers would you use to construct an argument supporting Jorge's conjecture?

2. How could you support Jorge's conjecture?

3. Is Jorge's conjecture true? Justify your answer.

Independent Practice

Construct Arguments

The population of Gerald's city is three hundred thousand, twenty-seven. Gerald wrote the number as 327,000. Emily lives in a city that has a population of three hundred sixteen thousand, forty-two. Gerald concluded that his city's population is greater than the population of Emily's city.

4. Does Gerald's explanation make sense? Identify any flaws in Gerald's thinking.

5. Construct a math argument that explains why Gerald did not write the population of his city correctly.

6. Correct Gerald's argument. Explain how to compare the populations of Gerald's and Emily's cities.

*For another example, see Set E on page 38.

Problem Solving

Performance Assessment — ISTEP+ Ready

Planets

The planets in our solar system are different sizes, as shown below. Nora conjectured that Jupiter's equator is about 10 times as long as Earth's equator.

Length of Equators for 4 Planets

Earth 40,030 km

Jupiter 439,264 km

Venus 38,025 km

Mars 21,297 km

7. **Make Sense and Persevere** What information do you have?

8. **Be Precise** What are possible estimates for the lengths of the equators of Jupiter and Earth?

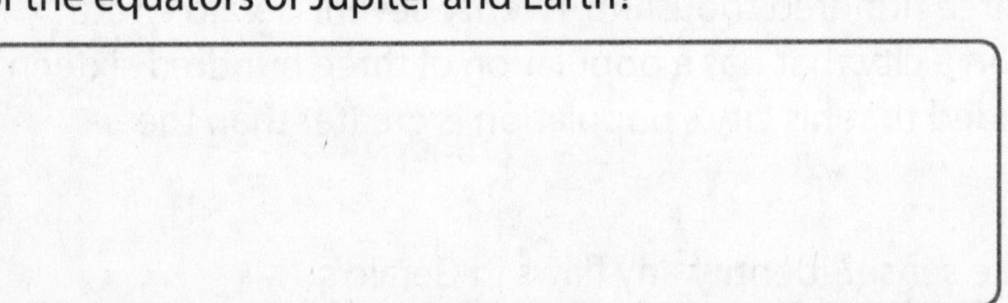

9. **Reasoning** What is the relationship between the estimates you found for the lengths of the two equators?

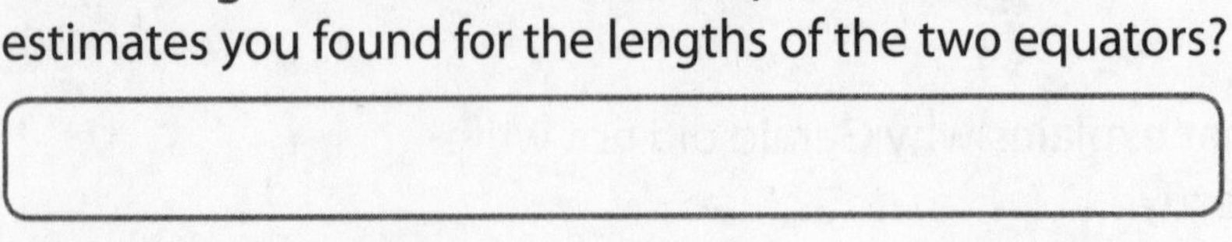

10. **Construct Arguments** Construct an argument justifying Nora's conjecture.

When you construct arguments, you explain clearly and completely.

Name ______________________________

Homework & Practice 1-5

Construct Arguments

Another Look!

In a recent year, Colorado issued 23,301 building permits and Vermont issued 2,296 building permits. Kyle said Colorado issued about 100 times as many permits as Vermont.

Tell how you can construct an argument to justify whether or not Kyle's conjecture is true.

- I can decide if the conjecture makes sense.
- I can use numbers to explain my reasoning.

When you construct arguments, you use numbers and symbols correctly to explain.

Construct an argument to justify whether or not Kyle's conjecture is true.

Kyle's conjecture is not true. Rounding to the nearest ten thousand, Colorado issued about 20,000 building permits. Vermont issued about 2,000 permits, rounding to the nearest thousand. One hundred times 2,000 is 200,000, so Colorado issued only about ten times as many building permits as Vermont, not 100 times as many.

Construct Arguments

Alisa says it is easier to compare the numbers in Set A than the numbers in Set B.

DATA

Set A	Set B
45,760	492,111
1,025,680	409,867

1. What is one way you could construct an argument justifying whether Alisa's conjecture is true?

2. Is Alisa's conjecture true? Justify your answer.

3. Alisa wrote a comparison for Set B using the ten thousands place. Explain what strategy she could have used.

Performance Assessment ISTEP+ Ready

Flight Distances

Chicago O'Hare is a busy international airport. The map shows the flight distance from Chicago O'Hare to several cities. Lee conjectured the flight distance from Chicago to Istanbul is the same as the flight distance from Chicago to Sao Paulo when the distances are rounded to the nearest thousand.

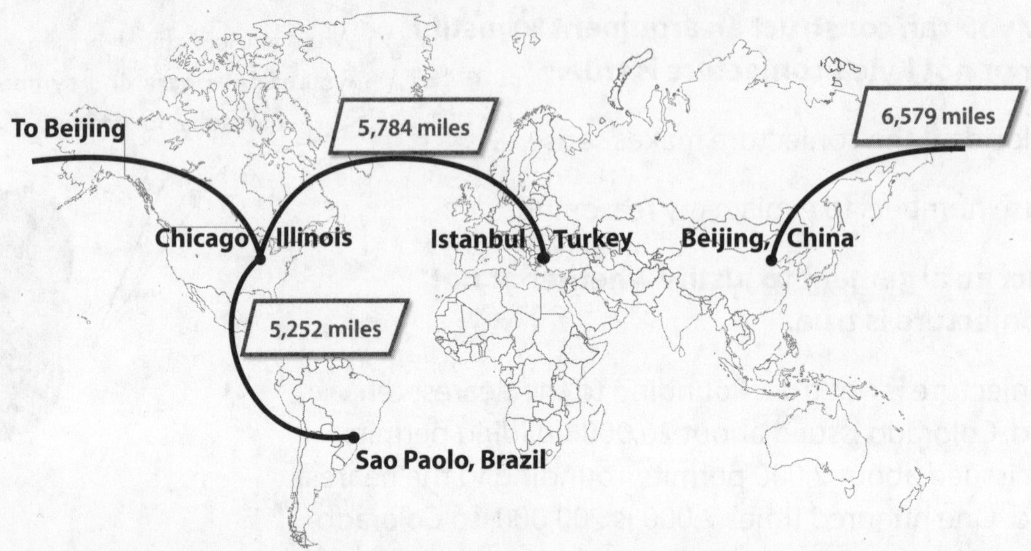

4. **Construct Arguments** Describe at least one way you could construct an argument justifying Lee's conjecture.

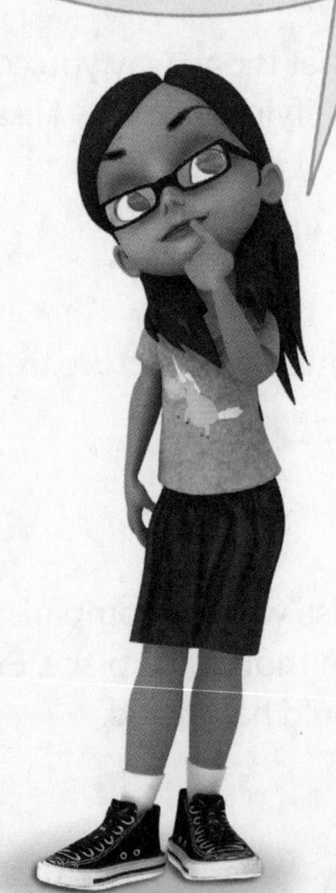

When you construct arguments, you can use place-value understanding.

5. **Be Precise** How can you round the two flight distances in Lee's conjecture?

6. **Reasoning** Is Lee's conjecture true? Justify your answer.

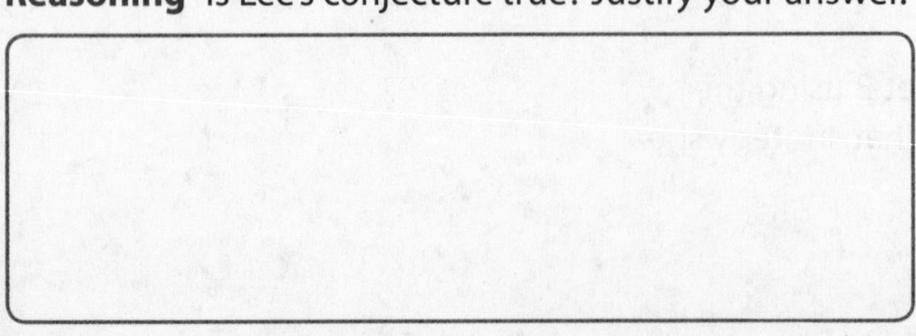

Name ____________________

TOPIC 1 Fluency Practice Activity

Find a partner. Get paper and pencil. Each partner chooses a different color: Light blue or dark blue.

Partner 1 and Partner 2 each point to a black number at the same time. Both partners multiply those numbers.

If the answer is on your color, you get a tally mark. Work until one partner has twelve tally marks.

I can ...
multiply within 100.

Partner 1

6
9
8
5
7

40	28	45	56
24	24	36	20
63	48	63	64
15	42	49	32
54	27	35	21
72	72	18	81

Partner 2

7
4
3
9
8

Tally Marks for Partner 1	Tally Marks for Partner 2

Word List

- conjecture
- expanded form
- greater than symbol (>)
- less than symbol (<)
- millions
- period
- place value
- rounding

Understand Vocabulary

Choose the best term from the box. Write it on the blank.

1. A group of three digits, separated by commas, starting from the right is called a ________________.
2. A process that determines which multiple of 10, 100, 1,000, and so on, a number is closest to is called ________________.
3. A statement that is believed to be true, but has not yet been proven is called a ________________.
4. The value given to a place a digit has in a number is called its ________________.
5. In a number, a period of three places to the left of the thousands period is called the ________________ period.

For each of these terms, give an example and a non-example.

	Example	Non-example
6. greater than symbol (>)	________	________
7. less than symbol (<)	________	________
8. expanded form	________	________

Use Vocabulary in Writing

9. Describe the value of the 9 in 926,415. Use at least 2 terms from the Word List in your explanation.

Name ______________________________

TOPIC 1

Reteaching

Set A pages 5–10

Use a place-value chart to write 301,400.

Expanded form: 300,000 + 1,000 + 400

Number names: three hundred one thousand, four hundred

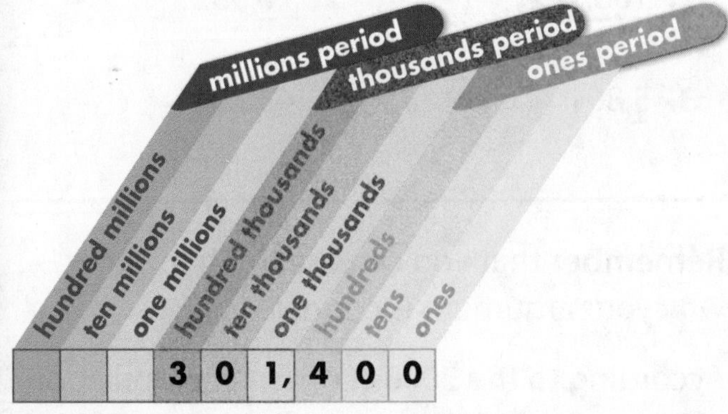

Remember that periods can help you read large numbers.

Write each number in expanded form and using number names.

1. 27,549

2. 792,065

Set B pages 11–16

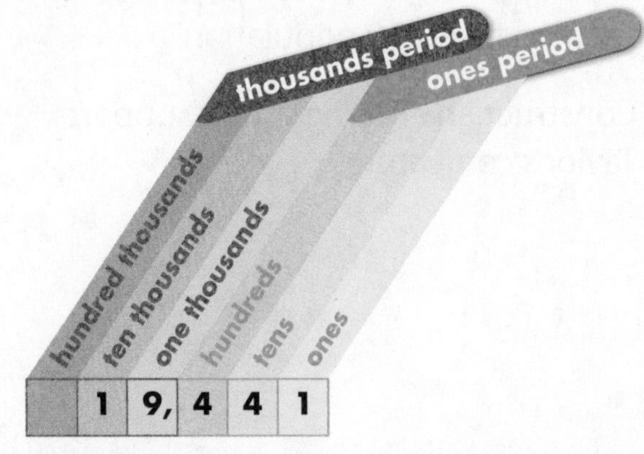

The first 4 is in the hundreds place. Its value is 400. The second 4 is in the tens place. The value of the 4 in the hundreds place is 10 times the value of the 4 in the tens place.

Remember that when two digits next to each other in a number are the same, the one on the left is 10 times greater than the one on the right.

For **1–2**, name the values of the given digits.

1. the 8s in 5,188

2. the 7s in 477,000

3. In 803,349, how is the value of the 3 in the thousands place related to the value of the 3 in the hundreds place?

Set C pages 17–22

Use place value to compare 45,423 and 44,897. Start comparing from the left. Look for the first digit that is different.

45,423   44,897

5 > 4

So, 45,423 > 44,897.

Remember that you can use place value to compare numbers.

Write < or > in the ◯.

1. 291,846 ◯ 291,864

2. 662,980 ◯ 66,298

3. 88,645 ◯ 87,645

Set D pages 23–28

Round 764,802 to the nearest hundred thousand.

hundred thousands place

$\underline{7}64,802$ The digit to the right of the rounding place is 6.

$\underline{8}00,000$ Since 6 > 5, round by adding 1 to the digit in the hundred thousands place.

So, 764,802 rounds to 800,000.

Remember to look at the digit to the right of the rounding place. Then change the digits to the right of the rounding place to zeros.

For **1–4**, round each number to the place of the underlined digit.

1. $16\underline{6},742$

2. $7\underline{6},532$

3. $\underline{5},861$

4. $43\underline{2},041$

Set E pages 29–34

Think about these questions to help you **construct arguments**.

Thinking Habits

- How can I use numbers, objects, drawings, or actions to justify my argument?
- Am I using numbers and symbols correctly?
- Is my explanation clear and complete?

Remember that you can use math to show why your argument is correct.

According to the 2000 census, the population of a city was 935,426. According to the 2010 census, the population of the same city was 934,578. Taylor says the 2000 population was greater than the 2010 population.

1. Construct an argument that supports Taylor's conjecture.

2. In 1870, the population was seventy-two thousand, five hundred six. Lupita wrote 72,560. Construct a math argument that explains whether Lupita wrote the number correctly.

Name ______________________________

1. Choose all the numbers that round to 100,000 when rounded to the nearest hundred thousand.

- ☐ 9,999
- ☐ 89,006
- ☐ 109,999
- ☐ 119,999
- ☐ 999,999

2. Which symbol makes the comparison true? Write the correct symbol from the box.

111,011 ◯ 110,111

< > =

3. Write three numbers that round to 40,000 when rounded to the nearest ten thousand.

4. Drew wrote a number that has a 7 in the hundreds place and a 7 in the ten-thousands place. Which could be Drew's number? Choose Yes or No.

4a. 177,871 ○ Yes ○ No

4b. 579,723 ○ Yes ○ No

4c. 777,075 ○ Yes ○ No

4d. 375,778 ○ Yes ○ No

5. The table shows the number of customers that have shopped at three pet stores over the past year.

Number of Customers	
For All Petkind	375,595
The Pet Lot	545,150
Pet Town	378,658

Part A

Write the expanded form of each number in the **Number of Customers** table.

Part B

Use the **Number of Customers** table. Which number has one digit that represents ten times the value of the digit to its right? Explain.

6. Miles writes the number for 160,060 in expanded form. What did Miles write?

7. Draw lines to match the value of the underlined digit in the numbers on the left to the numbers on the right.

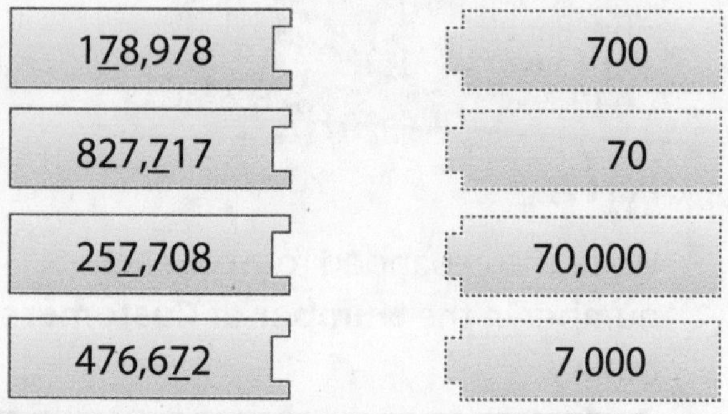

8. Which is one hundred twenty-one thousand, two hundred eleven using base-ten numerals?

Ⓐ 211,121

Ⓑ 121,211

Ⓒ 121,212

Ⓓ 112,211

9. Choose Yes or No to tell if the comparison is correct.

9a. 54,104 > 54,401 ○ Yes ○ No

9b. 101,199 < 110,199 ○ Yes ○ No

9c. 789,131 > 789,113 ○ Yes ○ No

9d. 909,999 < 999,999 ○ Yes ○ No

10. The table shows the areas of four states.

State	Area (square miles)
Montana	147,042
Oklahoma	68,898
Oregon	98,381
Wyoming	97,814

Part A

Which of the 4 states has the least area? the greatest area? Write the number name for the area of each of these states.

Part B

Draw a place-value chart. Record Oklahoma's area. Explain how the value of the 8 in the thousands place compares with the value of the 8 in the hundreds place.

Name ______________________________

Video Games

Tanji, Arun, and Juanita are playing a video game with 3 levels. The opportunity to earn points increases as the levels of the game increase. To keep track of their progress, Tanji, Arun, and Juanita record and examine their scores at each level.

1. Use the **Level 1** table to answer the following questions.

Part A

Tanji noticed he was the only player with 3s in his Level 1 score. What are the values of the 3s in Tanji's score?

DATA

Level 1	
Player	**Score**
Tanji	4,337
Arun	5,519
Juanita	2,868

Part B

Arun noticed the 5s in his score were next to each other. Describe the relationship between the 5s in Arun's score.

Part C

Juanita says the value of one 8 in her score is ten times greater than the value of the other 8. Construct an argument and draw a place-value chart to determine if Juanita is correct.

2. Use the **Level 2** table to answer the following questions.

DATA

Level 2	
Player	**Score**
Tanji	56,899
Arun	39,207
Juanita	60,114

Part A

Juanita had the greatest score at Level 2, followed by Tanji and Arun. Write each player's score in expanded form to compare each score by place value.

Part B

Write each player's score using number names.

Part C

Use >, =, or < to write comparisons between the Level 2 scores.

Part D

Arun noticed his Level 2 score has a greater value in the thousands place than Tanji's and Juanita's Level 2 scores. Round Arun's score to the nearest thousand.

Fluently Add and Subtract Multi-Digit Whole Numbers

Essential Questions: How can sums and differences of whole numbers be estimated? What are standard procedures for adding and subtracting whole numbers?

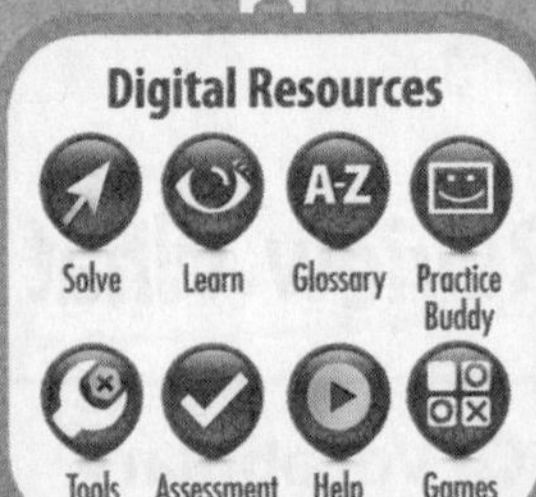

In 1970, a rocket-powered vehicle was the first to travel over 1,000 kilometers per hour!

The faster an object is moving, the more energy it has.

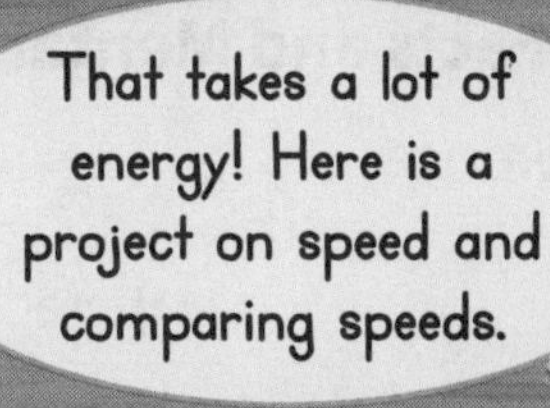

That takes a lot of energy! Here is a project on speed and comparing speeds.

Math and Science Project: The World's Fastest Vehicles

Do Research Since 1970, the speed record has been broken many times. Use the Internet or other sources to find five vehicles that can go faster than 1,000 kilometers per hour.

Journal: Write a Report Include what you found. Also in your report:

- Make a table that includes the type of vehicle, whether the vehicle moves on land, water, or in space, and the speed of the vehicle.
- Use place value to find the fastest and the slowest vehicle in your table.
- Calculate the difference between the speeds of two of the vehicles in your table.

Name ______________________________

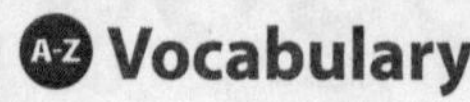

Review What You Know

Vocabulary

Choose the best term from the box. Write it on the blank.

- equation
- estimate
- period
- rounding

1. An ______________ is an approximate number or answer.

2. A process that determines which multiple of 10, 100, 1,000, and so on a number is closest to is called ______________.

3. A number sentence that uses the equal sign (=) to show two expressions have the same value is an ______________.

Addition Facts and Mental Math

Find each sum.

4. 4 + 6 **5.** 7 + 5 **6.** 29 + 8

7. 14 + 5 **8.** 13 + 7 **9.** 37 + 7

10. 289 + 126 **11.** 468 + 329 **12.** 157 + 211

Subtraction Facts and Mental Math

Find each difference.

13. 27 − 3 **14.** 6 − 4 **15.** 15 − 8

16. 11 − 8 **17.** 66 − 2 **18.** 17 − 8

19. 416 − 404 **20.** 220 − 205 **21.** 148 − 106

Rounding

22. Construct Arguments Why does 843,000 round to 840,000 rather than 850,000 when rounded to the nearest ten thousand?

A good math explanation should be clear, complete, and easy to understand.

A-Z Glossary

My Word Cards

Use the examples for each word on the front of the card to help complete the definitions on the back.

Commutative Property of Addition

$5 + 7 = 12$

$7 + 5 = 12$

Associative Property of Addition

$(4 + 3) + 8 = 15$

$4 + (3 + 8) = 15$

$(4 + 3) + 8 = 4 + (3 + 8)$

Identity Property of Addition

$2 + 0 = 2$

$4 + 0 = 4$

$17 + 0 = 17$

counting on

$400 - 165$

400

165	5	30	200

$5 + 30 + 200 = 235$

$400 - 165 = 235$

compensation

$135 + 48 = ?$

135	185
+ 50	− 2
185	183

I added 2 too many so I will subtract 2.

variable

$y = 5$ $x = 3$ $n = 7$

algorithm

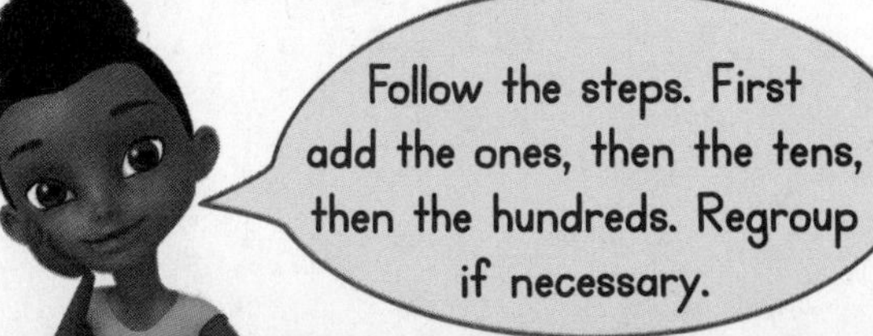

Follow the steps. First add the ones, then the tens, then the hundreds. Regroup if necessary.

inverse operations

addition		subtraction
$14 + 12 = 26$	↔	$26 - 12 = 14$
multiplication		**division**
$8 \times 9 = 72$	↔	$72 \div 9 = 8$

My Word Cards

Complete each definition. Extend learning by writing your own definitions.

The ______________________

______________________ states that addends can be regrouped and the sum remains the same.

The ______________________

______________________ states that numbers can be added in any order and the sum remains the same.

Counting up from the lesser number to the greater number to find the difference of two numbers is known as

______________________.

The ______________________

______________________ states the sum of any number and zero is that number.

A symbol or letter that stands for a number is a ______________________.

Choosing numbers close to the numbers in a problem to make the computation easier, and then adjusting the answer for the numbers chosen is called ______________________.

Operations that can undo each other are ______________________

______________________.

An ______________________ is a set of steps used to solve a math problem.

Name ____________________________________

Lesson 2-1
Mental Math: Find Sums and Differences

I can ...
use properties and strategies to change the structure of a problem to add and subtract with mental math.

Content Standard Prepares for 4.C.1
Process Standards PS.2, PS.3, PS.6, PS.7

Solve & Share

Luke collected 1,034 baseball cards, 1,289 football cards, and 1,566 hockey cards. Use mental math to find the number of cards in Luke's collection. ***Solve this problem any way you choose.***

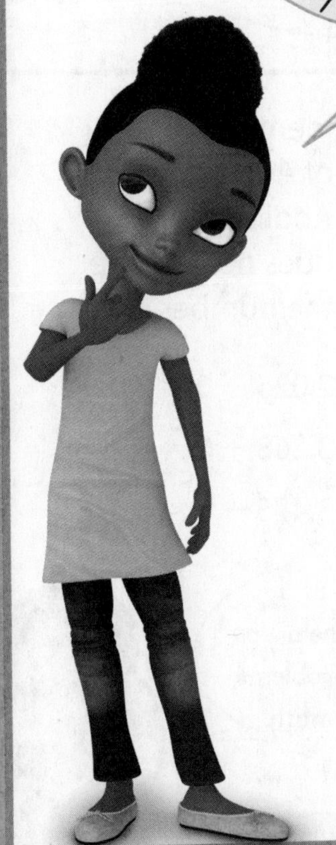

You can use structure. You can break apart the addends and use mental math to find the sum. *Show your work in the space below!*

Look Back! Construct Arguments Why is 1,034 + 1,566 an easier problem to solve mentally than 1,289 + 1,566?

How Can You Use Mental Math to Solve Problems?

A

The table shows how many windows a team of window washers cleaned on a skyscraper over three months. How many windows did they clean in September and October? What is the total number of windows they cleaned in three months?

DATA

Month	Windows Washed
September	2,025
October	3,268
November	3,475

You can use properties of operations and bar diagrams to help solve.

B

Commutative Property of Addition: You can add two numbers in any order.

Find 2,025 + 3,268.

5,293	
2,025	3,268

2,025 + 3,268 = 3,268 + 2,025

The window washers cleaned 5,293 windows in September and October.

C

Associative Property of Addition: You can change the grouping of addends.

Find 2,025 + 3,268 + 3,475.

8,768		
2,025	3,268	3,475

(2,025 + 3,268) + 3,475 = 2,025 + (3,268 + 3,475)

The window washers cleaned a total of 8,768 windows in three months.

D

Identity Property of Addition: Adding zero does not change the number.

2,025 + 0 = 2,025

3,268 + 0 = 3,268

3,475 + 0 = 3,475

Properties of operations can help you solve addition problems using mental math.

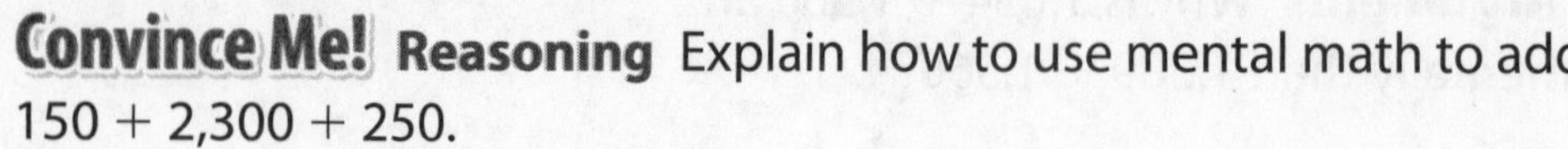

Convince Me! **Reasoning** Explain how to use mental math to add 150 + 2,300 + 250.

Name ____________________

Another Example!

Mental math strategies can help you add or subtract.

Break Apart

Find 2,864 + 1,136.

Break apart the addends.

2,000 + 1,000 = 3,000

800 + 100 = 900

64 + 36 = 100

Then add the sums.

3,000 + 900 + 100 = 4,000

So, 2,864 + 1,136 = 4,000.

Counting On

Find 1,136 − 897.

Use counting on to subtract.

3 + 200 + 30 + 6 = 239

So, 1,136 − 897 = 239.

Compensation

Find 4,260 − 2,170.

Use compensation.

It is easier to subtract 2,200 than 2,170.

4,260 − 2,200 = 2,060

I subtracted 30 too many, so I will add 30 to the difference.

2,060 + 30 = 2,090

So, 4,260 − 2,170 = 2,090.

Guided Practice*

Do You Understand?

1. **Use Structure** Sheri adds 135 + 1,048 using mental math. What properties and strategies can Sheri use to find the sum?

Do You Know How?

For **2–4**, use mental math strategies to solve.

2. 6,794 − 1,058

3. 72,314 + 35,525

4. (92,180 + 69,238) + 7,820

Independent Practice

For **5–13**, use mental math strategies to solve.

5. 7,100 − 827
6. 9,100 + 2,130 + 900
7. 5,491 − 2,860
8. 6,686 − 1,443
9. 58,375 + 31,842
10. 426,100 + 74,900
11. 1,700 − 315
12. 2,000 + 4,996
13. 11,219 − 1,219

*For another example, see Set A on page 85.

Problem Solving

For **14–15**, use the table at the right.

14. Which state has the greatest land area in square miles? Use number names to write the area.

State	Total Square Miles
Alaska	571,951
California	155,959
Montana	145,552
New Mexico	121,356
Texas	261,797

15. Round the land area of the state with the least number of total square miles to the nearest ten thousand.

16. The town of Worman Grove collected 9,645 blue pens and 18,836 black pens for a school supplies drive. Their goal is 30,000 pens. Show how to use counting on to find how many more pens they need to reach their goal.

17. Conservationists weigh two Northern elephant seals. An adult seal weighs 6,600 pounds, and its pup weighs 3,847 pounds. How much less does the pup weigh than the adult?

6,600

3,847	?

18. Reasoning Is 86,100 − 36,287 greater than or less than 50,000? Explain how you can tell using mental math.

19. Higher Order Thinking Kelly uses compensation to add 5,756 and 2,398. Her answer is 8,156. Is Kelly's answer correct? What mistake may she have made?

Assessment ISTEP+ Ready

20. Garry solves a subtraction problem. First he uses the Associative Property to group 6,145 and 2,145 together. Then he subtracts their difference from 17,422. Do you agree with Garry's reasoning? Explain.

Garry's Work

17,422 − 6,145 − 2,145
17,422 − (6,145 − 2,145)
17,422 − 4,000
13,422

Name ______________________

Homework & Practice 2-1

Mental Math: Find Sums and Differences

Another Look!

There are different strategies for adding and subtracting with mental math.

Addition Strategies

Find 3,728 + 2,420.

One Way

Break up the addends by place value.

3,000 + 2,000 = 5,000
700 + 400 = 1,100
20 + 20 = 40
8 + 0 = 8

$$\begin{array}{r} 5{,}000 \\ 1{,}100 \\ 40 \\ +\quad 8 \\ \hline 6{,}148 \end{array}$$

Another Way

Use compensation to find 3,728 + 2,420.

2,400 is easier to add than 2,420.

3,728 + 2,400 = 6,128.

Add 20 to the answer because 20 was subtracted earlier.

6,128 + 20 = 6,148

Subtraction Strategies

Find 40,000 − 7,985.

One Way

Use compensation.

8,000 is easier to subtract than 7,985.

40,000 − 8,000 = 32,000

Since you subtracted 15 too many, add 15 to your answer.

32,000 + 15 = 32,015

Another Way

Use counting on to find 40,000 − 7,985.

7,985 + 15 = 8,000
8,000 + 2,000 = 10,000
10,000 + 30,000 = 40,000

Add the parts.

30,000 + 2,000 + 15 = 32,015

For **1–10**, use mental math to solve.

You can choose the mental math strategy you think will work best.

1. 4,576 + 2,842

2. 56,211 − 6,189

3. 218,389 + 40,510

4. 72,000 − 41,426

5. 46,524 + (37,824 + 2,176)

6. 658,843 − 7,635

7. (86,765 + 36,235) + 24,215

8. 9,378 − 2,536

9. 8,452 + (917 + 0)

10. 12,211 + 11,298

11. Math and Science Write and solve a number sentence to find the difference between the speeds of the planets Venus and Saturn. Then write the difference using number names.

DATA

Speeds of Planets

Planet	Speed (Miles per hour)
Neptune	12,253
Saturn	21,637
Mars	53,979
Venus	78,341

12. Be Precise Use a mental math strategy to find 4,290 + 3,602. Explain how to check your answer using a different strategy.

13. Janelle needs to score 280,000 points on her computer game to get to the next level. So far, she has scored 96,675 points. How many more points does Janelle need to score to reach the next level? Use mental math strategies to find the answer.

14. A-Z **Vocabulary** June is working on an addition problem and starts with 17,985. After she adds, she still has 17,985. Which property of addition did June use? How do you know?

15. Higher Order Thinking Explain how you can use mental math to perform the following addition:

61,438 + 54,579 + 28,562

Assessment ISTEP+ Ready

16. Guy wants to add 7,145 and 8,265 and using mental math strategies. What steps could Guy take to add the numbers? Is Guy's answer correct? Explain.

Guy's Work

7,145 + 8,265 = 15,410

Name ______________________________ Solve

Lesson 2-2

Mental Math: Estimate Sums and Differences

I can ...
use rounding and place value to estimate sums and differences.

Content Standard Prepares for 4.C.1
Process Standards PS.1, PS.3, PS.5, PS.6

Solve & Share

A manufacturer in Detroit produces three new cars that weigh 6,127 pounds, 4,652 pounds, and 3,393 pounds. About how much do the three cars weigh in all? Use the bar diagram to show the problem. ***Solve this problem any way you choose.***

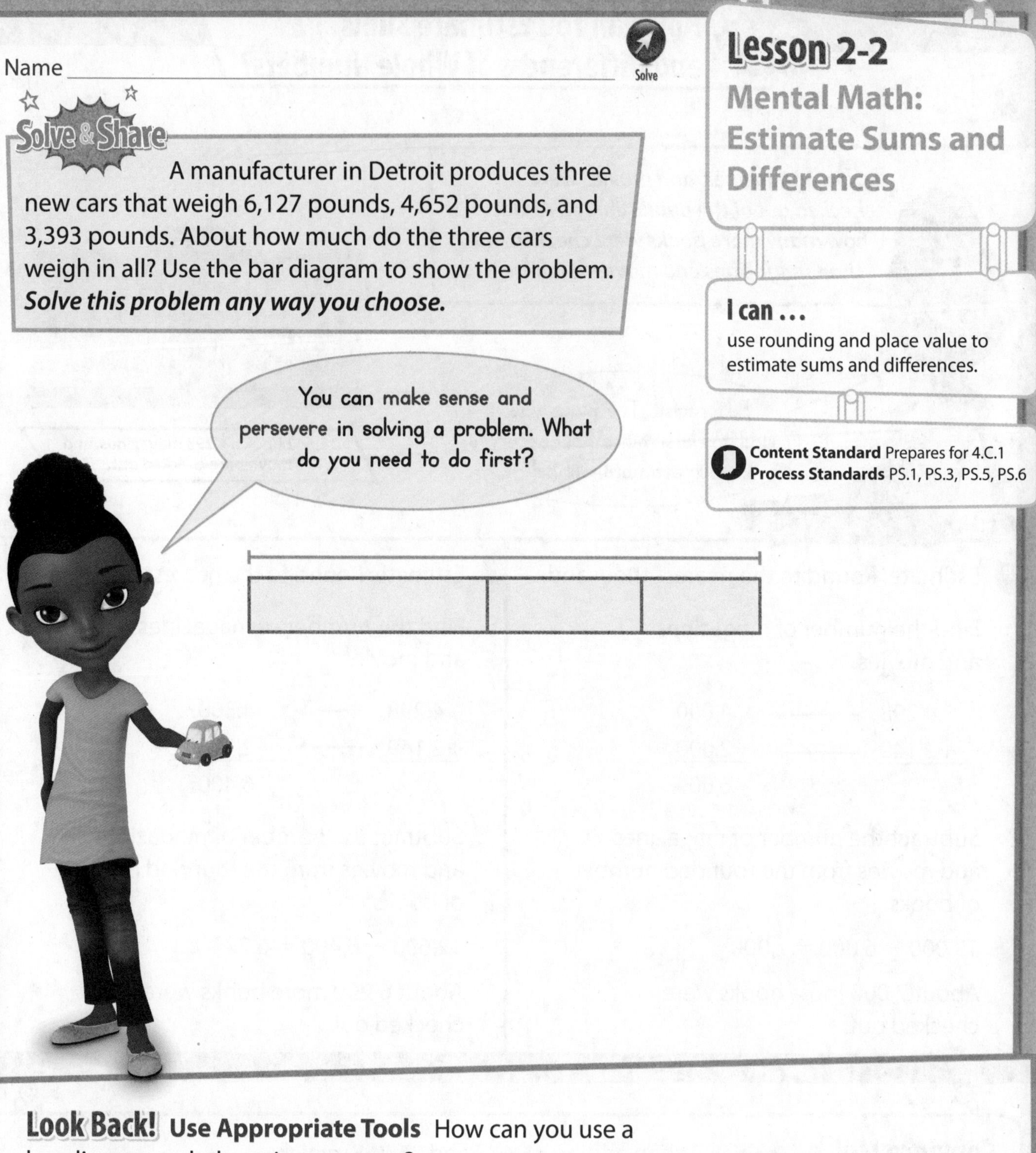

You can make sense and persevere in solving a problem. What do you need to do first?

Look Back! Use Appropriate Tools How can you use a bar diagram to help estimate a sum?

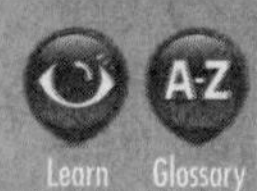

How Can You Estimate Sums and Differences of Whole Numbers?

A

Books, magazines, and movies were checked out of the public library. About how many more books were checked out than magazines and movies combined?

Be precise. The place you round to determines how accurate your estimate will be!

12,642 books, 4,298 magazines, and 2,149 movies are checked out.

B Estimate: Round to the nearest thousand.

Find the number of magazines and movies.

$$\begin{array}{r} 4{,}298 \\ +2{,}149 \\ \hline \end{array} \longrightarrow \begin{array}{r} 4{,}000 \\ +2{,}000 \\ \hline 6{,}000 \end{array}$$

Subtract the number of magazines and movies from the rounded number of books.

13,000 − 6,000 = 7,000

About 7,000 more books were checked out.

C Estimate: Round to the nearest hundred.

Find the number of magazines and movies.

$$\begin{array}{r} 4{,}298 \\ +2{,}149 \\ \hline \end{array} \longrightarrow \begin{array}{r} 4{,}300 \\ +2{,}100 \\ \hline 6{,}400 \end{array}$$

Subtract the number of magazines and movies from the rounded number of books.

12,600 − 6,400 = 6,200

About 6,200 more books were checked out.

Convince Me! **Be Precise** When adding 45,472 and 36,768, which gives the more precise estimate: rounding the addends to the nearest ten thousand, thousand, or hundred? Explain.

Name ______________________________

Guided Practice*

Do You Understand?

1. **Construct Arguments** To which place would you round to estimate 6,904 − 4,111? Explain.

2. The diameter of Saturn is 120,536 kilometers. Its widest rings have a diameter of 273,588 kilometers. To the nearest hundred thousand, about how much greater is the diameter of the rings than the diameter of Saturn?

Do You Know How?

For **3–8**, estimate each sum or difference.

3. 5,638 → ☐,☐00
 \+ 3,753 → ☐,☐00

4. 28,881 → ☐☐,000
 − 17,759 → − ☐☐,000

5. 63,526
 \+ 25,038

6. 262,262
 − 132,147

7. 9,524
 − 4,025

8. 30,098
 \+ 10,217

Independent Practice*

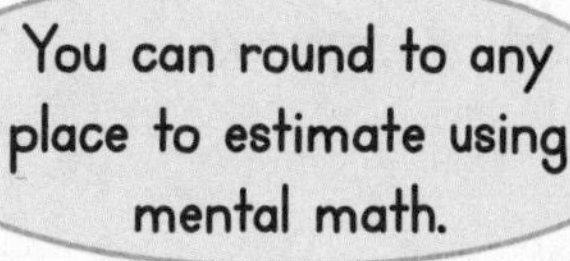

You can round to any place to estimate using mental math.

Leveled Practice For **9–20**, estimate each sum or difference.

9. 5,323 → ☐,000
 \+ 2,611 → + ☐,000

10. 542,817 → ☐☐☐,☐00
 − 27,398 → − ☐☐,☐00

11. 49,761 → ☐0,000
 \+ 59,499 → + ☐0,000

12. 4,225
 \+ 98

13. 738,775
 \+ 272,044

14. 24,300
 − 10,125

15. 485,635
 − 231,957

16. 9,668
 − 2,489

17. 368,545
 \+ 114,254

18. 150,499
 − 72,501

19. 95,487
 − 61,628

20. 5,317
 \+ 1,734

*For another example, see Set B on page 85.

Problem Solving

21. **Number Sense** The table shows the number of students at each school in the district. Estimate the total number of students at Wilson Elementary and Kwame Charter School. Explain.

DATA

Numbers of Students in District 37

School	Number of Students
Wilson Elementary	1,523
Hearst Academy	1,471
Kwame Charter School	1,458
Evers Elementary	1,697

22. **Math and Science** A satellite moves at a speed of about 27,000 kilometers per hour. Write four numbers that could be the actual speed of the satellite.

23. **Critique Reasoning** Elle says, "When rounding to the nearest thousand, 928,674 rounds to 930,000." Do you agree? Explain.

24. Jill climbed 3,240 feet up the mountain. Phil climbed a total of 3,600 up the same mountain. After Jill rested, she climbed up another 335 feet. Who climbed higher up the mountain? Explain.

25. **Higher Order Thinking** Suppose you want to estimate the sum of 10,234 and 10,563. Will rounding each number to the nearest hundred give an answer closer to the actual sum than rounding to the nearest ten? Explain.

Assessment ISTEP+ Ready

26. Last week, Mallory flew two round trips. They were 3,720 miles and 5,985 miles. Select all of the choices that are good estimates for the total miles Mallory flew last week by rounding to place values.

- ☐ 10,000
- ☐ 9,710
- ☐ 9,700
- ☐ 8,700
- ☐ 8,000

27. To the nearest ten thousand, Calvin estimates the difference of a subtraction problem at 220,000. Select all that could have been Calvin's original problem.

- ☐ 232,684 − 14,652
- ☐ 238,041 − 19,558
- ☐ 271,982 − 64,780
- ☐ 298,155 − 75,437
- ☐ 242,698 − 18,765

Name ______________________

Homework & Practice 2-2

Mental Math: Estimate Sums and Differences

Another Look!

You can use rounding to estimate sums and differences.

To estimate 64,236 + 15,542:	To estimate 452,776 − 186,257:
Round to the nearest hundred	Round to the nearest thousand
64,200 + 15,500 = 79,700	453,000 − 186,000 = 267,000
Round to the nearest thousand	Round to the nearest ten thousand
64,000 + 16,000 = 80,000	450,000 − 190,000 = 260,000
Round to the nearest ten thousand	Round to the nearest hundred thousand
60,000 + 20,000 = 80,000	500,000 − 200,000 = 300,000

For **1–10**, estimate each sum or difference.

1. 753,265 → ☐☐0,000
− 419,057 → − ☐☐0,000

2. 48,765 → ☐☐,000
+ 9,221 → + ☐,000

3. 7,792 → ☐,000
− 3,847 → − ☐,000

4. 2,189
+ 1,388

5. 9,245
− 4,033

6. 1,000,000
− 447,618

7. 65,327 − 14,231

8. 391,192 + 511,864

9. 8,475 + 1,329

10. 812,910 − 709,085

Your estimate may be different from someone else's estimate. That's okay if both estimates are reasonable.

For **11–12**, use the table at the right.

11. Make Sense and Persevere About how much greater is the area of the largest ocean than the area of the smallest ocean?

12. Write the area of the Pacific Ocean in expanded form.

DATA

Ocean Area

Ocean	Area (sq km)
Arctic Ocean	14,090
Atlantic Ocean	82,400
Indian Ocean	65,527
Pacific Ocean	165,760

13. Algebra In a local election, 138,201 people voted for the winning candidate. If she won by 29,288 votes, about how many votes did the other candidate receive?

14. In one weekend, a theatre sells 74,877 tickets to a new movie. Write the values for each of the 7s in 74,877.

15. Number Sense Is 9,760 − 5,220 more or less than 4,000? Explain how you can tell without finding the exact difference.

16. Higher Order Thinking The fourth graders sang on a two-day telethon for the local children's hospital. The hospital hoped to raise $750,000. On day one, they raised $398,622. On day two, they raised $379,873. Did they reach their goal? About how much more or less did they raise?

Assessment ISTEP+ Ready

17. Anya says, "62,996 rounds to 63,000." Select all the places to which she could have rounded the number.

- ☐ ones
- ☐ tens
- ☐ hundreds
- ☐ thousands
- ☐ ten thousands

18. Select all of the choices that are reasonable estimates for the difference of 874,169 − 387,245 by rounding to place values.

- ☐ 486,920
- ☐ 487,000
- ☐ 480,000
- ☐ 500,000
- ☐ 600,000

Name ______________________________ Solve

Lesson 2-3
Add Whole Numbers

I can ...
use the standard algorithm and place value to add multi-digit numbers.

Content Standards 4.C.1, 4.AT.1
Process Standards PS.1, PS.3, PS.5, PS.6

Solve & Share

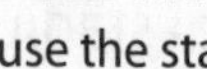

Erica's class collected 4,219 bottles for the recycling center. Ana's class collected 3,742 bottles. Leon's class collected 4,436 bottles. How many bottles did the three classes collect? ***Solve this problem any way you choose.***

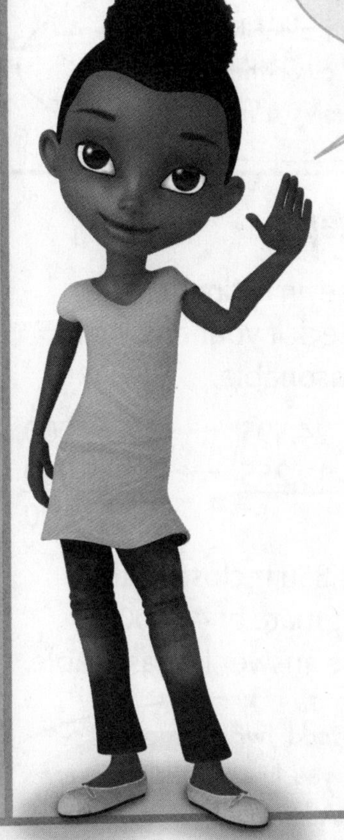

You can use structure to break up greater numbers by place value to help you add. *Show your work in the space below!*

Look Back! **Generalize** Which property states you can group numbers to add? How does the property make it easier to add two or more numbers?

Learn Glossary

How Do You Add Whole Numbers?

A

Plans for remodeling a sports stadium include adding an additional 19,255 seats. How many seats will be in the remodeled stadium?

Seats in the original stadium:
20,000 + 4,595 = 24,595

You can use a variable to represent the unknown value. The variable, *s*, represents the total number of seats in the remodeled stadium.

s	
24,595	19,255

You can use an algorithm to solve. Remember, an algorithm is a set of steps used to solve a math problem.

B

Step 1

Use the standard algorithm for addition.

To add 24,595 + 19,255, add the ones, then the tens, and then the hundreds. Regroup if necessary.

$$\begin{array}{r} \scriptstyle{1\,1} \\ 24{,}595 \\ +\ 19{,}255 \\ \hline 850 \end{array}$$

C

Step 2

Add the thousands and the ten thousands. Regroup if necessary.

$$\begin{array}{r} \scriptstyle{1}\scriptstyle{1\,1} \\ 24{,}595 \\ +\ 19{,}255 \\ \hline 43{,}850 \end{array}$$

s = 43,850

The remodeled stadium will have 43,850 seats.

D

Step 3

Use an estimate to check if your answer is reasonable.

$$\begin{array}{r} 24{,}595 \\ +\ 19{,}255 \\ \hline \end{array} \rightarrow \begin{array}{r} \scriptstyle{1} \\ 25{,}000 \\ +\ 19{,}000 \\ \hline 44{,}000 \end{array}$$

43,850 is close to the estimate of 44,000, so the answer is reasonable.

You can add two or more numbers when you line up the numbers by place value. Add one place at a time.

Convince Me! **Use Structure** If all of the seats at the basketball arenas listed in the table are filled, what is the total number of people in these three arenas?

DATA

Basketball Arena	Number of Seats
Memorial Dome	16,285
Park Center	18,187
Central Arena	20,557

Name ______

Practice Buddy Tools Assessment

Another Example!

Find 30,283 + 63,423 + 6,538.

Estimate:
30,000 + 63,000 + 7,000 = 100,000

```
  1 1 1 1
  30,283
  63,423
+  6,538
 100,244
```

The sum is reasonable because it is close to the estimate of 100,000.

Guided Practice*

Do You Understand?

1. **Construct Arguments** When adding 36,424 and 24,482, why is there no regrouping in the final step?

2. Science-volunteer teams catalog 7,836 species of insects and 4,922 species of spiders. How many species did the volunteers catalog?

Do You Know How?

For **3–6**, estimate. Then find each sum.

3. 14,926 + 3,382

4. 423,156 + 571,607

5. 3,258 + 1,761

6. 82,385 + 49,817

Independent Practice

Use estimation to check if your answer is reasonable.

For **7–16**, estimate. Then find each sum.

7. 14,312 + 9,617

8. 275,558 + 605,131

9. 38,911 + 45,681

10. 5,801 + 4,189

11. 8,818 + 1,182

12. 5,555 + 7,412

13. 21,009 + 5,529

14. 30,080 + 19,187

15. 29,634 + 12,958 + 6,835

16. 64,673 + 48,262 + 298,918

*For another example, see Set C on page 85.

Problem Solving

17. Beth ate $\frac{2}{8}$ of a pie. Jim ate $\frac{3}{8}$ of a same-size pie. Who ate more pie? Write a comparison.

18. Write the number name for 21,604.

19. **Construct Arguments** Explain the mistake made when finding the sum at the right. What is the correct sum?

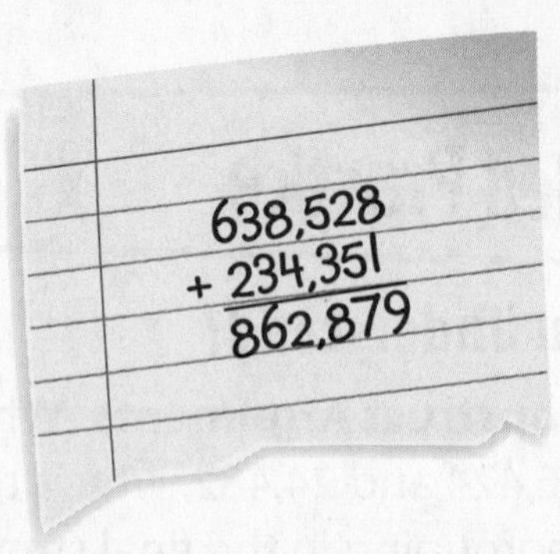

20. **Number Sense** Maria added 45,273 and 35,687 and got a sum of 70,960. Is Maria's answer reasonable? Explain.

21. **Higher Order Thinking** There were 130,453 pairs of skates rented at an ice rink in one year. The next year, 108,626 pairs were rented. The following year 178,119 pairs were rented. How many pairs were rented during the busiest two years? How many pairs were rented during all three years?

22. Aubrey writes a blog. 29,604 people read her first post. The next week, 47,684 people read her second post. Aubrey's third post has 41,582 readers.

Part A

Write to explain how you can round to estimate the total number of readers for Aubrey's first three blog posts.

Part B

What is the actual number of readers? How can you use the estimate to check if your answer is reasonable?

Name ______________________________

Homework & Practice 2-3
Add Whole Numbers

Another Look!

You can add two or more numbers when you line up the numbers by place value. Add one place at a time.

Find 3,456 + 2,139 + 5,547.

Estimate: 3,500 + 2,100 + 5,500 = 11,100

Step 1	Step 2	Step 3
Line up the numbers by place value. Add the ones. Regroup if needed. $\begin{array}{r} \scriptstyle 2 \\ 3{,}456 \\ 2{,}139 \\ +\ 5{,}547 \\ \hline 2 \end{array}$ Regroup 22 ones as 2 tens and 2 ones.	Add the tens and hundreds. Regroup if needed. $\begin{array}{r} \scriptstyle 1\ 1\ 2 \\ 3{,}456 \\ 2{,}139 \\ +\ 5{,}547 \\ \hline 142 \end{array}$ Keep digits in columns as you add.	Add the thousands. Remember to regroup for ten thousands if necessary. $\begin{array}{r} \scriptstyle 1\ 1\ 2 \\ 3{,}456 \\ 2{,}139 \\ +\ 5{,}547 \\ \hline 11{,}142 \end{array}$ 11,142 is close to the estimate of 11,100.

Use estimation to check if your answer is reasonable.

For **1–8**, find each sum.

1. $\begin{array}{r} 9{,}945 \\ +\ 3{,}343 \\ \hline \end{array}$

2. $\begin{array}{r} 12{,}566 \\ +\ 5{,}532 \\ \hline \end{array}$

3. $\begin{array}{r} 387{,}969 \\ +\ 562{,}031 \\ \hline \end{array}$

4. $\begin{array}{r} 629{,}979 \\ 294{,}116 \\ +\ \ 75{,}905 \\ \hline \end{array}$

5. $\begin{array}{r} 227{,}418 \\ 196{,}735 \\ +\ \ 48{,}062 \\ \hline \end{array}$

6. $\begin{array}{r} 82{,}011 \\ 96{,}489 \\ +\ 76{,}988 \\ \hline \end{array}$

7. $\begin{array}{r} 126{,}267 \\ 15{,}809 \\ +\ \ 8{,}764 \\ \hline \end{array}$

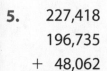

8. $\begin{array}{r} 45{,}101 \\ 35{,}099 \\ +\ 10{,}000 \\ \hline \end{array}$

9. Number Sense Estimate then add to find the combined length of the four highways shown in the table. Is your answer reasonable? Explain.

DATA

Lengths of Interstate Highways

Interstate	Length (miles)
I-90	3,102
I-10	2,460
I-70	2,153
I-80	2,899

10. Model with Math A shipping company delivered 38,728 letters and 41,584 packages. Write and solve an equation to find how many items the company delivered.

11. Algebra The total cost of the Fatigato family's two cars was $71,482. The cost of one car was $38,295. Write an equation using a variable to represent the cost of the family's other car.

12. Number Sense Leona added 206,425 + 128,579 + 314,004. Should Leona's sum be greater or less than 650,000?

13. Higher Order Thinking In one week, Katy walks 1,750 meters and runs 1,925 meters. She performs the same workouts for three weeks. How many meters does Katy walk and run in three weeks of workouts?

Assessment — ISTEP+ Ready

14. A recent census listed the population of a city as 831,982. Marisol rounds the population to 830,000, and Lindy rounds the population to 800,000.

Part A

Who rounded the population of the city correctly? Explain.

Part B

Which rounded population is a more accurate estimate?

Name ______________________________

Lesson 2-4
Subtract Whole Numbers

I can ...
use the standard algorithm and place value to subtract whole numbers.

Content Standards 4.C.1, 4.AT.1
Process Standards PS.1, PS.2, PS.3

Solve & Share Nevada has a land area of 109,781 square miles. Colorado has a land area of 103,642 square miles. How much larger is Nevada than Colorado? ***Solve this problem any way you choose.***

You can make sense of your answers by estimating before you subtract. *Show your work in the space below!*

Look Back! Construct Arguments How can you use addition to check your answer?

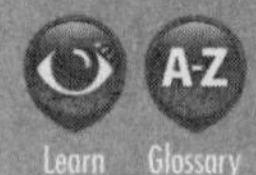

Essential Question How Do You Subtract Whole Numbers?

A

Three of the country's most scenic national parks are in Alaska. How much larger is the area of Gates of the Arctic than the combined area of Denali and Kenai Fjords?

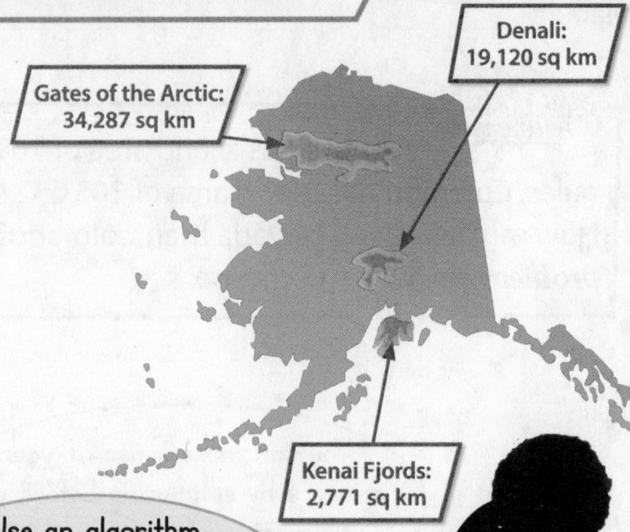

Find the total area of Denali and Kenai Fjords.

$$\begin{array}{r} 19{,}120 \\ +\ 2{,}771 \\ \hline 21{,}891 \end{array}$$ square kilometers

Then find the difference of the areas.

Use an algorithm to find the difference. Then use addition to check your answer.

34,287	
21,891	a

B

Step 1

Find 34,287 − 21,891.

Subtract the ones. Regroup if necessary.

$$\begin{array}{r} 34{,}287 \\ -\ 21{,}891 \\ \hline 6 \end{array}$$

C

Step 2

Subtract the tens, hundreds, thousands, and ten thousands.

Regroup if necessary.

$$\begin{array}{r} \scriptsize{3\ 11\ 18} \\ 3\not{4}{,}\not{2}87 \\ -\ 21{,}891 \\ \hline 12{,}396 \end{array}$$

Gates of the Arctic is 12,396 square kilometers larger.

D

Step 3

Operations that undo each other are inverse operations. Addition and subtraction have an inverse relationship. Add to check your answer.

$$\begin{array}{r} \scriptsize{1\ 1} \\ 12{,}396 \\ +\ 21{,}891 \\ \hline 34{,}287 \end{array}$$

Convince Me! **Critique Reasoning** The work shown below is **NOT** correct. What errors were made? Show how to find the correct answer.

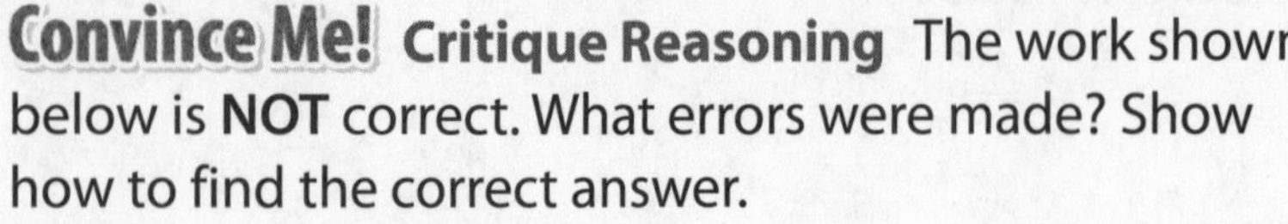

Name ____________________

Practice Buddy　Tools　Assessment

Another Example!

Find 68,792 − 33,215.

Estimate:
69,000 − 33,000 = 36,000

```
     812
  68,792
− 33,215
  35,577
```

You can use estimation to check if your answer is reasonable.

Guided Practice*

Do You Understand?

1. **Construct Arguments** In the Convince Me! problem on the previous page, why was the zero in the hundred thousands place not written in the answer?

2. The total land area of New Jersey is 19,047 square kilometers. Write and solve an equation to show how to find how much larger Gates of the Arctic is than New Jersey.

Do You Know How?

For **3–6**, subtract. Use inverse operations to check your differences.

3. 139,484 − 116,691

4. 2,164 − 1,398

5. 49,735 − 25,276

6. 281,311 − 3,427

Independent Practice

For **7–14**, subtract. Use inverse operations to check your differences.

7. 82,376 − 47,294

8. 653,642 − 562,410

9. 9,128 − 3,753

10. 42,648 − 8,169

11. 425,637 − 86,942

12. 8,457 − 1,946

13. 215,714 − 176,313

14. 85,968 − 74,084

*For another example, see Set D on page 86.

Problem Solving

15. **Reasoning** A crayon company makes 87,491 blue crayons, 36,262 red crayons, and 25,063 gray crayons. How many more blue crayons are made than red and gray crayons combined?

16. **Number Sense** Patrick subtracted 4,832 − 2,322 and got 2,510. Is his difference reasonable? Explain.

17. Nadia writes the following subtraction problem and answer. What mistake did Nadia make? What is the correct answer?

$$\begin{array}{r} 98{,}476 \\ -\ 82{,}185 \\ \hline 16{,}391 \end{array}$$

18. How many more people attended the street fair in 2016 than in 2014 and 2015 combined?

DATA

Attendance at Street Fair	
2014	81,129
2015	112,172
2016	362,839

19. **Higher Order Thinking** On Monday, from the peak of Mount Kilimanjaro, a group of mountain climbers descended 3,499 feet. On Tuesday, they descended another 5,262 feet. How many feet did the mountain climbers descend after 2 days? How many more feet do they have to descend to reach the botom?

Mount Kilimanjaro is 19,341 feet high.

Assessment

ISTEP+ Ready

20. Which of the following best describes the answer to the subtraction problem shown below?

3,775 − 1,831

Ⓐ The answer is less than 1,000.
Ⓑ The answer is about 1,000.
Ⓒ The answer is greater than 1,000.
Ⓓ The answer is 1,000.

21. Which problem can be used to check the answer for 62,179 − 31,211?

Ⓐ 30,968 + 31,211
Ⓑ 31,211 + 31,211
Ⓒ 62,179 − 31,211
Ⓓ 31,211 − 30,968

Name ______________________

Homework & Practice 2-4

Subtract Whole Numbers

Another Look!

Follow these steps to subtract whole numbers.

Find 7,445 − 1,368.

Estimate: 7,000 − 1,000 = 6,000

Step 1	Step 2	Step 3	Step 4
7,445 − 1,368 = 7 (regrouped: 3 15)	7,445 − 1,368 = 77 (regrouped: 13, 3 3 15)	7,445 − 1,368 = 077 (regrouped: 13, 3 3 15)	7,445 − 1,368 = 6,077 (regrouped: 13, 3 3 15)
To subtract 8 ones from 5 ones, you must regroup. Regroup 4 tens as 3 tens and 10 ones. Subtract 8 ones from 15 ones.	To subtract 6 tens from 3 tens, you must regroup. Regroup 4 hundreds as 3 hundreds and 10 tens. Subtract 6 tens from 13 tens.	Subtract 3 hundreds from 3 hundreds.	Subtract 1 thousand from 7 thousands. Check your answer using addition. 6,077 + 1,368 = 7,445 (carries: 1 1)

For **1–8**, find the difference. Use inverse operations or estimate to check if your answer is reasonable.

1. 8,737 − 6,754

2. 411,765 − 402,120

3. 43,429 − 17,101

4. 952,746 − 184,524

5. 17,863 − 3,747

6. 513,363 − 382,895

7. 4,226 − 2,958

8. 67,451 − 29,609

9. **Make Sense and Persevere** The Environmental Club's goal is to collect 9,525 cans by the end of four months. How can you find the number of cans the club needs to collect in September to meet their goal? How many more cans do they need?

DATA

Month	Cans Collected
June	1,898
July	2,643
August	2,287

10. **Number Sense** Naima's pedometer recorded 43,498 steps in one week. Her goal is 88,942 steps. Naima estimates she has about 50,000 more steps to meet her goal. Is Naima's estimate reasonable? Explain.

11. **Critique Reasoning** Mitch wrote the subtraction below. What mistake did Mitch make? What is the correct answer?

$$\begin{array}{r} 657{,}392 \\ -\ 434{,}597 \\ \hline 222{,}895 \end{array}$$

12. Compare the values of the 2s and 5s in 55,220.

13. **Higher Order Thinking** A restaurant has 1,996 forks, 1,745 knives, and 2,116 spoons. The owner wants to have 2,000 of each utensil. She can buy more utensils or donate extra utensils. How many additional forks and knives are needed? How many extra spoons are there?

Assessment ISTEP+ Ready

14. During his first year as a pilot, Rob flies 6,692 miles. He flies 16,429 miles the second year and 24,211 miles the third year. He wants to estimate how many more miles he flew in the third year than in the first and second years combined. Which shows one way Rob could estimate?

Ⓐ 24,000 − (7,000 + 16,000)

Ⓑ (24,000 + 7,000) − 16,000

Ⓒ (16,000 − 7,000) + 24,000

Ⓓ 24,000 + 16,000 + 7,000

Name ______________________________ Solve

Lesson 2-5
Subtract Across Zeros

I can ...
use number sense and regrouping to subtract from numbers with zeros.

Content Standards 4.C.1, 4.AT.1
Process Standards PS.2, PS.3, PS.5, PS.8

Solve & Share London, England, is 15,710 kilometers from the South Pole. Tokyo, Japan, is 13,953 kilometers from the South Pole. How much farther is London than Tokyo from the South Pole? ***Solve this problem any way you choose.***

You can use reasoning to identify the operation you use to compare two distances. *Show your work in the space below!*

Look Back! Generalize What do you need to do to subtract the 3 ones in 13,953 from the 0 ones in 15,710? How can you subtract across zeros? Explain.

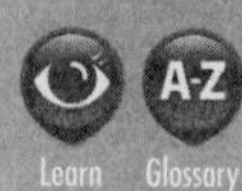

How Do You Subtract Across Zeros?

A

A concert hall is hosting a symphony. The hall sells 4,678 tickets to the show. How many tickets are still available?

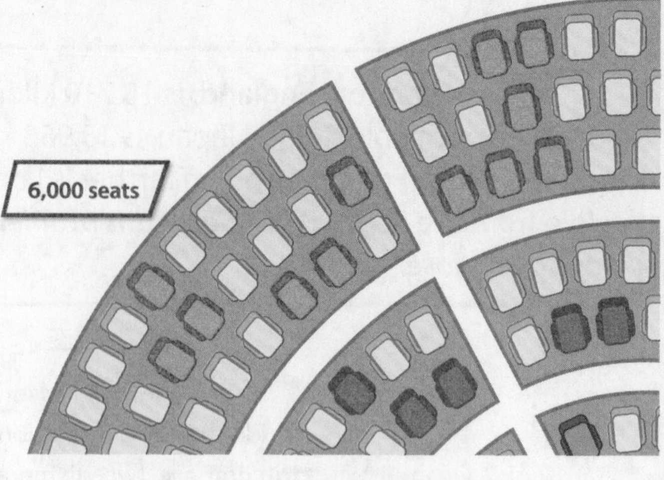

There is more than one way to record regroupings across zeros.

6,000

4,678	*t*

B

One Way

Find 6,000 − 4,678.
Estimate: 6,000 − 4,700 = 1,300

When necessary, regroup thousands to hundreds, hundreds to tens, and tens to ones.

$$\begin{array}{r} \scriptstyle 9\ 9\ \ \\ \scriptstyle 5\ 10\,10\,10 \\ \not{6},\not{0}\not{0}\not{0} \\ -\ 4,678 \\ \hline 1,322 \end{array}$$

6 thousands = 5 thousands, 9 hundreds, 9 tens, 10 ones

There are still 1,322 tickets available for the symphony.

C

Another Way

Find 6,000 − 4,678.
Estimate: 6,000 − 4,700 = 1,300

Think of 6,000 as 600 tens.
Then regroup tens as ones.

$$\begin{array}{r} \scriptstyle 5\ 9\ 9\,10 \\ \not{6},\not{0}\not{0}\not{0} \\ -\ 4,678 \\ \hline 1,322 \end{array}$$

6 thousands = 599 tens, 10 ones.

There are still 1,322 tickets available for the symphony.

Convince Me! **Generalize** How are the two methods shown above alike? Why might one be easier than the other?

Name ______________________________

Guided Practice*

Do You Understand?

1. **Construct Arguments** How would you check if the answer for the ticket problem on the previous page is correct?

2. One passenger flew from Oslo to Lima. The flight was 11,033 kilometers. Another passenger flew from Oslo to Los Angeles. The flight was 8,593 kilometers. How many more kilometers was the flight to Lima?

Do You Know How?

For **3–8**, subtract.

3. 6,000 − 1,773

4. 231,086 − 172,863

5. 76,810 − 22,645

6. 90,304 − 51,137

7. 101,001 − 8,915

8. 9,050 − 3,461

Independent Practice

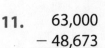

Estimate to check if your answer is reasonable.

For **9–24**, subtract.

9. 1,902 − 1,374

10. 6,502 − 5,380

11. 63,000 − 48,673

12. 84,010 − 3,992

13. 2,025 − 1,540

14. 31,030 − 27,426

15. 50,469 − 22,917

16. 1,830 − 644

17. 7,203 − 847

18. 726,003 − 282,942

19. 4,707 − 2,016

20. 30,900 − 22,855

21. 6,090 − 5,130

22. 11,246 − 9,489

23. 790,008 − 643,829

24. 39,603 − 30,922

*For another example, see Set E on page 86.

Problem Solving

25. Will the difference between 44,041 and 43,876 be greater or less than 1,000? Explain.

26. **Vocabulary** Define *variable* and give an example of how a variable is used in an equation.

For **27–28**, use the table at the right.

27. How many more hip-hop than country downloads were sold?

28. **Higher Order Thinking** Use the Music City Sales table on the right. How many more hip-hop and Latin downloads were sold than rock and country downloads? Explain.

DATA

Music City Sales	
Music style	**Downloads sold**
Rock	4,007
Hip-hop	7,097
Country	5,063
Latin	6,203

29. Find how much longer the Nile and Amazon rivers are combined than the Lower Tunguska and Ganges rivers combined. Write numbers in the boxes to show the missing lengths, sums, and difference.

DATA

World Rivers	
River	**Length (kilometers)**
Nile	6,650
Lower Tunguska	2,989
Senegal	1,641
Ganges	2,620
Amazon	6,400

Nile and Amazon	Lower Tunguska and Ganges	Difference
6,650 + □,□□□ □□,□□□	□,□□□ + 2,620 □,□□□	□□,□5□ − 5,6□□ □,□□□

Name ______________________

Homework & Practice 2-5

Subtract Across Zeros

Another Look!

Find 700,402 − 297,354.

Estimate: 700,000 − 300,000 = 400,000

Step 1

```
  700,402
− 297,354
```

You cannot subtract 4 ones from 2 ones, so you must regroup. Since there is a zero in the tens place, you must regroup 4 hundreds as 3 hundreds, 9 tens, and 10 ones.

```
       9
      31012
  700,4̸0̸2̸
− 297,354
```

Step 2

```
   9     9
  61010 31012
  7̸0̸0̸,4̸0̸2̸
− 297,354
```

Since there are zeros in the thousands and ten thousands places, you can regroup 700 thousands as 6 hundred thousand 9 ten thousands, and 10 thousands.

Step 3

```
   9     9
  61010 31012
  7̸0̸0̸,4̸0̸2̸
− 297,354
  403,048
```

Now you can subtract.

Step 4

```
   11  11
  297,354
+ 403,048
  700,402
```

You can check your answer by using addition.

You can use these steps to subtract across zeros.

For **1–12**, subtract.

1. 61,070 − 4,981

2. 5,707 − 2,058

3. 815,950 − 423,147

4. 90,800 − 37,638

5. 102,604 − 6,174

6. 22,700 − 20,487

7. 40,200 − 29,526

8. 600,470 − 307,299

9. 8,106 − 2,999

10. 214,507 − 83,569

11. 10,400 − 6,392

12. 45,500 − 9,450

13. Number Sense Este subtracts 9,405 from 11,038. Should Este's answer be greater or less than 2,000? Explain.

14. A park district holds a fundraiser over 4 weekends in which teams swim laps for donations. The park district's goal is 40,000 laps. Over three weekends the teams swam 8,597 laps, 11,065 laps, and 9,211 laps. How many laps do they need to swim the fourth weekend to reach their goal?

15. Reasoning Fill in themissing numbers:

106,984 − 37,639 = ___________, and

69,345 + ___________ = 106,984.

Explain why you use addition to check subtraction.

16. Construct Arguments Blaine subtracted 342,139 from 601,800. Is Blaine's answer correct? If not, explain why and write the correct answer.

$$\begin{array}{r} 601{,}800 \\ -\ 342{,}139 \\ \hline 359{,}661 \end{array}$$

17. Use Appropriate Tools There are 332,054 people in a city. Of these, 168,278 are under the age of eighteen. Draw a bar diagram and find how many people are eighteen or older.

18. Higher Order Thinking To most closely estimate the difference below, would you round the numbers to the nearest ten thousand, the nearest thousand, or the nearest hundred? Explain.

$$\begin{array}{r} 62{,}980 \\ -\ 49{,}625 \\ \hline \end{array}$$

Assessment ISTEP+ Ready

19. Sahira's company printed 37,652 books of the 70,000 that were ordered. How many more books does Sahira's company need to print? Write the missing numbers to complete the problem.

$$\begin{array}{r} 7\square{,}000 \\ -\ \square 7{,}6\square 2 \\ \hline \square\square{,}\square\square\square \end{array}$$

Name ______________________

Problem Solving

Lesson 2-6

Reasoning

I can ...

make sense of quantities and relationships in problem situations.

Process Standards PS.2 Also PS.1, PS.4, PS.8
Content Standards 4.C.1, 4.AT.1

Solve & Share

A group of students collected donations for a toy drive. They collected a total of 3,288 toys one week and 1,022 toys the next week. How many toys did they collect in all? They donated 1,560 toys to the Coal City Charity and the rest were donated to Hartville Charity. How many toys were donated to Hartville Charity? Use reasoning about numbers to show and explain how the two quantities are related.

Thinking Habits

Be a good thinker! These questions can help you.

- What do the numbers and symbols in the problem mean?
- How are the numbers or quantities related?
- How can I represent a word problem using pictures, numbers, or equations?

Look Back! Reasoning Over three weeks, the students collected a total of 8,169 toys. How many toys did they collect in the third week? Complete the bar diagram to show your reasoning. Did the students collect more toys in the third week than in weeks 1 and 2 combined? Explain.

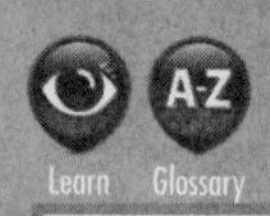

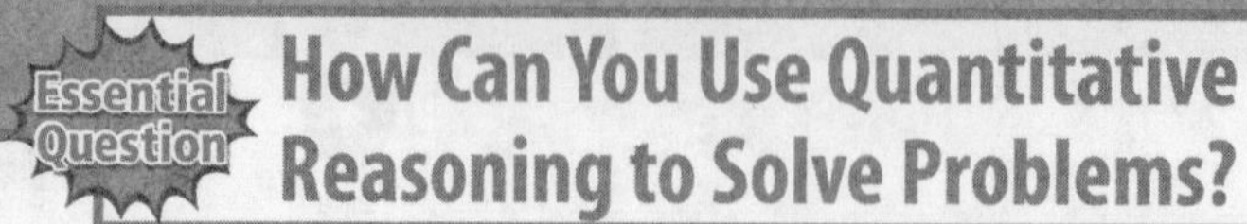

How Can You Use Quantitative Reasoning to Solve Problems?

A

Justine and her father are going on a fishing trip. The prices for supplies, including tax, are shown in the table. Justine and her father have $25. They bought 4 bottles of water and 2 box lunches. How many pounds of bait can they buy?

DATA

Captain Bob's Price List

Item	Price
Bait	$3 per pound
Hooks	50¢ each
Bottled Water	$1 each
Box Lunch	$6 each

How can you draw a diagram to help reason how the numbers in the problem are related?

I can represent the relationship between the numbers with a bar diagram.

Here's my thinking.

B

How can I use reasoning to solve this problem?

I can

- identify the quantities I know.
- draw diagrams to show relationships.
- give the answer using the correct unit.

C

Bottled water $4 \times \$1 = \$4$ Box lunch $2 \times \$6 = \$12$

Find the amount they spent.

amount spent → *s*

$6	$6	$1	$1	$1	$1

They spent $16. Subtract to find how much money they have left.

$25

$16	*m*

Divide to find how many pounds of bait they can buy.

$9 \div 3 = 3$

They can buy 3 pounds of bait.

Convince Me! **Reasoning** Write a problem that can be solved using the bar diagram below. Write an equation to solve. Use reasoning to think about the meaning of each number before starting.

16,792

2,550	*c*

Name ______________________________

Practice Buddy | Tools | Assessment

Guided Practice*

Reasoning

Kelly used 6 cups of apples, 4 cups of oranges, and 2 cups of grapes to make a fruit salad. She put an equal amount in 6 bowls. How many cups of fruit salad were in each bowl?

When you use reasoning, you use diagrams, numbers, or equations to show relationships.

1. What quantities are given in the problem, and what do the numbers mean?

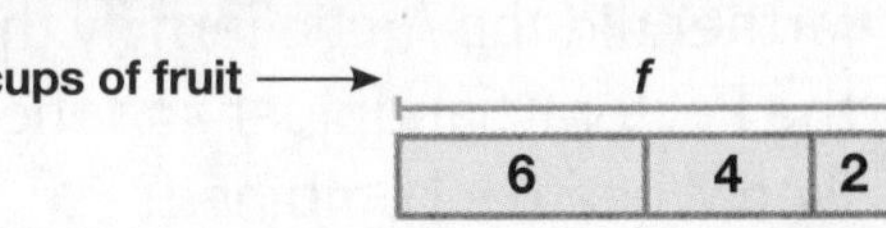

2. Use the bar diagrams that show the relationships of the numbers in the problem. Write and solve equations which could be used to find *f*, the number of cups of fruit used to make the salad and *c*, the number of cups of fruit in each bowl.

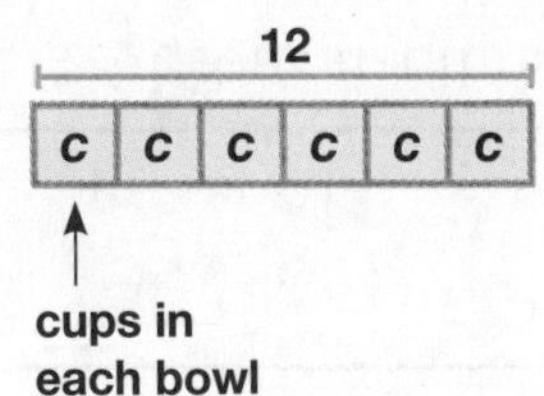

Independent Practice

Reasoning

A monument is going to be built from 16,351 stones. The builders have placed 8,361 stones, and have 7,944 stones left. How many more stones do they need? Use Exercises 3–5 to answer the question.

3. What quantities are given in the problem, and what do the numbers mean?

4. Complete the bar diagram to show how to find *s*, the number of stones the builders have in all. Then, write and solve an equation.

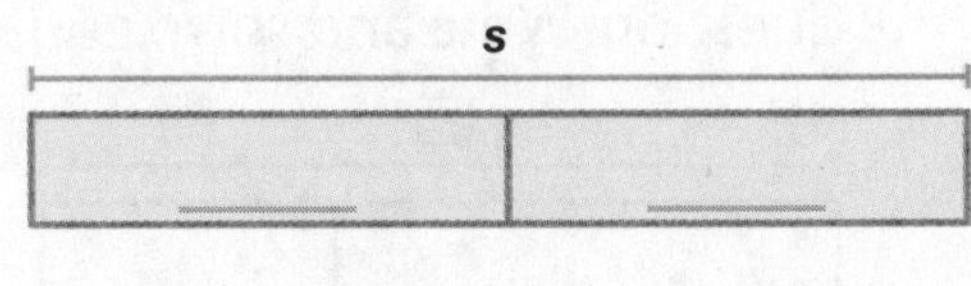

5. Complete the bar diagram to show how to find the difference, *d*, of how many more stones the builders need. Then, write and solve an equation.

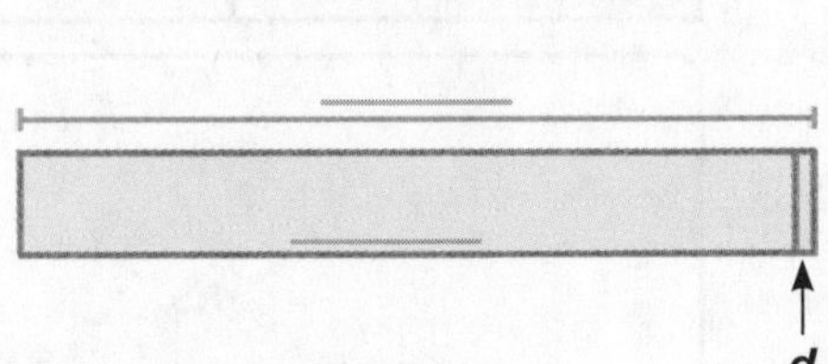

*For another example, see Set F on page 86.

Problem Solving

Performance Assessment — ISTEP+ Ready

Bird Migration
Ornithology is the scientific study of birds. Every year, some birds travel great distances, or migrate, to find food and start families. The table shows the distances five species of birds flew over one year, as observed by an ornithologist. How much farther did the Arctic Tern fly than the Pectoral Sandpiper and the Pied Wheatear combined?

DATA

Distances Traveled by Birds

Species	Distance in Miles
Sooty Shearwater	39,481
Pied Wheatear	11,184
Arctic Tern	44,819
Short-Tailed Shearwater	26,636
Pectoral Sandpiper	18,247

6. **Reasoning** What quantities are given in the problem and what do the numbers mean?

7. **Make Sense and Persevere** What strategy can you use to solve the problem?

8. **Make Sense and Persevere** What is the hidden question?

9. **Model with Math** Complete the bar diagrams to show how to find the answer to the hidden question and the main question. Write and solve equations.

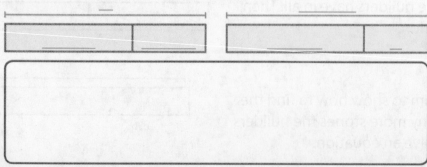

When you use reasoning, you give the answer using the correct unit.

Name ______________________

Homework & Practice 2-6
Reasoning

Another Look!

In a week, a farmer collected 3,978 red apples and 2,504 green apples. He sold a total of 4,856 apples. He took the rest of the apples to the Farmer's Market. How many apples did the farmer have left for the Farmer's Market?

When you use reasoning, you show how quantities are related.

Tell how you can use quantitative reasoning to find the answer.

- I can identify the quantities given.
- I can draw diagrams to show relationships.
- I can give the answer using the correct unit.

Identify quantities and the relationships between them to solve.

First find how many apples the farmer collected.

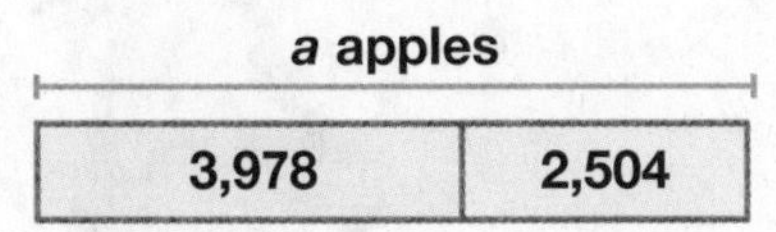

$3,978 + 2,504 = 6,482$

The farmer collected 6,482 apples.

Find how many apples were left for the Farmer's Market.

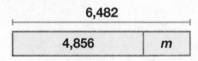

6,482

4,856	*m*

$6,482 - 4,856 = 1,626$

1,626 apples were left.

Reasoning

A census says that there were 659,000 French Creole speakers in the United States. There were 186,000 more Arabic speakers than French Creole speakers. How many Arabic speakers were there? Use Exercises 1–2 to answer the question.

1. What quantities are given in the problem, and what do the numbers mean?

2. What is the relationship between the quantities? Complete the bar diagram to find *a*, the number of Arabic speakers. Write and solve an equation.

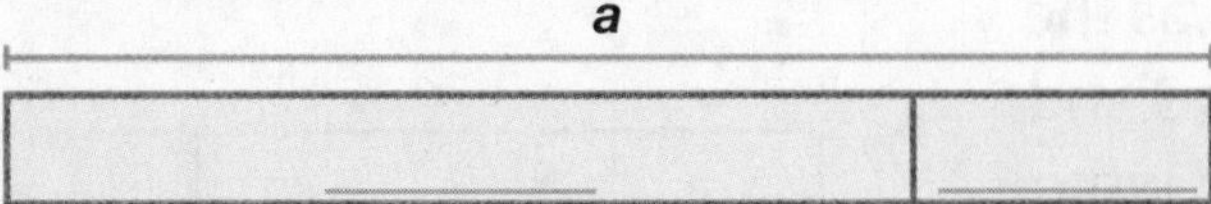

Performance Assessment — ISTEP+ Ready

Music
The table shows how many times a song was downloaded the first four days it was on sale. How many more times was it downloaded the first day than on days 3 and 4 combined?

DATA

Day	Times Downloaded
1	313,280
2	270,463
3	106,548
4	98,273

3. **Reasoning** What quantities are given in the problem and what do the numbers mean?

When you use reasoning, you identify the quantities given and their relationships.

4. **Make Sense and Persevere** What strategy can you use to solve the problem?

5. **Make Sense and Persevere** What hidden question must be answered first?

6. **Model with Math** Complete the bar diagram to show how to represent the hidden question. Then, write and solve an equation.

7. **Model with Math** How many more times was the song downloaded the first day than on days 3 and 4 combined? Complete the bar diagram and write and solve an equation.

Name ______________________________

Fluency Practice Activity

Shade a path from **START** to **FINISH**. Follow the sums that are correct. You can only move up, down, right, or left.

I can ...
add multi-digit whole numbers.

Start

213 + 675 = 888	264 + 632 = 896	887 + 112 = 999	124 + 345 = 461	414 + 111 = 515
810 + 172 = 762	212 + 486 = 678	511 + 228 = 739	245 + 322 = 667	613 + 282 = 891
454 + 545 = 919	187 + 412 = 499	676 + 322 = 998	101 + 116 = 218	454 + 432 = 876
409 + 390 = 697	340 + 340 = 620	124 + 65 = 189	911 + 64 = 975	674 + 115 = 789
374 + 613 = 978	318 + 121 = 429	177 + 311 = 478	612 + 317 = 939	678 + 321 = 999

Finish

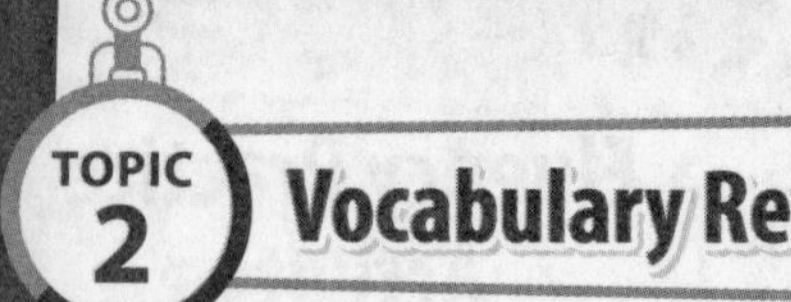

Vocabulary Review

Word List

- algorithm
- Associative Property of Addition
- Commutative Property of Addition
- compensation
- counting on
- Identity Property of Addition
- inverse operations
- variable

Understand Vocabulary

1. Circle the property of addition shown by $126 + 0 = 126$.

Associative Commutative Identity

2. Circle the property of addition shown by $21 + 34 = 34 + 21$.

Associative Commutative Identity

3. Circle the property of addition shown by $(1 + 3) + 7 = 1 + (3 + 7)$.

Associative Commutative Identity

4. Draw a line from each term to its example.

algorithm	$4 + 2 = 6 \rightarrow 6 - 2 = 4$
compensation	$130 - 31 \rightarrow 130 - 30 = 100$ $100 - 1 = 99$
counting on	Step 1: Add the ones. Step 2: Add the tens.
inverse operations	$x = 7$
variable	$6 + 20 + 300 = 326$

Use Vocabulary in Writing

5. Rob found $103 + 1{,}875 = x$ using mental math. Use at least 3 terms from the Word List to describe how Rob could find the sum.

Name ______________________________

TOPIC 2

Reteaching

Set A pages 47–52

Find 3,371 + 2,429. Use mental math.

Use the breaking apart strategy.
Break apart 2,429 into 2,400 + 29.

Adding 3,371 + 29 is easy.

3,371 + 29 = 3,400

3,400 + 2,400 = 5,800

So, 3,371 + 2,429 = 5,800.

Remember to adjust the sum or difference when you use the compensation strategy.

1. 4,153 + 2,988 **2.** 92,425 + 31,675

3. 5,342 + 1,999 **4.** 22,283 − 14,169

5. 47,676 − 16,521 **6.** 1,089 − 961

Set B pages 53–58

Estimate the sum by rounding each number to the nearest ten thousand.

$$\begin{array}{r} 241{,}485 \\ +\ 429{,}693 \\ \hline \end{array}$$

241,485 rounds to 240,000.

429,693 rounds to 430,000.

Add.
$$\begin{array}{r} 240{,}000 \\ +\ 430{,}000 \\ \hline 670{,}000 \end{array}$$

Remember that you can round numbers to any place when estimating sums and differences.

Estimate each sum or difference.

1. 652,198 + 49,753 **2.** 8,352 − 3,421

3. 17,586 − 9,483 **4.** 823,725 + 44,851

5. 1,440 − 933 **6.** 55,748 − 28,392

7. 4,981 + 6,193 **8.** 995,275 + 4,921

Set C pages 59–64

Find 72,438 + 6,854.

Estimate: 72,000 + 7,000 = 79,000

Add the ones. Regroup if necessary.

$$\begin{array}{r} \scriptstyle 1\ \ \\ 72{,}438 \\ +\ \ 6{,}854 \\ \hline 2 \end{array}$$

Add the other places, regrouping as necessary.

$$\begin{array}{r} \scriptstyle 1\ \ \ 1\ \ \\ 72{,}438 \\ +\ \ 6{,}854 \\ \hline 79{,}292 \end{array}$$

The answer 79,292 is close to the estimate of 79,000, so the answer is reasonable.

Remember to regroup if necessary when adding whole numbers.

1.
$$\begin{array}{r} 32{,}834 \\ +\ 17{,}384 \\ \hline \end{array}$$

2.
$$\begin{array}{r} 148{,}382 \\ +\ \ \ 9{,}243 \\ \hline \end{array}$$

3. 215 + 8,823 **4.** 142,968 + 44,456

5. 2,417 + 3,573 **6.** 572,941 + 181,662

Set D pages 65–70

Find 52,839 − 38,796.

Estimate: 53,000 − 39,000 = 14,000

Subtract the ones. Regroup if necessary.	Subtract the other places, regrouping as necessary.	Add to check your answer.
52,839 − 38,796 3	4 12 7 13 ~~5~~~~2~~,~~8~~~~3~~9 − 38,796 14,043	1 1 38,796 + 14,043 52,839

The answer is reasonable.

Remember that you may need to regroup to subtract.

1. $\begin{array}{r} 651{,}784 \\ -\ 482{,}638 \\ \hline \end{array}$
2. $\begin{array}{r} 18{,}465 \\ -\ 6{,}291 \\ \hline \end{array}$
3. 41,542 − 32,411
4. 4,978 − 2,766
5. 735,184 − 255,863
6. 44,558 − 22,613

Set E pages 71–76

Find 60,904 − 54,832.

Estimate: 61,000 − 55,000 = 6,000

Subtract the ones. Regroup if necessary.	Subtract the other places, regrouping as necessary.	Add to check your answer.
60,904 − 54,832 2	5 10 8 10 ~~6~~~~0~~,~~9~~~~0~~4 − 54,832 6,072	1 1 54,832 + 6,072 60,904

The answer is reasonable.

Remember to estimate to check if your solution is reasonable.

1. $\begin{array}{r} 40{,}700 \\ -\ 23{,}984 \\ \hline \end{array}$
2. $\begin{array}{r} 203{,}056 \\ -\ 5{,}213 \\ \hline \end{array}$
3. 70,000 − 25,228
4. 560,043 − 312,562
5. 8,052 − 1,205
6. 20,008 − 16,074

Set F pages 77–82

Think about these questions to help you **reason abstractly and quantitatively.**

Thinking Habits

- What do the numbers and symbols in the problem mean?
- How are the numbers or quantities related?
- How can I represent a word problem using pictures, numbers, or equations?

Remember that you can draw a bar diagram and use it to reason about a problem.

Raahil traveled 11,469 kilometers from home to visit his mother's family in Qatar. He then traveled 12,332 kilometers from Qatar to visit his father's family in Brisbane, Australia.

1. Draw a bar diagram that shows the distance Raahil traveled to Brisbane.

2. Write and solve an equation for your bar diagram.

Name ______________________________

TOPIC 2

Assessment

ISTEP+ Ready

1. The table shows the number of hot dogs Frank's hot dog stand sold this weekend.

Hot Dogs Sold	
Friday	3,825
Saturday	1,297
Sunday	4,175

Part A

Estimate the number of hot dogs sold by rounding each number in the table to the nearest thousand and finding the sum.

Part B

Write and solve an equation to find how many hot dogs were sold.

2. A band made 8,000 copies of an album. They sold 6,280 copies. How many copies are left?

Ⓐ 172 copies

Ⓑ 1,700 copies

Ⓒ 1,720 copies

Ⓓ 2,720 copies

3. Tom earned 134,867 points playing a video game, and Carlos earned 29,978 points. How many more points did Tom earn than Carlos?

Ⓐ 104,698 points

Ⓑ 104,886 points

Ⓒ 104,888 points

Ⓓ 104,889 points

4. Luis used compensation to find 6,572 − 239. Which of the following compensation methods can be used to find 6,572 − 239?

4a. Subtract 200, Subtract 40, Add 1 ○ Yes ○ No

4b. Subtract 200, Subtract 30, Add 9 ○ Yes ○ No

4c. Subtract 200, Subtract 40, Subtract 1 ○ Yes ○ No

4d. Subtract 200, Subtract 50, Add 11 ○ Yes ○ No

5. Write the number that makes the number sentence true, then write what property of addition the number sentence shows.

12,769 + 13,432 = ☐ + 12,769

6. Mount Steele is 5,029 meters tall. Mount Whitney is 4,421 meters tall. How much taller is Mount Steele than Mount Whitney?

7. Draw lines to match the problems on the left with the sums and differences on the right.

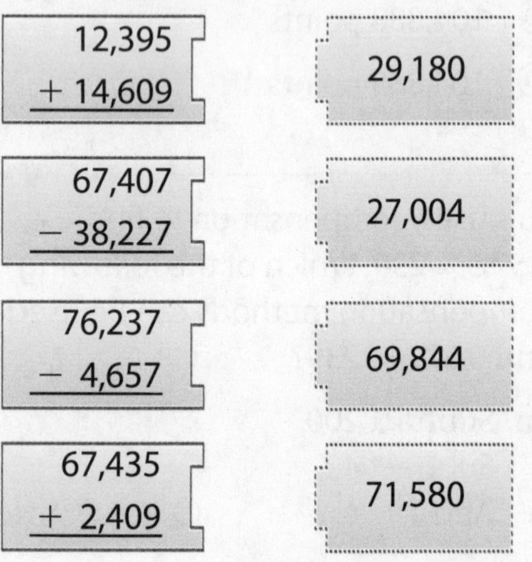

12,395
+ 14,609
29,180
67,407
− 38,227
27,004
76,237
− 4,657
69,844
67,435
+ 2,409
71,580

8. In May, 8,723 cans were recycled. In June, 6,419 cans were recycled. What is the total number of cans recycled?

9. Sandra used addition properties to rewrite the equation below. Select all the equations Sandra might have written.

$$450 + 125 + 50 = n$$

- ☐ $450 + 50 = n$
- ☐ $450 + 50 + 225 = n$
- ☐ $50 + 125 + 450 = n$
- ☐ $450 + 50 + 125 = n$
- ☐ $(450 + 50) + 125 = n$

10. Joe and Sara recorded the number of birds they saw in the park over two summers.

Birds in the Park

Year	Finches	Pigeons
Last Year	1,219	4,620
This Year	906	5,287

Part A

Write and solve equations to find how many more total birds Joe and Sara saw this year than last year.

Part B

Estimate how many more birds were seen in the park this year than last year by rounding each number in the table to the nearest hundred and solving the problem. Use the estimate to check if your answer to Part A is reasonable.

Name ____________________

TOPIC 2

Performance Assessment

ISTEP+ Ready

Taking Inventory

Jiao runs a wholesale art supply website. She fills bulk orders for craft and hobby stores.

1. Use the **Wooden Beads** table to answer the questions.

Part A

Crafts and Stuff ordered oak and ebony beads. Explain how to use properties of addition to find how many beads Jiao sent.

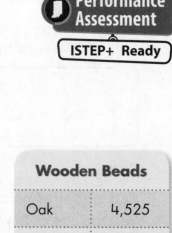

Wooden Beads	
Oak	4,525
Maple	6,950
Ash	3,720
Ebony	2,475
Bayong	1,250

Part B

Jiao sends an order of oak and bayong beads to Jill's Crafts and an order of ash and ebony beads to Create. How much larger is the order for Create? Explain.

2. Use the **Glass Beads** table to answer the questions.

Part A

Write and solve an equation to show how many glass beads Create will have if they order the bubble and smoky beads.

Glass Beads	
Smoky	25,236
Bubble	41,828
Stained	32,991
Molded	47,312

Part B

Jiao sends the molded and stained beads to Hometown Craft Supply. Explain how to use compensation to find how many more molded beads than stained beads were sent.

3. Use the **Metal Beads** table to answer the questions.

Part A

Write and solve an equation to show how many more beads are in an order of gold beads than in an order of platinum beads.

Metal Beads	
Gold	14,960
Silver	8,147
Platinum	6,488
Brass	30,019
Copper	20,605

Part B

Craftology orders the brass and copper beads. After they arrive, the store sells 29,735 of them. Use an algorithm to find how many beads Craftology has left from their order.

Use Strategies and Properties to Multiply by 1-Digit Numbers

Essential Questions: How can you multiply by multiples of 10, 100, and 1,000? How can you estimate when you multiply?

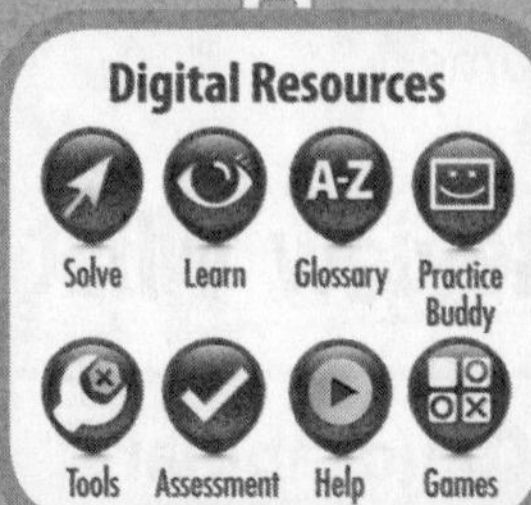

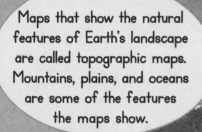

Maps that show the natural features of Earth's landscape are called topographic maps. Mountains, plains, and oceans are some of the features the maps show.

Did you know that Pikes Peak is the most visited mountain in North America?

We should visit! In the meantime, here is a project on maps and multiplication.

Math and Science Project: Maps and Math

Do Research Use the Internet or other sources to find information about three of Earth's features on a topographic map, such as mountains or oceans. Write two facts about each of the features you researched.

Journal: Write a Report Include what you found. Also in your report:

- Write the height or depth of each feature you researched.
- Estimate to find 10 times the heights or depths of the features you researched.

Name ____________________

Review What You Know

Vocabulary

Choose the best term from the box. Write it on the blank.

- breaking apart
- inverse operations
- compensation
- partial products

1. Multiplication and division are ____________________.

2. A mental math method used to rewrite a number as the sum of numbers to form an easier problem is called ____________________.

3. Choosing numbers close to the numbers in a problem to make the computation easier, and then adjusting the answer is called ____________________.

Multiplication

Find each product.

4. 6×2 **5.** 8×9 **6.** 6×5

7. 7×8 **8.** 4×8 **9.** 3×7

Rounding

Round each number to the nearest ten.

10. 16 **11.** 82 **12.** 35

13. 53 **14.** 24 **15.** 49

Round each number to the nearest hundred.

16. 868 **17.** 499 **18.** 625

19. 167 **20.** 341 **21.** 772

22. 919 **23.** 552 **24.** 321

Problem Solving

25. Critique Reasoning Tyler says, "9×7 is greater than 7×9 because the greater number is first." Explain Tyler's error.

A-Z Glossary

My Word Cards

Use the examples for each word on the front of the card to help complete the definitions on the back.

Associative Property of Multiplication

$(4 \times 3) \times 2 = 24$

$4 \times (3 \times 2) = 24$

$(4 \times 3) \times 2 = 4 \times (3 \times 2)$

numerical expression

6×3

$(8 \div 2) + 4 - 1$

$12 + 17 - 4$

Distributive Property

$6 \times (10 + 8) = (6 \times 10) + (6 \times 8)$

compensation

$3 \times 48 = n$

Think: $3 \times 50 = 150$

Adjust: $150 - 6 = 144$

Commutative Property of Multiplication

$4 \times 3 \times 2 = 24$

$4 \times 2 \times 3 = 24$

$3 \times 4 \times 2 = 24$

partial products

$$\begin{array}{r} 16 \\ \times\ 2 \\ \hline 12 \\ +\ 20 \\ \hline 32 \end{array}$$

Partial products (12 and 20)

My Word Cards

Complete each definition. Extend learning by writing your own definitions.

A ______________________ contains numbers and at least one operation.

The ______________________ ______________________ states that you can change the grouping of the factors and the product stays the same.

Choosing numbers close to the numbers in a problem to make the computation easier, and then adjusting the answer for the numbers chosen is called ______________________.

The ______________________ states that multiplying a sum (or difference) by a number is the same as multiplying each number in the sum (or difference) by that number and adding (or subtracting) the products.

______________________ are products found by breaking one factor in a multiplication problem into ones, tens, hundreds, and so on and then multiplying each of these by the other factor.

The ______________________ ______________________ states that the order of factors can be changed, but the product stays the same.

Name ______________________

Lesson 3-1

Mental Math: Multiply by Multiples of 10, 100, and 1,000

I can ...
find the products of multiples of 10, 100, and 1,000 using mental math and place-value strategies.

Content Standards 4.C.2, 4.C.4
Process Standards PS.2, PS.4, PS.7

Solve & Share

Find the products for 3 × 4, 3 × 40, 3 × 400, and 3 × 4,000. ***Solve these problems using any strategy you choose.***

You can look for relationships in the products. How can finding the first product help you find the remaining products? *Show your work in the space above!*

Look Back! Look for Relationships What pattern do you notice in the products?

How Can You Multiply by Multiples of 10, 100, and 1,000?

A

Calculate 3 × 50, 3 × 500, and 3 × 5,000 using basic multiplication facts and properties of operations. Then, calculate 6 × 50, 6 × 500, and 6 × 5,000.

The Associative Property of Multiplication states that you can change the grouping of the factors and the product stays the same.

n

B Find 3 × 50, 3 × 500, and 3 × 5,000.

$3 \times 50 = 3 \times (5 \times 10)$
$= (3 \times 5) \times 10$
$= 15 \times 10$
$= 150$

Shortcut rule for 3 × 50:
Multiply 3 × 5 and write 1 zero.
3 × 50 = 150

Shortcut rule for 3 × 500:
Multiply 3 × 5 and write 2 zeros.
3 × 500 = 1,500

Shortcut rule for 3 × 5,000:
Multiply 3 × 5 and write 3 zeros.
3 × 5,000 = 15,000

C Find 6 × 50, 6 × 500, and 6 × 5,000.

Apply the shortcut rules:

6 × 5 = 30
6 × 50 = 300
6 × 500 = 3,000
6 × 5,000 = 30,000

When the product of a basic fact ends in zero, the product will have an extra zero. The extra zero is part of the basic fact that you use.

Convince Me! Reasoning How many zeros will be in the product of 5 × 200? Explain.

Name ______________________

Practice Buddy Tools Assessment

Another Example!

Use place value to calculate 5 × 50, 5 × 500, and 5 × 5,000.

5 × 50 is 5 groups of 5 tens or 5 × 5 tens. 5 × 5 tens is 25 tens, or 250.

5 × 500 is 5 groups of 5 hundreds or 5 × 5 hundreds. 5 × 5 hundreds is 25 hundreds, or 2,500.

5 × 5,000 is 5 groups of 5 thousands or 5 × 5 thousands. 5 × 5 thousands is 25 thousands, or 25,000.

Guided Practice*

Do You Understand?

1. **Look for Relationships** Show how you can use the basic fact 5 × 8 = 40 to determine the product of 5 × 800.

2. Bob said 4 × 500 = 200. Explain his error.

Do You Know How?

For **3–5**, use strategies you learned to help multiply.

3. 8 × 7 = ______
   8 × 70 = ______
   8 × 700 = ______
   8 × 7,000 = ______

4. 7 × 70

5. 2 × 700

Independent Practice

You can use place-value strategies to calculate each product.

Leveled Practice For **6–11**, find each product.

6. 3 × 70 = ______
   3 × 700 = ______
   3 × 7,000 = ______

7. 6 × 40 = ______
   6 × 400 = ______
   6 × 4,000 = ______

8. 8 × 60 = ______
   8 × 600 = ______
   8 × 6,000 = ______

9. 4 × 2,000

10. 700 × 4

11. 6 × 60

*For another example, see Set A on page 157.

Problem Solving

12. Math and Science The Mississippi River is about 8 times the length of the Hudson River. If the Hudson River is about 300 miles long, about many miles long is the Mississippi River? Write and solve an equation.

13. Model with Math Ted, Jason, and Angelina are trying to raise $200 for a local shelter. Ted raised $30. Jason raised $90. How much money does Angelina need to raise in order to reach their goal?

$200

$30	$90	*m*

For **14–15**, use the table at the right.

14. There are 9 girls and 4 adults in Aimee's scout troup. How much did the troop pay for tickets to the amusement park?

15. Higher Order Thinking Tina visited Funland with her mom and a friend. They bought tickets for Plan C. How much money did they save on the two children's tickets for Plan C instead of buying separate tickets for Plan A and Plan B?

DATA

Funland Ticket Prices

Plans	Adult	Child
Plan A Waterpark	$30	$20
Plan B Amusement Park	$40	$30
Plan C Combined A + B	$60	$40

ISTEP+ Ready

16. Brandon says 4 × 800 is greater than 8 × 4,000. Renee says 4 × 800 is less than 8 × 4,000.

Part A

Without calculating the answer, explain how to use place-value strategies or the Associative Property to find which is greater.

Part B

Without calculating the answer, explain how to use relationships or basic facts to find which is less.

Name ______________________

Help Practice Buddy Tools Games

Homework & Practice 3-1

Mental Math: Multiply by Multiples of 10, 100, and 1,000

Another Look!

Use basic facts to multiply by multiples 10, 100, and 1,000.

$3 \times 7 = 21$	$8 \times 3 = 24$	$9 \times 5 = 45$
$3 \times 70 = 210$	$8 \times 30 = 240$	$9 \times 50 = 450$
$3 \times 700 = 2{,}100$	$8 \times 300 = 2{,}400$	$9 \times 500 = 4{,}500$

When one factor of a multiplication problem is a multiple of 10, first solve the basic multiplication fact. Then write the same number of zeros as in the factor that is a multiple of 10. For example:

$4 \times 5 = 20$ $4 \times 50 = 200$ $4 \times 500 = 2{,}000$

For **1–18**, find each product.

1. $8 \times 20 =$ ______
$8 \times 200 =$ ______
$8 \times 2{,}000 =$ ______

2. $9 \times 40 =$ ______
$9 \times 400 =$ ______
$9 \times 4{,}000 =$ ______

3. $3 \times 90 =$ ______
$3 \times 900 =$ ______
$3 \times 9{,}000 =$ ______

4. $7 \times 60 =$ ______
$7 \times 600 =$ ______
$7 \times 6{,}000 =$ ______

5. $5 \times 70 =$ ______
$5 \times 700 =$ ______
$5 \times 7{,}000 =$ ______

6. $2 \times 40 =$ ______
$2 \times 400 =$ ______
$2 \times 4{,}000 =$ ______

7. 3×40

8. $3{,}000 \times 9$

9. 80×3

10. $8{,}000 \times 5$

11. $8 \times 7{,}000$

12. 2×90

13. $3{,}000 \times 4$

14. $7 \times 6{,}000$

15. $5{,}000 \times 6$

16. 2×800

17. 90×8

18. $3{,}000 \times 6$

19. Adele has 6 sheets of stickers. Bea has 9 sheets of the same stickers. How many stickers do they have altogether?

20. Algebra There were 4 times the number of students in fourth grade at the basketball game. How many students attended the basketball game? Write and solve an equation.

DATA

School Population	
Grade	**Number of Students**
Fourth Grade	50
Fifth Grade	54
Sixth Grade	60

21. Model with Math Jenna saved $100. She wants to buy 6 games that cost $20 each. Does Jenna have enough money? Explain.

t total cost of games

$20	$20	$20	$20	$20	$20

Cost of each game

22. Higher Order Thinking Mr. Young has 30 times as many pencils as Jack. The whole school has 200 times as many pencils as Jack. If Jack has 2 pencils, how many pencils does Mr. Young have? How many pencils does the whole school have?

Mr. Young has ______ pencils.

The whole school has ______ pencils.

Assessment ISTEP+ Ready

23. How many zeros will be in the product of $7 \times 5{,}000$?

Part A

Without calculating the answer, explain how to use place-value strategies or the Associative Property to find the number of zeros in the product.

Part B

Without calculating the answer, explain how to use patterns or basic facts to find the number of zeros in the product.

Name ______________________________________

Lesson 3-2
Mental Math: Round to Estimate Products

I can ...
use rounding to estimate products and check if my answer is reasonable.

Content Standard Prepares for 4.C.2
Process Standard PS.2

Solve & Share

Sarah earns $48 a week babysitting. She saves all of her earnings for 6 weeks. Estimate to determine about how much money Sarah saves. ***Solve this problem using any strategy you choose.***

How can reasoning about place value make it easier to estimate products? *Show your work in the space above!*

Look Back! Reasoning Calculate how much Sarah earns babysitting. Is your estimate more or less than the amount Sarah actually earned? Explain.

How Can You Estimate When You Multiply?

A

Hoover School is holding a fundraiser. Any class that raises more than $5,000 will earn a prize. Mr. Hector and Mrs. Alan both estimate if their class sold enough items to earn a prize.

You can use place value to help round numbers. Rounding is one way to estimate products.

DATA

Class	Items Sold	Cost per Item
Mr. Hector	1,930	$4
Mrs. Alan	1,150	$3

B

Mr. Hector's Class

Estimate $4 × 1,930 using rounding.

4 × 1,930

Round 1,930 to 2,000.

4 × 2,000 = 8,000

Mr. Hector's class raised more than $5,000.

$8,000 > $5,000

His class earns a prize.

C

Mrs. Alan's Class

Estimate $3 × 1,150 using rounding.

3 × 1,150

Round 1,150 to 1,000.

3 × 1,000 = 3,000

Mrs. Alan's class raised less than $5,000.

$3,000 < $5,000

Her class does not earn a prize.

Convince Me! **Reasoning** Is the estimate for Mr. Hector's class greater than or less than the exact answer? Use reasoning to explain how the estimate and the exact answer are related.

Name ____

Practice Buddy Tools Assessment

Another Example!

Mr. Harm's class sold 1,475 items at $5 per item. He calculates his class raised $2,375. Is Mr. Harm's calculation reasonable?

You can estimate to check if an answer is reasonable.

Estimate: $5 × 1,475

Round 1,475 to the nearest thousand. Multiply 5 × 1,000 = 5,000.
$2,375 is not reasonable because it is not close to $5,000.

Guided Practice*

Do You Understand?

1. **Reasoning** Mrs. Alan's class sold 700 more items. Estimate to see if her class sold enough items to earn a prize.

Do You Know How?

For **2–5**, estimate the product.

2. 6 × 125
3. 4 × 2,610
4. 538 × 3
5. 314 × 7

Independent Practice

Leveled Practice For **6–8**, estimate the product.

6. 3 × 287
   Round 287 to ______.
   3 × ______ = ______

7. 6 × 1,310
   Round 1,310 to ______.
   6 × ______ = ______

8. 9 × 62
   Round 62 to ______.
   9 × ______ = ______

For **9–11**, estimate to check if the answer is reasonable.

9. 7 × 486 = 3,402
   Round 486 to ______.
   7 × ______ = ______
   Reasonable Not Reasonable

10. 5 × 1,240 = 9,200
    Round 1,240 to ______.
    5 × ______ = ______
    Reasonable Not Reasonable

11. 9 × 287 = 2,583
    Round 287 to ______.
    9 × ______ = ______
    Reasonable Not Reasonable

*For another example, see Set B on page 157.

Problem Solving

For **12–13**, use the graph at the right.

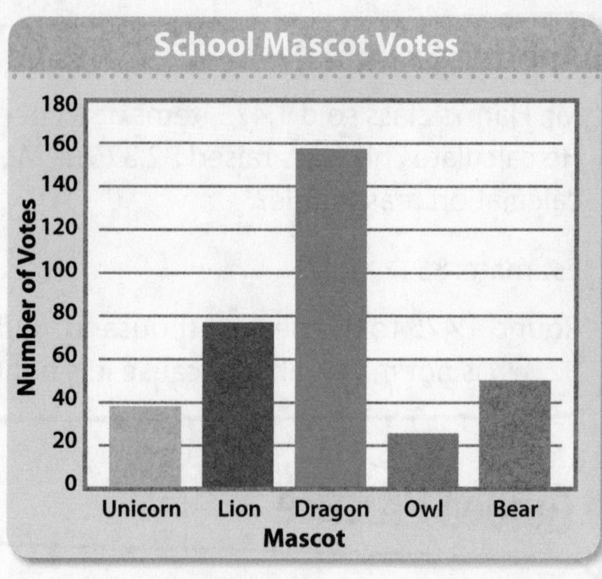

12. The students voted on a school mascot. Which mascot had as many votes as 4 times the number of votes for the unicorn?

13. Explain how you could estimate the number of students who voted on a school mascot. Then give your estimate.

14. Number Sense Ellie estimates the product of 211 and 6 is 1,800. Is this estimate reasonable? Explain.

15. Higher Order Thinking An adult sleeps about 480 minutes per day. An infant sleeps about 820 minutes per day. About how many more minutes does an infant sleep than an adult in one week? Solve the problem two different ways.

Assessment — ISTEP+ Ready

16. Beth calculated the cost for tuition and books for 4 years of college will be $31,800. Which expression shows an estimate to check if Beth's calculation is reasonable?

DATA

College Costs (per year)	
Tuition	$7,200
Books	$750

Ⓐ $10,000 × 8

Ⓑ ($7,000 × 4) + ($1,000 × 4)

Ⓒ ($8,000 × 4) + ($700 × 8)

Ⓓ 4 × ($10,000 + $1,000)

17. Sam and his two brothers want to fly to Boston. About how much will Sam and his brothers save buying the less expensive fare?

DATA

Airfare for Round Trip to Boston	
Skies the Limit Airline	$319
In the Clouds Airline	$405

Ⓐ About $100

Ⓑ About $200

Ⓒ About $300

Ⓓ About $400

Name ____________

Homework & Practice 3-2

Mental Math: Round to Estimate Products

Another Look!

To estimate, round 3-digit numbers to the nearest hundred and round 4-digit numbers to the nearest thousand.

Use rounding to estimate 7×215.

First, round 215 to the nearest hundred. 215 rounds to 200.

Then, multiply.
$7 \times 200 = 1{,}400$

So, 7×215 is about 1,400.

Check if $2{,}885 \times 4 = 11{,}540$ is reasonable.

First round 2,885 to the nearest thousand. 2,885 rounds to 3,000.

Then, multiply.
$3{,}000 \times 4 = 12{,}000$

So, $2{,}885 \times 4$ is about 12,000.

11,540 is a reasonable answer.

For **1–6**, estimate the product.

1. 4×279
↓ Round 279 to ______.
$4 \times$ ______ $=$ ______

2. $9 \times 4{,}720$
↓ Round 4,720 to ______.
$9 \times$ ______ $=$ ______

3. 8×89
↓ Round 89 to ______.
$8 \times$ ______ $=$ ______

4. 183×4

5. $3 \times 1{,}675$

6. $8{,}210 \times 2$

For **7–9**, estimate to check if the answer is reasonable.

7. $8 \times 578 = 4{,}624$
↓ Round 578 to ______.
$8 \times$ ______ $=$ ______
Reasonable Not Reasonable

8. $3 \times 8{,}230 = 2{,}469$
↓ Round 8,230 to ______.
$3 \times$ ______ $=$ ______
Reasonable Not Reasonable

9. $7 \times 289 = 2{,}023$
↓ Round 289 to ______.
$7 \times$ ______ $=$ ______
Reasonable Not Reasonable

10. **Vocabulary** Use *expanded form* or *number name* to complete the definition.

A number written as the sum of the value of its digits is written in ________________.

11. **Math and Science** The Ojos del Salado volcano has an elevation about 3 times as great as the Khangar volcano. If the Khangar volcano is 6,562 feet above sea level, what is the approximate elevation of the Ojos del Salado volcano?

For **12–13**, use the graph at the right.

12. **Number Sense** Estimate how many of Part B would be made in 3 months.

13. It costs the factory $4 to make each Part A. About how much does it cost to make Part A each month?

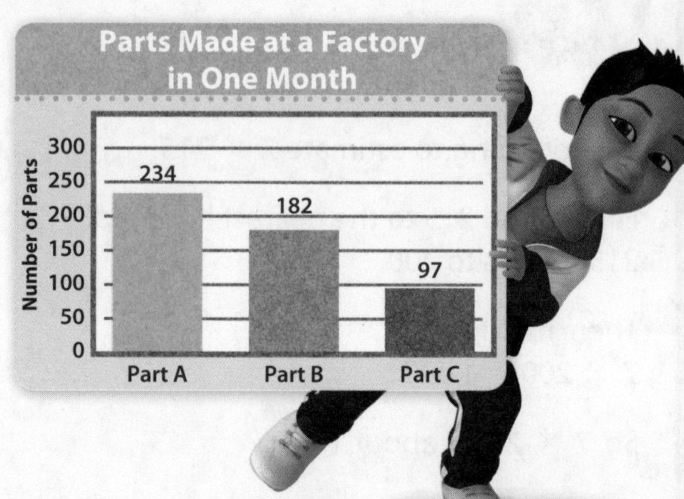

14. **Higher Order Thinking** A Deluxe Package costs $50 and includes one of each of the individual pictures listed in the table. Estimate about how much money you save with the Deluxe Package instead of buying one of each of the individual pictures. Explain.

DATA

Individual Picture Prices

Picture Size	Price
8 × 10	$18
5 × 7	$14
4 × 6	$10
8 wallets	$18

Assessment ISTEP+ Ready

15. The distance between Bill's house and his aunt's house is 485 miles. About how many miles would Bill drive if he made 4 round trips from his house to his aunt's house?

Ⓐ About 5,000 miles
Ⓑ About 4,000 miles
Ⓒ About 3,200 miles
Ⓓ About 2,000 miles

16. Fourth graders chose to have a read-a-thon for one hour. Each of the four fourth-grade classes read 408 pages. About how many pages did all the fourth graders read?

Ⓐ About 800 pages
Ⓑ About 1,000 pages
Ⓒ About 1,600 pages
Ⓓ About 2,400 pages

Name ______________________________

Lesson 3-3
The Distributive Property

I can ...
use place value and a property of operations to multiply larger numbers.

Content Standard 4.C.7
Process Standards PS.1, PS.2, PS.4, PS.7

Solve & Share

Use only the numbers shown on the diagram and the operation symbols (+, −, ×, ÷) to determine the area of the unshaded rectangle below. ***Solve this problem using any strategy you choose.***

Remember what you know about calculating area to make sense of this problem. *Show your work in the space below!*

Look Back! Use Structure Are these equations equal? Explain.

$8 \times (10 - 4) = n$

$(8 \times 10) - (8 \times 4) = n$

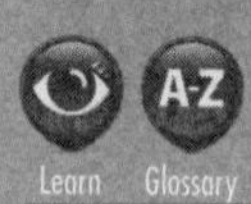

How Can You Use the Distributive Property to Multiply?

A

The Rails-to-Trails Preservation opened a new section of a biking trail. The section is 6 yards wide and 1,842 yards long. Calculate 6 × 1,842.

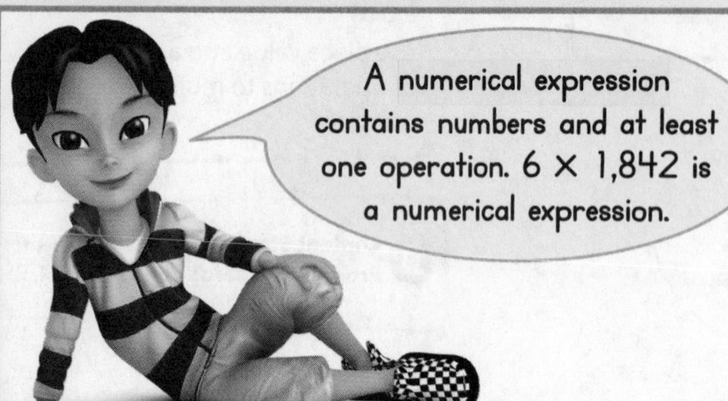

A numerical expression contains numbers and at least one operation. 6 × 1,842 is a numerical expression.

Trail Length: 1,842 yards

B

Use the Distributive Property to find $6 \times 1{,}842$.

$6 \times 1{,}842 = 6 \times (1{,}000 + 800 + 40 + 2)$

1,000 + 800 + 40 + 2

6 | 6 × 1,000 | 6 × 800 | 6 × 40 | 6 × 2

The Distributive Property says that multiplying a sum by a number is the same as multiplying each number in the sum by that number and adding the products.

Multiply. Then add the products of all four parts.

$$6 \times 1{,}842 = (6 \times 1{,}000) + (6 \times 800) + (6 \times 40) + (6 \times 2)$$
$$= (6{,}000) + (4{,}800) + (240) + (12)$$
$$= 11{,}052$$

6 yards × 1,842 yards is 11,052 square yards.

Convince Me! **Use Structure** Does $12 - (4 \times 2) = (12 - 4) \times (12 - 2)$? Explain.

Name ______________________________

Practice Buddy Tools Assessment

Another Example!

Find 7 × 560 using addition and the Distributive Property.

$560 = 500 + 60$

$7 \times 560 = (7 \times 500) + (7 \times 60)$
$= 3{,}500 + 420$
$= 3{,}920$

Find 7 × 560 using subtraction and the Distributive Property.

$560 = 600 - 40$

$7 \times 560 = (7 \times 600) - (7 \times 40)$
$= 4{,}200 - 280$
$= 3{,}920$

Guided Practice*

Do You Understand?

1. **Model with Math** Shade and label the figure to show $4 \times (10 + 3) = (4 \times 10) + (4 \times 3)$.

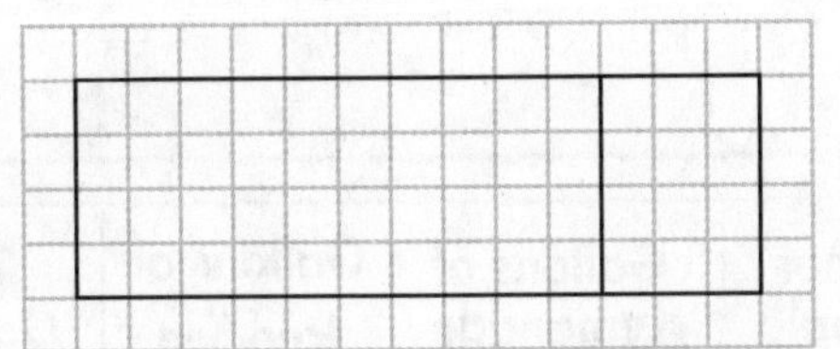

Do You Know How?

2. Use the Distributive Property and addition to complete the equation.

$2 \times 308 = 2 \times (300 + 8)$
$= (2 \times \_\_\_\_) + (2 \times \_\_\_\_)$
$= \_\_\_\_ + \_\_\_\_$
$= \_\_\_\_$

Independent Practice

Leveled Practice For **3–10**, use the Distributive Property to find each product.

3. $509 \times 7 = (500 + 9) \times 7$
$= (500 \times \_\_\_\_) + (9 \times \_\_\_\_)$
$= \_\_\_\_ + 63$
$= \_\_\_\_$

4. $2 \times 47 = 2 \times (50 - \_\_\_\_)$
$= (2 \times \_\_\_\_) - (2 \times 3)$
$= 100 - \_\_\_\_$
$= \_\_\_\_$

5. 7 × 86

6. 5 × 1,242

7. 9 × 504

8. 6 × 312

9. 5 × 811

10. 4 × 731

*For another example, see Set C on page 158.

Problem Solving

11. Show how you can use the Distributive Property to find the product of $4 \times 1{,}512$.

12. Show how multiplication distributes over subtraction to find the product of 3×298. Use $298 = 300 - 2$ and the Distributive Property.

13. **Reasoning** Wyatt said he used the Distributive Property to write $4 + (8 + 3) = (4 + 8) + (4 + 3)$. Explain Wyatt's error and use math to justify your explanation.

14. Todd Mountain is a mountain peak near Tyler, Texas. A ranger hiked 607 feet to and from the peak, each way. The ranger hiked 3 times in the past four weeks. How far did the ranger hike on Todd Mountain over the past four weeks?

15. **Higher Order Thinking** Wendy plans to bring beverages for the school picnic. She has 5 gallons of iced tea. Also, she will bring 2 gallons of lemonade for every 10 people. How many total gallons of lemonade and iced tea does Wendy need to bring for 40 people? Complete the table. Write and solve an equation to find how many total gallons of beverages Wendy will need.

Number of People	Gallons of Lemonade	Gallons of Iced Tea	Total Gallons
10	2	5	
20			
30			
40			

Assessment ISTEP+ Ready

16. Jane and Bob each used the Distributive Property to write 8×490 a different way. Write to explain who is correct.

Jane's Work

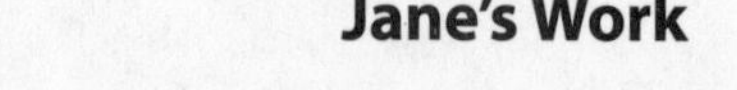

$$8 \times 490 = 8 \times (400 + 90)$$
$$= (8 \times 400) + (8 \times 90)$$

Bob's Work

$$8 \times 490 = 8 \times (500 - 10)$$
$$= (8 \times 500) - (8 \times 10)$$

Name ________________________

Homework & Practice 3-3

The Distributive Property

Another Look!

Hector's rock collection is stored in 7 cases. Each case holds 280 rocks. How many rocks are in Hector's collection?

You can use the Distributive Property to find the product of 7×280.

Step 1 Break apart 280 into 200 + 80
$7 \times 280 = 7 \times (200 + 80)$

or Break apart 280 into 300 − 20
$7 \times 280 = 7 \times (300 - 20)$

Step 2 Multiply 7 times each part of the sum.
$(7 \times 200) + (7 \times 80)$
$1{,}400 + 560$

or Multiply 7 times each part of the difference.
$(7 \times 300) - (7 \times 20)$
$2{,}100 - 140$

Step 3 Add.
$1{,}400 + 560 = 1{,}960$

or Subtract.
$2{,}100 - 140 = 1{,}960$

So, $7 \times 280 = 1{,}960$.
Hector has 1,960 rocks in his collection.

For **1–8**, use the Distributive Property to find each product.

1. $8 \times 46 = 8 \times (40 + \_\_\_\_)$
$= (8 \times 40) + (\_\_\_\_ \times \_\_\_\_)$
$= \_\_\_\_ + \_\_\_\_$
$= \_\_\_\_$

2. $39 \times 5 = 5 \times (\_\_\_\_ - 1)$
$= (5 \times \_\_\_\_) - (5 \times 1)$
$= \_\_\_\_ - \_\_\_\_$
$= \_\_\_\_$

3. $6 \times 310 = 6 \times (300 + \_\_\_\_)$
$= (6 \times \_\_\_\_) + (\_\_\_\_ \times 10)$
$= \_\_\_\_ + \_\_\_\_$
$= \_\_\_\_$

4. $9 \times 895 = 9 \times (\_\_\_\_ - \_\_\_\_)$
$= (9 \times \_\_\_\_) - (\_\_\_\_ \times 5)$
$= \_\_\_\_ - \_\_\_\_$
$= \_\_\_\_$

5. 5×108

6. 2×62

7. $4 \times 1{,}554$

8. $2 \times 2{,}568$

9. **Use Structure** Show how to use the Distributive Property to find 7 × 1,214.

10. A lodge at a state park has 49 rooms. Up to five people may stay in each room. What is the maximum number of people who can stay at the lodge at one time?

11. Lauren read 36 books during the year. If she reads the same number of books for 6 years in a row, how many total books will Lauren read?

12. A parking garage has 8 levels. Each level has parking spaces for 78 cars. How many cars can park in the garage at one time?

For **13–14**, use the table at the right.

13. A banquet room is being set up for a party using round tables. How many chairs are used for the round tables?

14. **Higher Order Thinking** Which of the three table types allows seating for the greatest number of people? Explain.

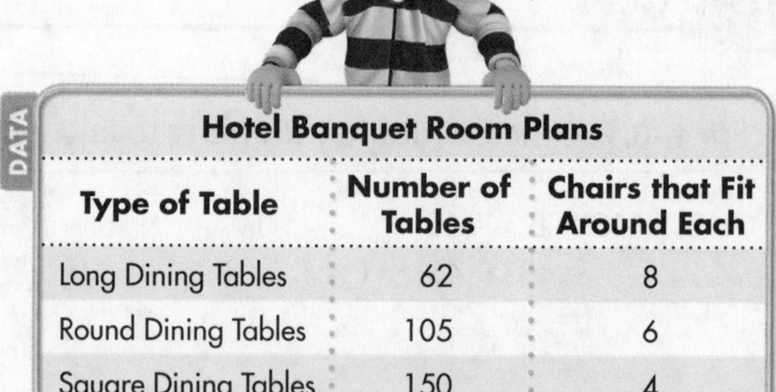

DATA

Hotel Banquet Room Plans

Type of Table	Number of Tables	Chairs that Fit Around Each
Long Dining Tables	62	8
Round Dining Tables	105	6
Square Dining Tables	150	4

15. Joey's grade has a goal to collect 4,000 cans for the school canned-food drive. There are 486 students in Joey's grade. If each student brings in 8 cans of food, will the class reach its goal? Explain.

Use place value to break apart numbers and the Distributive Property to help multiply.

Name ______________________________

Solve

Lesson 3-4
Mental Math Strategies for Multiplication

Solve & Share

Determine the products for the expressions given below. Use mental math to solve. Explain your thinking. ***Solve these problems using any strategy you choose.***

I can ...
use mental math strategies based on place value and properties of operations to multiply.

Content Standard 4.C.7
Process Standards PS.2, PS.3, PS.4, PS.7

You can use structure to break apart numbers into simpler parts to solve the problems. *Show your work in the space below!*

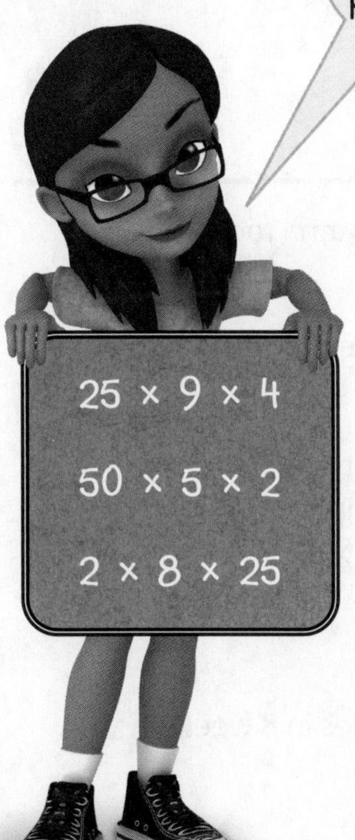

Look Back! Construct Arguments Is there more than one way to find 4 × 97? Is one way easier than the other to solve mentally? Explain.

How Can You Multiply Mentally?

A

Three cyclists rode their bikes the distances shown in the table. Use mental math to calculate the total distance Pam and Anna each rode.

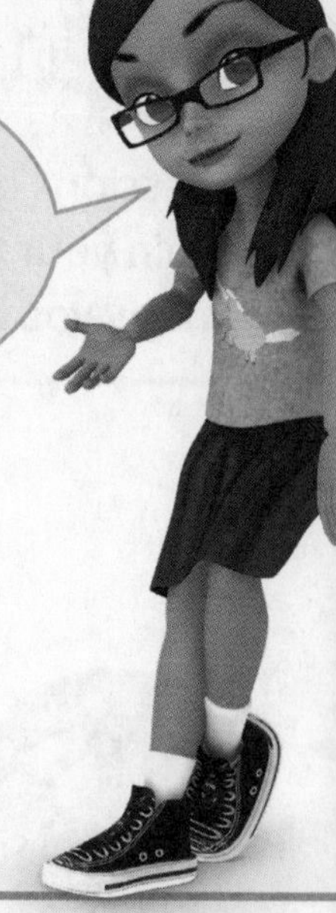

You can use properties of operations to help multiply mentally. According to the Commutative Property of Multiplication, you can multiply in any order.

DATA

Cyclist	Distance
Pam	325 miles a month for 4 months
Anna	25 miles a week for 8 weeks
George	398 miles a month for 3 months

B

Find the distance Pam rode.

Calculate 4×325.

Break apart 4×325.
Use the Distributive Property.
$4 \times 325 = (4 \times 300) + (4 \times 25)$

Multiply mentally, and then add.
$1{,}200 + 100 = 1{,}300$

Pam rode 1,300 miles in 4 months.

C

Find the distance Anna rode.

Calculate 8×25.

Break apart 8×25.
$8 \times 25 = (4 \times 2) \times 25$

Use the Commutative and Associative Properties to multiply.
$(2 \times 4) \times 25 = 2 \times (4 \times 25)$

Multiply mentally.
$2 \times 100 = 200$

Anna rode 200 miles in 8 weeks.

Convince Me! **Use Structure** Could you find how far Pam rode by calculating this expression, $4 \times (400 - 75)$? Explain.

Name ______________________________

Practice Buddy Tools Assessment

Another Example!

Determine the distance George rode.

Find 3 × 398. 400 is close to 398.
Find 3 × 400 and adjust the answer.

3 × 400 = 1,200
398 + 2 = 400   3 × 2 = 6

Adjust the answer by subtracting 6.
1,200 − 6 = 1,194
George rode 1,194 miles in 3 months.

You can use compensation to multiply mentally. Choose numbers close to the numbers in the problem and then adjust the answer.

Guided Practice*

Do You Understand?

1. **Reasoning** How can you tell if you need to add or subtract to adjust your answer when you use compensation? Explain.

Do You Know How?

2. How can you use compensation to find 8 × 903?

Independent Practice

Leveled Practice For **3–10**, use mental math to find each product.

3. 5 × 18 = 5 × (_____ × _____)
= (5 × _____) × _____
= _____ × _____
= _____

4. 4 × 506 = 4 × (_____ + _____)
= (4 × _____) + (4 × 6)
= _____ + _____
= _____

5. 4 × 1,995

6. 22 × 5

7. 404 × 6

8. 7 × 250

9. 2 × 395

10. 9 × 56

*For another example, see Set D on page 158.

Problem Solving

11. **Reasoning** Each elephant at a zoo eats 100 pounds of hay and 5 pounds of fruits and vegetables every day. How many pounds of food does the zoo need to feed one elephant for one week? Use mental math to solve.

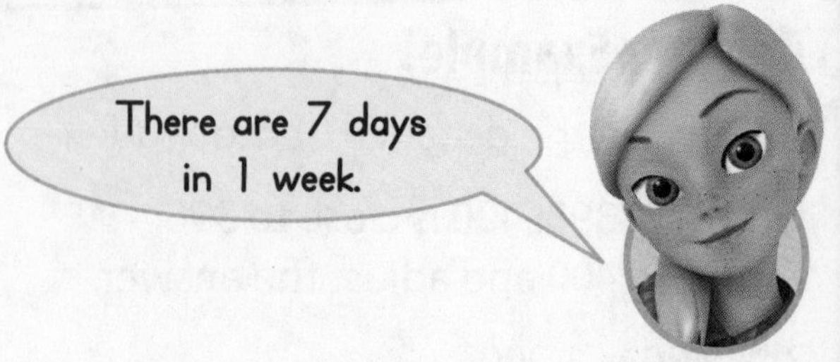
There are 7 days in 1 week.

12. **Model with Math** Ashley and 3 friends are planning a trip. The cost of the trip is \$599 per person. How much will the trip cost Ashley and her friends? Explain how to use mental math to find the answer.

13. Kyle has a rock collection. On Monday, he found 16 new rocks. On Tuesday, he gave 9 rocks to his friends. After giving away the rocks, Kyle had 122 rocks left in his collection. How many rocks did Kyle have to start with?

14. **Critique Reasoning** Quinn used compensation to find the product of 4×307. First, she found $4 \times 300 = 1{,}200$. Then she adjusted the product by subtracting 4 groups of 7 to get her final answer of 1,172. Explain Quinn's mistake and find the correct answer.

15. **Higher Order Thinking** Do you think it would be better to use breaking apart or compensation to find the product of 5×328? Explain why and show how to find the product.

Assessment ISTEP+ Ready

16. Which of the following expressions shows how to use mental math to find the product of 4×27? Select all that apply.

- ☐ $(4 \times 20) + (4 \times 7)$
- ☐ $4 \times (20 \times 7)$
- ☐ $(4 \times 30) - (4 \times 3)$
- ☐ $(4 \times 25) + (4 \times 2)$
- ☐ $4 \times 2 \times 7$

Some mental math strategies include both compensation and properties of operations.

Name ______________________________

Homework & Practice 3-4

Mental Math Strategies for Multiplication

Another Look!

Use mental math to calculate $4 \times 4{,}002$ and 8×60.

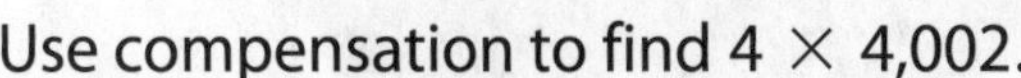

You can break numbers apart, use properties of operations, or use compensation to multiply mentally.

Use compensation to find $4 \times 4{,}002$.

4,000 is close to 4,002.
$4 \times 4{,}000 = 16{,}000$
$4{,}000 + 2 = 4{,}002$ $\quad 4 \times 2 = 8$
$16{,}000 + 8 = 16{,}008$

Use properties of operations to find 8×60.

$8 \times 60 = (4 \times 2) \times 60$
$= 4 \times (2 \times 60)$
$= 4 \times 120$
$= 480$

For **1–18**, use mental math to find each product.

1. $5 \times 395 = 5 \times (\_\_\_\_ - \_\_\_\_)$
$= (5 \times \_\_\_\_) - (5 \times \_\_\_\_)$
$= \_\_\_\_ - \_\_\_\_$
$= \_\_\_\_$

2. $7 \times 312 = 7 \times (\_\_\_\_ + \_\_\_\_)$
$= (7 \times \_\_\_\_) + (7 \times \_\_\_\_)$
$= \_\_\_\_ + \_\_\_\_$
$= \_\_\_\_$

3. 9×898

4. 2×144

5. 4×408

6. 8×15

7. 36×9

8. 3×496

9. 4×509

10. $3{,}004 \times 6$

11. 6×198

12. 5×999

13. 8×250

14. 4×525

15. 6×28

16. 7×156

17. $9 \times 1{,}276$

18. $3 \times 1{,}607$

For **19–20**, use the picture at the right.

19. Reasoning The longest blue whale on record was about 18 scuba divers in length. Use breaking apart to estimate the length of the blue whale.

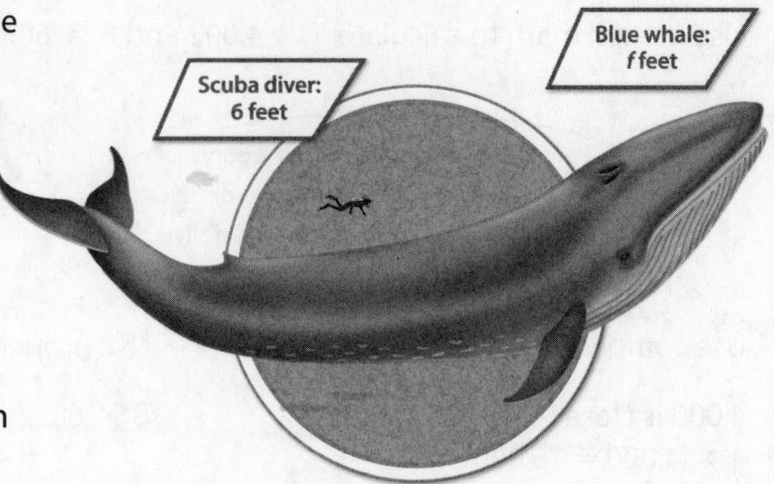

20. Explain how to estimate the length of the whale using compensation.

21. In an election, 589,067 people voted. Write 589,067 in expanded form and using number names.

22. Higher Order Thinking Davidson's Bakery bakes 108 cookies and 96 muffins every hour. How many baked goods are baked in 4 hours? Use mental math to solve.

Assessment ISTEP+ Ready

23. Which of the following expressions shows how to use mental math to find the product of 8×490? Select all that apply.

- ☐ $8 + (400 \times 90)$
- ☐ $(8 \times 400) + (8 \times 90)$
- ☐ $(8 \times 400) + (8 \times 9)$
- ☐ $(8 \times 500) - (8 \times 10)$
- ☐ $8 \times (500 \times 10)$

24. Which of the following expressions shows how to use mental math to find the product of $4 \times 2{,}025$? Select all that apply.

- ☐ $4 \times (2{,}000 + 20 + 5)$
- ☐ $(4 \times 2{,}000) + 25$
- ☐ $(4 \times 2{,}000) + (4 \times 25)$
- ☐ $4 \times (2{,}000 + 25)$
- ☐ $(4 \times 2{,}000 \times 25)$

Name ______________________________

Lesson 3-5
Arrays and Partial Products

I can …
use tools and multiplication strategies to help find products.

Content Standards 4.C.7, 4.AT.2
Process Standards PS.2, PS.4, PS.5

Solve & Share

A museum exhibit has 4 display cases. There are 118 coins in each case. How many coins are there in all the display cases? ***Solve this problem using any strategy you choose.***

You can use appropriate tools. Place-value blocks or drawings can help you visualize the problem. *Show your work in the space above!*

Look Back! Model with Math If you break apart 118 by place values to multiply, how many partial products would you have to add to determine the final product? Explain.

How Can You Record Multiplication?

A

A pet store bought 3 fish tanks to display different types of fish. Each tank holds the same amount of water. How much water will it take to fill all 3 tanks?

Partial products are products found by breaking one factor into ones, tens, hundreds, and so on and then using the Distributive Property to multiply each of these by the other factor.

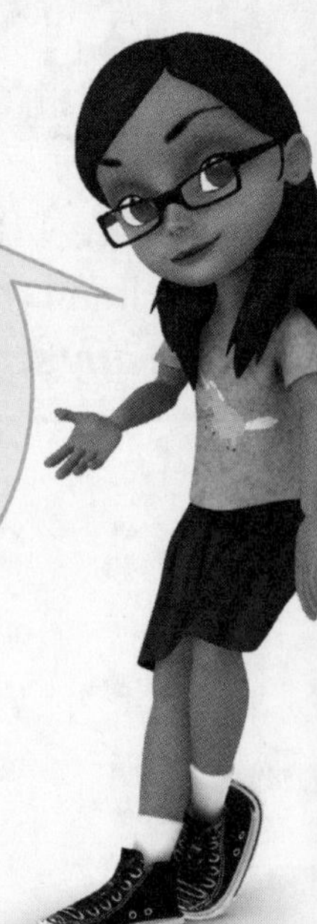

B

What You Show

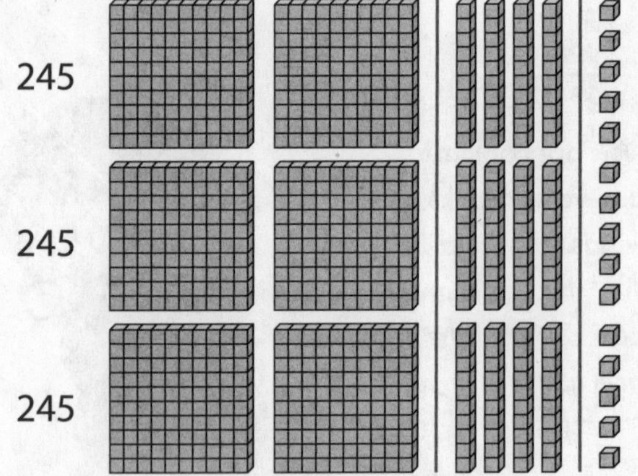

C

What You Write

$$
\begin{array}{rl}
245 & \\
\times \quad 3 & \\
\hline
15 & 3 \times 5 \\
120 & 3 \times 40 \\
+\ 600 & 3 \times 200 \\
\hline
735 &
\end{array}
$$

You can use place value to break factors apart and the Distributive Property to find partial products.

It will take 735 gallons of water to fill the 3 tanks.

Convince Me! **Model with Math** How are the partial products represented with the place-value blocks?

Name ____________________

Another Example!

The aquarium has 2 fish tanks that each hold 1,125 gallons of water. How much water does it take to fill these 2 tanks?

1,125 = 1,000 + 100 + 20 + 5

2 

```
   1,125
 ×     2
      10   2 × 5
      40   2 × 20
     200   2 × 100
 + 2,000   2 × 1,000
   2,250
```

You can draw a model to show partial products.

It takes 2,250 gallons to fill the tanks.

Guided Practice*

Do You Understand?

1. **Reasoning** What calculations were used to find the partial products 12, 30, and 300?

```
   114
 ×   3
    12
    30
 + 300
   342
```

Do You Know How?

For **2–3**, complete each calculation.

2. 124 × 2

3. 218 × 3

Independent Practice

Leveled Practice For **4–7**, complete each calculation. Use place-value blocks or arrays as needed.

4. 227 × 3

5. 122 × 4

6. 1,165 × 7

7. 391 × 5

*For another example, see Set E on page 159.

Problem Solving

8. **Model with Math** What multiplication equation do the place-value blocks show? Find the product. Then write a problem that could be solved using this model.

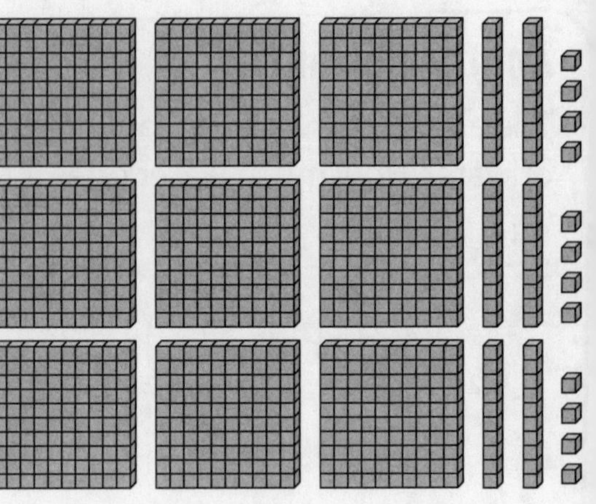

9. How many marbles are in 3 large bags and 4 small bags?

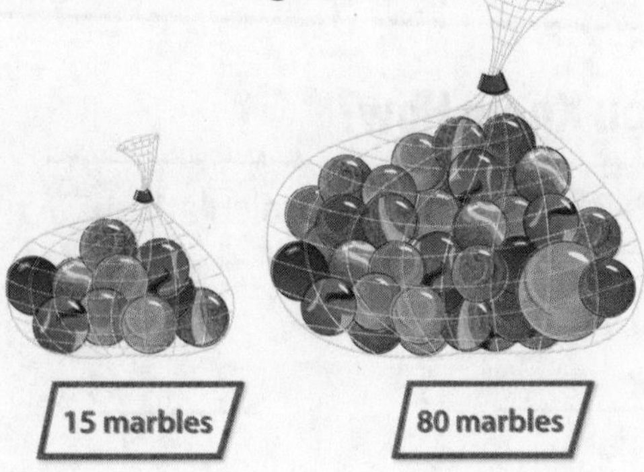

10. **Higher Order Thinking** How can the Distributive Property be used to find 4×875? Draw an array.

Assessment ISTEP+ Ready

11. Complete the calculation using the numbers from the box. Use each number once.

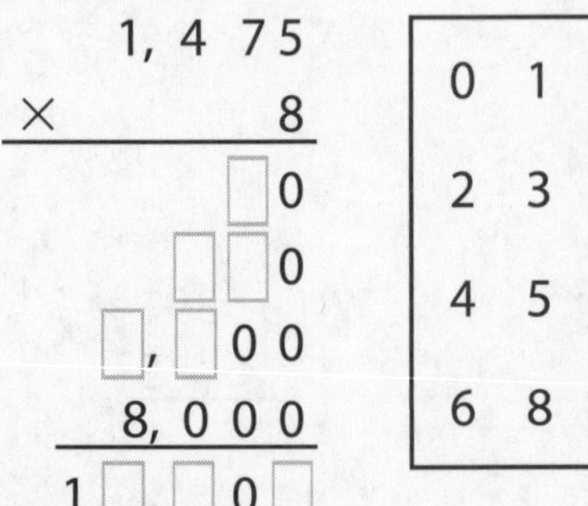

12. Complete the calculation using the numbers from the box. Use each number once.

```
   1, 6 1 8
 ×        9
        ☐ 2
        9 0
  ☐, ☐ 0 0
  ☐, 0 0 ☐
☐ 4, 5 ☐ ☐
```

0	1
2	4
5	6
7	9

Name ________________________________

Homework & Practice 3-5

Arrays and Partial Products

Another Look!

Find 3 × 124.

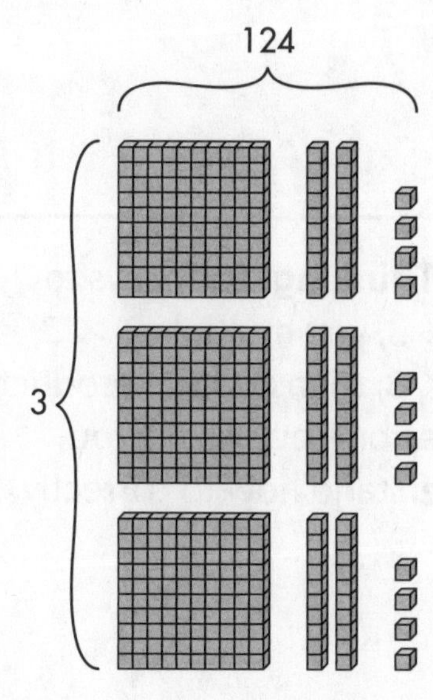

$3 \times 124 = 3 \times (100 + 20 + 4)$
$= (3 \times 100) + (3 \times 20) + (3 \times 4)$
$= 300 + 60 + 12$
$= 372$

The partial products are modeled by the drawing.

```
   124
 ×   3
    12   3 × 4 ones
    60   3 × 2 tens
 + 300   3 × 1 hundred
   372
```

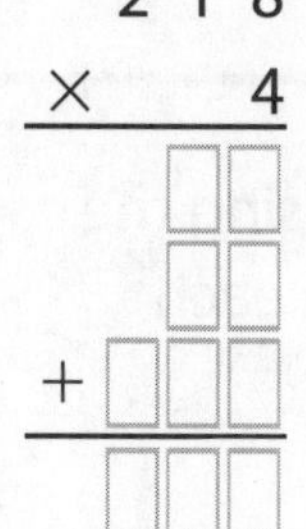

For **1–8**, complete each calculation. Use place-value blocks or draw arrays as needed.

1. 218 × 4

2. 411 × 2

3. 223 × 5

4. 316 × 3

5. 1,178 × 5

6. 2,148 × 3

7. 1,116 × 2

8. 2,136 × 4

9. James was able to correctly name 11 major highways, 4 mountains, 86 major cities, and 9 bodies of water on a map. How many places on the map did James identify? Explain how you can use compatible numbers to help calculate the sum.

10. **Use Appropriate Tools** Show how you can use place-value blocks or draw an array to find the partial products for 4×125.

11. A red tree frog can jump up to 150 times its body length. How far can this tree frog jump?

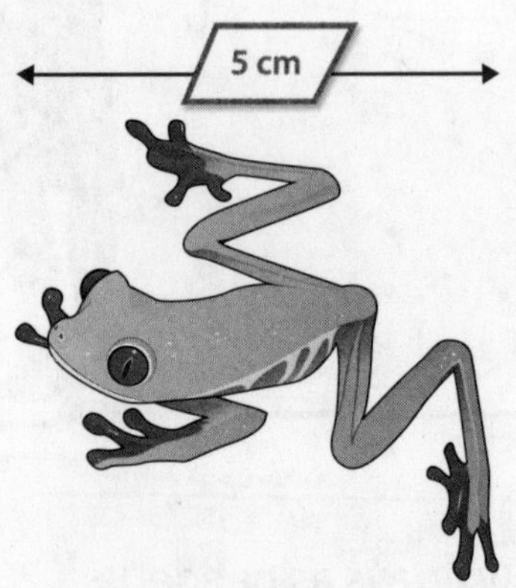

12. **Higher Order Thinking** Tony says to multiply 219×3, you multiply 2×3, 1×3, and 9×3, then add the products. Explain Tony's error. How would you help Tony understand how to correctly multiply 219×3?

13. Complete the calculation using the numbers from the box. Use each number once.

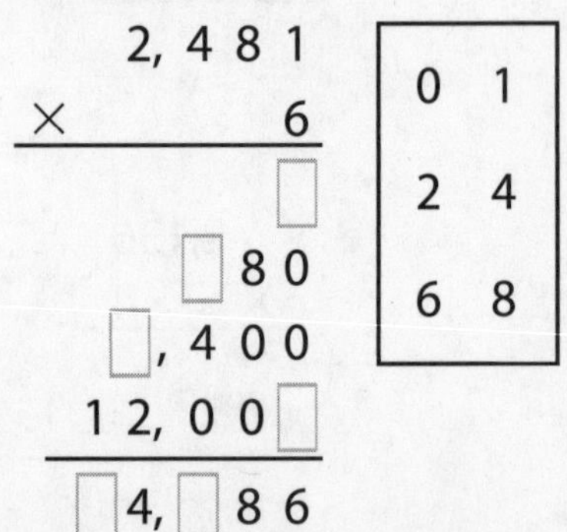

14. Complete the calculation using the numbers from the box. Use each number once.

```
    3, 0 4 9
×          6
         ☐ 4
       2 ☐ 0
           0
  1 ☐, 0 0 0
  ☐ 8, ☐ ☐ 4
```

1	2
4	5
8	9

Name ____________________

Lesson 3-6
Use Partial Products to Multiply by 1-Digit Numbers

I can ...
use place value and partial products to help multiply.

Content Standard 4.C.2
Process Standards PS.4, PS.5, PS.7, PS.8

Solve & Share There are 6 elementary schools in a school district. Each school has 412 students. How many students are in the district? ***Solve this problem using any strategy you choose.***

You can use appropriate tools. How can you use place-value blocks or drawings to solve this problem? *Show your work in the space above!*

Look Back! Generalize What shortcut could you use to check if your solution is reasonable?

What Is One Way to Record Multiplication?

A

David read that baseball bats are weighed in ounces and that baseballs are hand-sewn with double stitches. David wants to know how many ounces 6 baseball bats weigh and how many double stitches would be used in 6 baseballs.

You can record math with an algorithm.

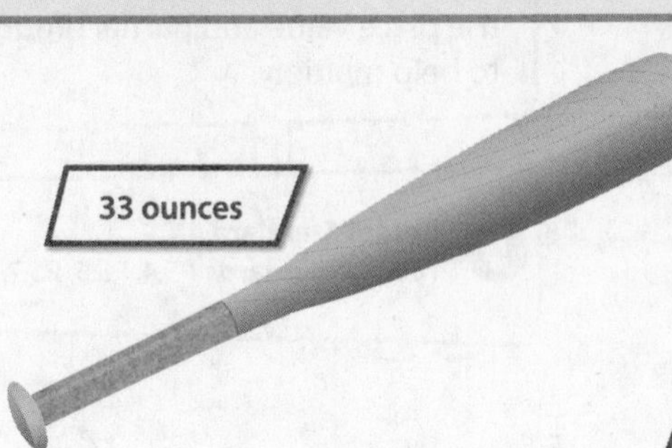

108 double stitches

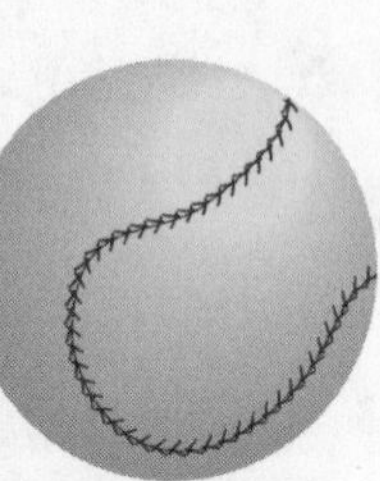

B

Find 6×33.

Multiply each place value to find the partial products. Then add the partial products.

$$\begin{array}{rl} 33 & \\ \times \ \ 6 & \\ \hline 18 & 6 \times 3 \\ +\ 180 & 6 \times 30 \\ \hline 198 & \end{array}$$

Six baseball bats weigh 198 ounces.

C

Find 6×108.

$$\begin{array}{rl} 108 & \\ \times \ \ 6 & \\ \hline 48 & 6 \times 8 \\ 0 & 6 \times 0 \\ +\ 600 & 6 \times 100 \\ \hline 648 & \end{array}$$

Use rounding to estimate.

$6 \times 100 = 600$

There are 648 double stitches in 6 baseballs. 600 is close to 648, so the answer is reasonable.

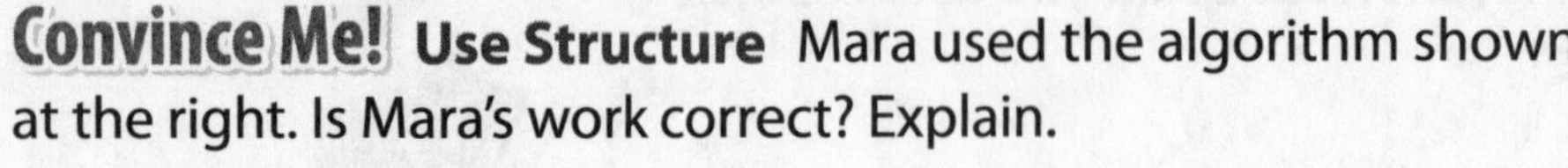

Convince Me! Use Structure Mara used the algorithm shown at the right. Is Mara's work correct? Explain.

$$\begin{array}{r} 124 \\ \times \ \ 4 \\ \hline 400 \\ 80 \\ +\ 16 \\ \hline 496 \end{array}$$

Name ________________________________

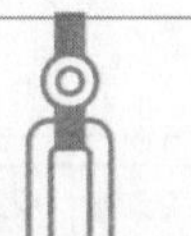

Guided Practice*

Do You Understand?

1. **Use Structure** Seth found 374 × 3. What partial product is missing from Seth's work? Explain.

$$\begin{array}{r} 374 \\ \times \quad 3 \\ \hline 12 \\ +\,900 \\ \hline 912 \end{array}$$

Do You Know How?

For **2–3**, find each product using an algorithm.

2. $\begin{array}{r} 117 \\ \times \quad 5 \\ \hline \end{array}$

3. $\begin{array}{r} 243 \\ \times \quad 3 \\ \hline \end{array}$

Use an estimate to check if your answer is reasonable.

Independent Practice

For **4–7**, find each product using an algorithm. Draw pictures if needed.

4. $\begin{array}{r} 223 \\ \times \quad 5 \\ \hline \end{array}$

5. $\begin{array}{r} 418 \\ \times \quad 8 \\ \hline \end{array}$

6. $\begin{array}{r} 193 \\ \times \quad 3 \\ \hline \end{array}$

7. $\begin{array}{r} 2{,}917 \\ \times \quad 7 \\ \hline \end{array}$

For **8–11**, find each product using an algorithm.

8. 6 × 138

9. 7 × 226

10. 8 × 242

11. 5 × 1,640

*For another example, see Set E on page 159.

Problem Solving

12. Model with Math The bar diagram shows 4 groups of 225. Calculate 4 × 225 using an algorithm.

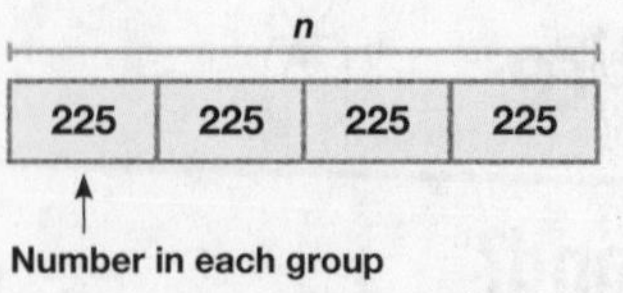

13. There are usually 365 days in each year. Every fourth year is called a leap year and has one extra day in February. How many days are there in 8 years if two of the years are leap years?

14. There are 1,250 seeds in each package. There are 5 packages. How many seeds are there in all?

15. A cat breeder has 6 Sphynx kittens and 7 Persian kittens for sale. If all 13 kittens sell, how much money will the breeder earn? Explain.

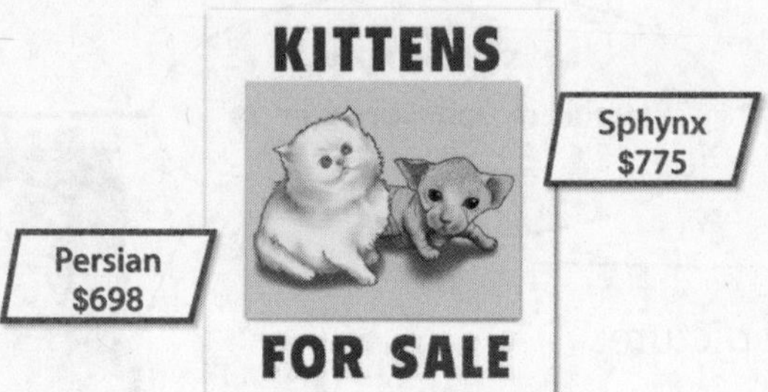

16. **Higher Order Thinking** Patricia creates a design using 163 tiles. She doubles the number of tiles to make a second design. Her third design uses 3 times as many tiles as the second design. How many tiles does Patricia use in her third design? Explain.

17. A charter boat holds 60 adults and 50 children. How many people can go on 4 charter boat rides? Which are the three partial products that will be added to find the number of people that can go on 4 charter boat rides?

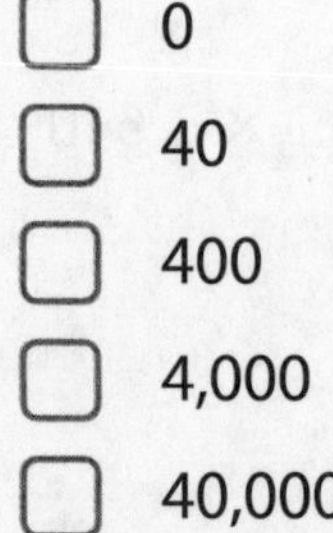

- ☐ 0
- ☐ 40
- ☐ 400
- ☐ 4,000
- ☐ 40,000

First add to find the number of people on each ride. Then multiply to find how many people can go on 4 rides.

Name ____________________

Homework & Practice 3-6

Use Partial Products to Multiply by 1-Digit Numbers

Another Look!

Three groups of 145 students attended the play. How many students attended the play?

Find 3 × 145.

Record the partial products.

```
   145
 ×   3
    15   3 × 5
   120   3 × 40
 + 300   3 × 100
   435
```

435 students attended the play.

You can use an algorithm to record the partial products when multiplying.

For **1–16**, find each product using an algorithm. Draw pictures, use arrays, or area models if needed. Check if your answer is reasonable.

1. 275 × 6

2. 164 × 5

3. 317 × 9

4. 3,933 × 4

5. 15 × 8

6. 137 × 4

7. 1,619 × 7

8. 4,269 × 5

9. 7 × 64

10. 96 × 3

11. 531 × 8

12. 5 × 2,111

13. 62 × 9

14. 217 × 4

15. 119 × 3

16. 1,231 × 2

17. **Model with Math** Complete the model showing how to use the Distributive Property to find the product of 7 and 16. Then write an equation showing how to find the product using the Distributive Property.

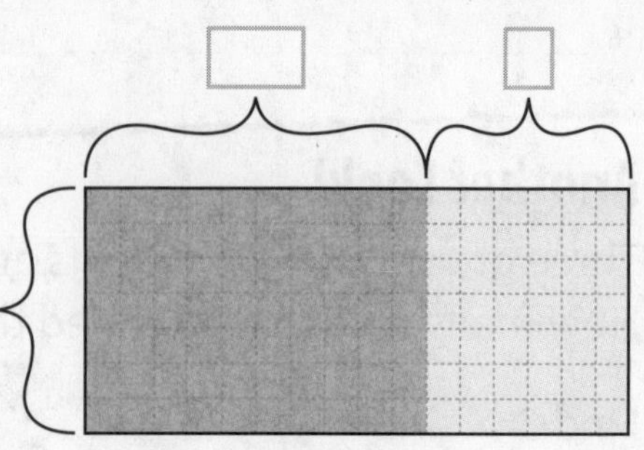

18. Fred's Auto Sales purchases 3 new vehicles for $11,219, $31,611, and $18,204. What was the total cost for all the vehicles?

19. Kinsey earns $54,625 a year. She purchases a snowmobile for $12,005. How much of Kinsey's yearly earnings does she have left?

20. **Number Sense** Dalton added 3,402 + 4,950 to get 8,352. Estimate the sum by rounding the addends to the nearest hundred. Is Dalton's sum reasonable? Explain.

n

3,402	4,950

21. **Higher Order Thinking** Josh used an algorithm to find the product for 9 × 239. His work is shown below. Is Josh's work correct? Explain.

$$\begin{array}{r} 239 \\ \times \quad 9 \\ \hline 1{,}800 \\ 270 \\ + \quad 81 \\ \hline 2{,}151 \end{array}$$

Assessment ISTEP+ Ready

22. DeShawn fuels 2 yachts and 6 barges. Each boat gets 126 gallons of fuel. To find how much fuel he needs for all the boats, DeShawn first finds the number of boats, then he uses an algorithm to multiply. Which are the three partial products DeShawn could add to find the final product?

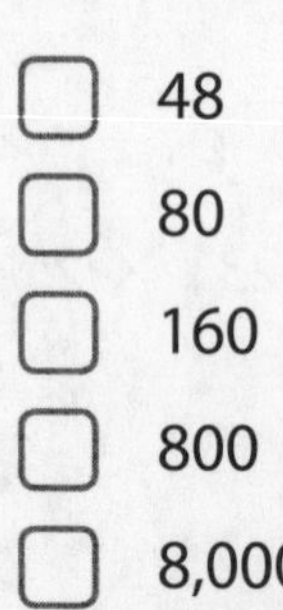

- ☐ 48
- ☐ 80
- ☐ 160
- ☐ 800
- ☐ 8,000

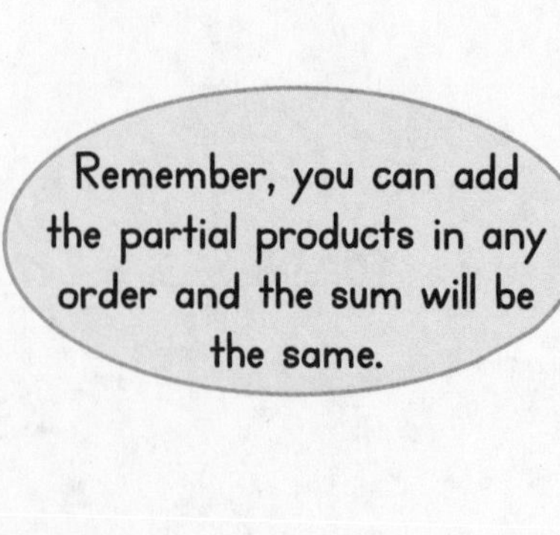

Remember, you can add the partial products in any order and the sum will be the same.

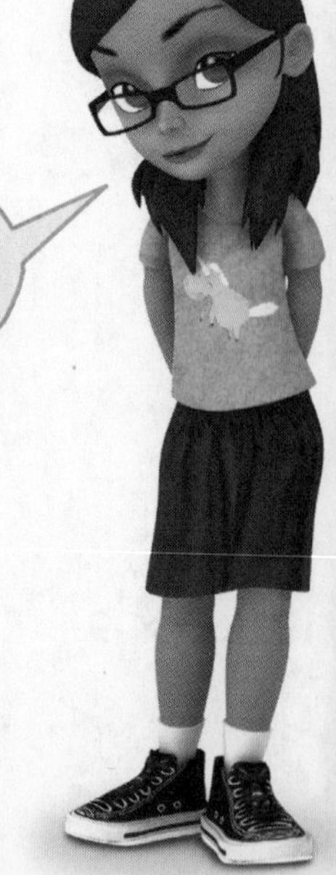

Name ____________________

Lesson 3-7
Multiply 2- and 3-Digit Numbers by 1-Digit Numbers

I can ...
use place-value strategies and algorithms to multiply 2-digit and 3-digit numbers.

Content Standard 4.C.2
Process Standards PS.1, PS.2, PS.3, PS.4, PS.7, PS.8

Solve & Share Suppose a school ordered 7 boxes of books. There are 25 books in each box. How can you use paper and pencil to find how many books were ordered? How can you check if your answer is reasonable? ***Solve these problems using any strategy you choose.***

You can make sense and persevere. Formulating a plan can help you solve problems. *Show your work in the space above!*

Look Back! Generalize What shortcut can you use to check if your solution is reasonable?

What Is a Common Way to Record Multiplication?

A

Ms. Stockton ordered 2 boxes of T-shirts with the phrase, **Keep Dreaming!** *and 4 boxes of T-shirts with the phrase,* **I ❤ Math.** *How many T-shirts did Ms. Stockton order?*

Phrase on T-shirt	Number of T-shirts per Box
I ❤ Math	26 T-shirts
Just sayin...	12 T-shirts
Life is better on a long board	24 T-shirts
Keep Dreaming	26 T-shirts

Some problems have more than one step to solve. First find how many boxes of T-shirts were ordered in all.

Ms. Stockton ordered a total of 6 boxes of T-shirts.

B

You can multiply and add the partial products in any order.

Find 6×26.

$$\begin{array}{rl} 26 & \\ \times\ 6 & \\ \hline 120 & 6 \times 20 \\ +\ 36 & 6 \times 6 \\ \hline 156 & \end{array}$$

Partial products → 120, 36

C

You can multiply each place value in order, beginning with the ones. Regroup if needed. Add any regrouped values to each place value.

Find 6×26.

Step 1: Multiply the ones.

$$\begin{array}{r} \overset{3}{2}6 \\ \times\ 6 \\ \hline 6 \end{array}$$

$6 \times 6 = 36$

Record the 6 ones and regroup the 3 tens.

Step 2: Multiply the tens.

$$\begin{array}{r} \overset{3}{2}6 \\ \times\ 6 \\ \hline 156 \end{array}$$

$6 \times 20 = 120$

12 tens + 3 tens = 15 tens

Ms. Stockton ordered 156 T-shirts.

Convince Me! **Critique Reasoning** A student did the calculation for 3 boxes of the *I ❤ Math* T-shirts and got the incorrect answer shown at the right. What did this student do wrong? What is the correct answer?

Incorrect Answer

$$\begin{array}{r} \overset{1}{2}6 \\ \times\ 3 \\ \hline 98 \end{array}$$

Name ______________________________

Another Example!

Ms. Stockton ordered 156 T-shirts each week. How many T-shirts did she order in 4 weeks? Find 156 × 4.

The algorithm works with any number of digits.

One Way

$$\begin{array}{rl} 156 & \\ \times\ \ 4 & \\ \hline 24 & 4 \times 6 \\ 200 & 4 \times 50 \\ +\ 400 & 4 \times 100 \\ \hline 624 & \end{array}$$

Another Way

$$\begin{array}{r} {}^{2\,2}\ \ \ \\ 156 \\ \times\ \ 4 \\ \hline 624 \end{array}$$

Multiply the ones, then the tens, and then the hundreds. Regroup if needed.

Ms. Stockton ordered 624 T-shirts.

Guided Practice*

Do You Understand?

1. Explain how to check if the answer to the Another Example above is reasonable.

2. Reasoning In the problem below, why is there a 5 recorded in the tens place of the product?

$$\begin{array}{r} 738 \\ \times\ \ 4 \\ \hline 2{,}952 \end{array}$$

Do You Know How?

For **3–10**, find each product. Estimate to check if your answer is reasonable.

3. $\begin{array}{r} 523 \\ \times\ \ 4 \\ \hline \end{array}$

4. $\begin{array}{r} 378 \\ \times\ \ 2 \\ \hline \end{array}$

5. $\begin{array}{r} 157 \\ \times\ \ 5 \\ \hline \end{array}$

6. $\begin{array}{r} 746 \\ \times\ \ 3 \\ \hline \end{array}$

7. 123 × 9

8. 445 × 5

9. 27 × 3

10. 204 × 6

Independent Practice

For **11–14**, find each product. Estimate to check if your answer is reasonable.

11. $\begin{array}{r} 519 \\ \times\ \ 4 \\ \hline \end{array}$

12. $\begin{array}{r} 28 \\ \times\ 3 \\ \hline \end{array}$

13. $\begin{array}{r} 72 \\ \times\ 5 \\ \hline \end{array}$

14. $\begin{array}{r} 138 \\ \times\ \ 5 \\ \hline \end{array}$

For another example, see Set F on page 159.

Problem Solving

For **15–17**, use the information in the pictures below to find each mass.

15. Elephant Seal **16.** Sports Car **17.** Bison

18. Model with Math Last year, Anthony's grandmother gave him 33 silver coins and 16 gold coins to start a coin collection. Now Anthony has six times as many coins in his collection. How many coins does Anthony have in his collection? Complete the bar diagram to show your work.

coins in all

coins now

coins to start

19. Vocabulary Use *Distributive* or *Commutative* to complete the definition.

According to the ____________ Property of Multiplication, factors can be multiplied in any order and the product remains the same.

20. Higher Order Thinking Do you think you could use a multiplication algorithm to multiply a 4-digit number by a 1-digit number? Explain.

21. Find the missing numbers in the multiplication problem. Write the missing numbers in the answer spaces at the right.

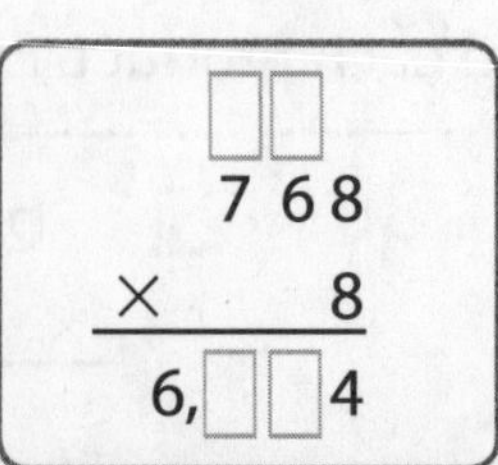

Name ______________________

Help Practice Buddy Tools Games

Homework & Practice 3-7

Multiply 2- and 3-Digit Numbers by 1-Digit Numbers

Another Look!

The steps below show one way to multiply 3-digit numbers by 1-digit numbers.

Step 1

Multiply the ones.
Regroup if necessary.

$$\begin{array}{r} \overset{1}{}\\ 154 \\ \times \quad 4 \\ \hline 6 \end{array}$$

Step 2

Multiply the tens.
Add any extra tens.
Regroup if necessary.

$$\begin{array}{r} {}^{2\,1}\\ 154 \\ \times \quad 4 \\ \hline 16 \end{array}$$

Step 3

Multiply the hundreds.
Add any extra hundreds.

$$\begin{array}{r} {}^{2\,1}\\ 154 \\ \times \quad 4 \\ \hline 616 \end{array}$$

For **1–16**, find each product.

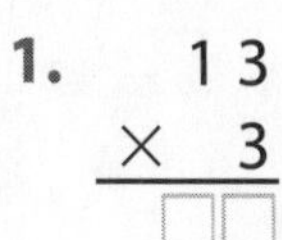

Remember to regroup if necessary.

1. $\begin{array}{r} 13 \\ \times \quad 3 \\ \hline \square\square \end{array}$

2. $\begin{array}{r} \square \\ 17 \\ \times \quad 7 \\ \hline \square\square\square \end{array}$

3. $\begin{array}{r} \square \\ 741 \\ \times \quad 3 \\ \hline \square\square\square\square \end{array}$

4. $\begin{array}{r} \square\square \\ 587 \\ \times \quad 3 \\ \hline \square\square\square\square \end{array}$

5. $\begin{array}{r} 413 \\ \times \quad 6 \\ \hline \end{array}$

6. $\begin{array}{r} 625 \\ \times \quad 6 \\ \hline \end{array}$

7. $\begin{array}{r} 36 \\ \times \quad 5 \\ \hline \end{array}$

8. $\begin{array}{r} 731 \\ \times \quad 9 \\ \hline \end{array}$

9. $\begin{array}{r} 88 \\ \times \quad 5 \\ \hline \end{array}$

10. $\begin{array}{r} 52 \\ \times \quad 8 \\ \hline \end{array}$

11. $\begin{array}{r} 352 \\ \times \quad 3 \\ \hline \end{array}$

12. $\begin{array}{r} 159 \\ \times \quad 5 \\ \hline \end{array}$

13. $\begin{array}{r} 164 \\ \times \quad 5 \\ \hline \end{array}$

14. $\begin{array}{r} 19 \\ \times \quad 8 \\ \hline \end{array}$

15. $\begin{array}{r} 478 \\ \times \quad 2 \\ \hline \end{array}$

16. $\begin{array}{r} 862 \\ \times \quad 7 \\ \hline \end{array}$

For **17–18**, use the table at the right.

17. What is the average length fingernails will grow in 12 months?

18. How much longer will hair grow than fingernails in 6 months?

Average Rate of Growth in Millimeters per Month	
Fingernails	5 mm
Hair	12 mm

19. Derek rides in three motorcycle races. Each race is 150 miles. How many miles does Derek ride?

20. Walt averages 98 miles per hour in 4 races. If each race is 95 miles in length, how many miles did Walt drive in the races?

21. The Puerto Rico Trench has a depth of 30,246 feet. Write the numbers that are 10,000 less than and 10,000 greater than this number.

22. Which place value would you look at to compare 225,998 and 225,988?

23. **Critique Reasoning** Martin multiplied 423 by 7 and said the product is 2,841. Do Martin's calculations make sense? Explain.

24. **Higher Order Thinking** Tyrone has 6 times as many marbles as Pam. Pam has 34 marbles. Louis has 202 marbles. Who has more marbles, Tyrone or Louis? Explain.

25. Find the missing numbers in the multiplication problem. Write the missing numbers in the answer spaces at the right.

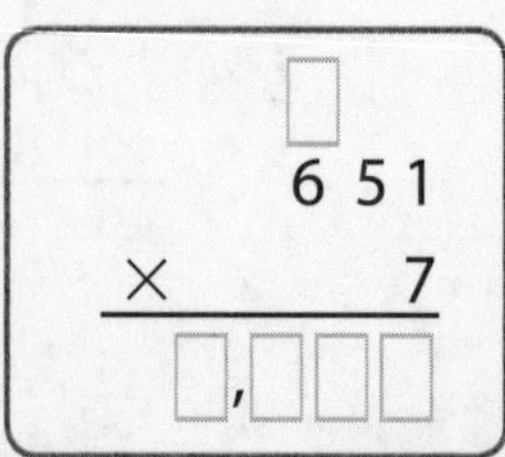

Name ______________________________  Solve

Lesson 3-8
Multiply 4-Digit by 1-Digit Numbers

I can ...
multiply greater numbers following the same steps as when multiplying smaller numbers.

Content Standard 4.C.2
Process Standards PS.2, PS.4, PS.8

Solve & Share A floor pattern contains 5,835 tiles. The same pattern is used 7 times. How many tiles are used all together? ***Solve this problem using any strategy you choose.***

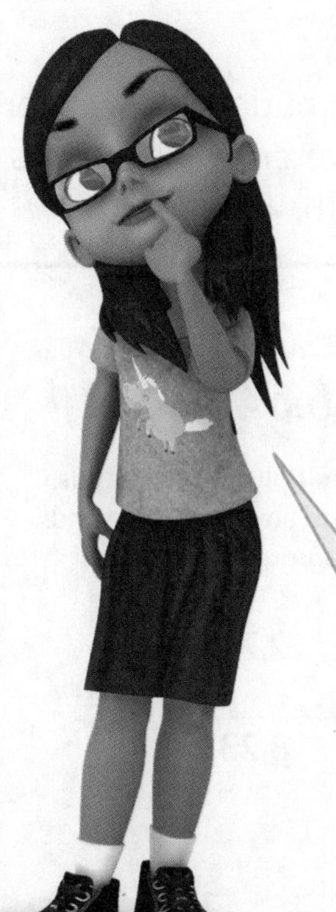

You can use reasoning. How are 4-digit numbers like 3-digit numbers? How are they different? *Show your work in the space above!*

Look Back! Reasoning Explain why you needed to regroup when multiplying in the problem above.

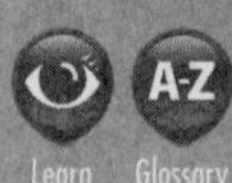

Essential Question

How Can You Multiply 4-Digit Numbers by 1-Digit Numbers?

A

A wildlife center budgets the amount shown below for food and veterinary expenses each month. What is the budget for food and veterinary expenses for a 3-month period?

You can use an algorithm to multiply thousands the same way you multiply hundreds or tens.

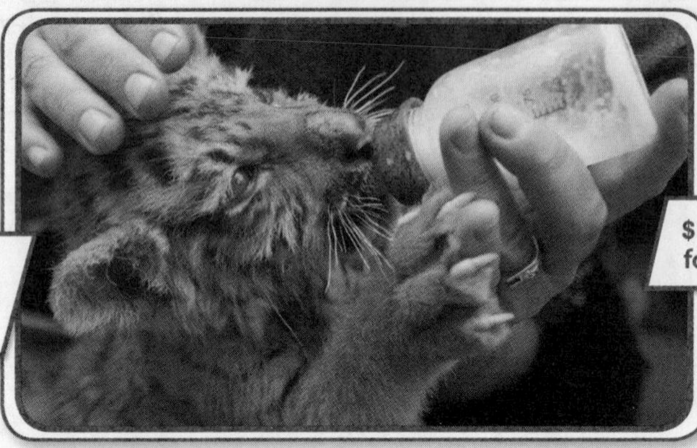

$1,215 is spent on veterinary expenses each month.

$1,531 is spent on food each month.

$$\begin{array}{r} \$1,215 \\ +\ \$1,531 \\ \hline \$2,746 \end{array}$$

The center budgets $2,746 for food and veterinary expenses each month.

B

Find 3 × 2,746.

Step 1

Multiply the ones.
Regroup if necessary.

$$\begin{array}{r} \scriptsize{1} \\ 2,746 \\ \times \quad\ \ 3 \\ \hline 8 \end{array}$$

Step 2

Multiply the tens.
Add any extra tens.
Regroup if necessary.

$$\begin{array}{r} \scriptsize{1\,1} \\ 2,746 \\ \times \quad\ \ 3 \\ \hline 38 \end{array}$$

Step 3

Multiply the hundreds.
Add any extra hundreds.
Regroup if necessary.

$$\begin{array}{r} \scriptsize{2\ 1\,1} \\ 2,746 \\ \times \quad\ \ 3 \\ \hline 238 \end{array}$$

Step 4

Multiply the thousands.
Add any extra thousands.
Regroup if necessary.

$$\begin{array}{r} \scriptsize{2\ 1\,1} \\ 2,746 \\ \times \quad\ \ 3 \\ \hline 8,238 \end{array}$$

The budget for food and veterinary expenses for 3 months is $8,238.

Convince Me! **Generalize** How can you use estimation to decide if a product is reasonable? Use the problem above to explain.

Name ____________________

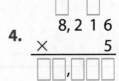

Guided Practice*

Do You Understand?

1. How is multiplying a 4-digit number like multiplying a 3-digit number?

2. **Reasoning** Explain when you would not need to regroup any hundreds into thousands when multiplying a 4-digit number by a 1-digit number.

Do You Know How?

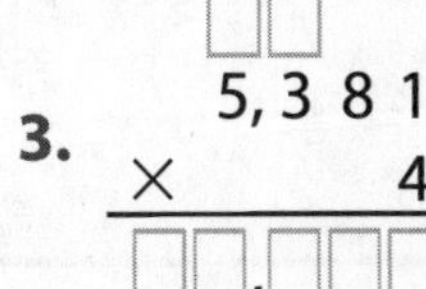

For **3–6**, find each product.

3. 5,381 × 4 = ☐☐,☐☐☐

4. 8,216 × 5 = ☐☐,☐☐☐

5. 9,734 × 6

6. 7,512 × 7

Independent Practice

Leveled Practice For **7–22**, find each product.

7. 1,842 × 3 = ☐,☐☐☐

8. 2,089 × 2 = ☐,☐☐☐

9. 9,152 × 7 = ☐☐,☐☐☐

10. 6,451 × 8 = ☐☐,☐☐☐

11. 3,287 × 1

12. 8,721 × 6

13. 1,428 × 3

14. 3,756 × 9

15. 6,912 × 4

16. 7,856 × 8

17. 4,005 × 5

18. 1,624 × 2

19. 4,569 × 3

20. 2,146 × 7

21. 1,002 × 4

22. 6,191 × 5

*For another example, see Set G on page 160.

Problem Solving

23. Algebra There are 5,280 feet in 1 mile. How many feet farther is it to Pickens Corner than Hobbs Landing? Write and solve an equation to explain how you found your answer.

Hobbs Landing	3 mi
Pickens Corner	9 mi

24. Describe the relationship between the 2s in 22,679.

25. There are 12,216 seats in the arena and 4,216 seats in the auditorium. How many more seats are in the arena than the auditorium?

26. Model with Math A restaurant sells 3,125 of its famous veggie burgers each month. At this rate, how many veggie burgers will be sold in 6 months?

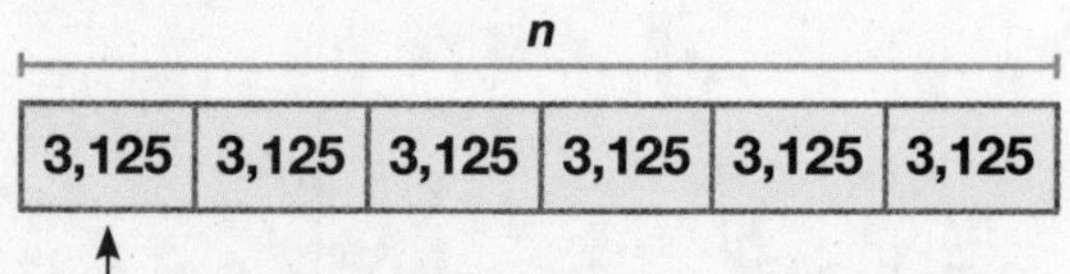

Number of veggie burgers sold each month

27. Higher Order Thinking A semi-truck trailer has a load capacity of 25,900 pounds. A trucker is asked to haul 5 crates on the trailer. Each crate weighs 4,450 pounds. Can the trucker haul all 5 crates in one load? Explain.

28. The driving distance from Boston, MA, to Colorado Springs, CO, and back again is 4,084 miles. A salesperson has already made the trip back and forth twice. A salesperson may drive up to 12,500 miles each month. Can she make the trip again and remain below the monthly miles allowed? If so, how many miles will she have left for the month?

Name ______________________________

Help Practice Buddy Tools Games

Homework & Practice 3-8

Multiply 4-Digit by 1-Digit Numbers

Another Look!

Find 1,214 × 7.

The steps below show how to multiply greater numbers.

Step 1

Multiply the ones. Regroup if necessary.

```
    2
 1,214
×    7
     8
```

Step 2

Multiply the tens. Add any extra tens. Regroup if necessary.

```
    2
 1,214
×    7
    98
```

Step 3

Multiply the hundreds. Add any extra hundreds. Regroup if necessary.

```
  1 2
 1,214
×    7
   498
```

Step 4

Multiply the thousands. Add any extra thousands.

```
  1 2
 1,214
×    7
 8,498
```

For **1–16**, find each product.

1. 1,324 × 2

2. 5,618 × 7

3. 4,810 × 3

4. 9,018 × 6

5. 2,721 × 4

6. 7,183 × 2

7. 8,734 × 5

8. 6,451 × 7

9. 2,649 × 8

10. 1,273 × 5

11. 6,019 × 2

12. 4,867 × 7

13. 3,258 × 2

14. 4,307 × 4

15. 2,894 × 8

16. 6,113 × 9

For **17–18**, use the table at the right.

17. Bailey rode Coaster B four times. How many feet did she ride? What is your answer rounded to the nearest thousand?

18. Janna rode each of the four roller coasters listed in the table twice. How many feet of roller coaster did she ride?

DATA

Roller Coaster Length	
Coaster A	6,595 ft
Coaster B	6,072 ft
Coaster C	5,843 ft
Coaster D	5,600 ft

19. The Appalachian Trail is 2,174 miles long. If a group of 7 people hike the entire trail, how many combined miles do they hike?

20. The Chisholm trail was approximately 800 miles long. If a cowboy walked the trail 9 times, about how many miles did the cowboy walk?

21. Model with Math The Appalachian Trail is 2,174 miles long. About how long would a trail be if it were 3 times the length of the Appalachian Trail?

n

2,174	2,174	2,174	3 times as long

2,174

22. Higher Order Thinking Describe the mistakes in the solution below. Show the correct solution.

$$\begin{array}{r} 1{,}892 \\ \times \quad 4 \\ \hline 8 \\ 36 \\ 320 \\ +\,4{,}000 \\ \hline 4{,}364 \end{array}$$

Assessment ISTEP+ Ready

23. Show two different ways to solve the following problem. Each wheel on a roller coaster turns 3,999 times during the ride. How many times will each wheel turn during 2 rides?

Name ______________________________ Solve

Lesson 3-9
Multiply by 1-Digit Numbers

I can ...
use an algorithm to multiply numbers and estimate to check if the answer is reasonable.

Content Standard 4.C.2
Process Standards PS.2, PS.3, PS.6, PS.8

Solve & Share A cineplex contains 4 movie theaters. Each theater can seat 312 people. How many people can the cineplex seat? ***Solve this problem using any strategy you choose.***

You can be precise and use the information given to calculate accurately. *Show your work in the space above!*

Look Back! Be Precise If the cineplex had 8 movie theaters with 312 seats each, how many seats would the cineplex have? Explain how to use the answer from above to solve this problem. Remember to label your answer.

What Are the Steps to Record Multiplication?

A

Paying for pothole damage to cars can be costly. The table shows the cost of some car repairs. Use the table to answer each question.

Repairs Due to Pothole Damage

Item	Cost
Shock Absorber	$69 each
Tires	$135 each
Paint	$1,450 per coat

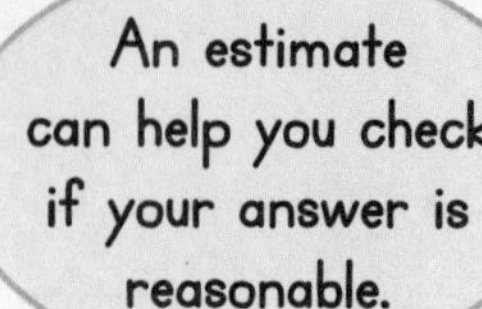

An estimate can help you check if your answer is reasonable.

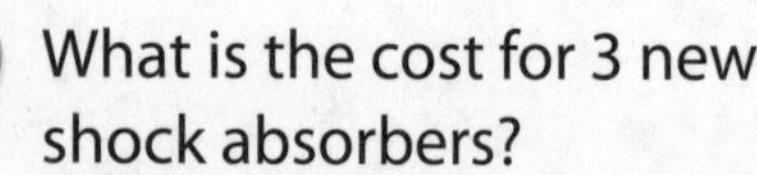

B What is the cost for 3 new shock absorbers?

Estimate:
$3 \times \$69$ is about
$3 \times 70 = 210$.

$$\begin{array}{r} {}^{2}\\ 69 \\ \times \quad 3 \\ \hline 207 \end{array}$$

Three shock absorbers cost $207. The answer is reasonable.

C What is the cost for 4 new tires?

Estimate:
$4 \times \$135$ is about
$4 \times 100 = 400$.

$$\begin{array}{r} {}^{1\,2}\\ 135 \\ \times \quad 4 \\ \hline 540 \end{array}$$

Four new tires cost $540. The answer is reasonable.

D What is the cost for 2 coats of paint?

Estimate:
$2 \times \$1,450$ is about
$2 \times 1,500 = 3,000$.

$$\begin{array}{r} {}^{1}\quad\\ 1,450 \\ \times \quad 2 \\ \hline 2,900 \end{array}$$

Two coats of paint cost $2,900. The answer is reasonable.

Convince Me! **Reasoning** Find each product at the right. Does the multiplication process change as the value of one factor increases?

$$\begin{array}{r} 21 \\ \times \quad 4 \\ \hline \end{array} \qquad \begin{array}{r} 321 \\ \times \quad 4 \\ \hline \end{array} \qquad \begin{array}{r} {}^{1}\quad\\ 4,321 \\ \times \quad 4 \\ \hline \end{array}$$

Name ______________________

Practice Buddy Tools Assessment

Guided Practice*

Do You Understand?

1. A road repair crew can usually fix 825 potholes each week. How many potholes can they fix in 6 weeks?

2. Construct Arguments A tire shop sells 3 tires that cost $175 each, which includes a fourth tire for free. Is this more or less expensive than buying 4 tires that cost $135 each?

Do You Know How?

For **3–10**, find each product.

3. 74×6

4. 819×5

5. 4×309

6. 3×175

7. 8×218

8. $6 \times 1{,}741$

9. 29×7

10. $1{,}461 \times 9$

Independent Practice

For **11–26**, find each product. Estimate to check if your answer is reasonable.

11. 77×6

12. 83×5

13. 62×4

14. 89×7

15. 245×3

16. 318×9

17. 736×2

18. 314×8

19. $4 \times 4{,}347$

20. $6 \times 2{,}716$

21. $7 \times 1{,}287$

22. $3 \times 1{,}942$

23. $2{,}319 \times 5$

24. $1{,}467 \times 5$

25. $2{,}138 \times 9$

26. $9{,}749 \times 5$

*For another example, see Set G on page 160.

Problem Solving

27. Maura's dance team wants to buy costumes that cost $56 each. They have $523 saved in a fund. How much money will they have left in the fund after they buy 9 costumes?

What is the hidden question you have to answer first?

28. Elaine rents a car for 5 days. It costs $44 each day to rent the car and $7 each day for insurance. At the end of the trip she spends $35 to fill the car with gas. What is the total cost for Elaine to use the car?

29. At the Math Club ceremony, there were 17 tables with 8 people seated at each table. Each guest received 2 certificates. How many certificates were distributed at the ceremony?

30. Water erupting from geysers can reach a temperature of 244°F. The average temperature in Yellowstone National Park is 35°F. Use compensation to calculate the difference between these two temperatures.

31. **Higher Order Thinking** On Monday, Paolo sold 21 tickets to the dance. On Tuesday, he sold three times as many tickets as he sold on Monday. On Wednesday, he sold twice as many tickets as he sold on Tuesday. How many total tickets did Paolo sell in the three days?

32. Mr. Tran would like to buy a new sofa that costs $934. He can pay the total all at once, or he can make a $125 payment each month for 8 months. Which plan costs less? Explain.

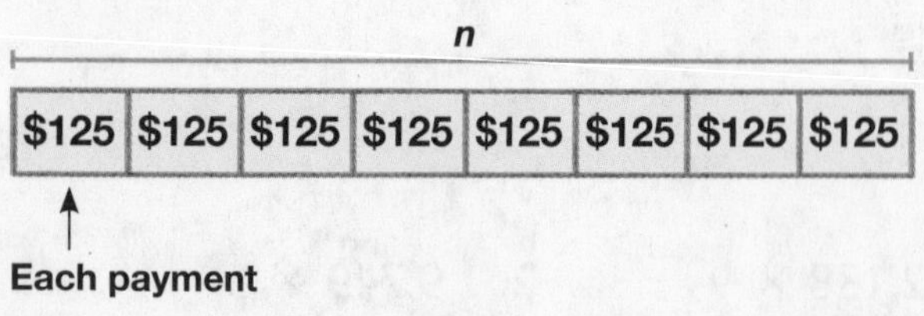

Name ______________________

Homework & Practice 3-9

Multiply by 1-Digit Numbers

Another Look!

Find 78 × 4.

Estimate by rounding to the nearest ten.

78 × 4 is about
80 × 4 = 320.

$$\begin{array}{r} \overset{3}{7}8 \\ \times\ 4 \\ \hline 312 \end{array}$$

312 is close to 320.
The answer is reasonable.

Find 2,802 × 2.

Estimate by rounding to the nearest thousand.

2,802 × 2 is about
3,000 × 2 = 6,000.

$$\begin{array}{r} \overset{1}{2},802 \\ \times\ \ \ \ 2 \\ \hline 5,604 \end{array}$$

5,604 is close to 6,000.
The answer is reasonable.

For **1–15**, find each product.

1. $\begin{array}{r} 538 \\ \times\ 4 \\ \hline \end{array}$

2. $\begin{array}{r} 214 \\ \times\ 8 \\ \hline \end{array}$

3. $\begin{array}{r} 3,721 \\ \times\ \ \ 7 \\ \hline \end{array}$

4. $\begin{array}{r} 7,956 \\ \times\ \ \ 8 \\ \hline \end{array}$

5. $\begin{array}{r} 92 \\ \times\ 4 \\ \hline \end{array}$

6. $\begin{array}{r} 37 \\ \times\ 8 \\ \hline \end{array}$

7. 6 × 505

8. 3 × 589

9. 5 × 6,384

10. 2 × 9,497

11. 7 × 3,218

12. 9 × 1,938

13. 5,219 × 3

14. 6,205 × 3

15. 1,236 × 8

Remember to use estimation to check if your answers are reasonable.

16. A grocery store orders 47 bags of onions and 162 bags of potatoes. The onions cost \$2 per bag, and the potatoes cost \$3 per bag. How much is spent on onions and potatoes?

17. The animal shelter charges \$119 to adopt a pet. On Saturday, 2 dogs and 7 cats were adopted. How much money did the animal shelter receive from those adoptions?

18. Algebra The insect exhibit at the museum has 8 display cases with 417 insects in each case. Write and solve an equation to show how many insects are displayed at the museum.

19. Kamiko and her 4 sisters each have 18 grandchildren. Calculate the total number of grandchildren of Kamiko and her 4 sisters.

20. Over the weekend, 1,719 tickets were sold for a musical. How much money did the musical bring in?

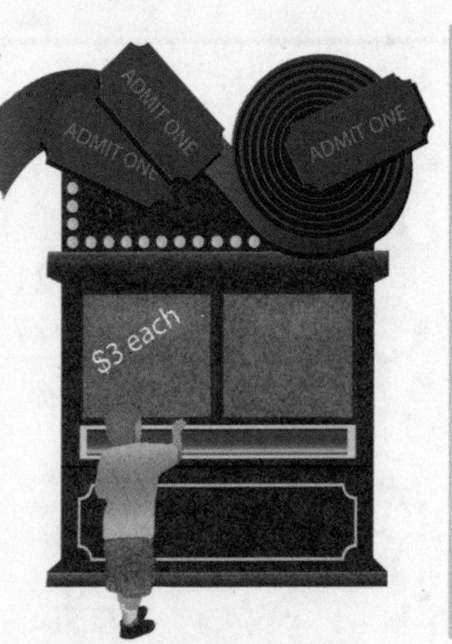

21. Higher Order Thinking Bo has 23 video games for sale. He plans to donate the money he makes from each sale to a local charity. What is the least amount of money in whole dollars Bo should charge for each game in order to raise \$100? Explain.

22. Zoe has 1,500 beads. She wants to make 6 friendship bracelets. She needs 215 beads for each bracelet. How many beads will Zoe have left after making all 6 of the bracelets? Explain.

In a multi-step problem, look back to be sure you answered the question asked.

Name ____________________

Problem Solving

Lesson 3-10
Model with Math

I can ...
apply the math I know to solve problems.

Process Standards PS.4 Also PS.1, PS.2, PS.5, PS.6
Content Standards 4.C.2, 4.AT.2

Solve & Share

Kevin took 120 color photos and 128 black and white photos on a field trip. Marco took 2 times as many photos as Kevin. How many photos did Marco take? ***Solve this problem using any strategy you choose. Use the bar diagrams to help.***

Kevin

Marco

Thinking Habits

Be a good thinker! These questions can help you.

- How can I use math I know to solve this problem?
- How can I use pictures, objects, or an equation to represent the problem?
- How can I use numbers, words, and symbols to solve the problem?

Look Back! Model with Math What representation did you use to solve the problem and show relationships?

How Can You Represent a Situation with a Math Model?

A

An art show uses 9 teams of art judges. If each team judges the work of 13 painters and 14 sculptors, how many artists attend the show?

What do you need to find?

I need to find how many artists each team judges.

I need to find the total number of artists.

t	
13	14

Each team judges 27 artists.

B **How can I model with math?**

I can

- use bar diagrams and equations to represent and solve this problem.
- decide if my results make sense.

C Find 9×27.

Here's my thinking.

Use a bar diagram. Write and solve an equation.

***a* artists**

27	27	27	27	27	27	27	27	27

number of artists for each team of judges

$a = 9 \times 27$

$a = 243$

There are 243 artists at the show.

Convince Me! **Model with Math** How could you decide if your answer makes sense?

Name ______________________

Guided Practice*

Model with Math

Sharon's Stationery Store contains 1,219 boxes of cards. May's Market contains 3 times as many boxes of cards. How many boxes, *b*, does May's Market contain?

When you model with math, you can write an equation to represent the relationships in the problem.

1. Explain how to use a picture to represent the problem and show relationships.

2. What equation can you write to represent the problem?

3. What is the solution to the problem?

Independent Practice

Model with Math

Annie has 6 albums of stamps in her stamp collection. Each album contains 440 stamps. How many stamps does Annie have in her collection? Use Exercises 4–6 to answer the question.

4. Draw a picture and write an equation to represent the problem.

5. What previously learned math can you use to solve the problem?

6. What is the solution to the problem? Explain why your solution makes sense.

*For another example, see Set H on page 160.

Problem Solving

Performance Assessment

ISTEP+ Ready

Hauling Fuel

A truck like the one shown delivers a load of gasoline to a gas station 3 times a week. The storage tank at the gas station holds 9 loads of fuel. How much more gas does the storage tank hold than the truck?

Hauls 2,700 gallons

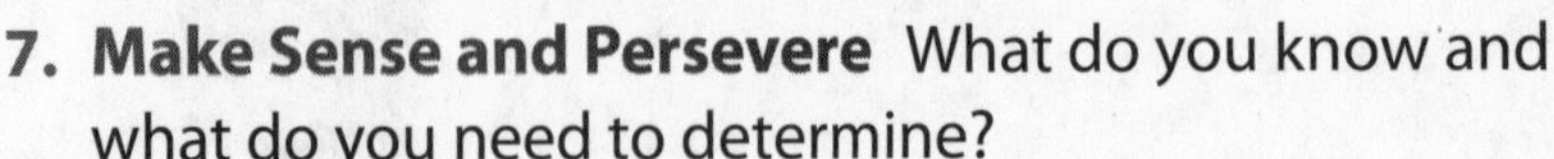

7. **Make Sense and Persevere** What do you know and what do you need to determine?

When you model with math, you use math to represent real-world situations.

8. **Reasoning** What do you need to know to determine how much more the tank holds than the truck?

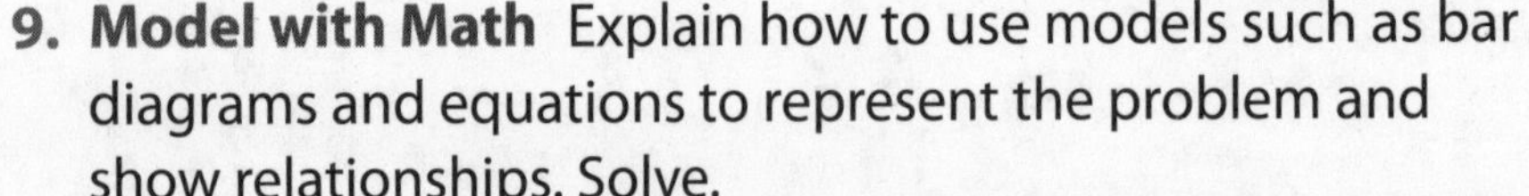

9. **Model with Math** Explain how to use models such as bar diagrams and equations to represent the problem and show relationships. Solve.

Name ____________________

Homework & Practice 3-10
Model with Math

Another Look!

A hardware store ordered 4 packs of large screws and 5 packs of smaller screws from a supplier. Each pack contains 150 screws. How many screws did the store order?

Tell how you can model with math.

- I can use bar diagrams and equations to represent and solve this problem.
- I can use previously learned concepts and skills.

When you model with math, you use pictures and objects to show how the quantities in the problem are related.

Draw a bar diagram and write an equation to solve.

$4 + 5 = 9$ packs

$9 \times 150 = s$

$s = 1{,}350$

The store ordered 1,350 screws.

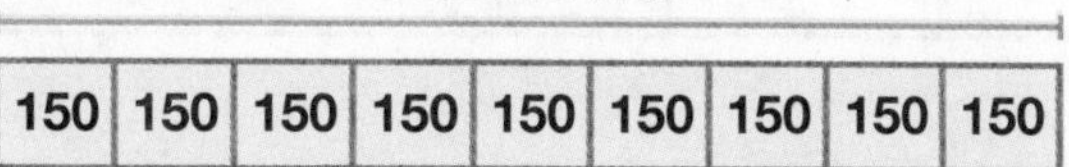

Model with Math

When Mary was born, she weighed 8 pounds. When she was 10 years old, she weighed 10 times as much. How much more did Mary weigh when she was 10 years old than when she was born? Use Exercises 1–2 to answer the question.

1. Draw a picture, write and solve an equation to find Mary's weight, *w*, when she was 10 years old.

2. Draw a picture, and write and solve an equation to find the difference, *d*, between Mary's weight when she was 10 years old and when she was born.

Performance Assessment — ISTEP+ Ready

School Supplies

A bookstore ordered 1,528 packs of pens and 1,823 packs of pencils at the prices shown. How much did the bookstore spend on pens?

$3 per pack

$4 per pack

3. **Make Sense and Persevere** Have you seen a problem like this before? Explain.

4. **Reasoning** What do the numbers that you need to use in the problem mean?

5. **Model with Math** What operation can you use to solve the problem? Draw a bar diagram to show the operation.

When you model with math, you use math you already know to solve a problem.

6. **Use Appropriate Tools** Would place-value blocks be a good tool to use to solve the problem? Explain.

7. **Be Precise** What was the total cost of the pens? Show that you computed accurately.

8. **Reasoning** Explain why your answer makes sense.

Name ____________________

Fluency Practice Activity

Shade a path from **START** to **FINISH**. Follow the differences that are correct. You can only move up, down, right, or left.

I can ...
subtract multi-digit whole numbers.

Start

812 − 44 = 768	929 − 879 = 150	511 − 423 = 112	767 − 31 = 636	698 − 12 = 586
621 − 85 = 536	341 − 299 = 142	486 − 230 = 256	825 − 789 = 36	333 − 111 = 222
543 − 97 = 446	836 − 788 = 48	178 − 98 = 80	123 − 53 = 30	342 − 88 = 254
111 − 87 = 76	876 − 55 = 72	912 − 842 = 170	282 − 32 = 150	293 − 95 = 198
684 − 485 = 299	922 − 87 = 865	312 − 219 = 193	986 − 887 = 199	876 − 543 = 333

Finish

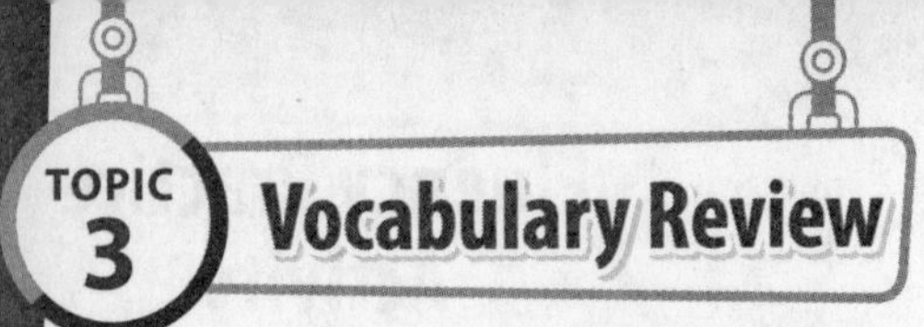

Word List

- array
- Associative Property of Multiplication
- Commutative Property of Multiplication
- compensation
- Distributive Property
- estimate
- numerical expression
- partial product

Understand Vocabulary

1. Circle the property shown by $4 \times (6 + 2) = (4 \times 6) + (4 \times 2)$.

Associative Commutative Distributive

2. Circle the property shown by $21 \times 34 = 34 \times 21$.

Associative Commutative Distributive

3. Circle the property shown by $(1 \times 3) \times 7 = 1 \times (3 \times 7)$.

Associative Commutative Distributive

4. Draw a line from each vocabulary word to its example.

array	7×19 is about 140.
compensation	7×9
estimate	$2 \times 19 = 2 \times 20 = 40$ $40 - 2 = 38$
numerical expression	$15 \times 2 = 10 + 20 = 30$
partial products	■■■■

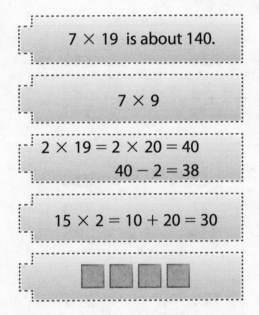

Use Vocabulary in Writing

5. Find 4×114. Use at least 3 terms from the Word List to describe how to find the product.

Name ________________________________

TOPIC 3

Reteaching

Set A pages 95–100

Use basic facts and multiplication properties to multiply by multiples of 10 and 100.

Find 4 × 60.

4 × 60 = 4 × (6 × 10)
4 × 60 = (4 × 6) × 10
4 × 60 = 24 × 10
4 × 60 = 240

Shortcut: Multiply 4 × 6 and write 1 zero.

Find 4 × 600.

4 × 600 = 4 × (6 × 100)
4 × 600 = (4 × 6) × 100
4 × 600 = 24 × 100
4 × 600 = 2,400

Shortcut: Multiply 4 × 6 and write 2 zeros.

Find 4 × 6,000.

4 × 6,000 = 4 × (6 × 1,000)
4 × 6,000 = (4 × 6) × 1,000
4 × 6,000 = 24 × 1,000
4 × 6,000 = 24,000

Shortcut: Multiply 4 × 6 and write 3 zeros.

Remember when the product of a basic fact ends in zero, the answer will have an extra zero.

1. 8 × 60 **2.** 3 × 10

3. 6 × 50 **4.** 5 × 300

5. 7,000 × 4 **6.** 2 × 900

7. 80 × 8 **8.** 400 × 5

9. 30 × 9 **10.** 5 × 8,000

11. 700 × 8 **12.** 9,000 × 6

13. 7 × 9,000 **14.** 5 × 100

15. 20 × 5 **16.** 5 × 4,000

17. 5 × 500 **18.** 3 × 2,000

Set B pages 101–106

Use rounding to estimate 9 × 1,993.

Round 1,993 to 2,000.

9 × 1,993
↓
9 × 2,000 = 18,000

So, 9 × 1,993 is about 18,000.

Remember to round a three-digit number to the nearest hundred and a four-digit number to the nearest thousand.

Estimate each product.

1. 8 × 7,632 **2.** 493 × 3

3. 9,379 × 5 **4.** 678 × 6

5. 707 × 4 **6.** 5,703 × 3

7. 483 × 6 **8.** 6 × 8,166

Set C pages 107–112

Use the Distributive Property to find $5 \times 2{,}345$.

Think of 2,345 as 2,000 + 300 + 40 + 5.

$$\begin{aligned} 5 \times 2{,}345 &= 5 \times (2{,}000 + 300 + 40 + 5) \\ &= (5 \times 2{,}000) + (5 \times 300) + (5 \times 40) + (5 \times 5) \\ &= 10{,}000 + 1{,}500 + 200 + 25 \\ &= 11{,}725 \end{aligned}$$

So, $5 \times 2{,}345 = 11{,}725$.

Remember that you can use the Distributive Property to help multiply larger numbers.

1. 7×45
2. $4{,}326 \times 9$
3. 720×6
4. 3×46
5. 371×8
6. 5×95
7. 88×3
8. $4 \times 1{,}865$
9. 57×3
10. 209×7

Set D pages 113–118

Use the Distributive Property to find $3 \times 1{,}275$.

$$\begin{aligned} 3 \times 1{,}275 &= 3 \times (1{,}000 + 200 + 70 + 5) \\ &= (3 \times 1{,}000) + (3 \times 200) + (3 \times 70) + (3 \times 5) \\ &= 3{,}000 + 600 + 210 + 15 \\ &= 3{,}825 \end{aligned}$$

Use the Commutative and Associative Properties to find 8×50.

$$\begin{aligned} 8 \times 50 &= (2 \times 4) \times 50 \\ &= (4 \times 2) \times 50 \\ &= 4 \times (2 \times 50) \\ &= 4 \times 100 \\ &= 400 \end{aligned}$$

Use compensation to find 3×175.

175 is close to 200.
$3 \times 200 = 600$
$200 - 25 = 175$ $3 \times 25 = 75$
$600 - 75 = 525$

Remember that you can use compensation or properties of operations to help multiply mentally.

1. $1{,}468 \times 4$
2. 361×3
3. 25×7
4. $2{,}189 \times 7$
5. 6×987
6. 8×22
7. 763×5
8. 14×9
9. 171×8
10. 22×9
11. $1{,}409 \times 5$
12. 17×6
13. 211×4
14. $7{,}800 \times 5$
15. $8{,}756 \times 2$
16. $2{,}105 \times 3$

You can break larger numbers apart to help multiply.

Name ____________________

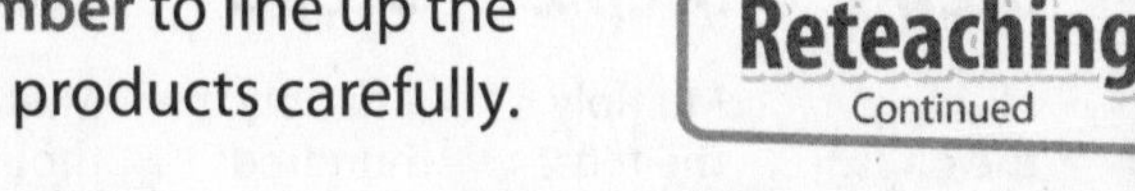

Set E pages 119–130

Use an array and partial products to find 3 × 121.

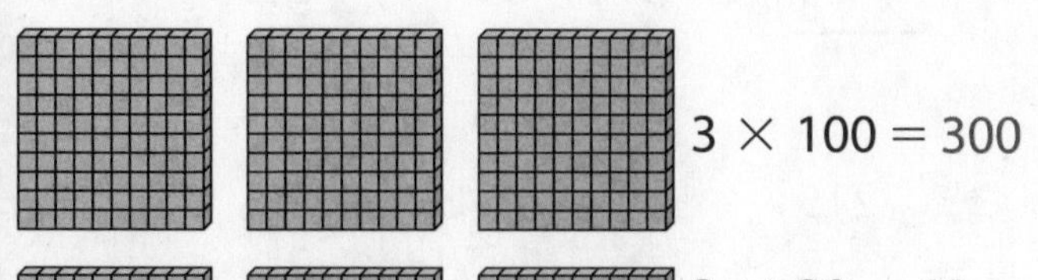

$3 \times 100 = 300$

$3 \times 20 = 60$

$3 \times 1 = 3$

$300 + 60 + 3 = 363$

Step 1

Multiply the ones.

```
  121
×   3
    3
```

Step 2

Multiply the tens.

```
  121
×   3
    3
   60
```

Step 3

Multiply the hundreds.

```
  121
×   3
    3
   60
+ 300
  363
```

Remember to line up the partial products carefully.

1. 75 × 5

2. 253 × 4

3. 214 × 7

4. 1,341 × 7

Set F pages 131–136

Find 8 × 24.

Step 1

Multiply the ones. Regroup if necessary.

```
  3
  24
×  8
   2
```

Step 2

Multiply the tens. Add any extra tens.

```
  3
  24
×  8
 192
```

Find 6 × 768.

Step 1

Multiply the ones. Regroup if necessary.

```
   4
  768
×   6
    8
```

Step 2

Multiply the tens. Add any extra tens. Regroup if necessary.

```
  44
  768
×   6
   08
```

Step 3

Multiply the hundreds. Add any extra hundreds.

```
  44
  768
×   6
4,608
```

Remember to estimate first to check that your answer is reasonable.

1. 18 × 2

2. 48 × 5

3. 52 × 7

4. 33 × 6

5. 97 × 7

6. 88 × 4

7. 239 × 4

8. 148 × 5

9. 233 × 6

10. 937 × 7

Set G pages 137–148

Find 8 × 1,649.

Step 1	Step 2	Step 3	Step 4
Multiply the ones. Regroup if necessary.	Multiply the tens. Add any extra tens. Regroup if necessary.	Multiply the hundreds. Add any extra hundreds. Regroup if necessary.	Multiply the thousands. Add any extra thousands.
regrouped: 7 1,649 × 8 2	regrouped: 3 7 1,649 × 8 92	regrouped: 5 3 7 1,649 × 8 192	regrouped: 5 3 7 1,649 × 8 13,192

Remember to use an estimate to check if your answer is reasonable.

1. $\begin{array}{r} 43 \\ \times\ 8 \\ \hline \end{array}$
2. $\begin{array}{r} 57 \\ \times\ 9 \\ \hline \end{array}$
3. $\begin{array}{r} 215 \\ \times\ 7 \\ \hline \end{array}$
4. $\begin{array}{r} 869 \\ \times\ 2 \\ \hline \end{array}$
5. $\begin{array}{r} 4,233 \\ \times\ 7 \\ \hline \end{array}$
6. $\begin{array}{r} 3,261 \\ \times\ 4 \\ \hline \end{array}$
7. $\begin{array}{r} 1,250 \\ \times\ 8 \\ \hline \end{array}$
8. $\begin{array}{r} 2,239 \\ \times\ 5 \\ \hline \end{array}$

Set H pages 149–154

Think about these questions to help you **model with math.**

Thinking Habits

- How can I use math I know to help solve this problem?
- How can I use pictures, objects, or an equation to represent the problem?
- How can I use numbers, words, and symbols to solve the problem?

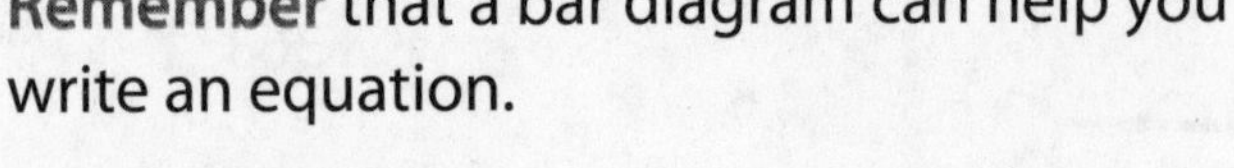

Remember that a bar diagram can help you write an equation.

Mia has a collection of 34 dolls. A toy store's warehouse has 5 times as many dolls.

1. Use pictures, a bar diagram, or an equation to find the number of dolls in the warehouse.

2. How can you decide if your answer makes sense?

Name ______________________

1. Rachel set up a display placing 126 painted rocks in each of 3 rows. How many rocks are in Rachel's display? Choose numbers from the box to complete and solve the equation.

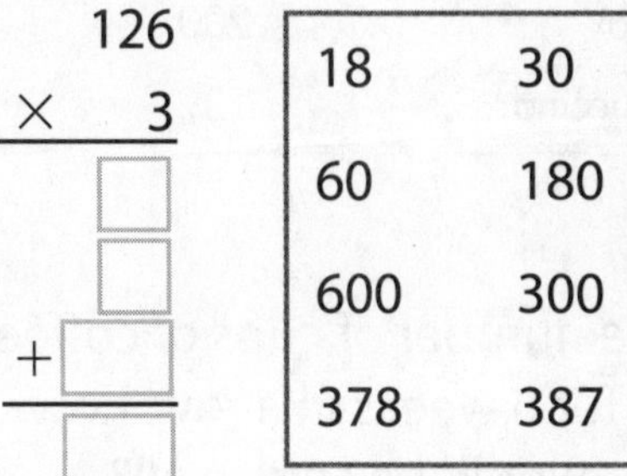

18	30
60	180
600	300
378	387

2. Alberto rode the train 198 miles round trip 4 times last month. Use compensation to find the total distance Alberto traveled. Explain.

3. Mr. Ortiz sells tortillas in bags of 25 and in bags of 50. If he sells 4 bags of 50, how many tortillas did Mr. Ortiz sell?

Ⓐ 8 tortillas

Ⓑ 20 tortillas

Ⓒ 200 tortillas

Ⓓ 2,000 tortillas

4. The Amnel family spends $1,874 for rent each month. How much does the family spend in 3 months?

5. A science class is growing some fruit and vegetable plants on a plot of land behind their school. Each section is laid out in rows.

DATA

Produce	Number of Rows
Strawberries	65
Peppers	18
Squash	11
Tomatoes	22

Part A

There are 9 strawberry plants planted in each row. Write and solve an equation to find how many strawberry plants were planted.

Part B

There are 9 pepper plants planted in each row. Draw an area model and show the partial products to find how many pepper plants are planted behind the school.

6. Select all the expressions that could be used to find the area of a field that is 1,235 yards long and 9 yards wide.

- ☐ $9 \times (1,000 + 200 + 20 + 5)$
- ☐ $9 \times (1,000 + 200 + 30 + 5)$
- ☐ $(9 \times 1,000) + (9 \times 200) + (9 \times 30) + (9 \times 5)$
- ☐ $9 \times 1,235$
- ☐ $1,235 + 9$

7. Draw an array to show and find the number of days in 3 years. Remember, there are 365 days in one year.

8. Tickets cost $1,182 each. Find the cost for 3 tickets. Explain how you know your answer is reasonable.

9. The table shows the number of hot drinks sold in a busy coffee shop in 1 week.

DATA

Type	Number
Coffee	835
Latte	567
Mocha	200
Cappuccino	139

Part A

If the same number of cups of coffee were sold for 6 weeks in a row, how many cups would be sold in all?

Part B

If the same number were sold each week, how many lattes and cappuccinos would be sold in 4 weeks? Explain.

Part C

The special drink of the month was an iced mocha. The shop sold 5 times as many iced mochas in one week as hot mochas. How many more iced mochas were sold than hot mochas in 4 weeks? Explain.

Name ______________________________

TOPIC 3

Assessment Continued

ISTEP+ Ready

10. Estimate to check if each product is reasonable. Choose numbers from the box to complete the equations. Then choose whether the product is reasonable.

200	300	800
900	2,400	2,700

$8 \times 296 = 2{,}368$

$8 \times$ ______ $=$ ______

Reasonable Not Reasonable

$3 \times 932 = 2{,}796$

$3 \times$ ______ $=$ ______

Reasonable Not Reasonable

11. Which expression shows how to use breaking apart to find 5×617?

Ⓐ $(5 \times 6) + (5 \times 1) + (5 \times 7)$

Ⓑ $(5 \times 60) + (5 \times 10) + (5 \times 70)$

Ⓒ $(5 \times 600) + (5 \times 1) + (5 \times 7)$

Ⓓ $(5 \times 600) + (5 \times 10) + (5 \times 7)$

12. Ivan earned $115 a month for working at the grocery store. Which are reasonable estimates for the amount of money Ivan would have if he saves all of the money he earns for 6 months?

☐ $200

☐ $600

☐ $700

☐ $1,200

☐ $1,500

13. A store clerk set 3 boxes filled with 312 pencils each on a shelf. How many pencils were placed on the shelf? Draw a bar diagram to solve the problem.

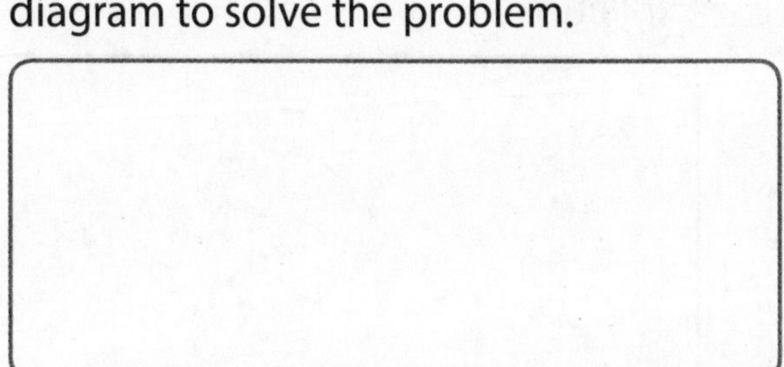

14. Bea's Bakery bakes 215 cookies and 45 muffins every hour. How many baked goods are baked in 4 hours?

15. Four buses are available for a field trip. Each bus can hold 48 people. Write and solve an equation that can be used to find the number of people the buses can hold.

b			
48	48	48	48

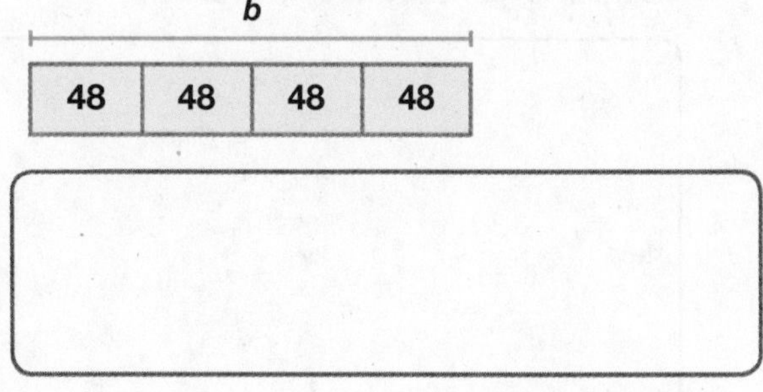

16. Mrs. Henderson bought 4 boxes of facial tissues. Each box has 174 tissues. Which is the best estimate for the total number of tissues Mrs. Henderson bought?

Ⓐ 200

Ⓑ 800

Ⓒ 1,200

Ⓓ 1,740

17. Mr. Luca would like to purchase a digital keyboard for each of his 3 nieces and 1 nephew. The keyboard costs $415.

Part A

Mr. Luca thinks the total cost should be about $1,200. Is this amount reasonable? Explain.

Part B

Write and solve an equation to find the total cost of the keyboards. Explain why your answer is reasonable.

18. Draw lines to match the number of boxes with the total number of that item.

DATA

Supply	Number per Box
Paper Clips	100
Small Erasers	300
Push Pins	500
Staples	3,000

5 boxes of ________	21,000
9 boxes of ________	2,500
4 boxes of ________	900
7 boxes of ________	1,200

19. Keira is on a rowing team. She practices by rowing 295 miles every month. Use mental math to find how many miles Keira rows in 6 months. Explain.

20. Select all the partial products for 8×321.

- ☐ 8
- ☐ 80
- ☐ 160
- ☐ 1,600
- ☐ 2,400

Name ______________________________

TOPIC 3

Performance Assessment

ISTEP+ Ready

Buying Classroom Computers

Jorge's school can purchase computers and printers for the prices shown. Information about the fourth-grade classes are given in the table.

Fourth Grade Classes

Teacher	Money Raised	Number of Students
Mr. Jones	$6,000	25
Ms. Sanchez	$9,000	24
Ms. Katz	$7,500	26

Desktop computer: $1,050

Laptop computer: $798

Printer: $128

1. Jorge's teacher is Ms. Sanchez. His class wants to buy 8 desktop computers and 3 printers.

Part A

What is the total cost of 8 desktop computers? Use place-value strategies and properties of operations.

Part B

What is the total cost of 3 printers? Draw an array and show the partial products to find the cost.

Part C

Did Jorge's class raise enough money to buy 8 computers and 3 printers? Explain.

2. Rachel's teacher is Mr. Jones. Her class wants to buy 7 computers and 2 printers.

Part A

How much more do 7 desktop computers cost than 7 laptop computers? Use bar diagrams and equations to represent and solve the problem.

Part B

What is another way to find the difference in the cost of 7 desktop computers and 7 laptop computers? Explain.

3. Miranda's teacher is Ms. Katz. Her class wants to buy 9 laptop computers and 4 printers. Miranda said the total cost should be $7,494. Is this amount reasonable? Explain. Does the class have enough money?

Use Strategies and Properties to Multiply by 2-Digit Numbers

Essential Questions: How can you use a model to multiply?
How can you use the Distributive Property to multiply?
How can you use multiplication to solve problems?

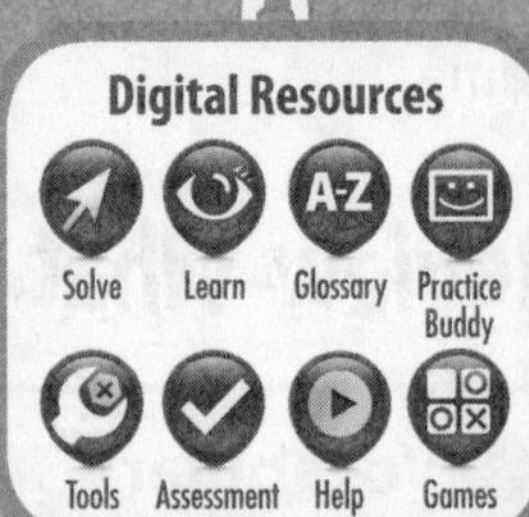

Renewable energy comes from natural resources that never run out.

These huge turbines harness wind energy to produce electric power and reduce pollution caused by fossil fuels.

Let me get my kite! Here is a project on energy and multiplication.

Math and Science Project: Renewable Energy and Multiplication

Do Research Use the Internet or other sources to find information about different sources of renewable energy.

Journal: Write a Report Include what you found. Also in your report:

- A wind farm is an area of land with a large number of turbines. Draw an array with 15 rows to show the turbines in a wind farm. How many turbines are in your wind farm?
- Some turbines produce 63 megawatt-hours of energy every week. Find how much energy one of these turbines would produce in one year. Remember, one year is 52 weeks.

Name ___

Review What You Know

Vocabulary

Choose the best term from the box. Write it on the blank.

- algorithm
- product
- array
- variable

1. You multiply numbers to find a(n) ___.
2. A(n) ___ shows the number of objects in rows and columns.
3. A symbol or letter that stands for a number is called a(n) ___.

Multiplication

Find each product.

4. 4 × 8 **5.** 2 × 9 **6.** 9 × 5

7. 6 × 8 **8.** 16 × 4 **9.** 6 × 68

10. 87 × 5 **11.** 19 × 9 **12.** 128 × 6

Rounding

Round each number to the nearest hundred.

13. 164 **14.** 8,263

15. 527 **16.** 2,498

17. 7,892 **18.** 472

You will use rounding to estimate products in this topic.

Round each number to the nearest thousand.

19. 8,685 **20.** 4,991 **21.** 62,549

22. 167,241 **23.** 77,268 **24.** 34,162

25. 1,372 **26.** 9,009 **27.** 121,619

28. Construct Arguments Explain how to round 608,149 to the nearest thousands place.

My Word Cards

Use the examples for each word on the front of the card to help complete the definitions on the back.

24 is close to 25.

38 is close to 40.

24×38

25×40

My Word Cards

Complete each definition. Extend learning by writing your own definitions.

Numbers that are easy to compute mentally are called ________________

______________________________.

Name ______________________________

Lesson 4-1

Mental Math: Multiply Multiples of 10

I can ...

use place-value strategies or patterns to multiply by multiples of 10.

Content Standard 4.C.2
Process Standards PS.2, PS.7

Solve & Share The principal of a school needs to order supplies for 20 new classrooms. Each classroom needs the following items: 20 desks, 30 chairs, and 40 pencils. How many of each item does the principal need to order? ***Solve these problems using any strategy you choose.***

You can use structure. What basic facts can you use to help solve these problems? How are they related? *Show your work in the space below!*

Look Back! Look for Relationships Look at the factors and products. What patterns do you notice?

Learn Glossary

How Can You Multiply by Multiples of 10?

A

The number of visitors of each age group for the Sunny Day Amusement Park are shown below. How many adults under 65 visit the park in 20 days? How many children visit the park in 30 days? How many adults 65 and over visit the park in 50 days?

You can use a pattern to multiply by a multiple of 10.

Number of visitors each day

B

Adults under 65 in 20 days

Find $20 \times 60 = a$.

To multiply 20×60, use a pattern.

$$2 \times 6 = 12$$
$$20 \times 6 = 120$$
$$20 \times 60 = 1{,}200$$

$a = 1{,}200$

1,200 adults under 65 visit the park in 20 days.

C

Children in 30 days

Find $30 \times 80 = c$.

The number of zeros in the product is the total number of zeros in both factors.

$$30 \times 80 = 2{,}400$$

1 zero 1 zero 2 zeros

$c = 2{,}400$

2,400 children visit the park in 30 days.

D

Adults 65 and over in 50 days

Find $50 \times 40 = a$.

If the product of a basic fact ends in zero, include that zero in the count.

$$5 \times 4 = 20$$
$$50 \times 40 = 2{,}000$$

$a = 2{,}000$

2,000 adults 65 and over visit the park in 50 days.

Convince Me! **Look for Relationships** Write the missing numbers for each of the following. Explain.

_______ $\times 7 = 280$ _______ $\times 40 = 1{,}600$ _______ $\times 50 = 3{,}000$

Name ______________________________

Practice Buddy Tools Assessment

Another Example!

Find 30 × 80. The product has the same number of zeros as in both factors.

$$30 \times 80 = 3 \times 10 \times 8 \times 10$$
$$= (3 \times 8) \times (10 \times 10)$$
$$= 24 \times 100$$
$$= 2{,}400$$

You can use the Commutative and Associative Properties of Multiplication to see why the patterns with zeros work!

Guided Practice*

Do You Understand?

1. **Reasoning** Find 50 × 20. How many zeros are in the product?

2. Fewer people go to the park in November than in May. There are 30 days in November. If 30 people visit the park each day in November, how many people visit for the whole month?

Do You Know How?

For **3–8**, use basic facts and place-value strategies to find each product.

3. 30 × 10 **4.** 50 × 10

5. 20 × 10 **6.** 60 × 20

7. 90 × 40 **8.** 80 × 50

Independent Practice

For **9–16**, use basic facts and place-value strategies to find each product.

9. 20 × 70 **10.** 70 × 90 **11.** 40 × 20 **12.** 40 × 30

13. 70 × 40 **14.** 20 × 30 **15.** 60 × 40 **16.** 60 × 90

For **17–22**, find the missing factor.

17. 10 × ________ = 100 **18.** ________ × 20 = 1,600 **19.** ________ × 30 = 1,500

20. 20 × ________ = 1,000 **21.** ________ × 90 = 8,100 **22.** 60 × ________ = 4,200

For another example, see Set A on page 239.

Problem Solving

23. **Reasoning** The product of two factors is 4,200. If one of the factors is 60, what is the other factor? Explain.

24. **Algebra** There are 30 players on each high school football team. Explain how you can find the total number of players if there are 40 teams. Write and solve an equation.

25. Bob uses 2 gallons of water while brushing his teeth. He uses 10 gallons of water to wash clothes. How many more cups of water did Bob use while washing his clothes than brushing his teeth?

There are 16 cups in 1 gallon.

26. **Look for Relationships** James walked 30 minutes each day for 90 days. Show how you can use basic facts to find how many minutes James walked.

27. **Higher Order Thinking** Explain why the product of 50 and 80 has three zeros when 50 and 80 each have one zero.

Assessment ISTEP+ Ready

28. Ms. Kim travels 10 weeks a year for work. She is home the other 42 weeks. There are 7 days in 1 week. Which of the following expressions can Ms. Kim use to mentally find the number of days she is home?

Ⓐ $(7 \times 2) + (4 \times 10)$

Ⓑ 7×100

Ⓒ $(7 \times 40) + (7 \times 10)$

Ⓓ $(7 \times 40) + (7 \times 2)$

29. Mr. Kim travels 32 weeks a year for work. He is home the other 20 weeks. There are 7 days in a week. Which of the following basic facts can Mr. Kim use to help find the number of days he is home?

Ⓐ 2×7

Ⓑ 3×7

Ⓒ $32 + 7$

Ⓓ $20 + 7$

Name ______________________

Homework & Practice 4-1

Mental Math: Multiply Multiples of 10

Another Look!

A kindergarten teacher wants to buy individual boxes of crayons for her students. Each box contains 50 crayons. How many crayons will she have if she buys 30 boxes of crayons?

Use a pattern to find 50×30.

$5 \times 3 = 15$
$50 \times 3 = 150$
$50 \times 30 = 1{,}500$

So, $50 \times 30 = 1{,}500$.

The kindergarten teacher will have 1,500 crayons.

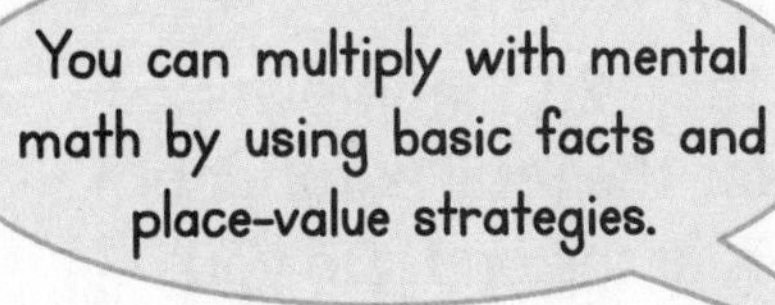

You can multiply with mental math by using basic facts and place-value strategies.

For **1–12**, use basic facts and place-value strategies to find each product.

1. $2 \times 2 =$ ______
$20 \times 2 =$ ______
$20 \times 20 =$ ______

2. $6 \times 3 =$ ______
$60 \times 3 =$ ______
$60 \times 30 =$ ______

3. $5 \times 6 =$ ______
$50 \times 6 =$ ______
$50 \times 60 =$ ______

4. 30×80

5. 60×60

6. 50×90

7. 30×70

8. 70×60

9. 40×50

10. 10×90

11. 40×10

12. 10×50

For **13–21**, find the missing factor.

13. $10 \times$ ______ $= 200$

14. $40 \times$ ______ $= 3{,}600$

15. $50 \times$ ______ $= 4{,}000$

16. $70 \times$ ______ $= 700$

17. $30 \times$ ______ $= 2{,}700$

18. ______ $\times 70 = 3{,}500$

19. ______ $\times 90 = 7{,}200$

20. $20 \times$ ______ $= 1{,}800$

21. $40 \times$ ______ $= 3{,}200$

22. Algebra Ms. Marks records the number of words each typist can type in 1 minute. How many more words could the fastest typist type in 30 minutes than the slowest typist? Use place-value strategies. Write and solve equations.

DATA

Typing Rates in 1 min	
Typist	**Words**
Lavon	50
Jerome	40
Charlie	60

23. Amy says, "To find 50×20, I multiply 5×2 and then place the total number of zeros in both factors at the end." Do you agree? Explain.

24. Algebra If in one year a city recorded a total of 97 rainy days, how many of the days did it **NOT** rain? Write and solve an equation.

365 days	
97	*d*

25. Name two 2-digit factors whose product is greater than 200 but less than 600.

26. Higher Order Thinking For every 30 minutes of television airtime, there are 8 minutes of commercials. If 90 minutes of television are aired, how many minutes of commercials will there be?

27. The product of two factors is 7,200. If one of the factors is 90, what is the other factor?

Ⓐ 8,000 Ⓒ 80
Ⓑ 800 Ⓓ 8

28. Derek solved 1,400 math problems in 70 days. If Derek solved the same number of math problems each day, how many math problems did Derek solve each day?

Ⓐ 2 Ⓒ 200
Ⓑ 20 Ⓓ 2,000

Use basic facts to help find the missing factors.

Name ______________________________

Lesson 4-2
Use Models to Multiply 2-Digit Numbers by Multiples of 10

There are 10 teams in a baseball league. Each team has 25 players. How many players are in the league? ***Solve this problem using any strategy you choose.***

I can ...
use models and properties of operations to help multiply.

Content Standard 4.C.2
Process Standards PS.1, PS.3, PS.4, PS.5

You can use appropriate tools. Place-value blocks or grid paper can help you visualize the problem. *Show your work in the space above!*

Look Back! Reasoning How do the digits in a number being multiplied by 10 compare to the digits in the product? Explain.

How Can You Use an Array or an Area Model to Multiply?

A

Max's Moving Company has boxes for packing books. If each box holds 24 books, how many books would fit into 20 boxes?

Making an array with place-value blocks or using an area model helps to visualize the partial products.

B Use place-value blocks to make an array.

Find $20 \times 24 = b$.

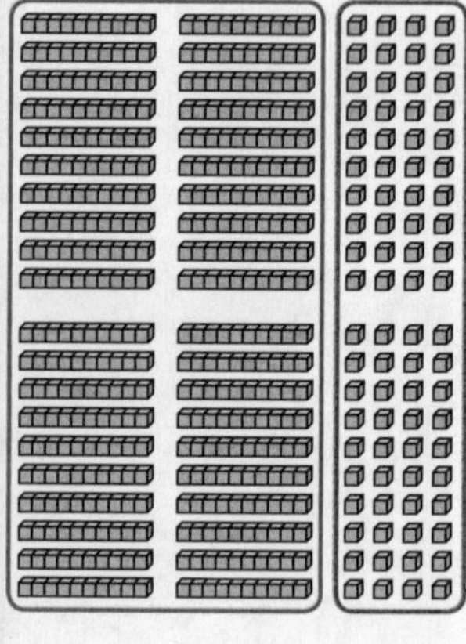

$$\begin{array}{r} 400 \\ +\ 80 \\ \hline 480 \end{array}$$ ← Partial Products

$20 \times 24 = 480$

$b = 480$

480 books will fit into 20 boxes.

C Draw an area model.

Find $20 \times 24 = b$.

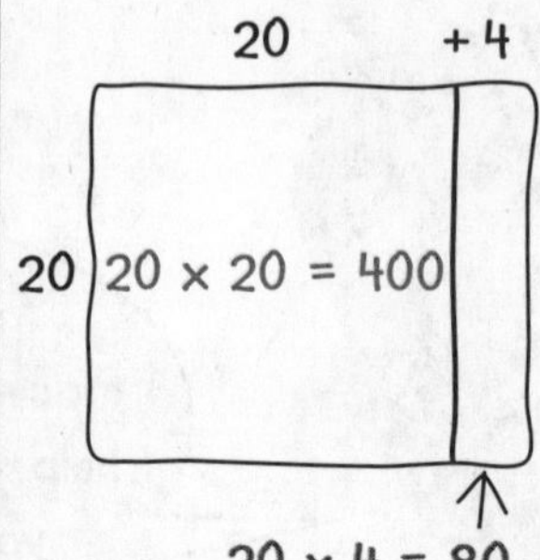

$$\begin{array}{r} 400 \\ +\ 80 \\ \hline 480 \end{array}$$ ← Partial Products

$20 \times 24 = 480$

$b = 480$

480 books will fit into 20 boxes.

Convince Me! **Model with Math** Use the grid to show an array for 20×27. What is the product? Explain.

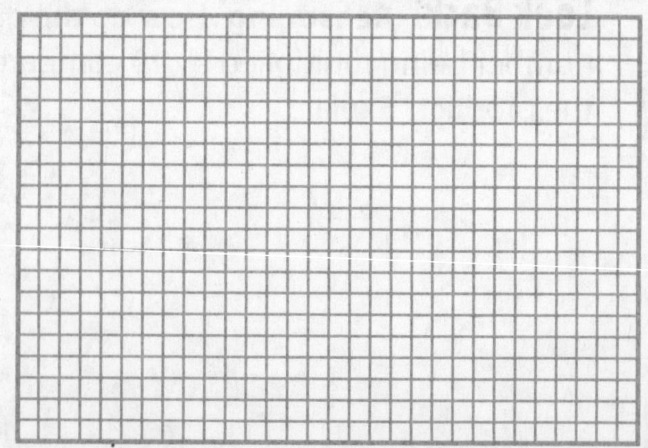

Name ______

Practice Buddy Tools Assessment

Guided Practice*

Do You Understand?

1. **Model with Math** Draw an area model to show 20 × 26. Then find the product.

Do You Know How?

2. The place-value block array shows 10 × 16. Find the product.

☐☐☐ ← 10 groups of 10
+ ☐☐ ← 10 groups of 6
☐☐☐ ← Add the partial products.

Independent Practice

For **3–12**, use place-value blocks, area models, or arrays to find each product.

3. 10 × 22

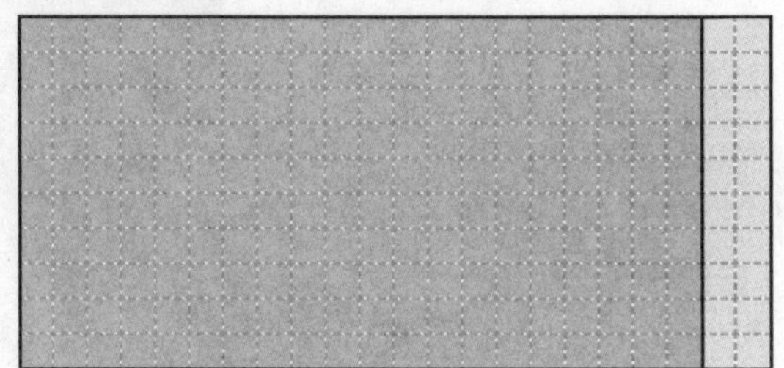

4. 10 × 13

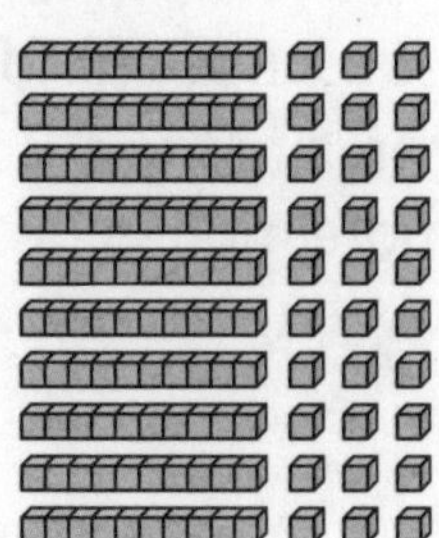

You can use a sheet of grid paper to draw arrays or area models.

5. 20 × 35 **6.** 20 × 41 **7.** 30 × 29 **8.** 40 × 37

9. 10 × 76 **10.** 50 × 12 **11.** 70 × 29 **12.** 80 × 43

For another example, see Set B on page 239.

Problem Solving

13. Algebra In the first 3 months of the year, an electronics store sold 1,446 cameras. How many cameras did the store sell in March? Write and solve an equation.

DATA

Camera Sales

Month	Number Sold
January	486
February	385

14. For every camera sold in February, the store donated \$2 to a charity. How much did the store donate?

15. Model with Math During a basketball game, 75 cups of fruit punch were sold. Each cup holds 20 fluid ounces. How many total fluid ounces of fruit punch were sold?

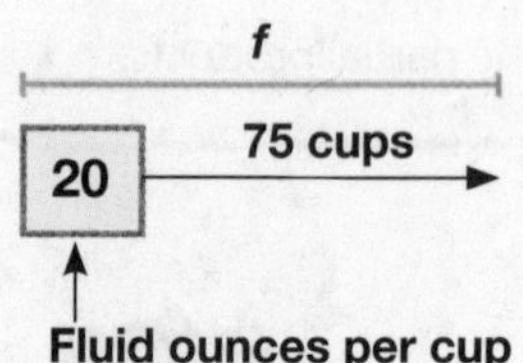

16. Higher Order Thinking There are 46 fourth graders at a school. Each fourth grader writes 3 book reports. Show how to use the Distributive Property to find the number of book reports written.

17. Angel sold 15 magazine subscriptions for \$30 each. Walt sold 22 subscriptions for \$20 each. Use arrays or area models to explain who raised more money.

Name ______________________________

Help Practice Buddy Tools Games

Homework & Practice 4-2

Use Models to Multiply 2-Digit Numbers by Multiples of 10

Another Look!

You can use arrays, area models, or place-value blocks to help find the product of 20 × 14.

20 × 14 means 20 groups of 14, or (20 groups of 10) + (20 groups of 4).

Add the partial products from the model.

20 groups of 10 = 200
20 groups of 4 = 80

200 + 80 = 280

So, 20 × 14 = 280.

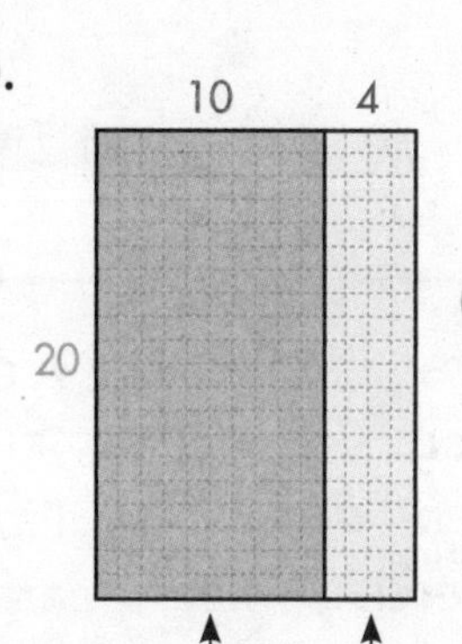

For **1–2**, use the array to find each product.

1. 10 × 12

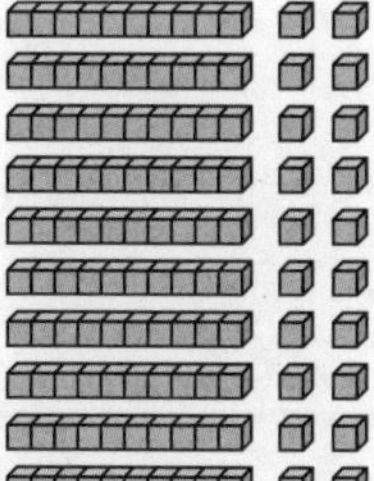

10 groups of 10 = ________
10 groups of 2 = ________
________ + ________ = ________
So, 10 × 12 = ________.

2. 20 × 18

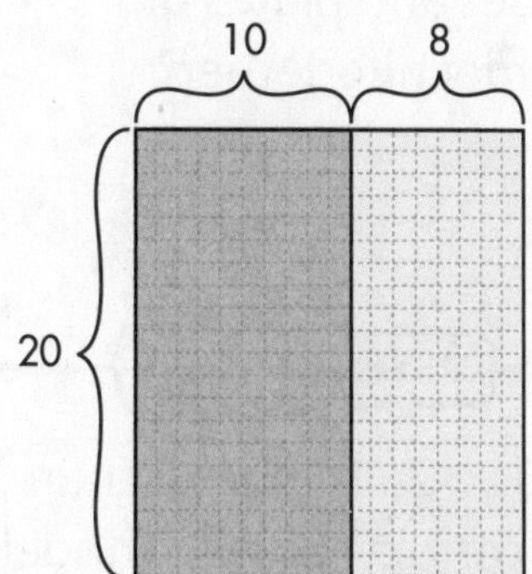

20 groups of 10 = ________
20 groups of 8 = ________
________ + ________ = ________
So, 20 × 18 = ________.

For **3–6**, find each product. Draw an array or an area model to help.

3. 50 × 15 **4.** 40 × 22 **5.** 30 × 39 **6.** 60 × 21

7. The height of each story of an apartment building is measured from the bottom of one floor to the bottom of the next floor. Each story has a height of 18 feet. How tall is the building?

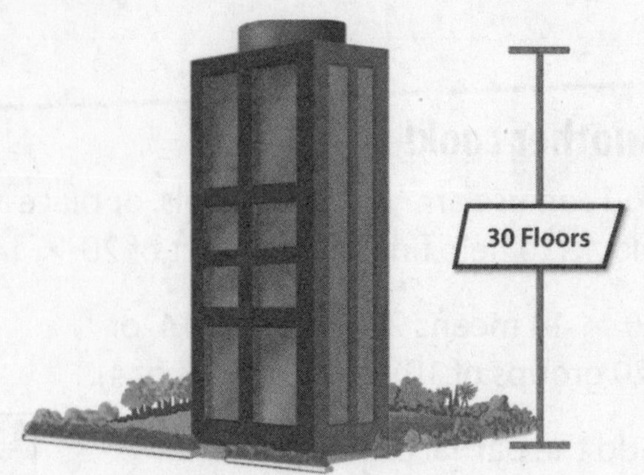

8. Make Sense and Persevere Marta exercises 30 minutes each day. Greg exercises 40 minutes each day. How many more minutes does Greg exercise than Marta in a month that has 31 days?

9. A dentist orders 15 boxes of floss and 20 boxes of toothbrushes each month. Floss is sold 70 to a box and toothbrushes are sold 50 to a box. How many items does the dentist order each month?

10. Mrs. Harrigan ordered 30 boxes of glasses for her restaurant. Each box holds 16 glasses. She also ordered 30 boxes of plates. There are 25 plates in each box. How many glasses and plates did Mrs. Harrigan order altogether?

11. Higher Order Thinking Without multiplying, is the product of 45×10 or 50×10 greater? Explain.

12. Miranda says 30×26 is greater than 20×36. Is she correct? Draw a model to explain if Miranda is correct.

You can draw an area model or an array to represent the problem.

Name ______________________________

Solve

Lesson 4-3
Estimate: Use Rounding

I can …
estimate products by rounding the factors.

Content Standard Prepares for 4.C.2
Process Standards PS.2, PS.3

Solve & Share

Find a product that is as close to 1,400 as possible. Choose two factors from the numbers 18, 42, 66, and 71. ***Solve this problem using any strategy you choose.***

Use reasoning. How can rounding help you choose two factors? *Show your work in the space below!*

1,400

Look Back! Reasoning What do the numbers you rounded have in common?

How Can You Use Rounding to Estimate?

A

The workers picked 50 dozen apples at Ms. Piper's apple grove and 37 dozen apples at Mr. Stuart's apple grove. There are 12 apples in one dozen. About how many apples did the workers pick?

1 dozen apples

You can use place value to help round numbers. Rounding is one way to estimate products.

B First, add to find how many dozens of apples were picked.

$$50 + 37 = 87 \text{ dozen apples}$$

Then, use rounding to estimate 87×12. To estimate the product, replace the factors with the closest multiple of ten.

Round 87 to the nearest ten.

87 is closer to 90 than 80, so 87 rounds to 90.

Round 12 to the nearest ten.

12 is closer to 10 than 20, so 12 rounds to 10.

C Estimate the product.

$$87 \times 12 = n$$
$$\downarrow \quad\quad \downarrow$$
$$90 \times 10 = 900$$

The workers picked about 900 apples.

Some problems do not need an exact answer.

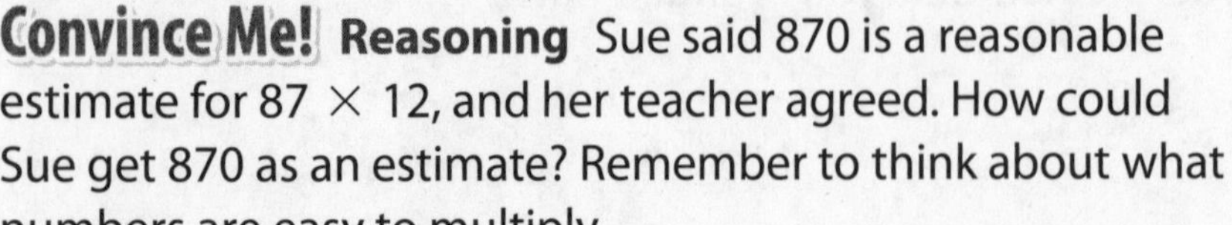

Convince Me! **Reasoning** Sue said 870 is a reasonable estimate for 87×12, and her teacher agreed. How could Sue get 870 as an estimate? Remember to think about what numbers are easy to multiply.

Name ___

Practice Buddy Tools Assessment

Guided Practice*

Do You Understand?

1. **Reasoning** In the example on the previous page, how do you know you only need an estimate and not an exact answer?

2. **Critique Reasoning** Howie used rounding to estimate the product of 35 × 42 and got 1,200. What did he do wrong?

Do You Know How?

For **3–6**, estimate each product.

3. 24 × 18 rounds to ___ × ___ = ___.

4. 33 × 31 rounds to ___ × ___ = ___.

5. 38 × 22

6. 45 × 48

Independent Practice

Leveled Practice For **7–12**, estimate each product.

7. 39 × 19 rounds to ___ × ___ = ___.

8. 28 × 27 rounds to ___ × ___ = ___.

9. 64 × 13

10. 42 × 17

11. 82 × 36

12. 54 × 18

For **13–14**, estimate to check if the given answer is reasonable.

13. 66 × 41 = 2,706
Rounds to ___ × ___ = ___
Reasonable Not Reasonable

14. 34 × 52 = 2,288
Rounds to ___ × ___ = ___
Reasonable Not Reasonable

Compare your estimate to the given answer to check if the answer is reasonable.

*For another example, see Set C on page 240.

Problem Solving

For **15–17**, use the table at the right.

15. Number Sense About how many more Valencia orange trees than Temple orange trees does Mr. Gonzalez have? Explain.

Your answer can be an estimate because an exact answer is not necessary.

16. Number Sense About how many orange trees does Mr. Gonzalez have? Explain.

17. Higher Order Thinking Mr. Gonzalez has the same number of which two types of trees? Use a property of multiplication to explain.

DATA

Mr. Gonzalez's Trees

Type of Orange Tree	Number of Rows	Number of Trees in Each Row
Hamlin	28	38
Temple	38	28
Valencia	31	46

ISTEP+ Ready

18. About how many books does Corner Books sell each year?

Ⓐ About 6,500 books

Ⓑ About 7,500 books

Ⓒ About 8,500 books

Ⓓ About 9,500 books

Remember, there are 52 weeks in 1 year.

19. About how many more nonfiction and children's books are sold than fiction books in 1 year?

Ⓐ About 2,000 books

Ⓑ About 1,500 books

Ⓒ About 1,000 books

Ⓓ About 500 books

DATA

Corner Books Weekly Sales

Type of Book	Number of Books
Fiction	72
Nonfiction	38
Children's	59

Name ______________________________

Homework & Practice 4-3

Estimate: Use Rounding

Another Look!

Estimate 28 × 36.
Replace the factors with the closest multiple of 10.

You can use place value to round and use rounding to estimate products.

Step 1

Round both numbers in 28 × 36.

Round 28 to the nearest ten.
28 is closer to 30 than 20, so 28 rounds to 30.

Round 36 to the nearest ten.
36 is closer to 40 than 30, so 36 rounds to 40.

Step 2

Estimate the product.

$28 \times 36 = n$

↓ ↓

$30 \times 40 = 1{,}200$

So, the product is about 1,200.

For **1–10**, estimate each product.

1. 31 × 12 rounds to ________ × ________ = ________.

2. 28 × 17 rounds to ________ × ________ = ________.

3. 54 × 14

4. 44 × 22

5. 45 × 19

6. 34 × 48

7. 64 × 76

8. 15 × 38

9. 88 × 23

10. 11 × 68

For **11–12**, estimate to check if the given answer is reasonable.

11. 39 × 37 = 2,183

Rounds to ________ × ________ = ________

Reasonable   Not Reasonable

12. 27 × 83 = 2,241

Rounds to ________ × ________ = ________

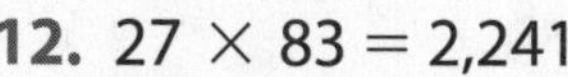
Reasonable   Not Reasonable

Round each factor to the nearest ten to estimate the product.

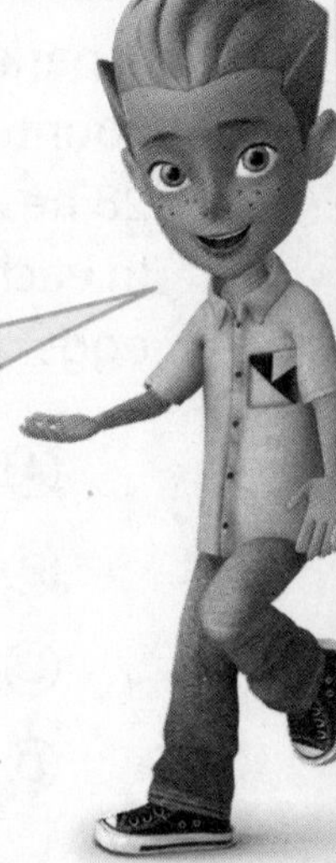

13. Sean baked 18 dozen chocolate cupcakes and 13 dozen vanilla cupcakes. About how many cupcakes did Sean bake? Explain.

There are 12 cupcakes in 1 dozen.

14. The art teacher has 30 boxes of crayons with 16 crayons in each box. She gives the students 10 of the boxes to use. Explain how to find the number of crayons the art teacher has left.

15. **Number Sense** Eric estimated 28×48 by finding 30×50. He estimated the product to be 1,500. Eric thinks the actual product will be greater. Is Eric correct? Explain.

16. **Math and Science** Wind turbines generate large amounts of electricity from wind energy. The blades on a wind turbine can revolve 22 times per minute. If a wind turbine runs for 1 hour, about how many times do the blades revolve? Remember, there are 60 minutes in 1 hour.

17. **Higher Order Thinking** Lenore rounds each factor to the nearest ten to estimate the product of 51×37 as 1,500. Is Lenore's estimate reasonable? Explain.

Assessment ISTEP+ Ready

18. A park ranger in Everglades National Park counted the number of alligator eggs in 28 nests. On average, there were 40 eggs in each nest. About how many alligator eggs did the ranger count?

   Ⓐ About 80 eggs
   Ⓑ About 120 eggs
   Ⓒ About 800 eggs
   Ⓓ About 1,200 eggs

19. A deep-sea fisherman went fishing 14 times last month. He caught 28 fish each time. About how many fish did the fisherman catch last month?

   Ⓐ About 100 fish
   Ⓑ About 200 fish
   Ⓒ About 300 fish
   Ⓓ About 400 fish

Name ________________________________

Lesson 4-4
Estimate: Use Compatible Numbers

I can ...
use compatible numbers to estimate products when multiplying two 2-digit numbers.

Content Standard Prepares for 4.C.2
Process Standards PS.2, PS.3

Solve & Share Choose two factors from the numbers below to find a product that is as close to 1,600 as possible. ***Solve this problem using any strategy you choose.***

24	32	61	78

Use reasoning. What strategies do you know can help you estimate a product? *Show your work in the space below!*

Look Back! Construct Arguments Why did you choose the two factors that you did? How do you know your factors will give the closest estimate of the product?

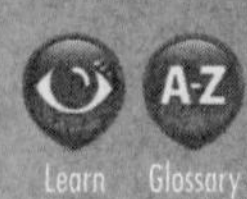

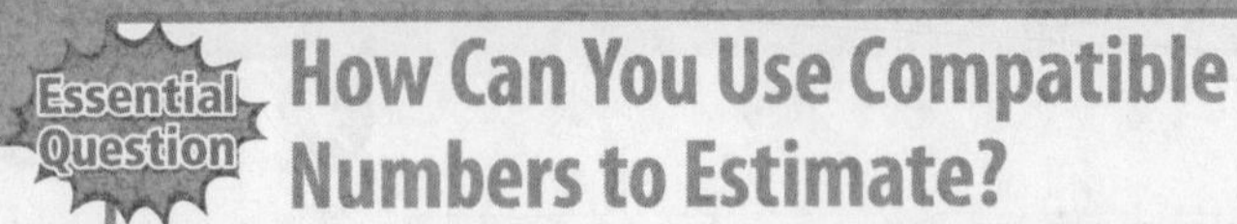

How Can You Use Compatible Numbers to Estimate?

A

Nolan set up a blog for his friends to visit. Estimate the number of hits Nolan will have in 24 days.

There is more than one strategy to estimate.

B Estimate 24 × 41.

Rounding to the nearest ten gives 20 × 40 = 800 as an estimate.

However, you can get a closer estimate by using compatible numbers. Compatible numbers are numbers that are easy to compute mentally.

Replace the factors with numbers that are close and easy to multiply.

24 is close to 25. 41 is close to 40.

C It is easy to find 25 × 40, since 25 and 40 are compatible numbers. Remember:

25 × 4 = 100

So, 25 × 40 = 1,000.

Notice that 24 is closer to 25 than to 20.

So, 25 × 40 gives a closer estimate than 20 × 40. However, either method can be used to find an estimate.

Nolan will have about 1,000 hits in 24 days.

Convince Me! **Critique Reasoning** To estimate 76 × 24, which student's explanation is correct? Explain.

Michelle's Explanation

I rounded 76 to 80 and 24 to 20. 80 × 20 = 1,600, so 76 × 24 is about 1,600.

Diana's Explanation

I used compatible numbers. 76 is close to 80 and 24 is close to 25. 80 × 25 = 2,000, so 76 × 24 is about 2,000.

Name ______

Practice Buddy Tools Assessment

Guided Practice

Do You Understand?

1. In the example on the previous page, suppose the average number of hits per day was 61. If you estimate 24×61 as 25×60, what is the new estimate for the number of hits?

2. **Reasoning** Rounding would give 20×60 as an estimate for 24×61. Why does 25×60 give a closer estimate than 20×60?

Do You Know How?

For **3–7**, estimate each product.

3. 24×18
   24 is close to 25.
   18 is close to ______.
   Multiply $25 \times$ ______ = ______

4. 24×37

5. 52×27

6. 25×59

7. 18×19

Independent Practice

For **8–22,** estimate each product.

8. 26×43
9. 31×46
10. 21×25
11. 58×12
12. 22×26
13. 78×21
14. 36×49
15. 66×31
16. 64×24
17. 21×19
18. 76×39
19. 32×24
20. 89×43
21. 79×79
22. 46×18

Practice using compatible numbers when you estimate.

For another example, see Set D on page 240.

Problem Solving

23. **Algebra** Write a multiplication equation for the area model at the right. Use the Distributive Property to find the product.

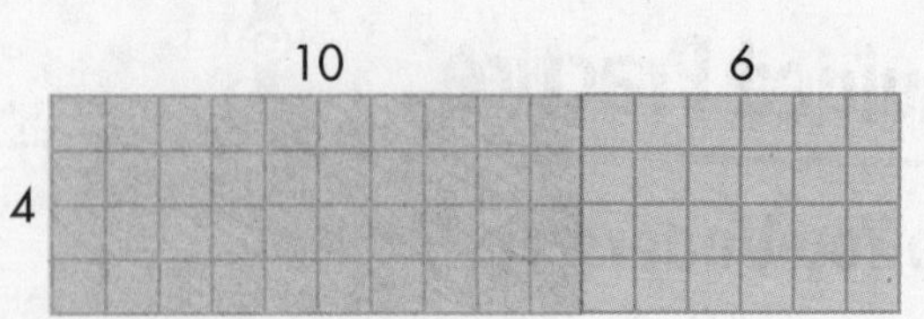

24. In 1858, two ships connected a telegraph cable across the Atlantic Ocean for the first time. Use the diagram below to calculate the total amount of cable used.

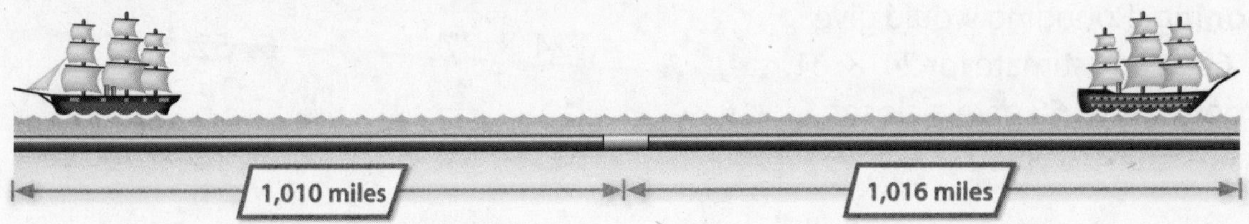

25. **Construct Arguments** Explain how you would use estimation to decide which has the greater product, 39×21 or 32×32.

26. **Higher Order Thinking** How is using compatible numbers to estimate simila to using rounding? How is it different?

27. A company ordered 28 cartons of tape. Each carton contained 24 rolls. Choose compatible numbers from the box to write two different estimates for the total number of rolls ordered. Use each number one time.

Name ____________________

Homework & Practice 4-4

Estimate: Use Compatible Numbers

Another Look!

A roller coaster has 38 seats for passengers. The roller coaster runs 24 times each hour. About how many passengers can ride the roller coaster each hour?

Choose numbers close to 38 and 24 that you can multiply mentally.

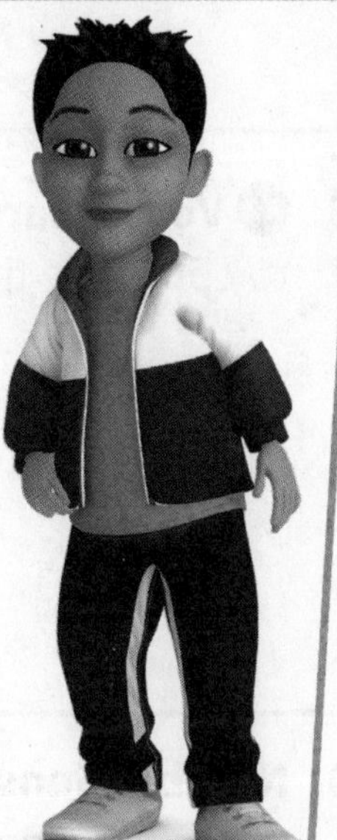

Step 1

Choose compatible numbers.

24 is close to 25.

38 is close to 40.

$$24 \times 38$$
$$\downarrow \quad \downarrow$$
$$25 \times 40$$

Step 2

Multiply the compatible numbers.

$25 \times 40 = 1{,}000$

So, 24×38 is about 1,000.

About 1,000 passengers can ride the roller coaster each hour.

For **1–16,** estimate each product.

1. 23×12
23 is close to 25.
12 is close to ______.
$25 \times$ ______ = ______

2. 24×31
24 is close to 25.
31 is close to ______.
______ $\times$ ______ = ______

3. 19×24

4. 51×17

5. 82×78

6. 12×26

7. 24×62

8. 48×29

9. 53×39

10. 51×23

11. 53×54

12. 68×39

13. 29×43

14. 62×87

15. 36×42

16. 91×77

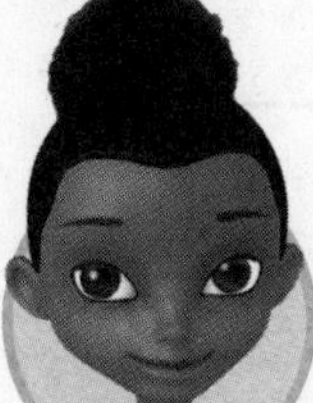

There is more than one way to estimate a product.

17. About how many gallons of water are used to refill the bathtub everyday for 31 days? Explain.

18. **Vocabulary** Use a vocabulary term to complete the definition.

_______________ are numbers that are easy to compute mentally.

19. A store sells about 45 gadgets a day, 7 days a week. About how many gadgets might the store sell in 4 weeks? Explain.

20. **Number Sense** Nathan estimates 67×36 by finding 70×40. Will Nathan's estimate be greater than or less than the actual product? Explain.

21. **Higher Order Thinking** What might you consider when deciding whether to use rounding or compatible numbers to estimate? Explain.

22. A tour guide leads groups of 26 people through a museum. She led 42 groups last year. Choose compatible numbers from the box to write two different estimates for the total number of people she led last year. Use each number one time.

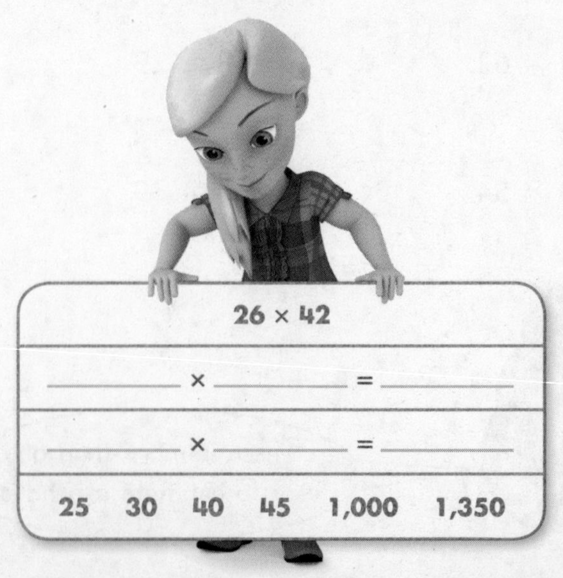

Name ______________________________

Lesson 4-5
Arrays and Partial Products

I can ...
use arrays, place value, partial products, and properties of operations to help multiply.

Content Standard 4.C.7
Process Standards PS.4, PS.7

Solve & Share

A theater contains 14 rows of seats with 23 seats in each row. How many seats are in the theater? ***Solve this problem using any strategy you choose.***

You can model with math using grid paper or arrays to show the problem. *Show your work in the space below!*

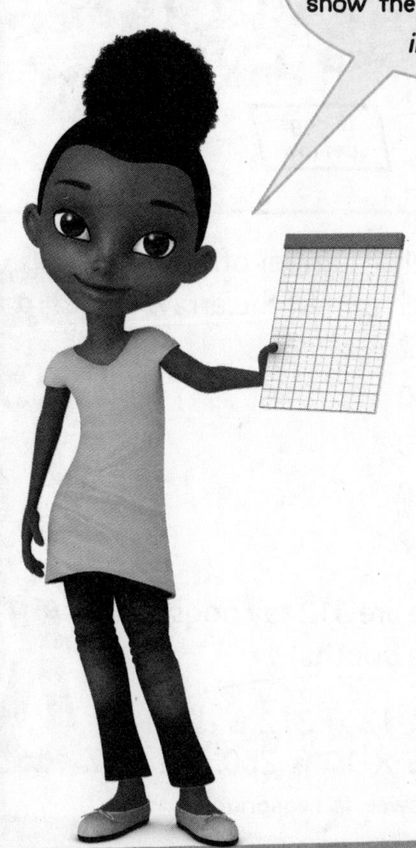

Look Back! Use Structure Theater seating is an example of objects that are arranged in rows and columns, or arrays. What are the dimensions of the array for the theater seating described above?

Learn A-Z Glossary

Essential Question

How Can You Multiply Using an Array?

A

There are 13 toy dogs in each row of a carnival booth. Twenty rows contain toy bulldogs and 4 rows contain toy huskies. How many toy dogs are there?

To solve this problem, you need to first find how many rows of toy dogs are in the booth.
13 dogs per row

20 rows of toy bulldogs
+ 4 rows of toy huskies
24 rows of toy dogs

There are 24 rows of toy dogs with 13 toy dogs in each row.

B

Use an array to find 24 × 13.

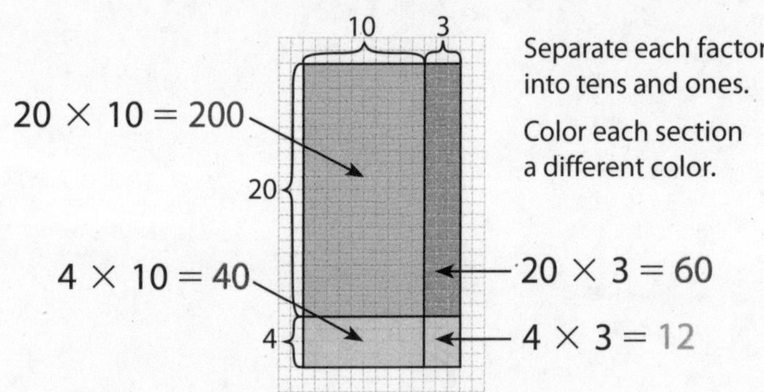

10
3
20 × 10 = 200
20
4 × 10 = 40
4
20 × 3 = 60
4 × 3 = 12
Separate each factor into tens and ones.
Color each section a different color.

12, 40, 60, and 200 are partial products.

C

Add the number of squares in each part of the array.

$$\begin{array}{r} 12 \\ 40 \\ 60 \\ +\ 200 \\ \hline 312 \end{array}$$

There are 312 toy dogs in the booth.

24 × 13 = 312 is close to 25 × 10 = 250. The answer is reasonable.

Convince Me! Model with Math What 2-digit by 2-digit multiplication is shown by the model at the right? What is the product? Explain how you used the model to find the product.

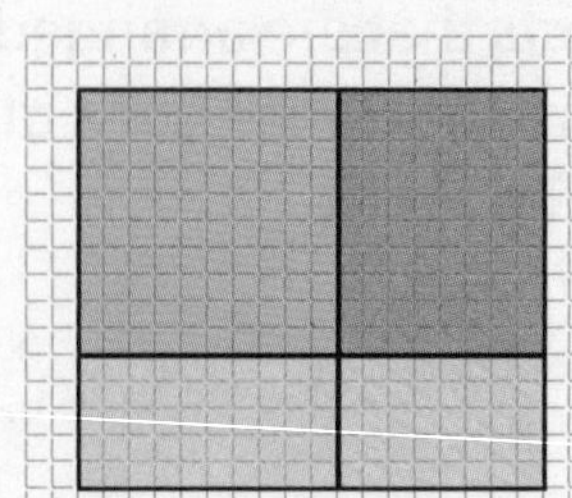

Name ______________________________

Practice Buddy | Tools | Assessment

Guided Practice*

Do You Understand?

1. **Model with Math** In the example on the previous page, what four simpler multiplication problems were used to find 24 × 13?

2. How can you use properties of operations to help find the product of 24 × 13?

Do You Know How?

For **3**, use the array drawn on a grid to find the product. Check if your answer is reasonable.

3. 24 × 16

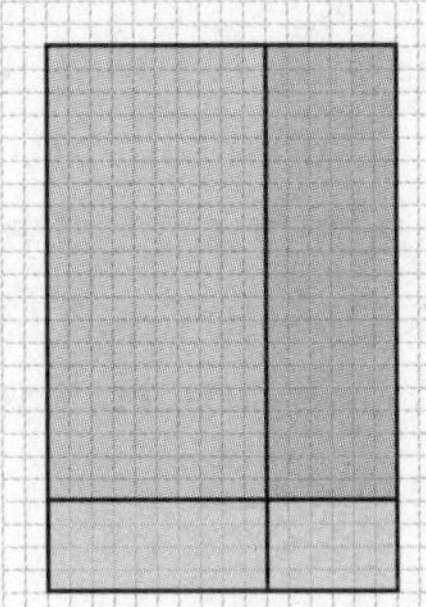

Independent Practice

For **4–7**, use the array drawn on a grid to find each product.

4. 14 × 21

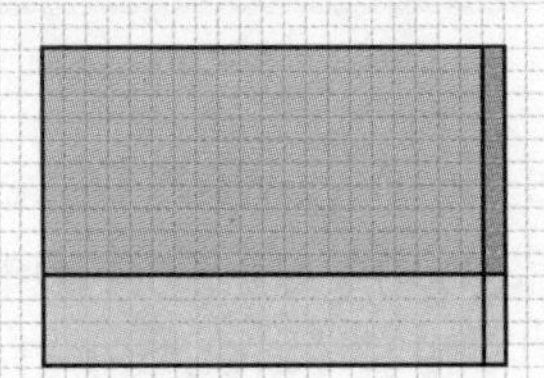

5. 14 × 12

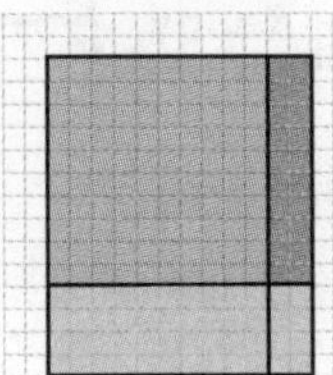

Using the Commutative Property of Addition, you can add the partial products in any order.

6. 18 × 18

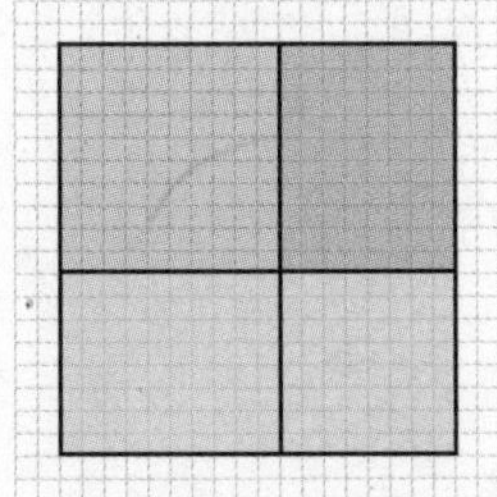

7. 15 × 13

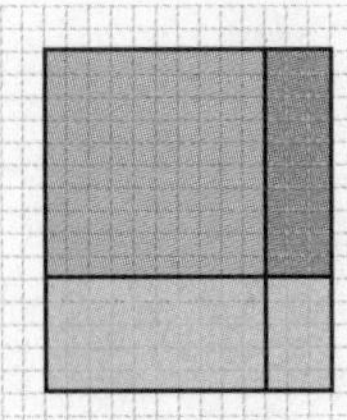

*For another example, see Set E on page 240.

Problem Solving

8. The flagpole in front of City Hall in Lou's town is 35 feet tall. How many inches tall is the flagpole? Remember, there are 12 inches in 1 foot.

9. **Vocabulary** Use *Associative* or *Commutative* to complete the definition.

The ______________ Property of Multiplication states you can change the grouping of the factors and the product stays the same.

For **10–11**, use the array at the right.

10. **Model with Math** Maggie is making a balloon game for the school fair. Students throw darts to pop the balloons. Draw lines on the array to separate each factor into tens and ones. How many balloons are used to set up the game?

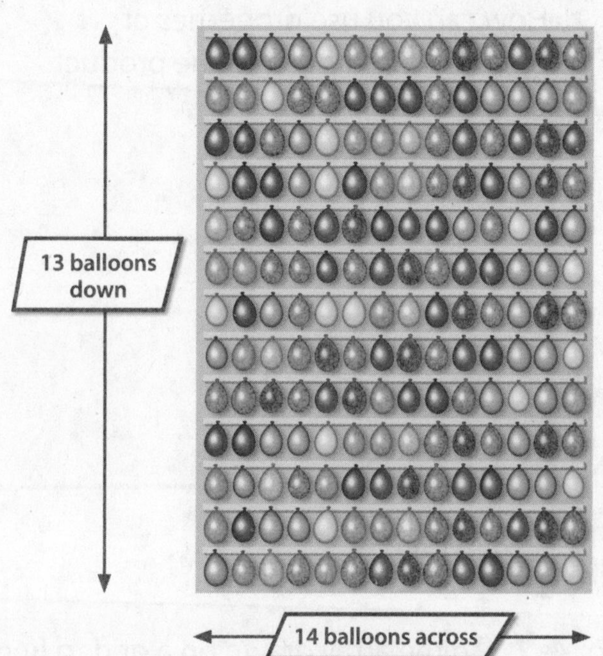

11. **Higher Order Thinking** Maggie knows she will have to completely refill the balloon board about 15 times. Write an equation to show the number of balloons Maggie will need.

12. Write to explain why the product of 15×32 is equal to the sum of 10×32 and 5×32.

13. A theater contains 17 rows with 14 seats in each row. Draw an array to find the number of seats in the theater. Separate each factor into tens and ones in the array.

Name ____________________

Help | Practice Buddy | Tools | Games

Homework & Practice 4-5

Arrays and Partial Products

Another Look!

One way to find the product of 12×24 is to use an array.

Draw an array on a grid. Divide the array into tens and ones for each factor. Find the number of squares in each smaller rectangle. Then add the numbers of squares in the four smaller rectangles.

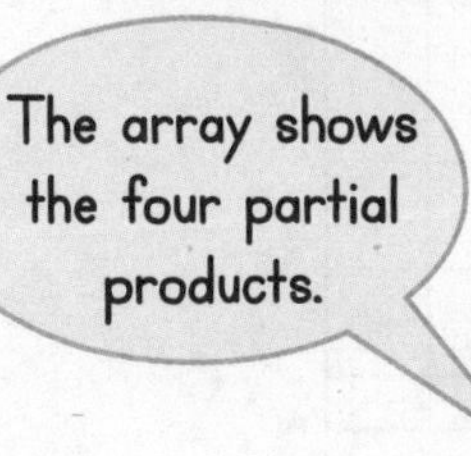

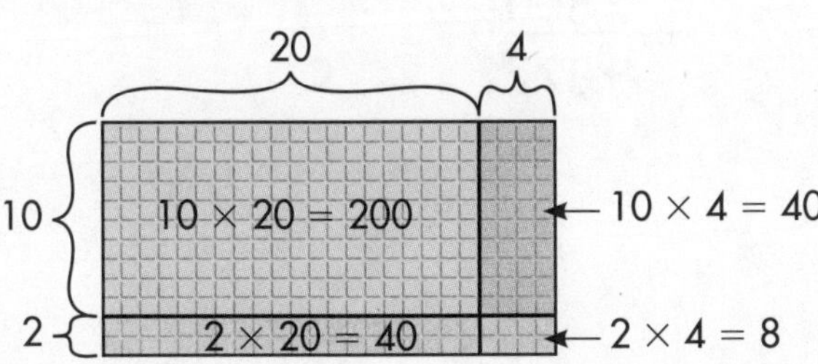

$$\begin{array}{r} 8 \\ 40 \\ 40 \\ +\ 200 \\ \hline 288 \end{array}$$

So, $12 \times 24 = 288$.

For **1–4**, find each product. Use the arrays drawn on grids to help.

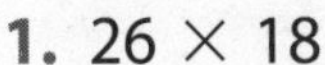

1. 26×18

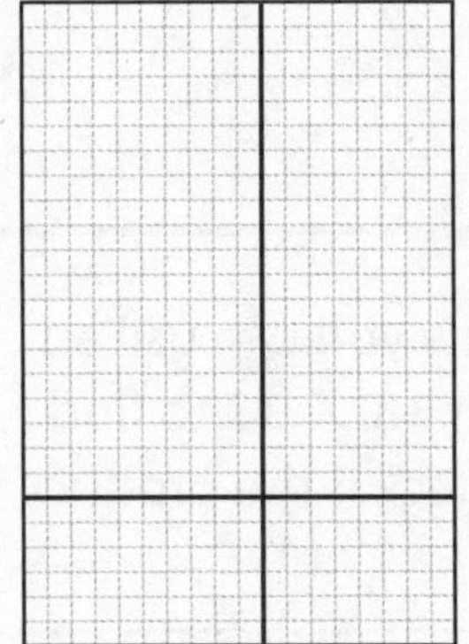

2. 23×23

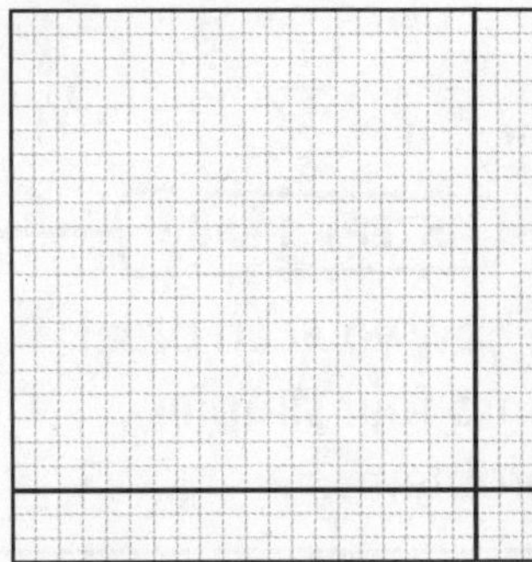

3. 19×27

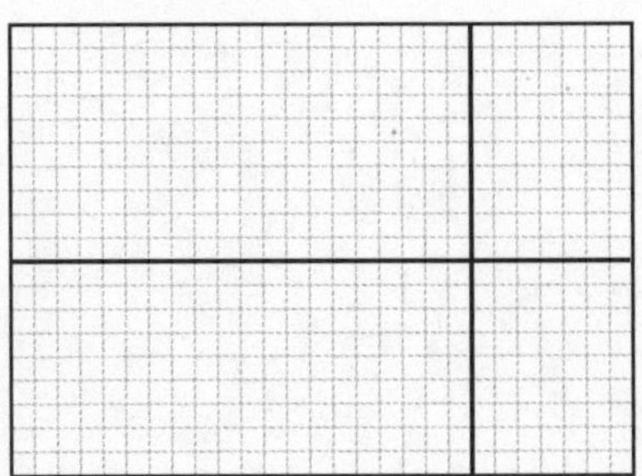

4. 11×16

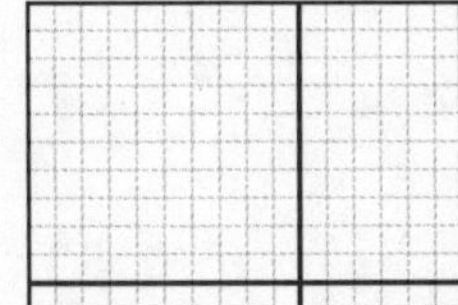

5. Barb exercises for 22 hours each week. How many hours does she exercise in 14 weeks? Use the array drawn on the grid to help multiply.

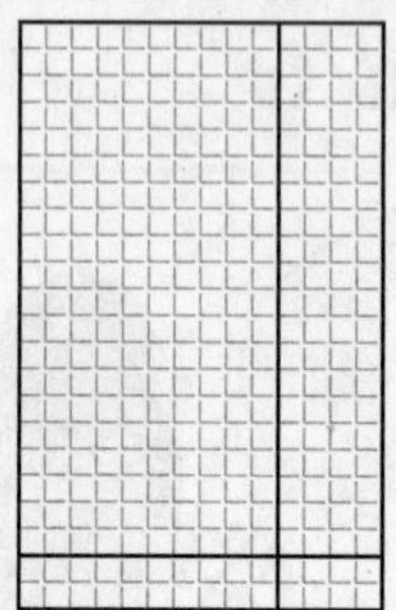

6. Teri used an algorithm to find the product below. Is Teri's answer reasonable? Explain.

$$\begin{array}{r} 4{,}296 \\ \times \quad 7 \\ \hline 42 \\ 630 \\ 1{,}400 \\ 2{,}800 \\ \hline 4{,}872 \end{array}$$

7. **Higher Order Thinking** The prices at Nolan's Novelties store are shown at the right. If 27 boxes of neon keychains and 35 boxes of glow-in-the-dark pens were sold, what were the total sales in dollars?

DATA

Item	Price per Box
Neon keychains	$15
Glow-in-the-dark pens	$10

Assessment ISTEP+ Ready

8. Write to explain how you can break apart 16×34 into four simpler multiplication problems.

9. Write to explain how you can use an array to break apart 18×12 to find the product and check if the product is reasonable.

Name ____________________

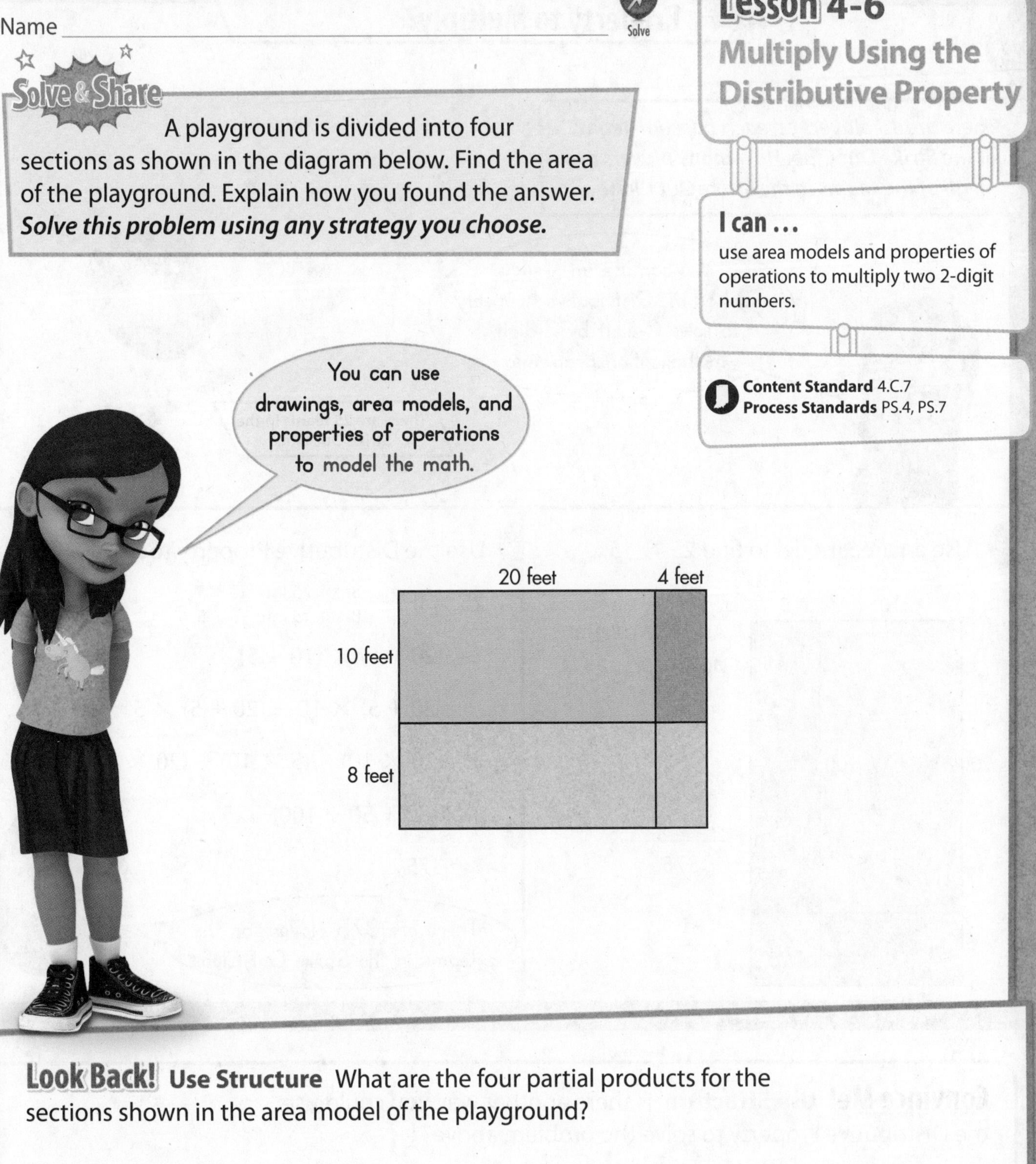

A playground is divided into four sections as shown in the diagram below. Find the area of the playground. Explain how you found the answer. ***Solve this problem using any strategy you choose.***

Lesson 4-6
Multiply Using the Distributive Property

I can ...
use area models and properties of operations to multiply two 2-digit numbers.

Content Standard 4.C.7
Process Standards PS.4, PS.7

Look Back! Use Structure What are the four partial products for the sections shown in the area model of the playground?

How Can You Use the Distributive Property to Multiply?

A

There are 15 players on each baseball team of the Strike Out Club. How many players are on all of the teams in the Strike Out Club?

You can use an area model or the Distributive Property to solve 2-digit by 2-digit multiplication problems.

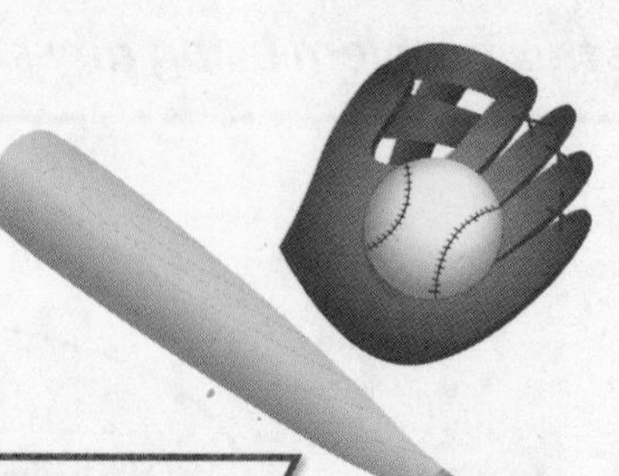

There are 25 teams in the Strike Out Club.

B Use an area model to find 25 × 15.

	10	5
20	20 × 10 = 200	20 × 5 = 100
5	5 × 10 = 50	5 × 5 = 25

Add the partial products.

$$\begin{array}{r} 200 \\ 50 \\ 100 \\ +\ 25 \\ \hline 375 \end{array}$$

C Use the Distributive Property to find 25 × 15.

25 × 15 Break 25 into 20 + 5. Break 15 into 10 + 5.

$= (20 + 5) \times (10 + 5)$

$= (20 + 5) \times 10 + (20 + 5) \times 5$

$= (20 \times 10) + (5 \times 10) + (20 \times 5) + (5 \times 5)$

$= 200 + 50 + 100 + 25$

$= 375$

There are 375 players on the teams in the Strike Out Club.

Convince Me! **Use Structure** Is there another way you could use the Distributive Property to solve the problem above?

Name ____

Practice Buddy Tools Assessment

Guided Practice*

Do You Understand?

1. Model with Math Use the area model and the Distributive Property to find 24 × 23.

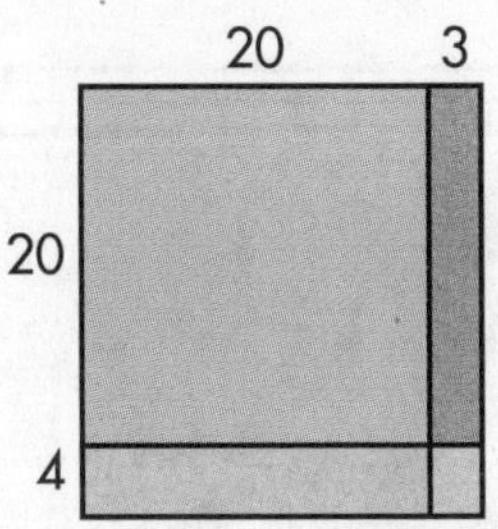

2. How can an area model and the Distributive Property help you multiply? Use 12 × 16 to explain.

Do You Know How?

3. Use the area model and the Distributive Property to find 35 × 12.

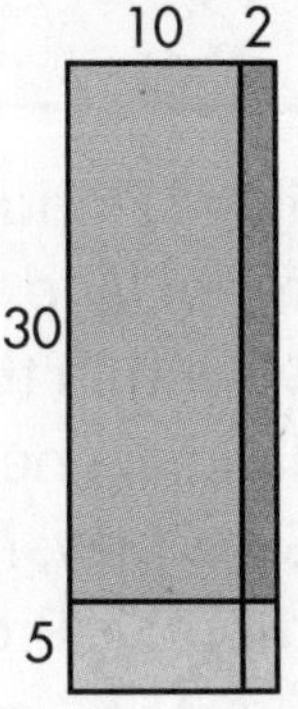

35 × 12

= (30 + ____) × (10 + ____)

= (30 + 5) × ____ + (30 + 5) × ____

= (30 × 10) + (5 × 10) +

(30 × 2) + (5 × 2)

= ____ + ____ + ____ + ____

= ____

Independent Practice

For **4–6**, draw an area model to find each product.

4. 18 × 25

5. 16 × 27

6. 22 × 88

For **7–11**, find each product. Use properties of operations.

7. $\begin{array}{r} 41 \\ \times\ 12 \\ \hline \end{array}$

8. $\begin{array}{r} 38 \\ \times\ 27 \\ \hline \end{array}$

9. $\begin{array}{r} 58 \\ \times\ 19 \\ \hline \end{array}$

10. $\begin{array}{r} 29 \\ \times\ 15 \\ \hline \end{array}$

11. $\begin{array}{r} 73 \\ \times\ 47 \\ \hline \end{array}$

**For another example, see Set F on page 241.*

Problem Solving

12. Write 652,079 using number names and in expanded form.

13. Number Sense Sara estimated 23×43 using 20×40. Sam estimated 23×43 using 25×40. Will Sara's or Sam's method give an estimate closer to the exact answer? Explain.

14. Use Structure Each family of Florida Scrub Jays inhabits 25 acres of land. No other scrub jay families live within this area. How many acres of land are needed for 24 families of Florida Scrub Jays? Show how you can use the Distributive Property to solve this problem.

15. Marla wants to buy a new tablet that costs $565, including tax. She saved $15 per week for 30 weeks. Does Marla have enough money saved to buy the tablet? Explain.

16. Higher Order Thinking Which costs less: 13 oranges that cost 29 cents each or 17 apples that cost 25 cents each? How much less?

ISTEP+ Ready

17. Part A

Write the partial product in each rectangle of the area model.

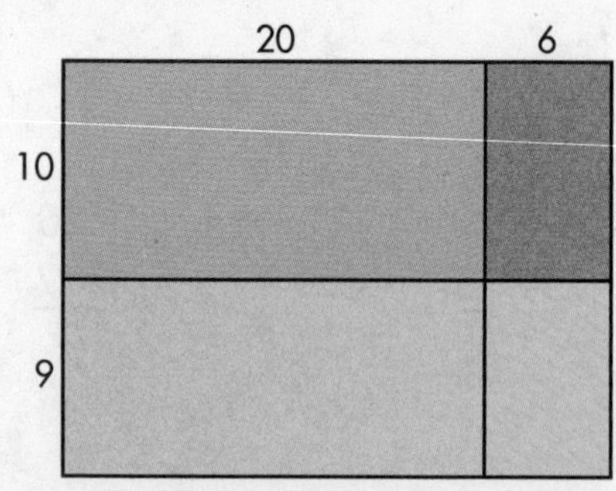

Part B

Find the sum of the partial products.

Name ________________________________

Homework & Practice 4-6
Multiply Using the Distributive Property

Another Look!

Find 23 × 18.

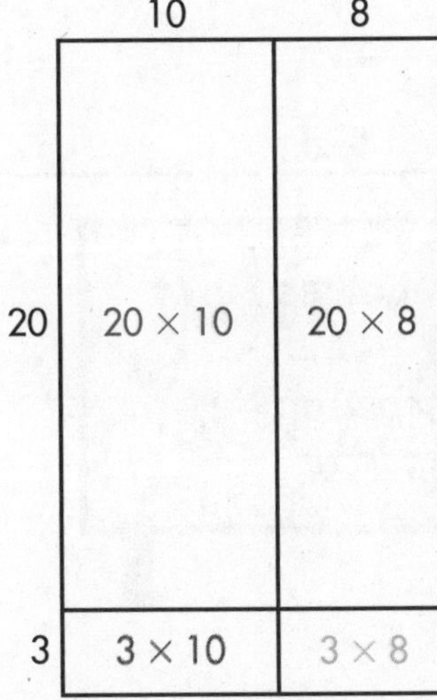

You can use an area model and the Distributive Property to help multiply.

$$23 \times 18 = (20 + 3) \times (10 + 8)$$
$$= (20 + 3) \times 10 + (20 + 3) \times 8$$
$$= (20 \times 10) + (3 \times 10) + (20 \times 8) + (3 \times 8)$$
$$= 200 + 30 + 160 + 24$$
$$= 414$$

For **1–3**, use the area model to find each product.

1. 14 × 19

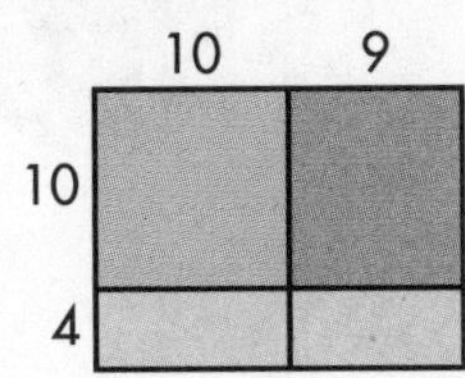

2. 12 × 22

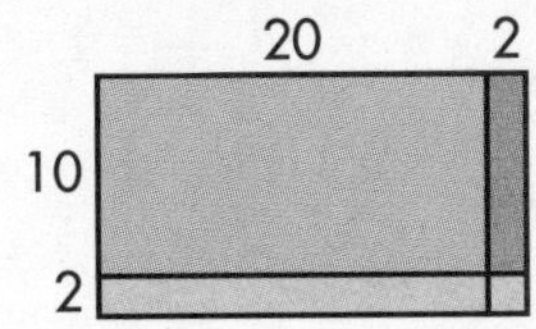

3. 21 × 51

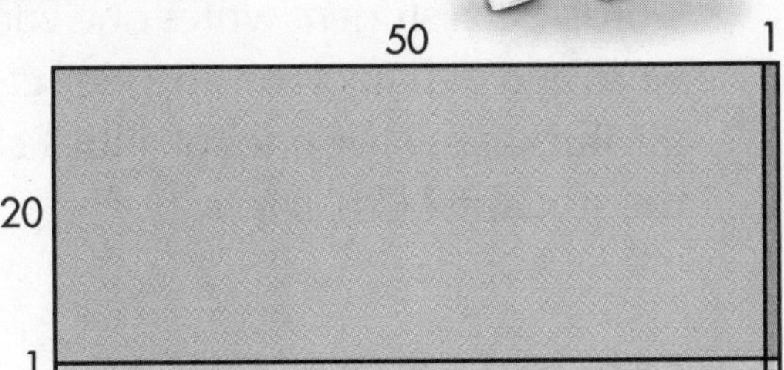

For **4–13**, find each product. Use properties of operations.

4. 10 × 18

5. 28 × 38

6. 51 × 12

7. 73 × 13

8. 99 × 11

9. 16 × 14

10. 17 × 38

11. 56 × 17

12. 11 × 13

13. 29 × 64

14. There are 27 students in Ms. Langley's class. Each student is assigned 15 different math problems. How many math problems are assigned to the whole class?

15. An arena hosts a concert on Friday and a rodeo on Saturday. If 12,211 people attend the concert and 9,217 attend the rodeo, how many people visit the arena on Friday and Saturday?

16. **Number Sense** On one trip, 82 people and 49 cars rode the ferry. About how much money did the ferry service collect for the one trip?

Cape May–Lewes Ferry

$3 per person
$34 per car

17. **Higher Order Thinking** Mr. Buckham teaches vocabulary to a class of 27 fourth grade students. There are 63 new vocabulary words. Each student writes one vocabulary word and definition on an index card. Does Mr. Buckham have enough index cards for all the students? Explain.

Mr. Buckham has 1,500 index cards.

Assessment ISTEP+ Ready

18. **Part A**

Write the partial product in each rectangle of the area model.

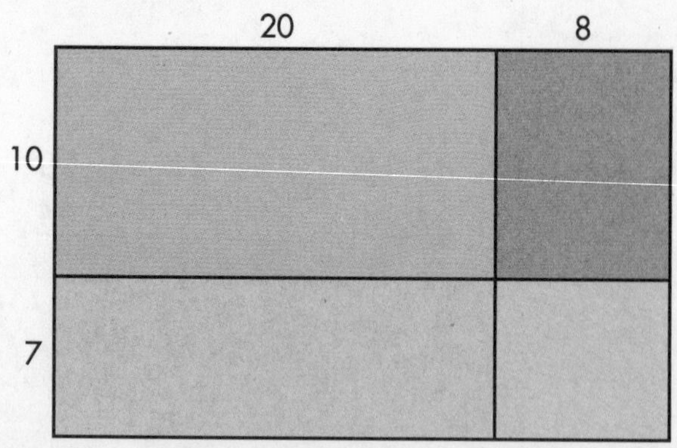
20
8
10
7

Part B

Find the sum of the partial products.

Name ___

Lesson 4-7
Use Partial Products to Multiply by 2-Digit Numbers

Solve & Share There are 11 regular players and 5 substitute players on a professional soccer team. How many players are on 15 soccer teams? ***Solve this problem using any strategy you choose.***

I can ...
use place value and partial products to multiply.

Content Standard 4.C.2
Process Standards PS.3, PS.4, PS.7

You can use structure. Use what you know about multiplying by 1-digit numbers to multiply by 2-digit numbers. *Show your work in the space below!*

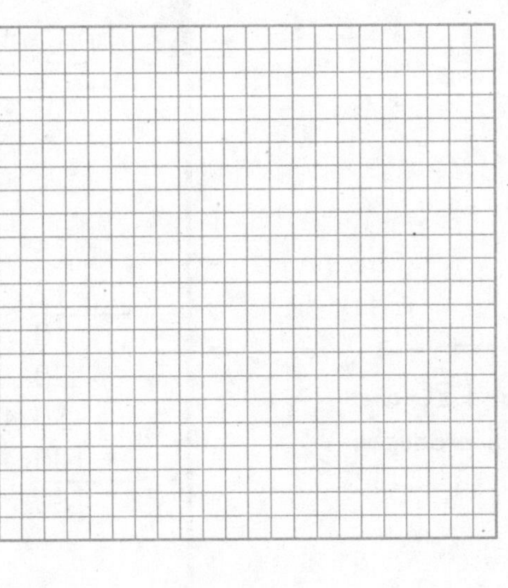

Look Back! Model with Math How could you use an array and rounding or an array and compatible numbers to estimate the product for the problem above?

How Can You Record Multiplication?

A

Marcia put 7 oranges and 8 apples into each of 12 bags. How many pieces of fruit did Marcia put into all of the bags?

Some problems have more than one step to solve.

7 + 8 = 15

Marcia put 15 pieces of fruit in each of the 12 bags.

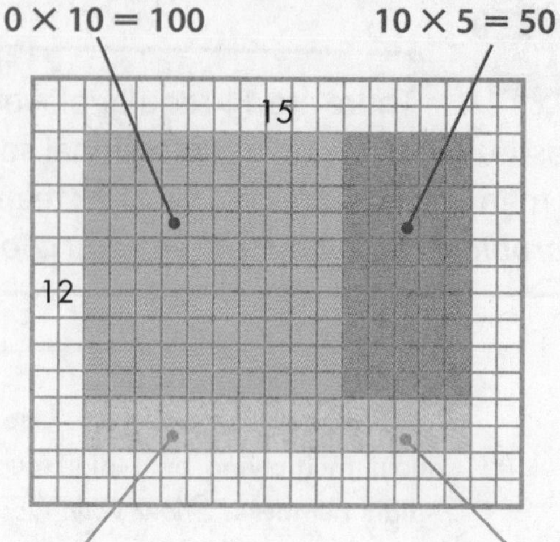

B

Find 12 × 15.

First, multiply the ones.

$$\begin{array}{r} 15 \\ \times\ 12 \\ \hline 10 \\ 20 \end{array}$$

10 $2 \times 5 = 10$

20 $2 \times 10 = 20$

10 and 20 are partial products.

C

Then, multiply the tens.

The partial products match the area model.

$$\begin{array}{r} 15 \\ \times\ 12 \\ \hline 10 \\ 20 \\ 50 \\ +\ 100 \\ \hline 180 \end{array}$$

50 $10 \times 5 = 50$

100 $10 \times 10 = 100$

Marcia put 180 pieces of fruit into the bags.

Convince Me! **Model with Math** Write the partial products in each rectangle of the area model. What is the final product?

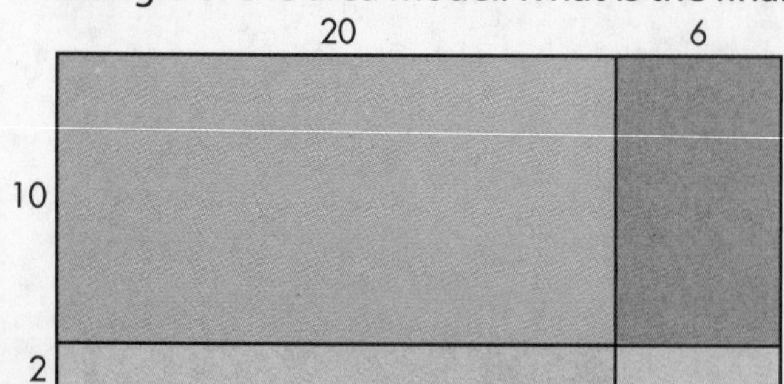

$$\begin{array}{r} 26 \\ \times\ 12 \\ \hline \end{array}$$

Name ____________________

Practice Buddy Tools Assessment

Guided Practice*

Do You Understand?

1. **Reasoning** In the example on the previous page, why do you find 2×10, rather than 2×1?

2. In the example on the previous page, could you record the 4 partial products in a different order? Explain.

Do You Know How?

For **3–4**, find all the partial products. Then add to find the final product. Draw area models as needed.

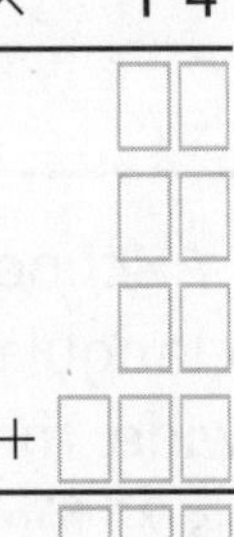

3. $$\begin{array}{r} 23 \\ \times\ 14 \\ \hline \end{array}$$

4. $$\begin{array}{r} 41 \\ \times\ 25 \\ \hline \end{array}$$

Independent Practice

Leveled Practice For **5–12**, find all the partial products. Then add to find the final product. Draw area models as needed.

5. $$\begin{array}{r} 34 \\ \times\ 51 \\ \hline \end{array}$$

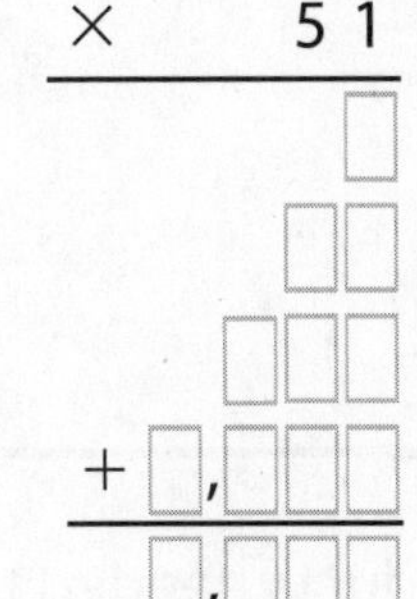

6. $$\begin{array}{r} 73 \\ \times\ 81 \\ \hline \end{array}$$

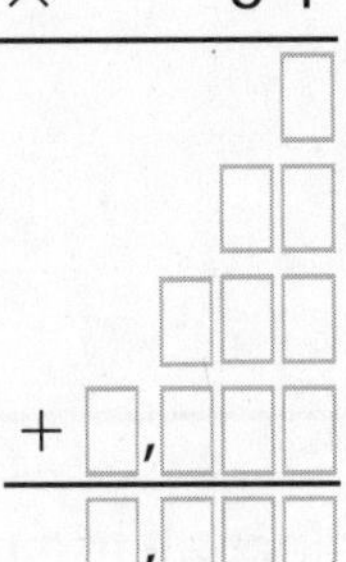

7. $$\begin{array}{r} 64 \\ \times\ 32 \\ \hline \end{array}$$

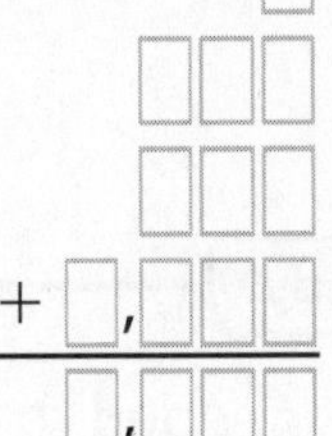

8. $$\begin{array}{r} 26 \\ \times\ 53 \\ \hline \end{array}$$

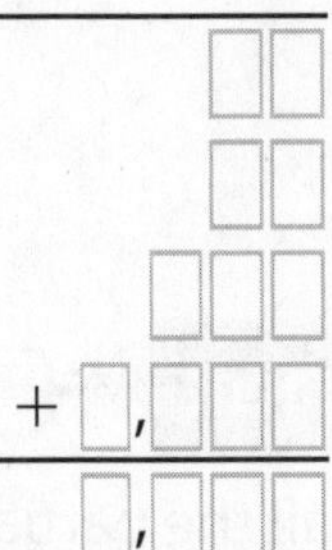

9. $$\begin{array}{r} 38 \\ \times\ 17 \\ \hline \end{array}$$

10. $$\begin{array}{r} 24 \\ \times\ 33 \\ \hline \end{array}$$

11. $$\begin{array}{r} 19 \\ \times\ 43 \\ \hline \end{array}$$

12. $$\begin{array}{r} 19 \\ \times\ 52 \\ \hline \end{array}$$

*For another example, see Set G on page 241.

Problem Solving

13. The Castillo de San Marcos is a Spanish fortress that was built between 1672 and 1695.

    a. Rounded to the nearest ten thousand, how many pesos did it cost to build the fortress?

    b. How many years did it take to build the fortress?

It cost 138,375 pesos to build this fortress.

14. **Construct Arguments** A school has 2 large patios. One is rectangular and is 24 feet long by 18 feet wide. The other is square and each side is 21 feet long. Which patio has a greater area? Explain.

15. **Higher Order Thinking** Explain how you can use the area model below to find 14 × 22. List the partial products and solve.

20 2

10

4

Assessment — ISTEP+ Ready

16. Select all the partial products needed to find the final product.

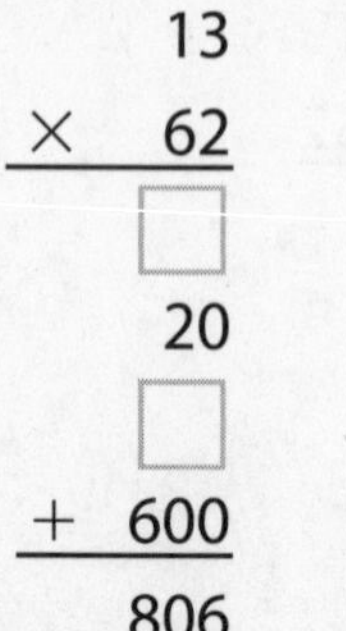

$$\begin{array}{r} 13 \\ \times \quad 62 \\ \hline \square \\ 20 \\ \square \\ + \; 600 \\ \hline 806 \end{array}$$

- ☐ 6
- ☐ 16
- ☐ 18
- ☐ 180
- ☐ 600

17. Select all the partial products needed to find the final product.

$$\begin{array}{r} 19 \\ \times \; 24 \\ \hline \square \\ 40 \\ \square \\ + \; \square \\ \hline 456 \end{array}$$

- ☐ 6
- ☐ 36
- ☐ 180
- ☐ 200
- ☐ 280

Name ______________________________

Help | Practice Buddy | Tools | Games

Homework & Practice 4-7

Use Partial Products to Multiply by 2-Digit Numbers

Another Look!

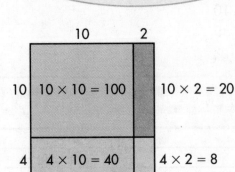

Golf balls come in a box of 12. How many golf balls are in 14 boxes?

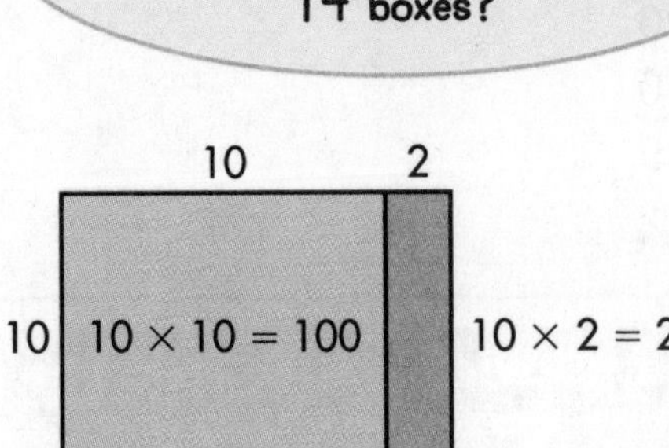

$$\begin{array}{rl} 12 & \\ \times\ 14 & \\ \hline 8 & 4 \times 2 = 8 \\ 40 & 4 \times 10 = 40 \\ 20 & 10 \times 2 = 20 \\ +\ 100 & 10 \times 10 = 100 \\ \hline 168 & \end{array}$$

For **1–8**, find all the partial products. Then add to find the final product. Draw area models as needed.

1. $\begin{array}{r} 16 \\ \times\ 15 \\ \hline \end{array}$

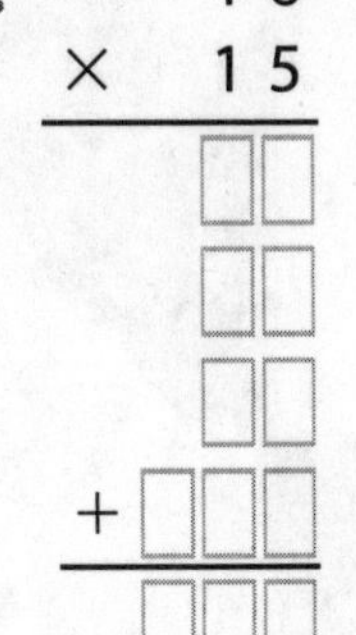

2. $\begin{array}{r} 16 \\ \times\ 12 \\ \hline \end{array}$

3. $\begin{array}{r} 19 \\ \times\ 13 \\ \hline \end{array}$

4. $\begin{array}{r} 24 \\ \times\ 12 \\ \hline \end{array}$

5. $\begin{array}{r} 32 \\ \times\ 23 \\ \hline \end{array}$

6. $\begin{array}{r} 79 \\ \times\ 47 \\ \hline \end{array}$

7. $\begin{array}{r} 23 \\ \times\ 46 \\ \hline \end{array}$

8. $\begin{array}{r} 82 \\ \times\ 74 \\ \hline \end{array}$

9. Reasoning Why can the calculations in red be thought of as simpler problems?

$$\begin{array}{rl} 34 & \\ \times\ 24 & \\ \hline 16 & 4 \times 4 \\ 120 & 4 \times 30 \\ 80 & 20 \times 4 \\ +\ 600 & 20 \times 30 \\ \hline 816 & \end{array}$$

10. Explain the mistakes in the calculation below. Show the correct calculation.

$$\begin{array}{r} 12 \\ \times\ 13 \\ \hline 6 \\ 3 \\ 20 \\ +\ 10 \\ \hline 39 \end{array}$$

11. A movie theater charges $10 for an adult ticket and $9 for a child ticket. The goal is to make $1,200 on adult tickets each week. Did the theater make its goal this week? How much more or less than the goal did the theater make?

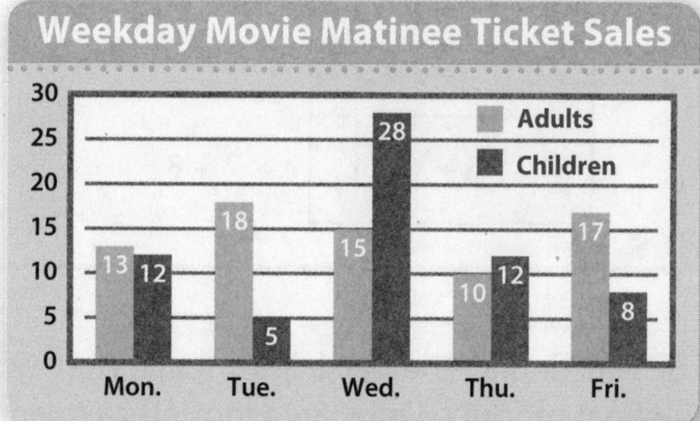

12. Higher Order Thinking A golf practice range has 245 balls. The owner bought a carton of golf balls. How many golf balls does the owner have after buying the carton?

ISTEP+ Ready

13. Select all the partial products needed to find the final product.

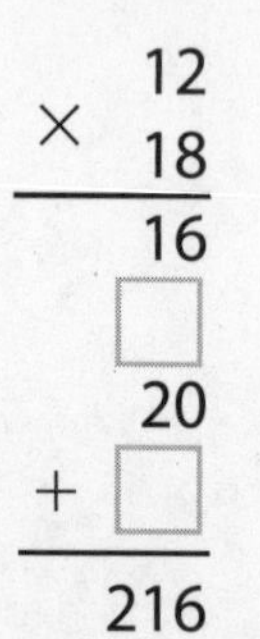

- ☐ 8
- ☐ 80
- ☐ 100
- ☐ 180
- ☐ 600

14. Select all the partial products needed to find the final product.

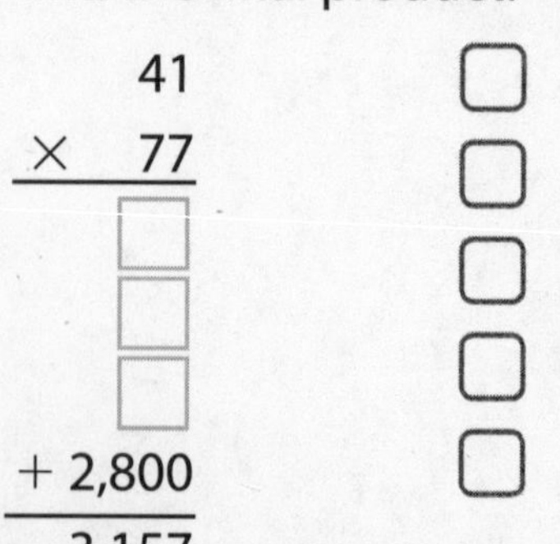

- ☐ 7
- ☐ 70
- ☐ 280
- ☐ 700
- ☐ 2,800

Name ______________________________________  Solve

Last year, Tim's Fish Shop had 23 guppies. This year, the shop has 90 times as many guppies. How many guppies does Tim's Fish Shop have this year? ***Solve this problem using any strategy you choose.***

Lesson 4-8
Multiply 2-Digit Numbers by Multiples of 10

I can ...
use area models and place-value strategies to multiply by multiples of 10.

Content Standard 4.C.2
Process Standards PS.2, PS.7

You can use structure. How can breaking up each factor using place value help you solve this problem? *Show your work in the space below!*

Look Back! Reasoning How is multiplying 23 by 90 like multiplying 23 by 9?

Essential Question How Can You Multiply by Multiples of 10?

A

Mr. Jeffrey bought 20 rock identification kits for his science classes. Each kit has 12 igneous rocks, 9 sedimentary rocks, and 7 metamorphic rocks. How many rocks are in all the kits?

Add to find how many rocks are in each kit. Then multiply to find how many rocks are in all the kits.

20 rock kits

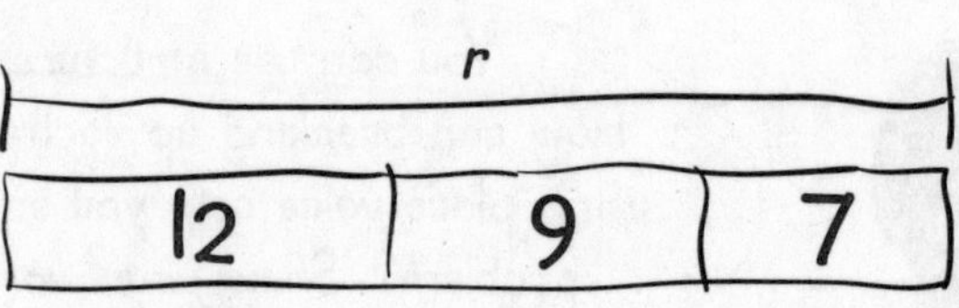

There are 28 rocks in each kit.

B

One Way

Find 20 × 28. Draw an area model and break 28 into tens and ones: 28 = 20 + 8.

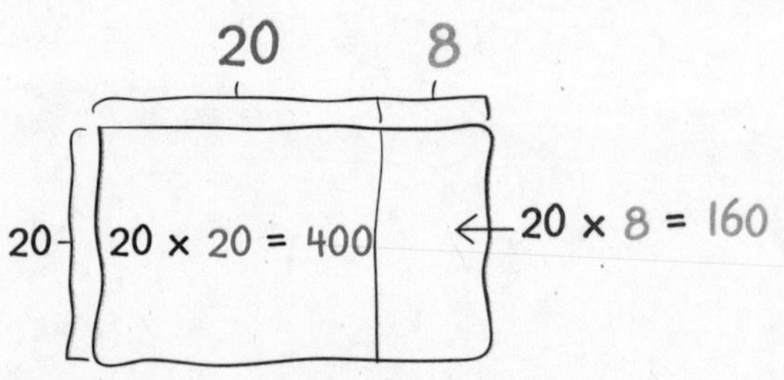

$$
\begin{aligned}
20 \times 28 &= 20 \times (20 + 8) \\
&= (20 \times 20) + (20 \times 8) \\
&= 400 + 160 \\
&= 560
\end{aligned}
$$

C

Another Way

Find 20 × 28.

Multiply 2 tens × 28.

$$
\begin{array}{r} \overset{1}{2}8 \\ \times\ 20 \\ \hline 560 \end{array}
$$

Record a 0 in the ones place of the answer.

The 0 in the ones place shows the product is a multiple of ten.

There are 560 total rocks in the kits.

Convince Me! **Look for Relationships** Amanda said, "To find 68 × 30, I'll just find 68 × 3 and write a zero at the end." Is Amanda correct? Explain.

Name ______________________________

Guided Practice*

Do You Understand?

1. When you multiply by 20, why is there a zero in the ones place of the product?

2. **Use Structure** What simpler multiplication problem can help you find 38 × 70?

Do You Know How?

For **3–6**, multiply to find each product.

3.
$$\begin{array}{r} 12 \\ \times\ 20 \\ \hline \square\square 0 \end{array}$$

4.
$$\begin{array}{r} 21 \\ \times\ 30 \\ \hline \square\square 0 \end{array}$$

5. 27 × 60

6. 66 × 40

Independent Practice

Leveled Practice For **7–20**, multiply to find each product. Draw models as needed.

7.
$$\begin{array}{r} 12 \\ \times\ 30 \\ \hline \square\square 0 \end{array}$$

8.
$$\begin{array}{r} 24 \\ \times\ 50 \\ \hline \square,\square\square 0 \end{array}$$

9.
$$\begin{array}{r} 33 \\ \times\ 20 \\ \hline \square\square 0 \end{array}$$

10.
$$\begin{array}{r} 71 \\ \times\ 30 \\ \hline \square,\square\square 0 \end{array}$$

11. 18 × 30

12. 20 × 51

13. 32 × 30

14. 40 × 22

15. 24 × 40

16. 34 × 50

17. 40 × 73

18. 88 × 30

19. 10 × 52

20. 30 × 97

If there is a zero in the ones place in one of the factors, there will be a zero in the ones place in the product.

*For another example, see Set H on page 241.

Problem Solving

21. Algebra A roller coaster ride ran 50 times one afternoon. If all of the rides were full, how many people rode the roller coaster that afternoon? Write and solve an equation.

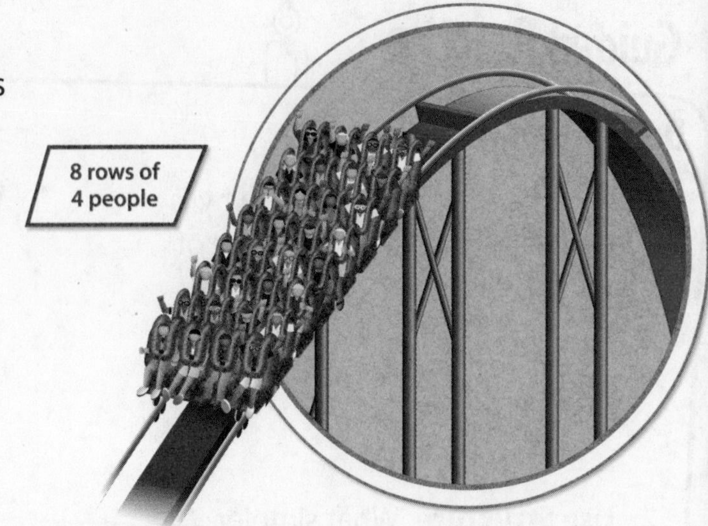

22. The roller coaster ran 30 times in the morning. If all the rides were full, how many rode in the morning?

23. Danika sold 285 items the first week and 374 items the second week. If each item costs $6, how much did Danika make in sales?

24. Higher Order Thinking Each year, Logan School orders 100 rock kits. Each kit contains 28 rocks. How many rocks are there in all of the kits? Remember, there are 2 zeros when you multiply by hundreds.

25. Jared says it is easier to place a number with 0 ones as the second factor rather than the first. Jasmine says it does not matter which order the factors are placed in the problem.

Jared $\begin{array}{r} 24 \\ \times\ 10 \\ \hline \end{array}$

Jasmine $\begin{array}{r} 10 \\ \times\ 24 \\ \hline \end{array}$ $\begin{array}{r} 24 \\ \times\ 10 \\ \hline \end{array}$

Remember, a good explanation is correct, simple, complete, and easy to understand.

Part A

Write to explain why Jared might find it easier to place the number with the 0 ones as the second factor.

Part B

Write to explain why it does not matter which order the factors are placed.

Name ____________________

Homework & Practice 4-8

Multiply 2-Digit Numbers by Multiples of 10

Another Look!

Find 30 × 26 by breaking one of the factors apart.

You can find 30 × 26 two different ways.

Break 26 into tens and ones.
26 = 20 + 6

Multiply to find the partial products.
30 × 20 = 600 and 30 × 6 = 180

Add the partial products.
600 + 180 = 780
So, 30 × 26 = 780.

Find 30 × 26 using a pattern.

$$\begin{array}{r} \overset{1}{26} \\ \times\ 30 \\ \hline 780 \end{array}$$

Record 0 in the ones place of the product. Then find 3 tens × 26.

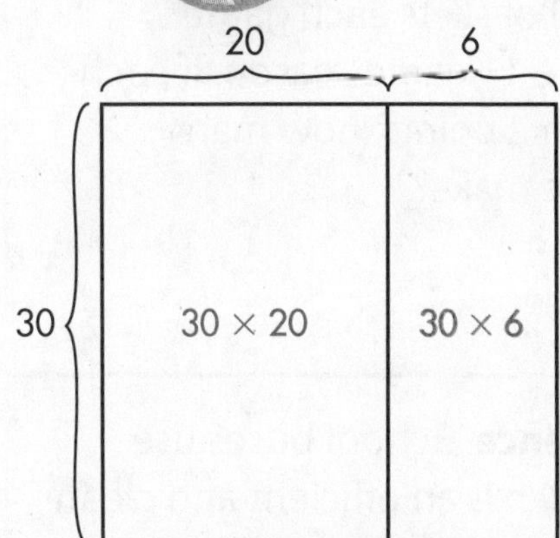

30 × 26 = 30 × (20 + 6)
= (30 × 20) + (30 × 6)
= 600 + 180
= 780

For **1–2**, use the area model to find each product.

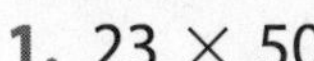

1. 23 × 50

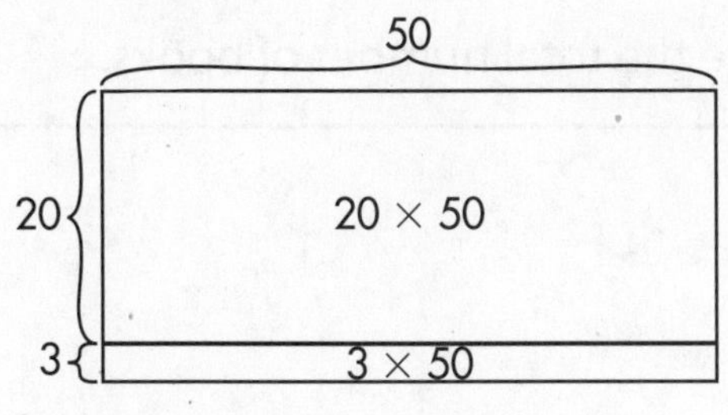

2. 30 × 82

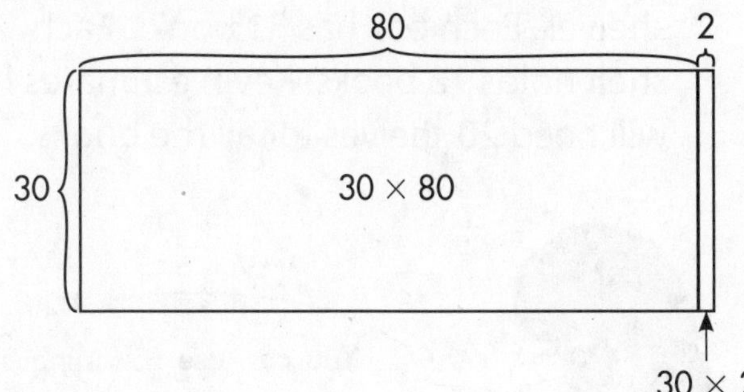

For **3–10**, use a pattern to find each product.

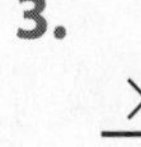

3.

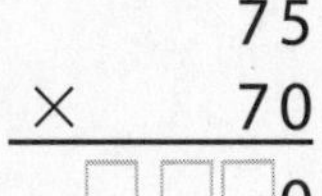

$$\begin{array}{r} 75 \\ \times\ 70 \\ \hline \square,\square\square 0 \end{array}$$

4.

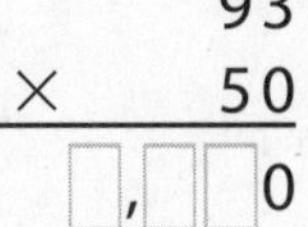

$$\begin{array}{r} 93 \\ \times\ 50 \\ \hline \square,\square\square 0 \end{array}$$

5.

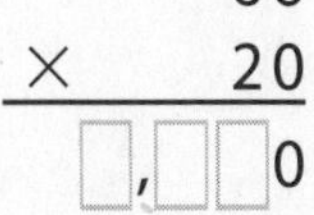

$$\begin{array}{r} 66 \\ \times\ 20 \\ \hline \square,\square\square 0 \end{array}$$

6.

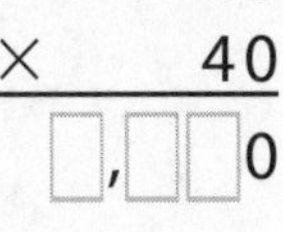

$$\begin{array}{r} 53 \\ \times\ 40 \\ \hline \square,\square\square 0 \end{array}$$

7. 32 × 20

8. 82 × 80

9. 60 × 14

10. 50 × 52

11. Reasoning How many fossil kits with 10 samples each have the same number of fossils as 30 fossil kits with 8 samples each?

12. Write 975,204 in expanded form.

13. Julie scored 10 baskets each game throughout the 11 game season. If each basket is worth 2 points, how many points did Julie make?

14. It costs $20 for admission to the zoo. If a family of 12 wants to go to the zoo, what would it cost?

15. Math and Science School buses use diesel fuel, which is an efficient and clean form of petroleum. One school has 60 buses. Each school bus carries 34 students. If all of the school buses are full, how many students are on the school buses?

16. Higher Order Thinking Explain how you can solve 40×16 by breaking apart the factors.

Assessment ISTEP+ Ready

17. There are 12 boxes of books to put on shelves. Each box has 31 books. Each shelf holds 18 books. Kevin estimates he will need 20 shelves for all the books.

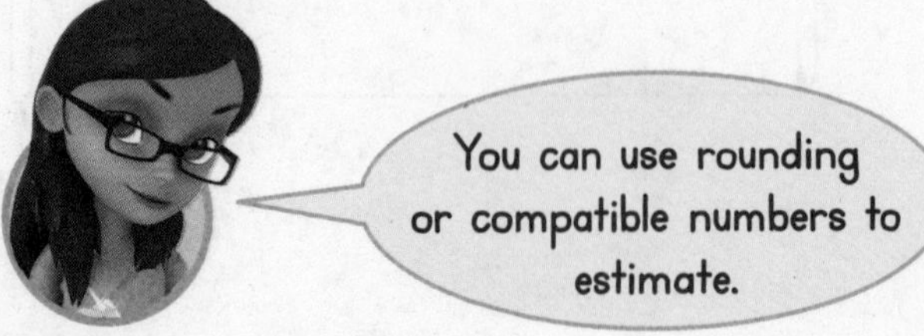

You can use rounding or compatible numbers to estimate.

Part A

Estimate the total number of books.

Part B

Write to explain if you agree with Kevin's estimate for 20 shelves.

Name ______________________________________

Lesson 4-9
Multiply 2-Digit by 2-Digit Numbers

I can ...
use area models, place-value strategies, and properties of operations to help multiply 2-digit by 2-digit numbers.

Content Standard 4.C.2
Process Standards PS.1, PS.3, PS.4, PS.7

Solve & Share

Ms. Silva has 12 weeks to train for a race. Over the course of one week, she plans to run 15 miles. If she continues this training, how many miles will Ms. Silva run before the race? ***Solve this problem using any strategy you choose.***

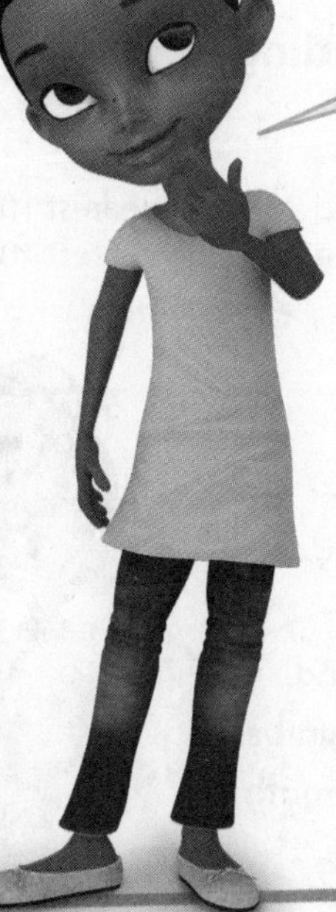

You can use partial products to help make sense of the problem and persevere in solving it. *Show your work in the space below!*

Look Back! **Critique Reasoning** Dwayne estimated 60 miles as an answer to the above problem. Is this estimate reasonable? If not, what mistake do you think Dwayne made?

What Is a Common Way to Record Multiplication?

A

A ferry carried 37 cars per trip on the weekend. If the ferry made 11 trips on Saturday and 13 trips on Sunday, how many cars did it carry on the weekend?

11 trips on Saturday
+ 13 trips on Sunday
24 trips on the weekend

You can add to find 24 trips were made on Saturday and Sunday.

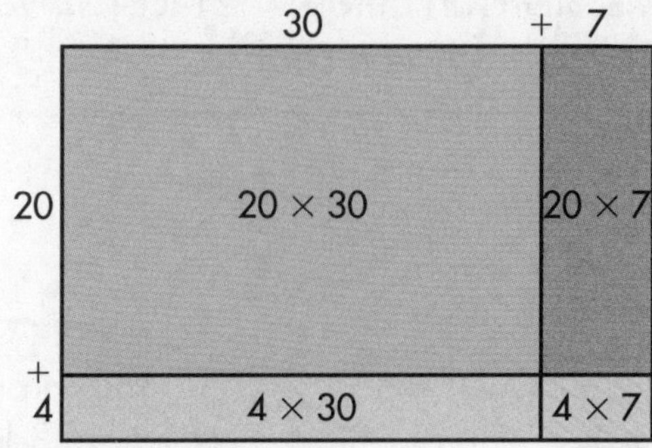

B

Use Partial Products

Use the area model to find the partial products for 24 × 37.

$$\begin{array}{r} 37 \\ \times\ 24 \\ \hline 28 \\ 120 \\ 140 \\ +\ 600 \\ \hline 888 \end{array}$$

The ferry carried 888 cars on the weekend.

C

Use an Algorithm

$$\begin{array}{r} \overset{2}{37} \\ \times\ 24 \\ \hline 148 \end{array}$$ Multiply by 4 ones.

$$\begin{array}{r} \overset{1}{\overset{2}{37}} \\ \times\ \ 24 \\ \hline 148 \\ +\ 740 \\ \hline 888 \end{array}$$ Multiply by 2 tens. Add the partial products.

The ferry carried 888 cars on the weekend.

D

Use Rounding to Check

$$\begin{array}{r} 40 \\ \times\ 20 \\ \hline 800 \end{array}$$

Round 37 to the nearest 10.
Round 24 to the nearest 10.

800 is close to 888. The answer is reasonable.

You can round, use compatible numbers, or use mental math to estimate.

Convince Me! **Look for Relationships** Nannette said, "The algorithm above broke 24 × 37 into two simpler problems."

$$\begin{array}{r} 37 \\ \times\ 20 \\ \hline \end{array} \qquad \begin{array}{r} 37 \\ \times\ \ 4 \\ \hline \end{array}$$

Is Nannette correct? What are the products for the simpler problems? What is the product for 24 × 37?

Name

Guided Practice*

Do You Understand?

1. **Make Sense and Persevere** The ferry made 18 one-way trips on Monday and 18 one-way trips on Tuesday. It carried 21 cars on each trip. How many cars were ferried on Monday and Tuesday? Use estimation and mental math to check if your answer is reasonable.

Do You Know How?

For **2**, use an algorithm or partial products to find the product. Estimate to check if your answer is reasonable.

2.
```
   4 1
×  2 3
   1 2 □
+ □ 2 0
   9 □ □
```

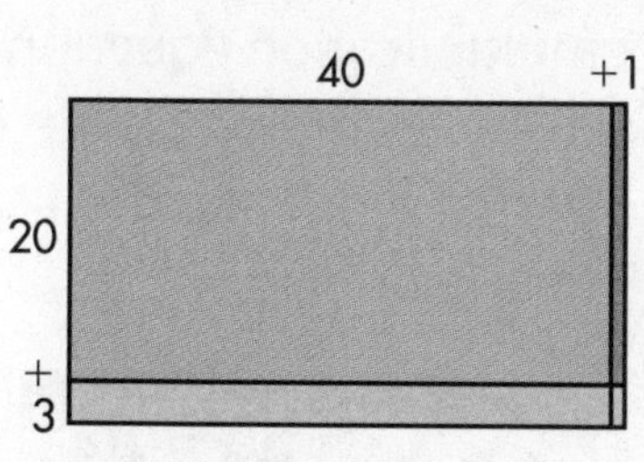

Independent Practice

Leveled Practice For **3–16**, use an algorithm or partial products to find the product. Draw area models as needed.

3.
```
    1 6
×   2 2
    □ 2
+ □ □ 0
  □ □ □
```

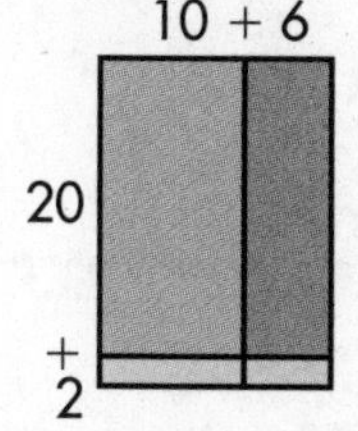

4.
```
    1 5
×   1 6
    □ □
+ □ □ □
  □ □ □
```

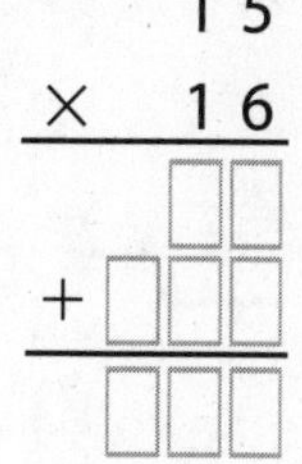

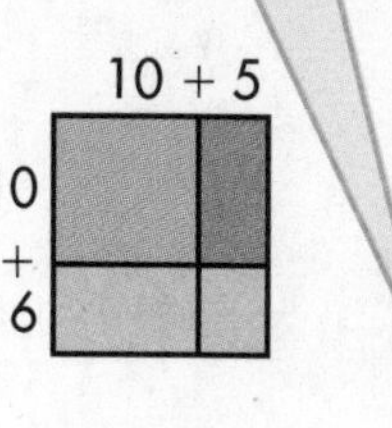

Use estimation to check if your answers are reasonable.

5. 27 × 12
6. 36 × 23
7. 18 × 42
8. 34 × 21
9. 53 × 17
10. 81 × 46
11. 15 × 16
12. 17 × 21
13. 12 × 22
14. 38 × 41
15. 42 × 52
16. 38 × 19

*For another example, see Set I on page 242.

Problem Solving

17. **Number Sense** The *Queen Mary 2's* height above water is about the same as a 14-story bulding. What is the Queen Mary 2's height above water?

Each story is
12 feet tall.

18. **Model with Math** Write the multiplication equation illustrated by the array drawn on the grid. Find the partial products. Then calculate the final product.

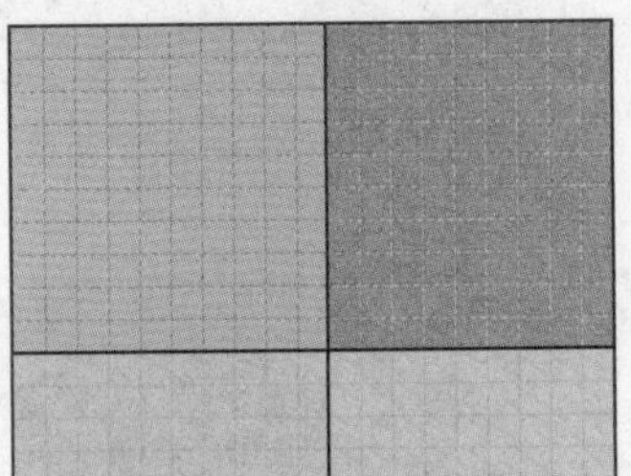

19. **Higher Order Thinking** An elevator can carry 15 adults or 20 children at one time. During the course of a day, the elevator carries a full passenger load 52 times. If all the passengers were children, how many more people would the elevator carry than if all the passengers were adults?

Assessment
ISTEP+ Ready

20. Ten years ago, Melissa planted a tree in her backyard. She has taken a photo of the tree every week so she can see how it has grown as time passed. How many photos of the tree does Melissa now have?

Ⓐ 62 photos
Ⓑ 120 photos
Ⓒ 520 photos
Ⓓ 620 photos

There are 52 weeks in one year.

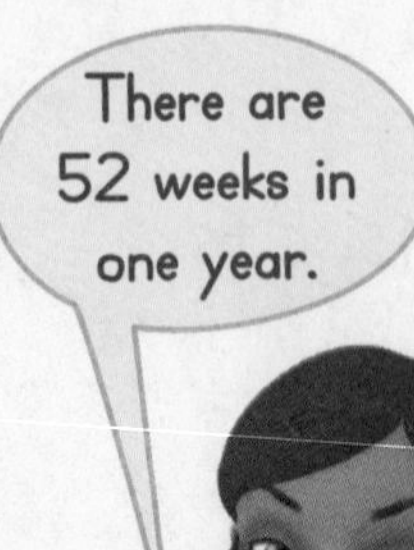

21. Mr. Morris bought sketchpads for 24 of his students. Each pad contained 50 sheets. How many sheets of paper were in all the pads?

Ⓐ 1,000 sheets
Ⓑ 1,200 sheets
Ⓒ 1,400 sheets
Ⓓ 1,600 sheets

Name ______________________

Help Practice Buddy Tools Games

Homework & Practice 4-9
Multiply 2-Digit by 2-Digit Numbers

Another Look!

There are 24 cars in the Speedy Cup Series. Each car has 13 workers in the pit area. How many pit-area workers are at the race?

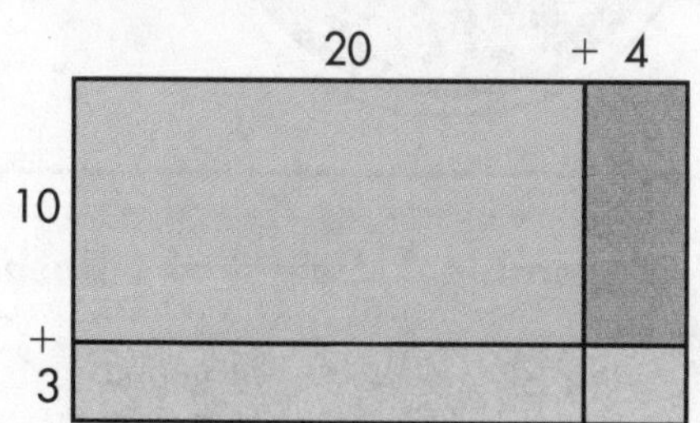

There is more than one way to multiply.

Use Partial Products

$$\begin{array}{r} 24 \\ \times\ 13 \\ \hline 12 \\ 60 \\ 40 \\ +\,200 \\ \hline 312 \end{array}$$

Use an Algorithm

Multiply by the ones. Regroup if necessary.

$$\begin{array}{r} \overset{1}{2}4 \\ \times\ 13 \\ \hline 72 \end{array}$$

Multiply by the tens. Regroup if necessary.

$$\begin{array}{r} \overset{1}{2}4 \\ \times\ 13 \\ \hline 72 \\ +\,240 \\ \hline 312 \end{array}$$

Add the partial products.

There are 312 pit-area workers at the race.

For **1–10**, use an algorithm or partial products to find the product. Draw area models as needed.

You can use rounding or compatible numbers to estimate and check if your answer is reasonable.

1. 18 × 26 = ☐☐☐ ; + ☐☐0 ; ☐☐☐

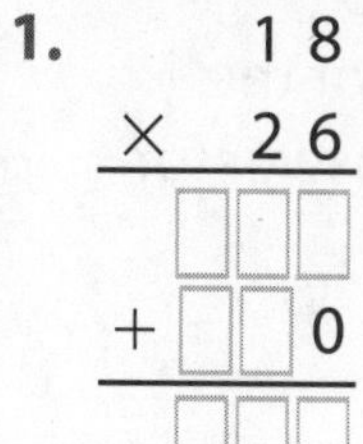

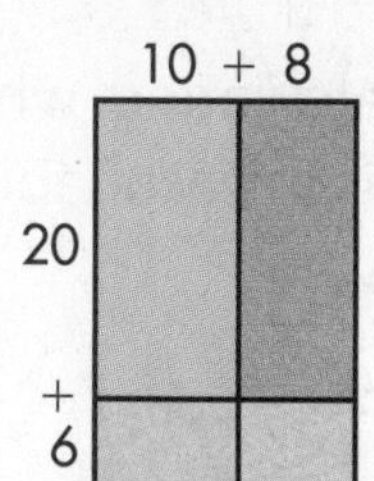

2. 17 × 25 = ☐☐ ; + ☐☐0 ; ☐☐☐

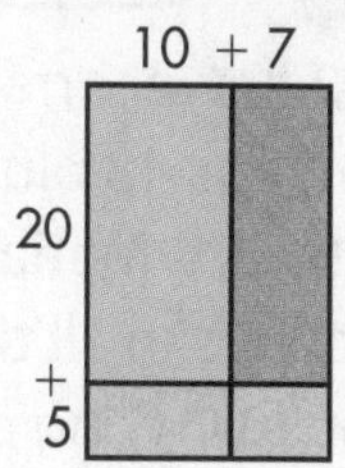

3. 88×32

4. 53×48

5. 18×77

6. 67×27

7. 67×34

8. 91×46

9. 56×31

10. 67×57

11. An ultralight airplane tracked monarch butterflies migrating to Mexico during the month of September. There are 30 days in September. How many miles did the ultralight travel in September?

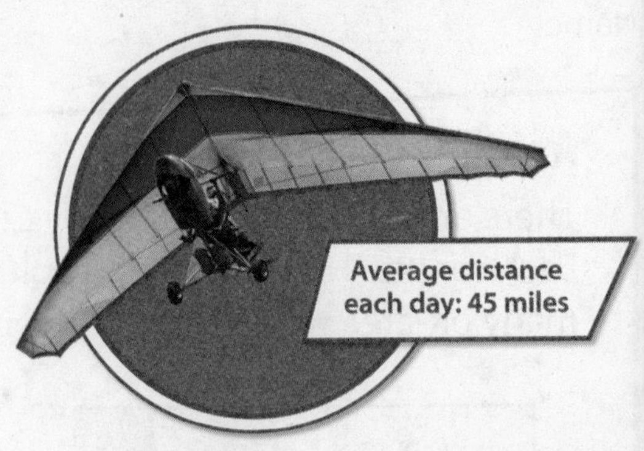

For **12–13**, use the table at the right.

12. How much do 21 bushels of sweet corn weigh?

13. How much do 18 bushels of asparagus and 7 bushels of carrots weigh?

DATA

Vegetable	Weight of 1 Bushel
Asparagus	24 pounds
Beets	52 pounds
Carrots	50 pounds
Sweet corn	35 pounds

14. Rob purchased a rug for his apartment. The rug is 72 inches by 96 inches. Calculate the area of the rug in square inches.

15. **Higher Order Thinking** Corina found $62 \times 22 = 1{,}042$. Is Corina's answer reasonable? Explain.

Assessment ISTEP+ Ready

16. Maria has 92 flower arrangements. Each arrangement has 48 blue flowers and 50 yellow flowers. Maria calculates there are 9,016 flowers in all the arrangements. Which of the following expressions shows how to use an estimate to check Maria's calculation?

Ⓐ $90 + 50 + 50$

Ⓑ 90×10

Ⓒ $90 \times (50 + 50)$

Ⓓ $90 \times (50 \times 50)$

17. Without calculating, which of the following is a reasonable answer for 28×32?

Ⓐ 196

Ⓑ 496

Ⓒ 896

Ⓓ 12,096

Name ______________________________

Lesson 4-10
Continue to Multiply by 2-Digit Numbers

I can ...
use area models and algorithms to multiply 2-digit by 2-digit numbers.

Content Standard 4.C.2
Process Standards PS.1, PS.6, PS.7, PS.8

Solve & Share The sports club at Carmel School bought 23 grandstand tickets. The sports club at Valley School bought 34 infield tickets. Which club paid more? How much more? ***Solve these problems using any strategy you choose.***

You can make sense of the problems and persevere in solving them. What operations do you need to solve the problem? *Show your work in the space below!*

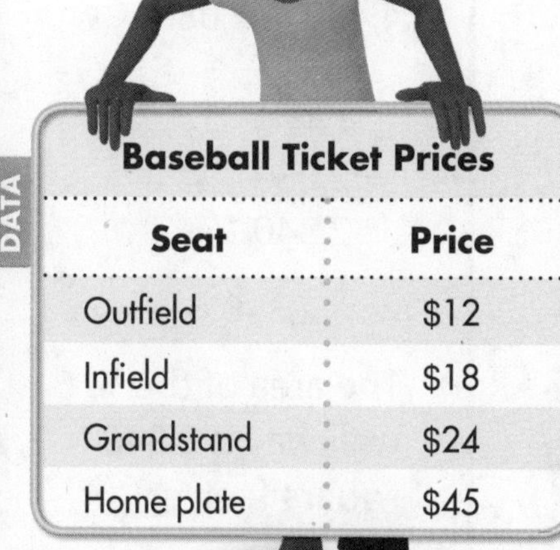

DATA

Baseball Ticket Prices

Seat	Price
Outfield	$12
Infield	$18
Grandstand	$24
Home plate	$45

Look Back! Generalize What general method could you use to estimate the products for these problems and check if your answers are reasonable?

How Can You Use Multiplication to Solve Problems?

A

The park has a large garden with a walkway around it. What is the area of the walkway?

You can multiply the length by the width to find the area of each rectangle.

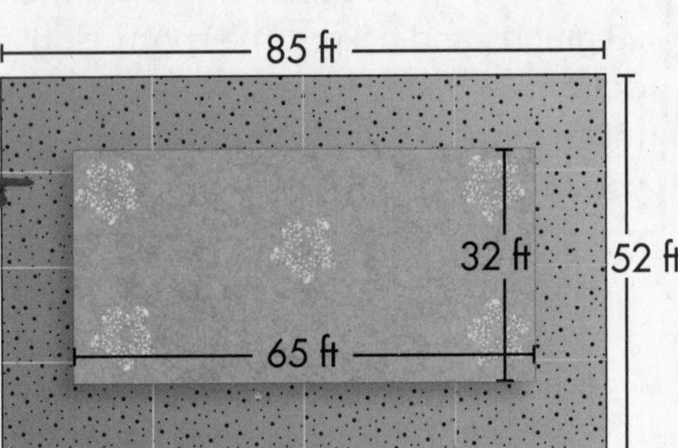

B Find the area of the park.

$52 \times 85 = p$

$$\begin{array}{r} \overset{2}{\overset{1}{8}}5 \\ \times \quad 52 \\ \hline 170 \\ + 4,250 \\ \hline 4,420 \end{array}$$

$p = 4,420$

The area of the park is 4,420 square feet.

C Find the area of the garden.

$32 \times 65 = g$

$$\begin{array}{r} \overset{1}{\overset{1}{6}}5 \\ \times \quad 32 \\ \hline 130 \\ + 1,950 \\ \hline 2,080 \end{array}$$

$g = 2,080$

The area of the garden is 2,080 square feet.

D Find the area of the walkway.

$4,420 - 2,080 = w$

$$\begin{array}{r} 4,\overset{3}{\cancel{4}}\overset{12}{\cancel{2}}0 \\ - 2,080 \\ \hline 2,340 \end{array}$$

$w = 2,340$

The area of the walkway is 2,340 square feet.

Convince Me! **Be Precise** Sally's work to find the area of the park is shown below. How is her work different than the work above? Is Sally's work correct? Explain. What is Sally missing from her answer?

$$\begin{array}{r} \overset{2}{\overset{1}{8}}5 \\ \times \quad 52 \\ \hline 170 \\ + 4,25 \\ \hline 4,420 \end{array}$$

Name ____________________

Practice Buddy | Tools | Assessment

Guided Practice*

Do You Understand?

1. What is the missing factor?

$$\begin{array}{r} 47 \\ \times \;\square\square \\ \hline 94 \\ +\;1,410 \\ \hline 1,504 \end{array}$$

2. **Look for Relationships** When you use the algorithm shown on the previous page to multiply two 2-digit numbers, why does the second partial product end in 0?

Do You Know How?

For **3–6**, find the products. Draw area models as needed.

3. $\begin{array}{r} 37 \\ \times \;83 \\ \hline \square\square\square \\ +\;\square,\square\square\square \\ \hline \square,\square\square\square \end{array}$

4. $\begin{array}{r} 62 \\ \times \;17 \\ \hline \square\square\square \\ +\;\square\square\square \\ \hline \square,\square\square\square \end{array}$

5. $\begin{array}{r} 43 \\ \times \;56 \\ \hline \end{array}$

6. $\begin{array}{r} 67 \\ \times \;39 \\ \hline \end{array}$

Independent Practice

For **7–21**, find each product.

You can draw arrays, area models, or use an algorithm to find the products.

7. $\begin{array}{r} 36 \\ \times \;29 \\ \hline \end{array}$

8. $\begin{array}{r} 84 \\ \times \;37 \\ \hline \end{array}$

9. $\begin{array}{r} 47 \\ \times \;46 \\ \hline \end{array}$

10. $\begin{array}{r} 71 \\ \times \;63 \\ \hline \end{array}$

11. $\begin{array}{r} 89 \\ \times \;52 \\ \hline \end{array}$

12. $\begin{array}{r} 25 \\ \times \;64 \\ \hline \end{array}$

13. $\begin{array}{r} 77 \\ \times \;33 \\ \hline \end{array}$

14. $\begin{array}{r} 92 \\ \times \;19 \\ \hline \end{array}$

15. $\begin{array}{r} 54 \\ \times \;64 \\ \hline \end{array}$

16. $\begin{array}{r} 75 \\ \times \;35 \\ \hline \end{array}$

17. 18×21

18. 12×17

19. 72×55

20. 67×14

21. 99×11

*For another example, see Set I on page 242.

Problem Solving

22. Fill in the missing digits to complete the calculation.

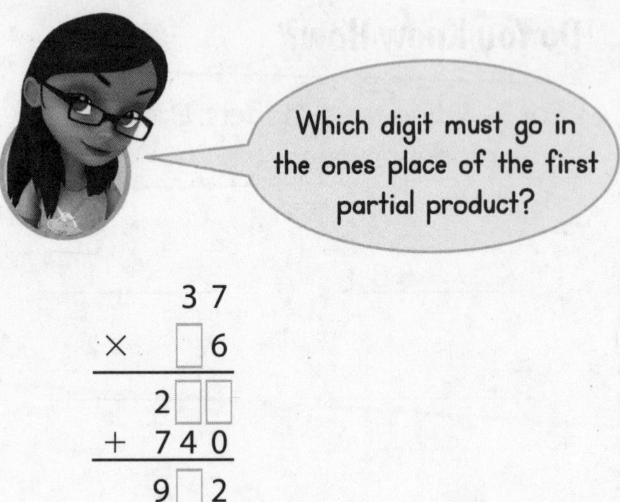

Which digit must go in the ones place of the first partial product?


```
    3 7
×   □ 6
-------
  2 □ □
+ 7 4 0
-------
  9 □ 2
```

23. One pine tree produced 78 pinecones with an average of 42 seeds in each pinecone. Another tree produced 72 pinecones with an average of 53 seeds in each pinecone. Estimate to find which pine tree produced more seeds. Multiply to check your estimate.

24. **Higher Order Thinking** A picture is 13 inches long and 17 inches wide. It is placed in a wood frame. What is the area of the frame?

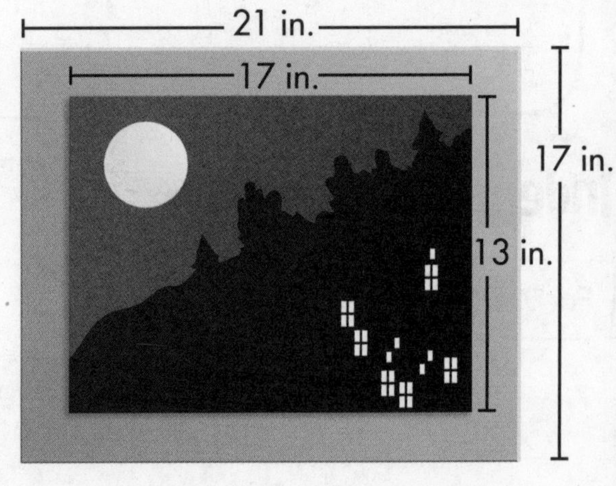

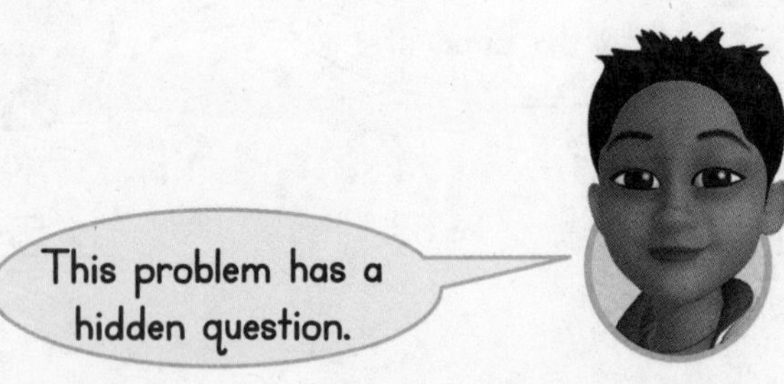

This problem has a hidden question.

25. An airport serves 14 different airlines. Each airline schedules 45 departing flights each day. How many flights depart from the airport in one day?

Ⓐ 205 flights
Ⓑ 550 flights
Ⓒ 610 flights
Ⓓ 630 flights

26. Patrick picks 18 apples from each of 24 trees. How many apples did Patrick pick?

Ⓐ 432 apples
Ⓑ 622 apples
Ⓒ 834 apples
Ⓓ 934 apples

Name ____________________

Homework & Practice 4-10

Continue to Multiply by 2-Digit Numbers

Another Look!

An office building is 27 stories tall. Each story has 42 windows that need to be washed. How many windows need to be washed?

Find 27 × 42.

```
    1
   42
 × 27
  294  ←— Multiply by 7 ones
+ 840  ←— Multiply by 2 tens
1,134  ←— Add the partial products
```

1,134 windows need to be washed.

The algorithm for multiplying by 2-digit numbers is an extension of the algorithm for multiplying by 1-digit numbers.
Remember to write a zero in the ones place when multiplying by the tens.

For **1–20**, find each product. Draw area models or use partial products as needed. Use estimation to check if your answer is reasonable.

1. 70 × 39

2. 58 × 90

3. 97 × 42

4. 64 × 88

5. 51 × 47

6. 62 × 69

7. 34 × 82

8. 98 × 23

9. 59 × 44

10. 13 × 31

11. 85 × 18

12. 36 × 29

13. 24 × 31

14. 62 × 48

15. 36 × 93

16. 41 × 11

17. 21 × 22

18. 59 × 78

19. 43 × 37

20. 90 × 24

21. Admission to a science museum is $22 for an adult. The cost for a child is $5 less than the cost for an adult. What would be the total cost of admission for 12 adults and 15 children? Explain.

Sometimes it takes more than one step to solve a problem.

22. **Number Sense** Bags of potatoes weigh 35 pounds each. Cases of onions weigh 19 pounds each. Estimate which weighs more: 23 bags of potatoes or 32 cases of onions?

23. **Algebra** An average person in the U.S. eats about 17 gallons of popcorn each year. How many gallons of popcorn does the average person eat in 12 years? Write and solve an equation.

24. **Higher Order Thinking** How is using partial products to find the product of two 2-digit factors similar to how you have used partial products in the past? How is it different? Explain.

25. A train is pulling 23 red cars and 36 blue cars. Each car has 32 boxes of freight. Which is the best estimate for the number of boxes on the train?

   Ⓐ 3,600 boxes
   Ⓑ 2,000 boxes
   Ⓒ 1,800 boxes
   Ⓓ 1,500 boxes

26. There are 13 bike racks at the park. Each bike rack holds 18 bicycles. There are 93 bikes in the racks already. How many more bikes can the bike racks hold? Which equation is correct?

   Ⓐ $(18 \times 93) - 13 = 121$ bikes
   Ⓑ $(13 \times 18) - 93 = 131$ bikes
   Ⓒ $(13 \times 18) - 93 = 141$ bikes
   Ⓓ $(13 \times 93) - 98 = 151$ bikes

Name ________________________________

Solve

Problem Solving

Lesson 4-11

Make Sense and Persevere

I can . . .

make sense of problems and keep working if I get stuck.

Process Standards PS.1 Also PS.2, PS.4, PS.6, PS.7
Content Standard 4.C.2

Solve & Share The table shows how far 5 students walked to raise money for charity. Sponsors donated $25 for each mile the students walked. How much money did the students raise? ***Solve this problem using any strategy you choose.***

DATA

Student	Miles Walked
Susan	3
Maxine	2
Charlie	2
Fillip	4
Rachael	3

Thinking Habits

Be a good thinker!
These questions can help you.

- What do I need to find?
- What do I know?
- What's my plan for solving the problem?
- What else can I try if I get stuck?
- How can I check that my solution makes sense?

Look Back! Make Sense and Persevere Is there more than one way to solve the problem? Explain.

Essential Question

How Can You Make Sense of and Persevere in Solving Problems with More Than One Step?

A

Maya and José were preparing for a bike race. Every day for 12 days, they rode their bicycles 15 miles in the morning and 22 miles in the afternoon. How far did they ride during the 12 days?

Rode the same distance 12 days in a row

What is a good plan for solving the problem?

Find the hidden question or questions to help solve the problem.

B

How can I make sense of and solve this problem?

I can

- identify the quantities given.
- understand how the quantities are related.
- choose and implement an appropriate strategy.
- check to be sure my work and answer make sense.

C

First, find how many miles Maya and José rode each day.

Here's my thinking.

They rode 37 miles each day.

m	
15	22

$m = 15 + 22$
$m = 37$ miles

Use the answer to the first question to determine how far they rode in 12 days.

d

37 → 12 days

$d = 12 \times 37$
$d = 444$ miles

They rode 444 miles in 12 days.

Convince Me! **Make Sense and Persevere** Can you solve the problem using a different strategy and still calculate the same answer? Explain.

What property lets you break apart a problem?

Name ________________________________

Practice Buddy Tools Assessment

Guided Practice*

Make Sense and Persevere

On her vacation, Julia filled 3 memory cards like the one shown. She printed 2 copies of each picture. How many pictures did Julia print?

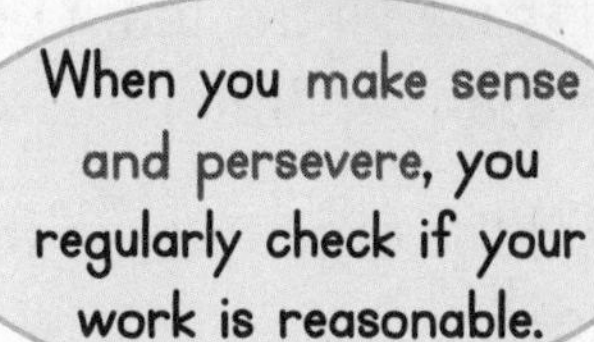

A memory card holds 28 pictures.

1. What do you know and what do you need to find?

When you make sense and persevere, you regularly check if your work is reasonable.

2. What steps might you take to solve the problem?

3. How many pictures did Julia print? Explain.

Independent Practice

Make Sense and Persevere

Jarrod delivers 63 newspapers each Monday through Saturday and 78 newspapers each Sunday. Last month consisted of 4 Sundays and 26 other days. How many newspapers did Jarrod deliver last month? Use Exercises 4–6 to solve this problem.

4. What strategies can you use to find how many newspapers Jarrod delivered last month?

5. How are the quantities related?

6. Explain how to solve the problem.

*For another example, see Set J on page 242.

Problem Solving

Performance Assessment — ISTEP+ Ready

Uniforms

The Stillwater Storm soccer team consists of 16 players. Each player needs a uniform set. The uniform set includes two jerseys, a pair of shorts, and a pair of socks. The price for each separate item is shown. Nine of the players need a medium size and the others need a small size. If the team buys more than 10 sets, the team price for each set is $56. How much money is saved if the team buys all the uniform sets together rather than separately?

DATA

Uniform Item	Price
Jersey	$23
Pair of Shorts	$17
Pair of Socks	$8

7. **Reasoning** What are the quantities in the problem and how are they related?

8. **Model with Math** Use the bar diagrams to write equations and find the total cost of the uniform sets when purchased separately or if 10 sets or more are purchased.

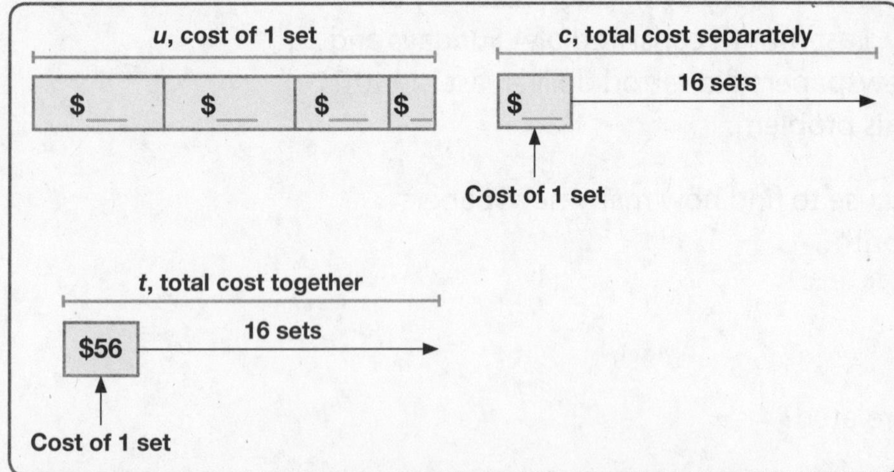

When you make sense and persevere, you think about the amounts given.

9. **Be Precise** What is the difference in cost if the team bought all the uniform sets together or if they bought them separately?

Name ______________________________

Homework & Practice 4-11

Make Sense and Persevere

Another Look!

April needs to arrange 18 baskets with each containing 15 silk plants. She needs 8 silk flowers on each plant. How many silk flowers will be in all the baskets?

Tell how you can make sense of the problem to solve.

When you make sense and persevere, you use objects, pictures, or diagrams to make sense of problems.

- I can identify the quantities given.
- I can understand how the quantities are related.
- I can choose and implement an appropriate strategy.

Find how many silk plants April needs.

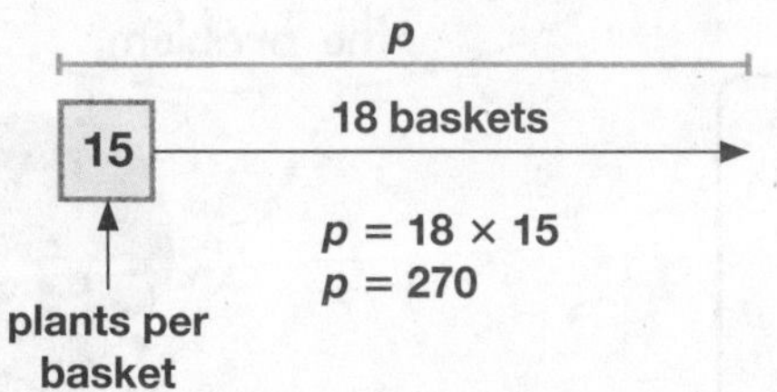

April needs 270 silk plants.

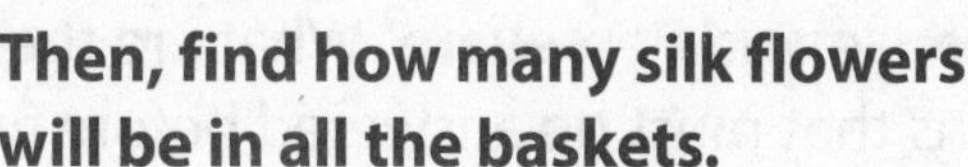

Then, find how many silk flowers will be in all the baskets.

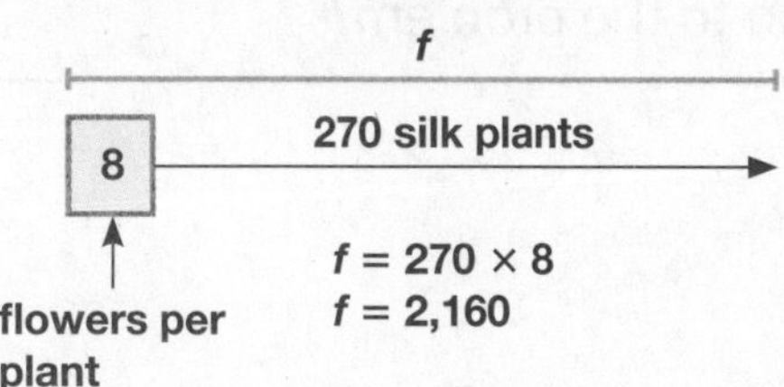

There will be 2,160 flowers in all the baskets.

Make Sense and Persevere

A store received a shipment of 4 boxes of peanuts. All four boxes were stacked on top of each other and measured 12 feet high. How many ounces of peanuts did the store receive? Use Exercises 1–4 to answer the question.

PEANUTS
Contents: 24 bags
12 oz in each bag

1. What do you know and what do you need to find?

2. What steps might you take to solve the problem?

3. Do you think the store got more or less than 800 ounces of peanuts? Justify your answer.

4. How many ounces of peanuts did the store receive? Explain.

Performance Assessment — ISTEP+ Ready

Cameras

A purchasing manager for an electronics store has a choice between two digital cameras. Information about each camera is shown below. How much money can the store make with Camera 1? The money a store makes is the difference in the price of what the store sells the camera for minus the price of what the store pays to buy the camera.

Camera 1
Store price: \$46
Selling price: \$85
Store can buy: 21

Camera 2
Store price: \$62
Selling price: \$98
Store can buy: 16

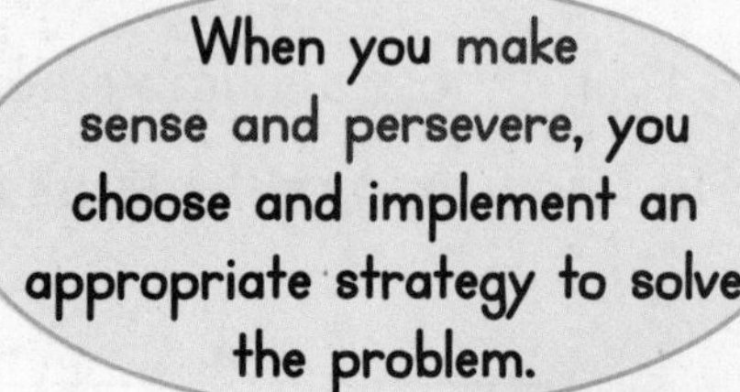
When you make sense and persevere, you choose and implement an appropriate strategy to solve the problem.

5. **Make Sense and Persevere** What are the hidden questions that must be answered before finding the solution to the problem?

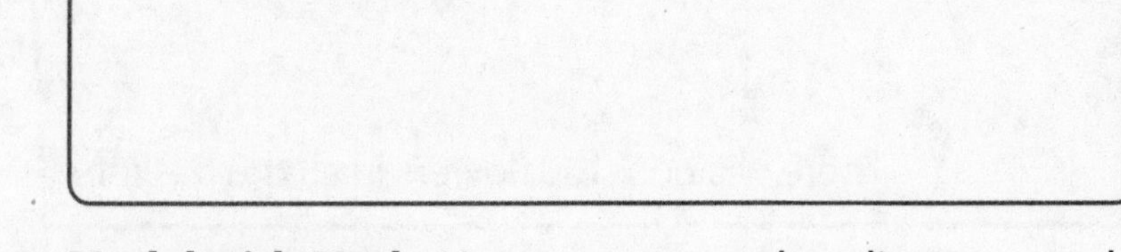

6. **Model with Math** How can you use bar diagrams and equations to represent and solve this problem?

7. **Look for Relationships** How can you tell that your answer makes sense? Explain.

Name ______________________________

Fluency Practice Activity

I can ...
add and subtract multi-digit whole numbers.

Work with a partner. Point to a clue. Read the clue.

Look below the clues to find a match. Write the clue letter in the box next to the match.

Find a match for every clue.

Clues

A The difference is between 950 and 1,000.

B The difference is exactly 913.

C The sum is between 600 and 700.

D The sum is exactly 500.

E The difference is between 700 and 800.

F The sum is greater than 300 but less than 400.

G The sum is exactly 753.

H The difference is exactly 413.

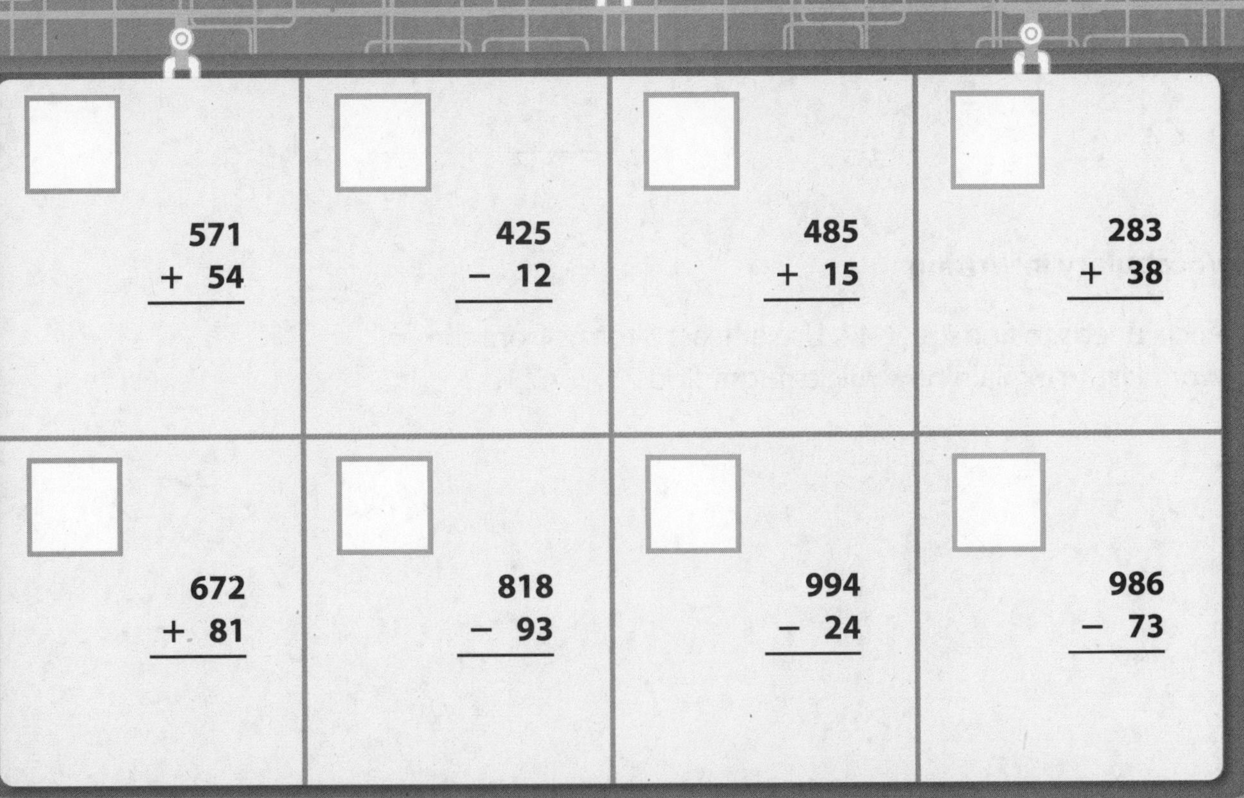

☐ 571 + 54	☐ 425 − 12	☐ 485 + 15	☐ 283 + 38
☐ 672 + 81	☐ 818 − 93	☐ 994 − 24	☐ 986 − 73

TOPIC 4 Vocabulary Review

Glossary

Word List

- array
- compatible numbers
- estimate
- factors
- partial product
- product
- rounding
- variable

Understand Vocabulary

1. Cross out the numbers that are **NOT** factors of 12.

1 3 5 6 8

2. Cross out the numbers that are **NOT** good estimates for 17×23.

600 400 300 200 100

3. Cross out the numbers that are **NOT** partial products for 12×41.

2 10 18 80 400

Label each example with a term from the Word List.

4.  ____________

5. n ____________

6. 2,318 to the nearest thousand is 2,000 ____________

7. $3 \times 4 = \underline{12}$ ____________

Use Vocabulary in Writing

8. Alicia needs to find 23×47. Use at least 3 terms from the Word List to explain how Alicia might find 23×47.

Name ______________________________

TOPIC 4

Reteaching

Set A pages 171–176

Use mental math to find 20 × 80.

Think about the pattern.

2 × 8 = 16

20 × 8 = 160

20 × 80 = 1,600

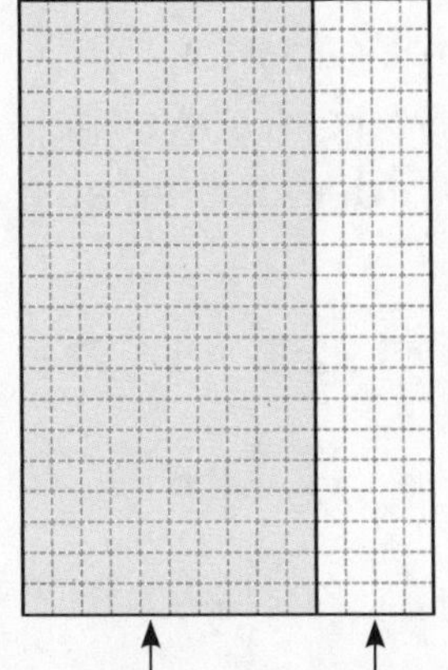

The number of zeros in the product is equal to the number of zeros in both factors.

Remember when the product of a basic fact has a zero, there is one more zero in the answer.

Use a pattern to find each product.

1. 40 × 10
2. 60 × 20
3. 80 × 50
4. 30 × 90
5. 80 × 70
6. 60 × 60
7. 80 × 30
8. 20 × 50

Set B pages 177–182

Use an array or an area model to multiply 20 × 14.

20 groups of 10 = 200
20 groups of 4 = 80

200 + 80 = 280

So, 20 × 14 = 280

Remember you can draw arrays or area models to represent multiplication problems.

Draw a model to find each product.

1. 10 × 23
2. 16 × 20
3. 10 × 17
4. 18 × 30

Set C pages 183–188

Use rounding to estimate 24×16.

Round each number to the nearest ten.

24 rounds to 20.
16 rounds to 20.

$20 \times 20 = 400$

So, 24×16 is about 400.

Remember the digit to the right of the rounding place determines how to round.

Estimate each product.

1. 27×21
2. 64×16
3. 53×32
4. 44×51
5. 35×42
6. 71×24

Set D pages 189–194

Use compatible numbers to estimate 28×19.

28 is close to 25.
19 is close to 20.

If $25 \times 2 = 50$, then
$25 \times 20 = 500$.

So, 28×19 is about 500.

Remember that compatible numbers are numbers that are easy to compute with mentally.

Estimate each product.

1. 29×31
2. 42×49
3. 73×18
4. 24×38
5. 19×31
6. 63×87

Set E pages 195–200

Find 14×12. Draw a 14×12 array.

Separate each factor into tens and ones. Color each section a different color. Add each part to find the product.

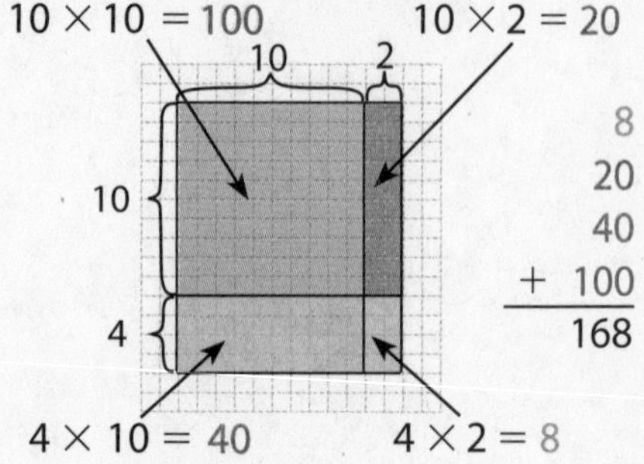

Remember when you break apart a multiplication problem, you can solve the simpler problems in any order and the answer will remain the same.

1. 14×32
2. 64×12
3. 56×17
4. 72×15
5. 26×63
6. 47×27
7. 19×51
8. 12×56
9. 76×23
10. 84×37
11. 14×72
12. 21×51

Name ______________________________

TOPIC 4

Reteaching
Continued

Set F pages 201–206

Use the Distributive Property to find 13 × 55.

13 × 55
= (10 + 3) × (50 + 5)
= (10 + 3) × 50 + (10 + 3) × 5
= (10 × 50) + (3 × 50) + (10 × 5) + (3 × 5)
= 500 + 150 + 50 + 15
= 715

Remember you can break numbers apart in more than one way when using the Distributive Property to solve multiplication problems.

1. 12 × 19
2. 38 × 12
3. 19 × 25
4. 45 × 23
5. 62 × 11
6. 46 × 26

Set G pages 207–212

Find 16 × 35. List the partial products.

Multiply the ones:

```
   16
 × 35
   30 ←——— 5 × 6
   50 ←——— 5 × 10
```

Multiply the tens:

```
   16
 × 35
   30
   50
  180 ←——— 30 × 6
+ 300 ←——— 30 × 10
```

Add: 30 + 50 + 180 + 300 = 560

Remember that to multiply two 2-digit factors, you can find four partial products.

1. 18 × 34
2. 51 × 15
3. 53 × 17
4. 26 × 28
5. 22 × 66
6. 41 × 54
7. 64 × 86
8. 32 × 71
9. 93 × 44
10. 57 × 91

Set H pages 213–218

Find 16 × 30.
Multiply 16 × 3 tens.

```
   1
   16
 × 30
  480
```

The 0 in the ones place shows the product is a multiple of 10.

Remember to check that your answer has a 0 in the ones place.

1. 39 × 10
2. 56 × 30
3. 41 × 20
4. 60 × 30

Set I pages 219–230

Use an algorithm to find 14 × 19.

Multiply the ones. Regroup if necessary.

$$\begin{array}{r} \overset{3}{1}9 \\ \times\ 14 \\ \hline 76 \end{array}$$

Multiply the tens. Regroup if necessary.

$$\begin{array}{r} 19 \\ \times\ 14 \\ \hline 76 \\ +\ 190 \\ \hline 266 \end{array}$$

Add the partial products.

Estimate to check.

$$\begin{array}{r} 20 \\ \times\ 10 \\ \hline 200 \end{array}$$

Round 19 to the nearest 10.
Round 14 to the nearest 10.

200 is close to 266.
The answer is reasonable.

Remember to estimate to check if your answer is reasonable.

1. $\begin{array}{r} 53 \\ \times\ 36 \\ \hline \end{array}$
2. $\begin{array}{r} 23 \\ \times\ 18 \\ \hline \end{array}$
3. $\begin{array}{r} 73 \\ \times\ 33 \\ \hline \end{array}$
4. $\begin{array}{r} 23 \\ \times\ 12 \\ \hline \end{array}$
5. $\begin{array}{r} 76 \\ \times\ 19 \\ \hline \end{array}$
6. $\begin{array}{r} 91 \\ \times\ 56 \\ \hline \end{array}$
7. $\begin{array}{r} 43 \\ \times\ 94 \\ \hline \end{array}$
8. $\begin{array}{r} 77 \\ \times\ 11 \\ \hline \end{array}$
9. $\begin{array}{r} 93 \\ \times\ 36 \\ \hline \end{array}$

Set J pages 231–236

Think about these questions to help you **make sense and persevere** in solving problems.

Thinking Habits

- What do I need to find?
- What do I know?
- What's my plan for solving the problem?
- What else can I try if I get stuck?
- How can I check that my solution makes sense?

Remember to use the information given to solve the problem.

Rose visited 14 cities on her vacation. She bought 8 souvenirs in each city to send to her friends. Rose paid $2 in postage for each souvenir she sent.

1. What hidden question do you need to answer to find how much it cost Rose to send all of the souvenirs?

2. What strategies can you use to find how much Rose spent?

3. How much did Rose spend?

Name ______________________________

TOPIC 4

Assessment

ISTEP+ Ready

1. Don works 18 hours a week. Which expression shows a good way to use rounding to estimate how many hours Don will work in 52 weeks?

Ⓐ 10 × 50

Ⓑ 10 × 60

Ⓒ 20 × 50

Ⓓ 18 × 60

2. There are 24 cheer teams competing in a contest. There are 18 cheerleaders on each team. Select all the expressions that are **NOT** good ways to use compatible numbers to estimate the number of cheerleaders competing.

☐ 20 × 20

☐ 25 × 18

☐ 18 × 24

☐ 10 × 10

☐ 20 × 15

3. There are 21 rows of seats. Each row has 42 seats. Use rounding to estimate the total number of seats.

4. A movie theater sells 50 tickets for each showing of a movie. The theater showed the movie 40 times. How many tickets did the theater sell?

Ⓐ 20,000 tickets

Ⓑ 2,000 tickets

Ⓒ 200 tickets

Ⓓ 20 tickets

5. Margo hiked 12 miles 13 times last month. She hiked 14 miles 12 times this month.

Part A

Draw arrays or area models to find the number of miles Margo hiked during the past two months.

Part B

Write and solve equations to represent your arrays or area models.

6. Elaine is making 20 pinecone wreaths to sell at a fair. She needs 13 pinecones for each wreath. How many pinecones does Elaine need in all?

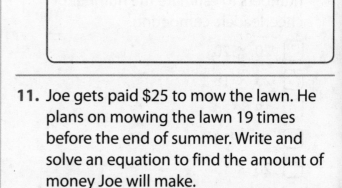

7. Mr. Hans bought tiles for his tile business. Each box of tiles costs \$30. Draw lines to match the number of boxes with the total cost.

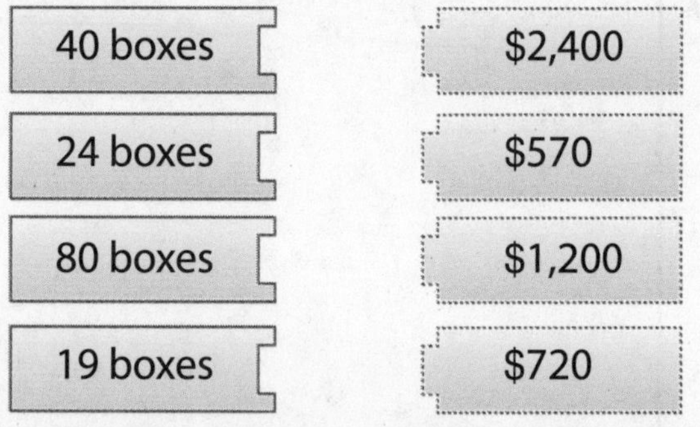

8. A florist makes centerpieces. He puts 18 roses in each centerpiece. Which is the best way to use compatible numbers to estimate the number of roses the florist needs for 24 centerpieces?

Ⓐ $10 \times 25 = 250$
Ⓑ $20 \times 25 = 500$
Ⓒ $25 \times 30 = 750$
Ⓓ $30 \times 30 = 900$

9. Elizabeth makes necklaces. Each necklace has 16 beads. Write each number from the box in the correct space in the table to show the number of beads needed for each number of necklaces.

50
90
160
480
1,440

Number of Necklaces	Number of Beads
10	
30	
	800

10. Justine's plant shop has 12 shelves. Each shelf holds 18 plants. Use properties of operations to find the number of plants the shelves can hold. Use rounding to check if your answer is reasonable.

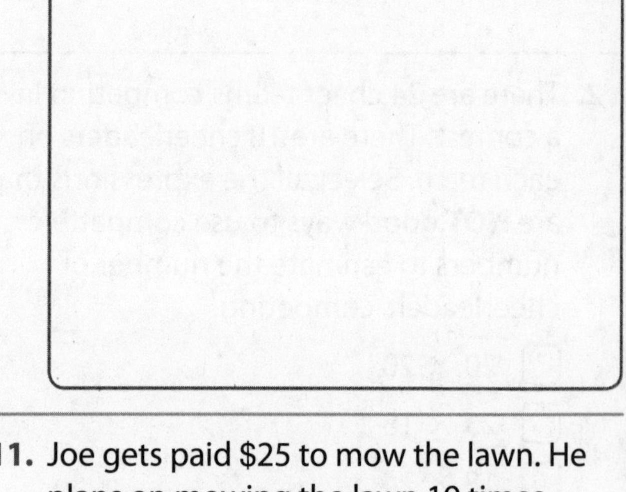

11. Joe gets paid \$25 to mow the lawn. He plans on mowing the lawn 19 times before the end of summer. Write and solve an equation to find the amount of money Joe will make.

12. When the Discount Tire Store sells a new tire, the profit is \$15. Which expression would you use to find the profit the store receives if they sell 60 new tires in one day?

Ⓐ 15×15
Ⓑ 60×60
Ⓒ 60×1
Ⓓ 60×15

Name ____

13. Tess has 15 pages in her coin collector's album. Each page holds 32 coins. Tess wants to find how many coins will fit in her entire album. Which partial product is missing from Tess's work?

Ⓐ 15

Ⓑ 150

Ⓒ 315

Ⓓ 480

$$\begin{array}{r} 32 \\ \times\ 15 \\ \hline 10 \\ \square \\ 20 \\ +\ 300 \\ \hline 480 \end{array}$$

14. Jonah bought 25 postcards that cost 17 cents each. He used partial products to find the total cost in cents. Which are **NOT** possible partial products for 25 × 17?

- ☐ 35
- ☐ 50
- ☐ 60
- ☐ 140
- ☐ 170

15. Lorin drew an area model to find 19 × 15. Write the partial product for each rectangle in the area model.

	10	5
10	A	B
9	C	D

A ☐

B ☐

C ☐

D ☐

16. The librarian ordered 29 sets of bookmarks. Each set contained 20 bookmarks. How many bookmarks did the librarian order?

☐

17. Large tables in the library have 18 chairs and small tables have 12 chairs.

Part A

Draw an array or an area model to find how many chairs are at 15 large tables.

☐

Part B

Use place-value strategies or properties of operations to find how many chairs are at 19 small tables. Use rounding to check if your answer is reasonable.

☐

18. LuAnn is practicing for her school's math Olympiad. Which expression shows one way LuAnn can use partial products to find 60×78?

Ⓐ $(60 \times 70) + (60 \times 8)$

Ⓑ $(60 \times 70) + (60 \times 78)$

Ⓒ $(60 \times 70) + (60 \times 80)$

Ⓓ $(6 \times 70) + (6 \times 8)$

19. Jack's landscape service charges \$78 to plant a tree. What is the total cost to plant 18 trees on Tuesday and 23 trees on Wednesday? Write and solve equations.

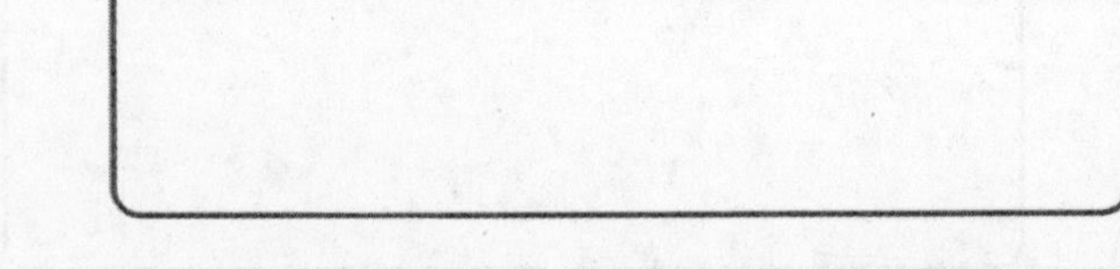

20. A school bought 28 new microscopes. The price for each microscope was \$87. What was the cost for all the microscopes? Use each number from the box once to complete and solve the equation.

```
       28
  ×    87
  -------
       56
     1 4□
     6□0
 + □,6 0 0
  -------
 $ □,4□□
```

0	1
2	3
4	6

21. Tori's goal is to learn 15 new Spanish words each day. If Tori meets her goal, how many new Spanish words will she have learned after 40 days?

22. Philip earns \$11 an hour. He recorded the number of hours he worked over a one-month period.

DATA

Philip's Hours

Week	Number of Hours Worked
Week A	15
Week B	24
Week C	22
Week D	18

Use compatible numbers to estimate how much Philip earned during the one-month period.

Name ____________________

TOPIC 4

Performance Assessment

ISTEP+ Ready

Raising Money

The fourth-grade students at Skyline School sold candles to raise money. The money raised will be used to buy toys for children who live in a group home. The **Candle Fundraiser** table shows how many candles each class sold.

Bee-hive candles sell for $20 each. The class raised $12 for each candle sold.

Soy bean candles sell for $22 each. The class raised $14 for each candle sold.

DATA

Candle Fundraiser

Teacher	Number Sold	Amount Raised for Each
Mr. Li	32	$12
Ms. Schmidt	25	$14
Ms. Picard	18	$14
Ms. Goldwasser	47	$12

1. About how much money did the fourth-grade students raise? Explain.

2. The school secretary needs to know exactly how much money was raised.

Part A

How much money did Ms. Schmidt's class raise? Use an area model and partial products to find the product.

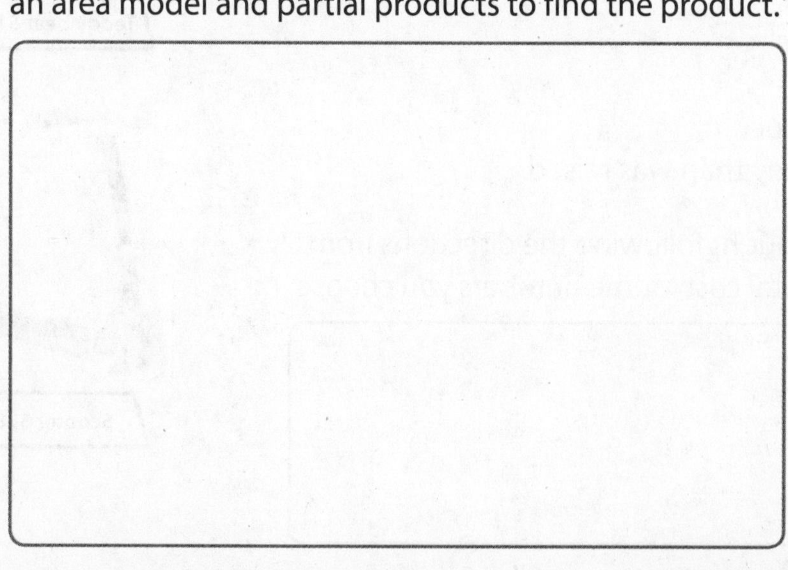

Part B

How much money did Ms. Picard's class raise? Use the Distributive Property to find the product.

Part C

How much money did the fourth-grade students raise? Explain.

Part D

Is the total amount of money raised from Part C reasonable based on the estimate you found in Exercise 1? Explain.

The fourth grade students at Skyline School decide to buy the toys shown.

Buying Toys

- They buy 68 toys in all.
- They buy at least 25 of each type.
- They cannot spend more money than was raised.

Teddy bear $17

Scooter $28

3. How many of each toy can be bought following the directions from the **Buying Toys** list? Find the total cost for the numbers you choose.

Use Strategies and Properties to Divide by 1-Digit Numbers

Essential Questions: How can mental math be used to divide? How can quotients be estimated? How can the steps for dividing be explained?

Musical instruments make sounds when motion that causes vibrations creates sound waves.

This piano uses a series of keys and hammers to strike the strings, which play different notes depending on their length.

Instruments use energy to make sounds in all different ways! Here is a project about music and division.

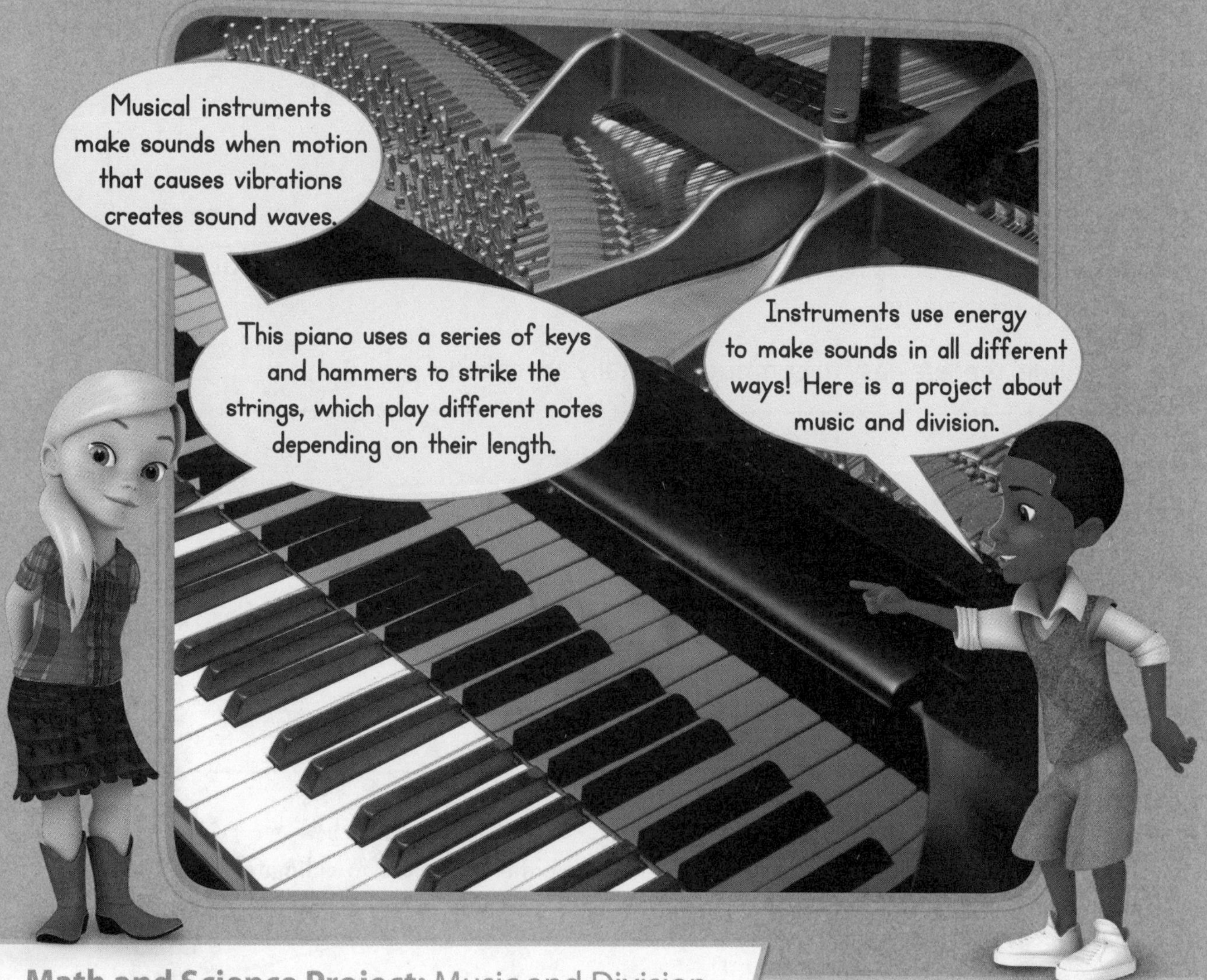

Math and Science Project: Music and Division

Do Research: Use the Internet or other resources to find an example of a woodwind instrument, a brass instrument, a stringed instrument, and a percussion instrument.

Journal: Write a Report Include what you found. Also in your report:

- Explain how each instrument you researched uses energy to make sounds. Include information about how the sounds are produced.
- Most instruments produce notes across ranges called octaves, which are made up of 8 notes. How many octaves do 51 notes span? Explain how you used division to calculate the answer.

Name ______________________

Review What You Know

Vocabulary

Choose the best term from the box. Write it on the blank.

- compatible numbers
- divisible
- division
- equation
- round
- variable

1. A(n) __________ uses the equal sign (=) to show two expressions have the same value.

2. One way to estimate a product is to __________ each factor.

3. A number is __________ by another number if it can be divided without leaving a remainder.

4. Numbers that are easy to compute mentally are called __________.

Division Facts

Find each quotient.

5. 27 ÷ 9
6. 30 ÷ 5
7. 32 ÷ 4
8. 54 ÷ 9
9. 28 ÷ 7
10. 72 ÷ 9
11. 56 ÷ 8
12. 18 ÷ 3
13. 15 ÷ 5

Rounding

Round each number to the nearest hundred.

14. 864
15. 651
16. 348
17. 985
18. 451
19. 749

You will round or use compatible numbers to estimate quotients in this topic.

Division as Sharing

20. **Make Sense and Persevere** Julio has 47 marbles. He keeps his two favorite marbles, then equally shares the remaining marbles between 5 friends. How many marbles does each friend receive? Explain.

My Word Cards

Use the examples for each word on the front of the card to help complete the definitions on the back.

A-Z Glossary

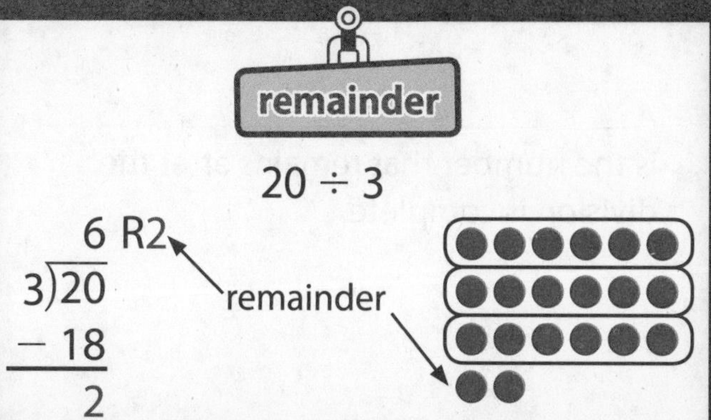

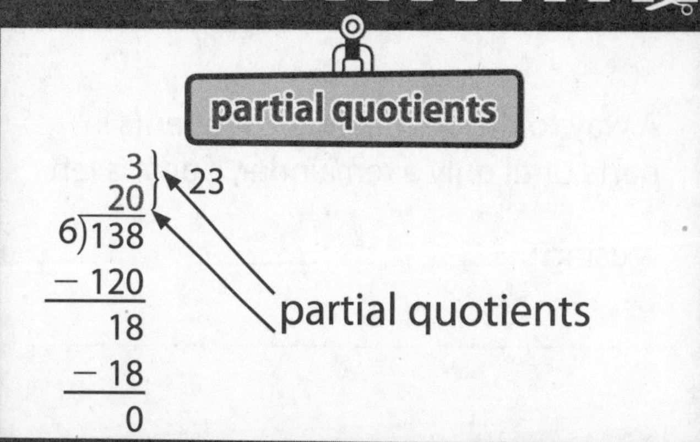

My Word Cards

Complete each definition. Extend learning by writing your own definitions.

A way to divide that finds quotients in parts until only a remainder, if any, is left

is using ____________________

____________________.

A ____________________ is the number that remains after the division is complete.

Name ______________________________

Lesson 5-1

Mental Math: Find Quotients

I can ...
make sense of quantities and use mental math and place-value strategies to divide.

Content Standard 4.C.3
Process Standards PS.2, PS.3, PS.4, PS.7

Solve & Share

José has 270 hockey cards to arrange equally in 9 boxes. Each box can hold the same number of cards. How many cards should José place in each box? ***Solve this problem using any strategy you choose.***

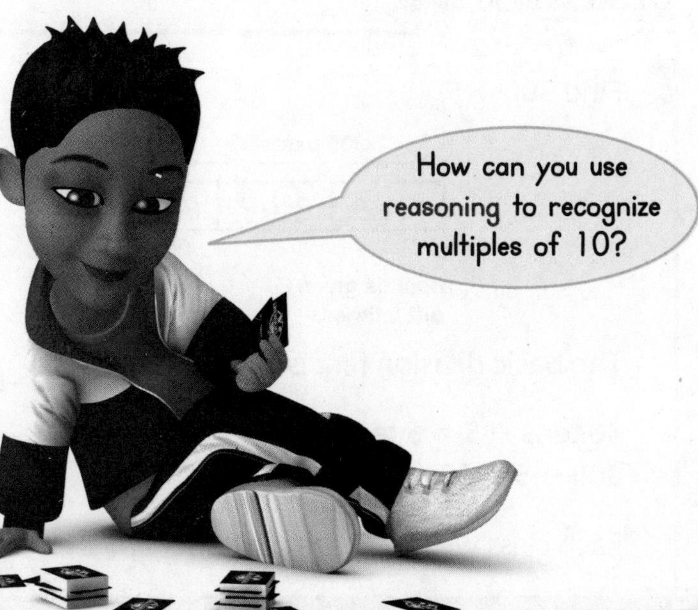

How can you use reasoning to recognize multiples of 10?

Look Back! Reasoning What multiplication equation could help you find the number of cards José should place in each box?

Learn Glossary

How Can You Divide Mentally?

Essential Question

A

Mr. Díaz ordered a supply of 1,800 pastels. He wants to divide them equally among his class and 5 other art classes. How many pastels does each class receive?

If Mr. Diaz stores the pastels so each class will receive new pastels 5 times a year, how many pastels are handed out each of the 5 times?

1,800 pastels

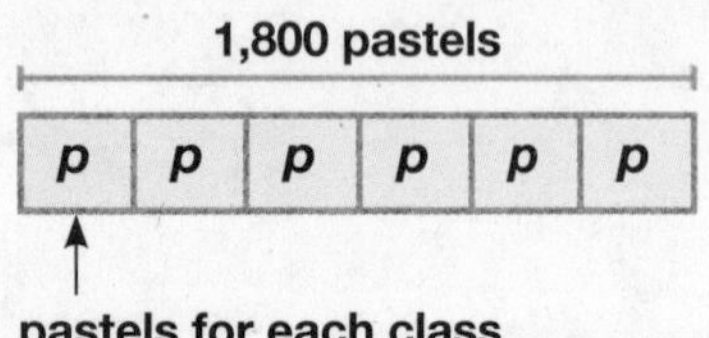

Division is used to find equal groups. Dividend ÷ Divisor = Quotient

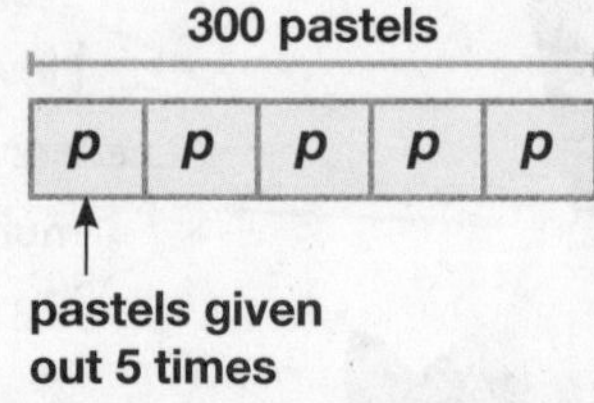

You can use basic division facts and place value to divide.

B Find $1{,}800 \div 6$.

1,800 pastels

p	p	p	p	p	p

↑ pastels for each class

The basic division fact is $18 \div 6 = 3$.

18 hundreds $\div 6 = 3$ hundreds or 300.
$1{,}800 \div 6 = 300$

Each class will receive 300 pastels.

C Find $300 \div 5$.

300 pastels

p	p	p	p	p

↑ pastels given out 5 times

The basic division fact is $30 \div 5 = 6$.

30 tens $\div 5 = 6$ tens or 60.
$300 \div 5 = 60$

Each class will receive 60 pastels 5 times a year.

Convince Me! **Use Structure** Write the missing dividends for each of the following equations. How did you determine each dividend?

_____ $\div 7 = 70$ _____ $\div 8 = 50$ _____ $\div 4 = 800$

Name ______

Practice Buddy | Tools | Assessment

Guided Practice*

Do You Understand?

1. **Reasoning** Explain how 32 ÷ 4 can help you solve 320 ÷ 4.

2. Mrs. Gall orders 240 folders and divides them equally among 3 classes. How many folders does each class receive? What basic fact did you use?

Do You Know How?

For **3–4**, use basic facts and patterns to find each quotient.

3. 28 ÷ 7 = ______
   280 ÷ 7 = ______
   2,800 ÷ 7 = ______

4. 64 ÷ 8 = ______
   640 ÷ 8 = ______
   6,400 ÷ 8 = ______

Independent Practice

Leveled Practice For **5–24**, use basic facts, patterns, or mental math to divide.

5. 36 ÷ 9 = ______
   360 ÷ 9 = ______
   3,600 ÷ 9 = ______

6. 10 ÷ 2 = ______
   100 ÷ 2 = ______
   1,000 ÷ 2 = ______

7. 45 ÷ 5 = ______
   450 ÷ 5 = ______
   4,500 ÷ 5 = ______

8. 24 ÷ 8 = ______
   240 ÷ 8 = ______
   2,400 ÷ 8 = ______

9. 2,000 ÷ 5

10. 360 ÷ 4

11. 540 ÷ 9

12. 160 ÷ 4

13. 900 ÷ 3

14. 3,200 ÷ 8

15. 360 ÷ 6

16. 1,800 ÷ 3

17. 7,200 ÷ 8

18. 500 ÷ 5

19. 350 ÷ 7

20. 6,300 ÷ 9

21. 1,600 ÷ 2

22. 210 ÷ 7

23. 4,800 ÷ 6

24. 600 ÷ 6

*For another example, see Set A on page 315.

Problem Solving

25. **Use Structure** If you know $20 \div 5 = 4$, how does that help you calculate $200 \div 5$?

26. A bakery produced two batches of bread with 80 loaves in each batch. It sold 30 loaves each hour. How many loaves of bread were sold in 4 hours? How many loaves of bread were left to sell?

27. At the North American Solar Challenge, teams use up to 1,000 solar cells to design and build solar cars for a race. If there are 810 solar cells arranged in 9 rows, how many solar cells are in each row?

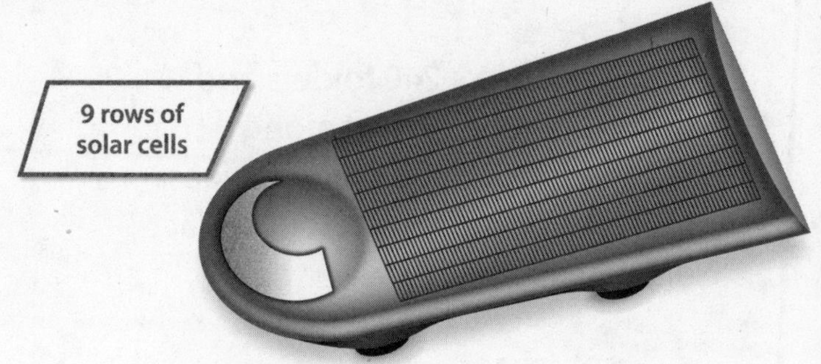

28. **Model with Math** On Saturday afternoon, 350 people attended a play. The seating was arranged in 7 equal rows. How many people sat in each row? Draw a bar diagram. Write and solve an equation.

29. **Higher Order Thinking** Molly and five friends picked a total of 300 oranges. If each girl picked the same number of oranges, how many oranges did Molly pick? Explain.

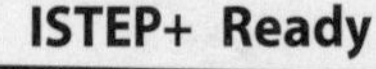

30. Three dock workers load 240 crates equally onto 8 ships. How many crates are loaded onto each ship?

Ⓐ 3 crates
Ⓑ 10 crates
Ⓒ 30 crates
Ⓓ 80 crates

31. Selena used a basic fact to help solve $180 \div 6$. What basic fact did Selena likely use? What is $180 \div 6$?

Ⓐ $18 \div 3$; 60
Ⓑ $18 \div 3$; 30
Ⓒ $18 \div 6$; 60
Ⓓ $18 \div 6$; 30

Name ______________________

Homework & Practice 5-1

Mental Math: Find Quotients

Another Look!

When dividing numbers that end in zero, use basic division facts and patterns to help divide mentally.

Find 210 ÷ 7.

What is the basic fact?

21 ÷ **7** = 3

21 tens ÷ **7** = 3 tens or 30

210 ÷ 7 = 30

Find 4,200 ÷ 6.

What is the basic fact?

42 ÷ **6** = 7

42 hundreds ÷ **6** = 7 hundreds or 700

4,200 ÷ 6 = 700

For **1–20**, use basic facts, patterns, or mental math to divide.

1. 25 ÷ 5 = ______
250 ÷ 5 = ______
2,500 ÷ 5 = ______

2. 14 ÷ 2 = ______
140 ÷ 2 = ______
1,400 ÷ 2 = ______

3. 30 ÷ 5 = ______
300 ÷ 5 = ______
3,000 ÷ 5 = ______

4. 16 ÷ 4 = ______
160 ÷ 4 = ______
1,600 ÷ 4 = ______

5. 120 ÷ 6

6. 720 ÷ 9

7. 200 ÷ 4

8. 2,800 ÷ 7

9. 5,000 ÷ 5

10. 240 ÷ 8

11. 3,600 ÷ 4

12. 1,600 ÷ 2

13. 4,200 ÷ 7

14. 640 ÷ 8

15. 2,000 ÷ 5

16. 320 ÷ 8

17. 810 ÷ 9

18. 270 ÷ 3

19. 1,200 ÷ 2

20. 300 ÷ 6

For **21–23**, use the graph at the right.

21. Barry charged $4 for each copy of *Return of the Dinosaurs*. How many copies did Barry sell?

22. Barry charged $9 for each copy of *America's National Parks*. How many copies did Barry sell?

23. Barry charged $7 for each copy of *Musa the Great*. How many copies did Barry sell?

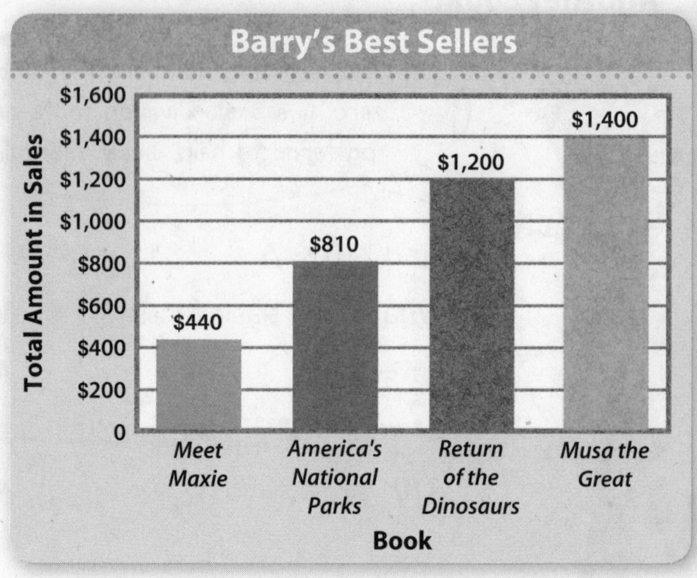

24. Construct Arguments Explain why the following quotient is incorrect: 1,000 ÷ 5 = 2,000.

25. Higher Order Thinking The band boosters collected $2,400 from the sale of hamburgers and hot dogs. The amounts earned from hamburgers and hot dogs were equal. A hamburger sold for $3, and a hot dog sold for $2. How many of each were sold?

Assessment ISTEP+ Ready

26. Jessica has 120 stamps in a collection. She bought 60 more. Jessica wants to place the stamps equally on 6 pages of a book. How many stamps will be on each page of the book?

Ⓐ 20 stamps
Ⓑ 25 stamps
Ⓒ 30 stamps
Ⓓ 40 stamps

27. There are 7 days in 1 week. Some months consist of 30 days. How many weeks are there in 280 days?

Ⓐ 37 weeks
Ⓑ 40 weeks
Ⓒ 70 weeks
Ⓓ 73 weeks

Name ___________________________________

Lesson 5-2
Mental Math: Estimate Quotients

I can . . .
use compatible numbers to estimate quotients when dividing with 3-digit dividends.

Content Standard Prepares for 4.C.3
Process Standards PS.2, PS.3, PS.4

Solve & Share Three friends at a video arcade win a total of 248 tickets. They decide to share the tickets equally. About how many tickets will each friend receive? ***Solve this problem using any strategy you choose.***

You can use reasoning to estimate quotients using mental math. *Show your work in the space below!*

Look Back! Reasoning Identify some other situations when you might want to estimate the answer to a division problem.

How Can You Estimate Quotients to Solve Problems?

A

Max wants to make 9 rubber band balls using about the same number of rubber bands for each ball. He bought a jar of 700 rubber bands. Estimate to find about how many rubber bands Max can use for each ball.

Max does not need to know the exact number of rubber bands to use for each ball. An estimate is all that is needed.

There is more than one way to estimate a quotient.

B **Use Compatible Numbers**

Estimate 700 ÷ 9.

What number close to 700 is easily divided by 9?

Try multiples of ten near 700.
710 is not easily divided by 9.
720 is 72 tens and can be divided by 9.
$720 \div 9 = 80$

Max can use about 80 rubber bands for each ball.

C **Use Multiplication**

Estimate 700 ÷ 9.

9 times what number is about 700?

$9 \times 8 = 72$, so $9 \times 80 = 720$.
$700 \div 9$ is about 80.

Max can use about 80 rubber bands for each ball.

Convince Me! **Reasoning** What compatible numbers can you use to estimate 132 ÷ 6? Why is rounding not a good way to estimate 132 ÷ 6?

Name ___

Practice Buddy | Tools | Assessment

Guided Practice*

Do You Understand?

1. **Construct Arguments** In the problem on the previous page, if Max uses 80 rubber bands to make each ball, will Max be able to make more or fewer balls than he wanted?

2. Max decides to use 700 rubber bands to make 8 balls. Is it reasonable to say he would use about 90 rubber bands to make each ball? Explain.

Do You Know How?

For **3–10**, estimate each quotient. Use multiplication or compatible numbers. Show your work.

3. 48 ÷ 5
4. 235 ÷ 8
5. 547 ÷ 6
6. 192 ÷ 5
7. 662 ÷ 8
8. 362 ÷ 3
9. 41 ÷ 2
10. 211 ÷ 4

Independent Practice*

For **11–26**, estimate each quotient.

Think of basic multiplication facts to help find compatible numbers.

11. 430 ÷ 9
12. 620 ÷ 7
13. 138 ÷ 5
14. 232 ÷ 6
15. 342 ÷ 8
16. 652 ÷ 6
17. 59 ÷ 9
18. 813 ÷ 8
19. 637 ÷ 6
20. 481 ÷ 4
21. 747 ÷ 8
22. 232 ÷ 9
23. 552 ÷ 7
24. 52 ÷ 5
25. 392 ÷ 2
26. 625 ÷ 3

*For another example, see Set B on page 315.

Problem Solving

For **27–28**, use the table at the right.

27. Ada sold her mugs in 3 weeks. About how many mugs did Ada sell each week?

28. Ben sold his mugs in 6 weeks. About how many mugs did Ben sell each week?

29. The International Space Station takes 644 minutes to orbit Earth 7 times. About how long does each orbit take?

30. There are 60 minutes in 1 hour and 24 hours in 1 day. About how many times does the International Space Station orbit Earth each day?

7 orbits take 644 minutes

31. Number Sense Complete by writing > or < in the ◯. Without dividing, explain how you know which quotient is greater.

$930 \div 4 \bigcirc 762 \div 4$

32. Higher Order Thinking Explain how to find a better estimate for $260 \div 5$ than the one shown below.

Round 260 to 300, and then estimate $300 \div 5$.

$300 \div 5 = 60$, so $260 \div 5$ is about 60.

Assessment ISTEP+ Ready

33. Kaylee wanted to divide 133 pieces of candy equally into 7 boxes. She decides to put 19 pieces in each box. Use estimation to determine if this answer seems reasonable.

Name ______________________________

Homework & Practice 5-2

Mental Math: Estimate Quotients

Another Look!

Estimate 460 ÷ 9.

Here are two ways to estimate quotients.

One Way

Use compatible numbers.

What number close to 460 can be easily divided by 9? Try 450.

450 ÷ 9 = 50

460 ÷ 9 is about 50.

Another Way

Use multiplication.

Nine times what number is about 460?

9 × 5 = 45, so 9 × 50 = 450.

460 ÷ 9 is about 50.

For **1–20**, estimate each quotient. Show your work.

1. 165 ÷ 4

2. 35 ÷ 4

3. 715 ÷ 9

4. 490 ÷ 8

5. 512 ÷ 5

6. 652 ÷ 8

7. 790 ÷ 9

8. 200 ÷ 7

9. 311 ÷ 6

10. 162 ÷ 2

11. 418 ÷ 6

12. 554 ÷ 7

13. 92 ÷ 3

14. 351 ÷ 7

15. 497 ÷ 5

16. 61 ÷ 2

17. 202 ÷ 2

18. 153 ÷ 3

19. 98 ÷ 9

20. 174 ÷ 9

For **21–23**, use Franny's To-Do List.

Franny's To-Do List
- Put 64 pictures in a photo album.
- Finish reading 113 pages of a book.
- Buy presents for Kate, Wendy, and Tia.
- Put shoes on rack.

21. Franny has 5 pages left in the album. About how many pictures can she place on each remaining page?

22. Franny plans to spend 4 hours reading. About how many pages would she need to read each hour to finish the book?

23. Franny wants to spend an equal amount of money on the presents for her friends. If she has $62, about how much money can she spend on each present?

---

24. Model with Math The veterinarian has seen 47 dogs, 19 cats, 7 exotic birds, and 3 horses this week. Complete the bar diagram and find the total number of animals seen by the veterinarian this week.

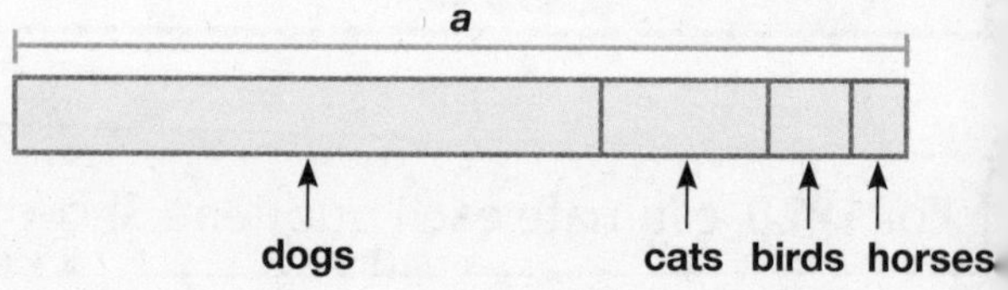

---

25. Wayne has 303 marbles. If he gives away 123 of the marbles equally to 3 friends, about how many marbles will Wayne give each friend? How many marbles does Wayne have left?

26. Higher Order Thinking Tessa wants to separate 187 ears of corn into bags of 6 ears each. She has 35 bags. Estimate to find whether Tessa has enough bags. Explain.

Assessment ISTEP+ Ready

27. Deon set a goal to ride his bicycle 310 miles in a month. He has biked 145 miles so far. If there are 4 days left in the month, about how many miles should Deon ride each day to reach his goal? Explain.

Name ____________________

Help Practice Buddy Tools Games

Homework & Practice 5-3

Mental Math: Estimate Quotients for Greater Dividends

Another Look!

Estimate 2,946 ÷ 5.

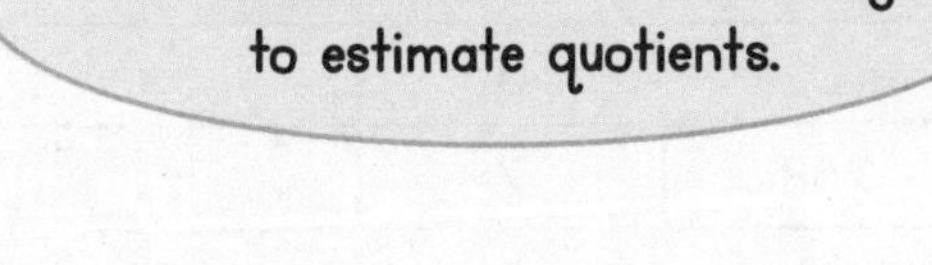

You can use mental math strategies to estimate quotients.

Use rounding.

2,946 rounds to 3,000.

3,000 ÷ 5 = 600

So, 2,946 ÷ 5 is about 600.

Use patterns.

5 × 6 = 30
5 × 600 = 3,000

So, 2,946 ÷ 5 is about 600.

For **1–18**, estimate each quotient.

1. 1,561 ÷ 8

What is 8 × 2? ________

What is 8 × 20? ________

What is 8 × 200? ________

What is 1,600 ÷ 8? ________

So, 1,561 ÷ 8 is about ________.

2. 2,008 ÷ 7

What is 7 × 3? ________

What is 7 × 30? ________

What is 7 × 300? ________

What is 2,100 ÷ 7? ________

So, 2,008 ÷ 7 is about ________.

3. 461 ÷ 9

4. 2,356 ÷ 6

5. 5,352 ÷ 9

6. 279 ÷ 9

7. 2,449 ÷ 8

8. 3,124 ÷ 6

9. 4,519 ÷ 5

10. 915 ÷ 3

11. 2,120 ÷ 5

12. 423 ÷ 4

13. 3,305 ÷ 7

14. 1,803 ÷ 2

15. 8,167 ÷ 9

16. 1,216 ÷ 6

17. 1,007 ÷ 2

18. 4,170 ÷ 8

For **19–21**, use the table at the right.

19. Bob and Kate are making bracelets to sell at a craft fair. Determine about how many bracelets Bob and Kate can make with each color of bead. Complete the table.

Color	Number of Beads	Beads per Bracelet	Estimated Number of Bracelets
Blue	258	6	
Silver	428	9	
Rose	102	3	
White	258	7	

20. About how many bracelets can they make before they run out of at least one color of bead? Which color of bead will they run out of first?

21. There is a special-rush order for 7 bracelets of each color. How many beads are needed for 7 bracelets of each color?

This table shows how many beads Bob and Kate have of each color. A table helps organize data.

22. Reasoning The students who run the school store ordered 1,440 pencils. They are putting them in packages of 6 pencils. About how many packages can they make? Will the exact answer be more or less than the estimate? Explain.

23. Higher Order Thinking Find two estimates for 4,396 ÷ 4 by rounding the dividend to the nearest hundred and also to the nearest thousand. Compare the estimates.

Assessment ISTEP+ Ready

24. Select all the expressions that have an estimated quotient close to 400.

- ☐ 6,321 ÷ 2
- ☐ 1,193 ÷ 3
- ☐ 5,055 ÷ 8
- ☐ 3,705 ÷ 9
- ☐ 1,649 ÷ 4

25. Select all the expressions that have an estimated quotient close to 600.

- ☐ 4,900 ÷ 7
- ☐ 1,234 ÷ 6
- ☐ 5,366 ÷ 9
- ☐ 1,332 ÷ 2
- ☐ 1,795 ÷ 3

Name ____________________

Homework & Practice 5-4
Interpret Remainders

Another Look!

Jamal has 20 marbles to put into bags. He plans to put 6 marbles in each bag. How many bags will Jamal be able to fill?

Find 20 ÷ 6.

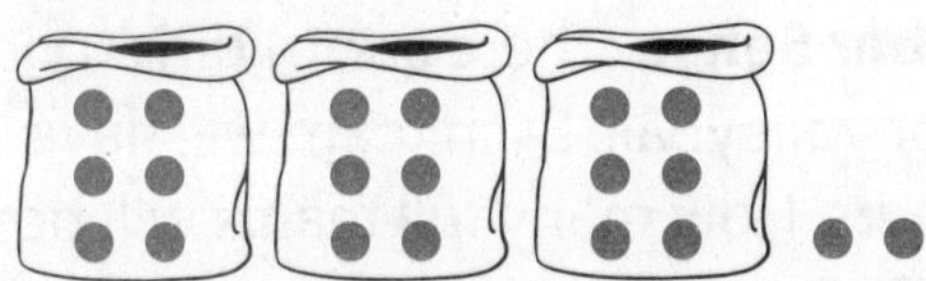

The remainder is the number left after the division is complete. Remember, the remainder should be less than the divisor.

Jamal can fill 3 bags with 6 marbles.
There will be 2 marbles left over.

There are 3 ways to interpret a remainder.

The remainder can be ignored.	The remainder can be the answer.	You need to add 1 to the quotient.
How many bags did Jamal fill? 3 bags	*How many marbles are not in the bags?* 2 marbles	*How many bags are needed for all of the marbles to be in bags?* 4 bags

For **1–4**, find the number of equal groups and the number left over.

1. 66 ÷ 5 = ____ with ____ left over

2. 94 ÷ 6 = ____ with ____ left over

3. 29 ÷ 9 = ____ with ____ left over

4. 46 ÷ 8 = ____ with ____ left over

For **5–6**, divide. Then interpret the remainder.

5. 77 apples
3 apples in each bag
77 ÷ 3 = ____ with ____ left over

How many apples are not in bags? ________

6. 71 cards
5 cards in each box
71 ÷ 5 = ____ with ____ left over

How many boxes are needed for all the cards? ________

7. Why should the remainder be less than the divisor?

8. There are 25 students in Ms. Morris's class. She wants to divide the class into 3, 4, or 5 equal teams with all students on a team. Which number of teams can Ms. Morris make? Explain.

9. Tammy decorated her art project with 12 different colors of sequins. If she used 15 of each color, how many sequins did Tammy use?

10. **Number Sense** There are 14 girls trying out for volleyball. Each team will have 6 players. How many full teams will be made? How many girls will not make a team?

11. **Model with Math** How many strings are used to make 4 guitars like the ones in the picture? Draw a bar diagram to show how you found your answer.

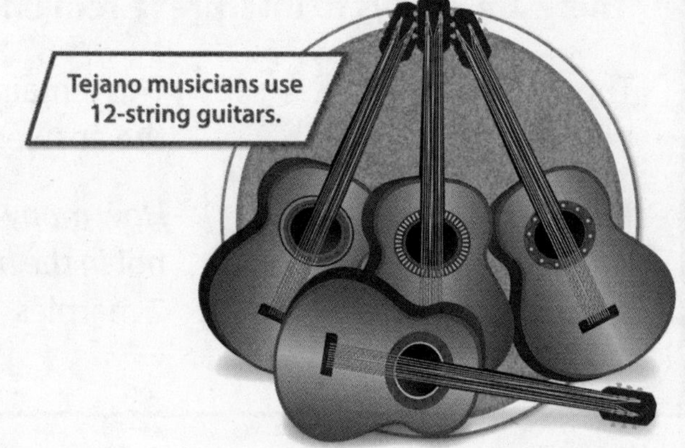
Tejano musicians use
12-string guitars.

12. There are 26 students in Dante's class. One student is out sick today. The students want to split into teams of six for a game. How many full teams can they make?

13. **Higher Order Thinking** Carl has 98 pictures to put in an album. He can put 8 pictures on each page. How many pictures will Carl put on the last page? Explain.

Assessment
ISTEP+ Ready

14. Jada bought an art kit with 58 colored pencils. She and her 3 sisters will share the pencils equally. How many pencils will each person receive? Will there be any pencils left over? If so, how many?

Name ______________________________

Lesson 5-5
Division as Sharing

I can . . .
sort objects into equal-sized groups to divide.

Content Standard 4.C.3
Process Standards PS.2, PS.3, PS.4, PS.5

Solve & Share

Paulo has 39 patches from states he and his relatives have visited. He wants to pin them onto a board and arrange them equally in 3 rows. How many patches will be in each row? ***Solve this problem using any strategy you choose.***

Using appropriate tools like place-value blocks can help you divide.

Look Back! **Reasoning** When might you need to divide something into equal groups in everyday life?

How Can Place Value Help You Divide?

A

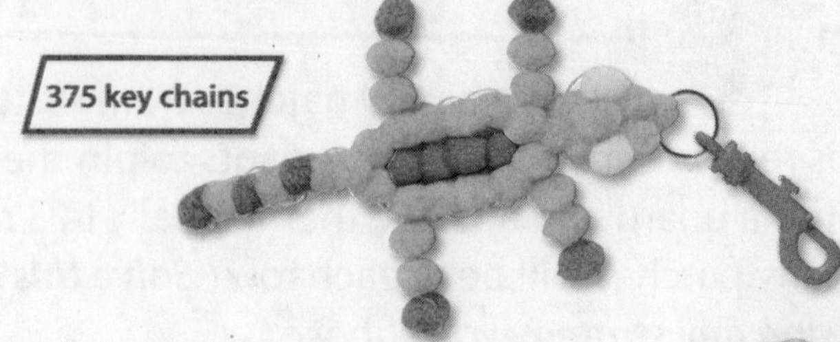

The craft club made 375 key chains. They sold 137 of the key chains at the school fair. The rest need to be packed into 2 boxes with the same number of key chains in each box. How many key chains will go in each box?

First, subtract to find how many key chains need to be packed.

375 − 137 = 238

Draw hundreds, tens, and ones to show 238. Then divide.

B Find 238 ÷ 2.

Divide the hundreds into two equal groups.

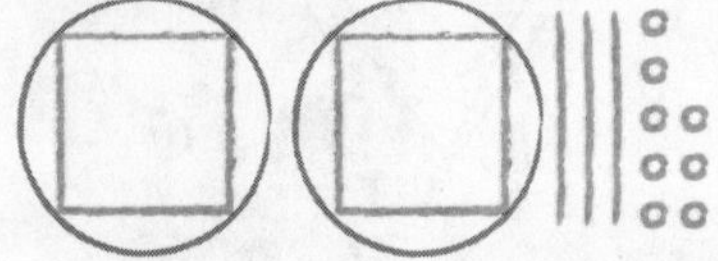

C Next, divide the tens into two equal groups.

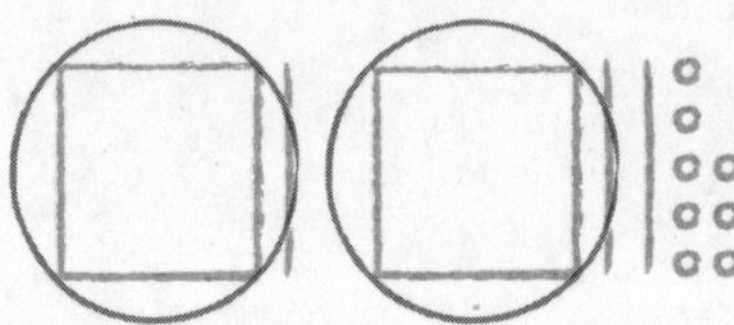

Unbundle 1 ten for 10 ones.

10 ones + 8 ones = 18 ones

D Divide the 18 ones into two equal groups.

Convince Me! **Use Appropriate Tools** Tell how you would evenly divide the money shown among 4 people only using $10 bills or $1 bills.

Name ______

Practice Buddy | Tools | Assessment

Another Example!

Find 55 ÷ 4.

Divide the tens equally into 4 groups. Regroup 1 ten as 10 ones and then divide the ones equally into 4 groups. There are 3 ones left over.

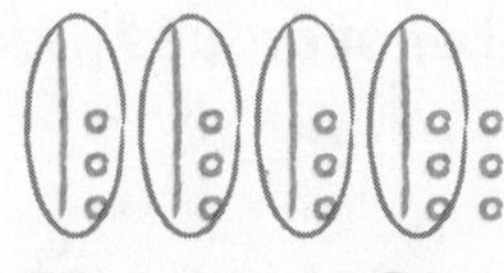

55 ÷ 4 = 13 R3

Guided Practice*

Do You Understand?

1. **Model with Math** Draw a picture to explain why 423 ÷ 3 = 141.

2. The art teacher displayed 48 paintings on 3 walls. If each wall had the same number of paintings, how many paintings were on each wall?

Do You Know How?

For **3–4**, tell how many are in each group and how many are left over. Draw pictures as needed.

3. 176 magazines divided equally into 5 boxes

4. 56 marbles divided equally into 3 bags

Independent Practice

For **5–6**, use the drawing to complete each division sentence.

5. 71 ÷ ____ = ____ R2

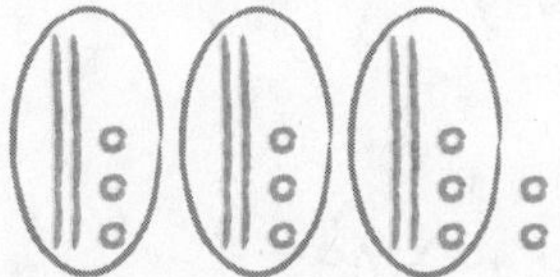

6. 176 ÷ ____ = ____

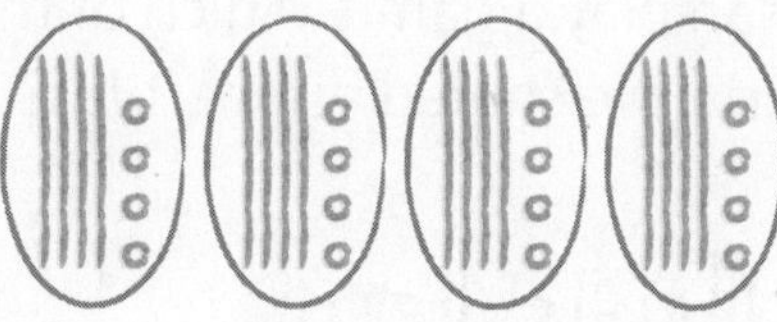

For **7–8**, draw pictures to solve.

7. 46 ÷ 3

8. 65 ÷ 4

*For another example, see Set D on page 316.

Problem Solving

9. Model with Math A company with 65 employees is moving to a new location. All of the employees are divided into groups of 5 for the move. Write an equation and find the number of groups used for the move.

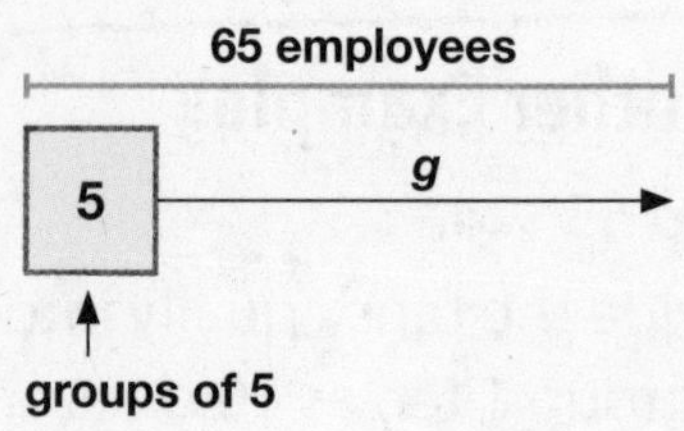

10. Maya used a drawing to divide 86. She made groups of 17 with 1 left over. Draw a picture to determine how many groups Maya made.

11. Number Sense A science museum has 2,400 gemstones displayed equally in 3 cases. How many gemstones are in each case? What basic fact did you use to determine the quotient?

12. Construct Arguments Mr. Harold has 268 books on 4 shelves in the classroom library. He has the same number of books on each shelf. To find the number of books on each shelf, he divided 268 by 4. How many tens did he regroup as ones? How many books are on each shelf?

13. Higher Order Thinking Five fourth-grade classes from an elementary school took a trip to the United States Capitol. There were 25 students in each class. At the Capitol, a maximum of 40 students were allowed on a tour at one time. What is the least number of tours needed so all the students were able to take a tour?

Assessment ISTEP+ Ready

14. Ken has 72 marbles. He shares the marbles equally with some friends so they can play a game. Which of the following drawings shows a way Ken could have shared his marbles?

Ⓐ 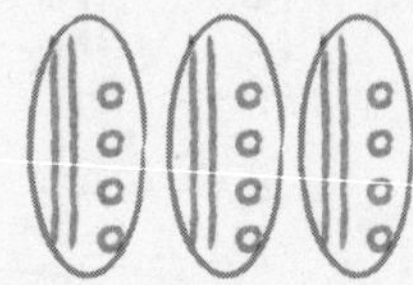

Ⓒ 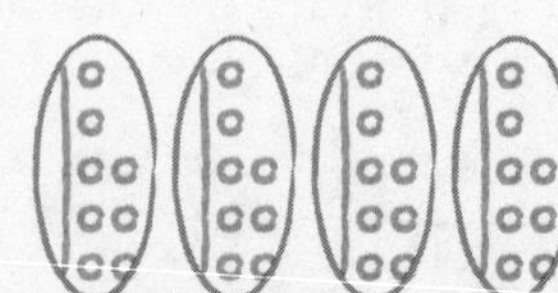

Ⓑ 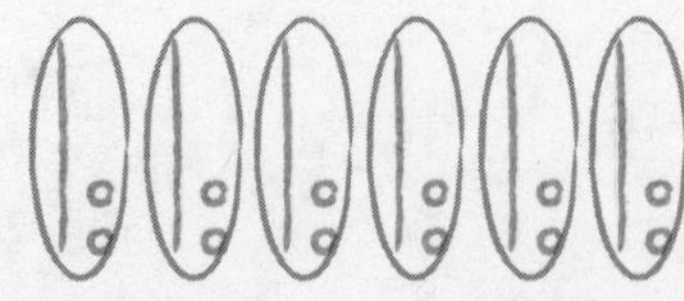

Ⓓ All of the models shown

Name ______________________

Homework & Practice 5-5

Division as Sharing

Another Look!

Find 78 ÷ 5.

You can draw pictures to help solve division problems.

First, divide the tens.

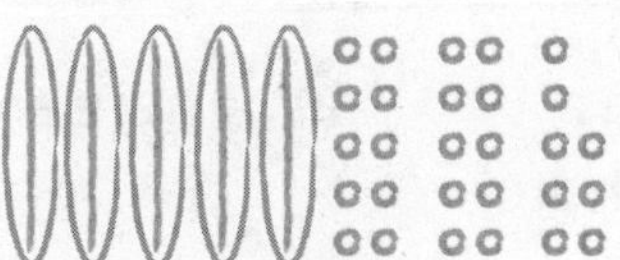

There is 1 ten in each of the 5 groups.

Then, unbundle the 2 tens for 20 ones.

20 ones and 8 ones are equal to 28 ones.

Lastly, divide the ones.

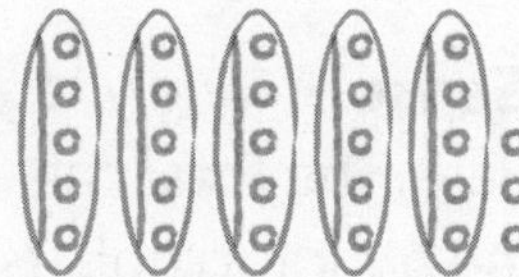

Each of the 5 groups has 1 ten and 5 ones. There are 3 ones remaining.

78 ÷ 5 = 15 R3

For **1–4**, Use the drawing to complete each division sentence.

1. 66 ÷ ____ = ____ R2

2. 136 ÷ 4 = ____

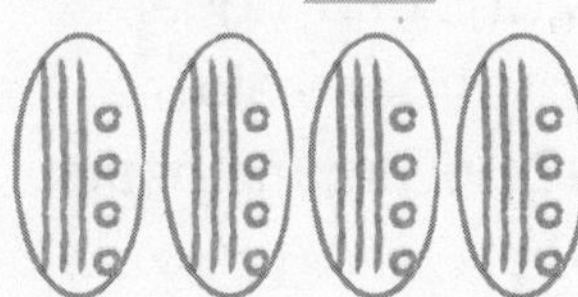

3. 131 ÷ ____ = ____ R1

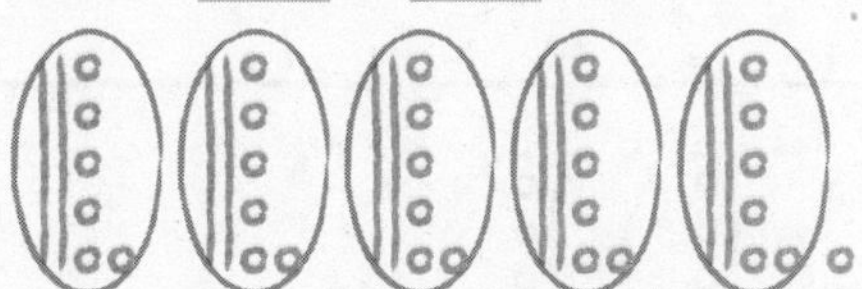

4. 76 ÷ ____ = ____ R ____

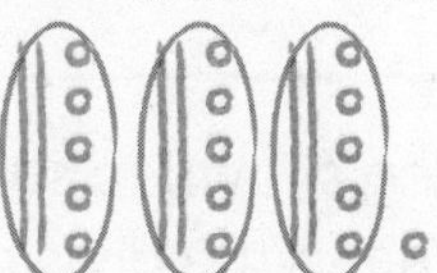

For **5–8**, draw pictures to solve.

5. 140 ÷ 6

6. 95 ÷ 2

7. 96 ÷ 8

8. 51 ÷ 2

9. Marcos has 78 toy cars. He arranges the toy cars into 6 equal groups. How many toy cars are in each group? Complete the diagram started below to show your work.

Pictures can help you solve problems.

10. Number Sense A family is going on a trip for 3 days. The total cost for the hotel is $336. One hundred dollars a day was budgeted for food. How much will each day of the trip cost?

11. There are 37 chairs and 9 tables in a classroom. Mrs. Kensington wants to put an equal number of chairs at each table. How many chairs can she put at each table? Will there be any chairs left over?

12. Higher Order Thinking Mrs. Dryson divided her collection of 52 glass bears into equal groups. She had 1 bear left over. How many groups did Mrs. Dryson make? How many bears are in each group?

13. Ben has 165 pictures from his summer trip to Austria. He put 6 pictures on each page of a photo album. How many pages of the album did Ben fill? How many pages did Ben use?

14. Adrian used the drawing shown to solve a division sentence. What is the division sentence? Explain.

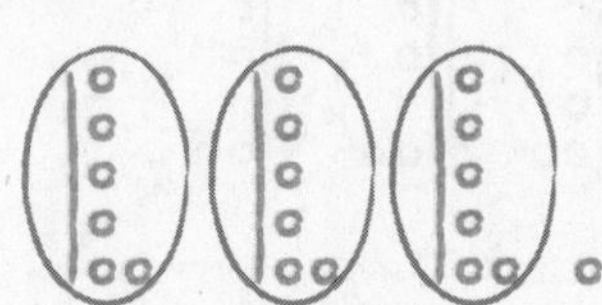

Assessment ISTEP+ Ready

15. Nancy planted 44 plants in rows. If there are 7 plants in each row, how many plants are left over?

Ⓐ 6 plants Ⓒ 2 plants

Ⓑ 3 plants Ⓓ 1 plant

16. A shipment of 8 boxes was delivered to Mason's Bookstore. Each box holds the same number of books. If there are 744 books in the shipment, how many books are in each box?

Ⓐ 90 books Ⓒ 95 books

Ⓑ 93 books Ⓓ 100 books

Name ____________________

Lesson 5-6
Use Partial Quotients to Divide

I can ...
divide by thinking about multiplication, estimation, and place value.

Content Standards 4.C.3, 4.AT.2
Process Standards PS.1, PS.3, PS.4, PS.7

Solve & Share Sally's bird feeder holds 6 cups of bird feed. How many times can Sally's bird feeder be filled using a 72-cup bag of bird feed? ***Solve this problem using any strategy you choose.***

You can use reasoning. Think about how many times you can take away groups of six from your original number.

Look Back! Use Structure How can you use multiplication to check your answer?

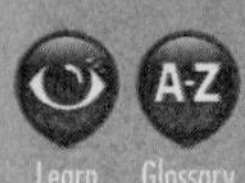

How Can You Use Partial Quotients to Solve Division Problems?

A

There are 3 seats in each row of an airplane for passengers. If there are 63 people boarding the airplane, how many rows of seats are needed for the passengers?

This bar diagram shows the problem.

63 people

3 | r

people in each row

You can divide using partial quotients to find quotients in parts until only a remainder, if any, is left.

3 seats per row

B One Way

$$\begin{array}{r} 1 \\ 10 \\ 10 \\ 3\overline{)63} \\ -30 \\ \hline 33 \\ -30 \\ \hline 3 \\ -3 \\ \hline 0 \end{array} \quad 1 + 10 + 10 = 21$$

Estimate: How many 3s are in 63? Try 10.

Multiply 10 × 3 and subtract.

Estimate: How many 3s are in 33? Try 10.

Multiply 10 × 3 and subtract.

How many 3s are in 3? Use 1.

	10 +	10 +	1
3	63 −30 33	33 −30 3	3 −3 0

=21 rows of seats

C Another Way

$$\begin{array}{r} 1 \\ 20 \\ 3\overline{)63} \\ -60 \\ \hline 3 \\ -3 \\ \hline 0 \end{array} \quad 1 + 20 = 21$$

Estimate: How many 3s are in 63? Try 20.

Multiply 20 × 3 and subtract.

Estimate: How many 3s are in 3? Use 1.

Multiply 1 × 3 and subtract.

	20 +	1
3	63 −60 3	3 −3 0

=21 rows of seats

Convince Me! **Use Structure** How can you use the relationship between multiplication and division to check your answer?

Name ______________________________

Help Practice Buddy Tools Games

Homework & Practice 5-7

Use Partial Quotients to Divide: Greater Dividends

Another Look!

A honeybee can travel 2,925 feet in 3 minutes. How many feet would that be each minute?

	900	+ 70 +	5 = 975
3	2,925 − 2,700 = 225	225 − 210 = 15	15 − 15 = 0

$$\begin{array}{r} 5 \\ 70 \\ 900 \end{array}\Big\} 975$$

$$\begin{array}{r} 3\overline{)2,925} \\ -2,700 \\ \hline 225 \\ -210 \\ \hline 15 \\ -15 \\ \hline 0 \end{array}$$

You can think about multiplication and use partial quotients to divide.

The honeybee traveled 975 feet each minute.

For **1–16**, use partial quotients to divide.

1. $9\overline{)126}$ **2.** $7\overline{)474}$ **3.** $2\overline{)179}$ **4.** $6\overline{)237}$

5. $4\overline{)3,264}$ **6.** $8\overline{)3,349}$ **7.** $3\overline{)6,334}$ **8.** $5\overline{)8,248}$

9. $6\overline{)5,769}$ **10.** $3\overline{)441}$ **11.** $7\overline{)4,999}$ **12.** $6\overline{)4,272}$

13. $3\overline{)3,791}$ **14.** $9\overline{)756}$ **15.** $5\overline{)4,271}$ **16.** $4\overline{)1,847}$

17. Algebra Five students ran an equal distance in the one-mile relay race. How many feet did each student run? Use the bar diagram to write and solve an equation.

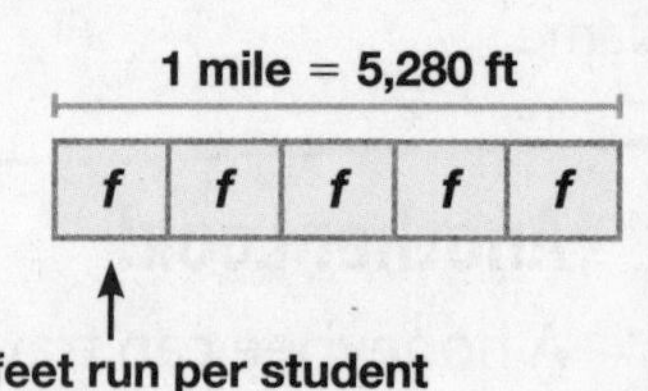

18. Math and Science The function of a hydroelectric plant is to change the energy from the motion of water into electricity. How long does it take the hydroelectric plant shown to produce 384-kilowatt hours of electricity?

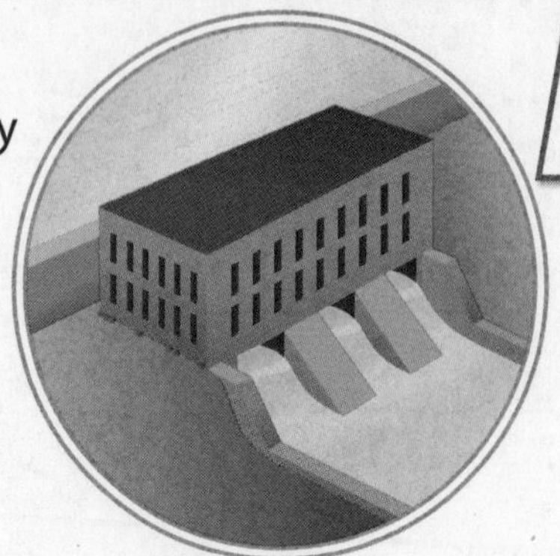

A hydroelectric plant can produce 8 kilowatt hours of electricity each hour.

19. Critique Reasoning Tell whether Miranda's or Jesse's reasoning is correct. Explain.

Miranda
$6{,}050 \div 5 = (6{,}000 + 50) \div 5$
$= (6{,}000 \div 5) + (50 \div 5)$
$= 1{,}200 + 10$
$= 1{,}210$

Jesse
$6{,}050 \div 5 = (6{,}000 + 50) \div (3+2)$
$= (6{,}000 \div 3) + (50 \div 2)$
$= 2{,}000 + 25$
$= 2{,}025$

20. Kelli signed up for 38 gymnastics lessons. Each lesson lasts for 2 hours. How many hours of lessons did Kelli sign up for?

21. Higher Order Thinking Edgar Elementary School is having a reading contest. Six fourth-grade classes each set a goal to read 1,266 pages. Six fifth-grade classes each set a goal of 2,212 pages. How many more pages does each fifth-grade class have to read than each fourth-grade class?

22. Write the correct numbers in the boxes to complete the area model and the equation shown.

$4{,}306 \div 9 =$ ☐ R ☐

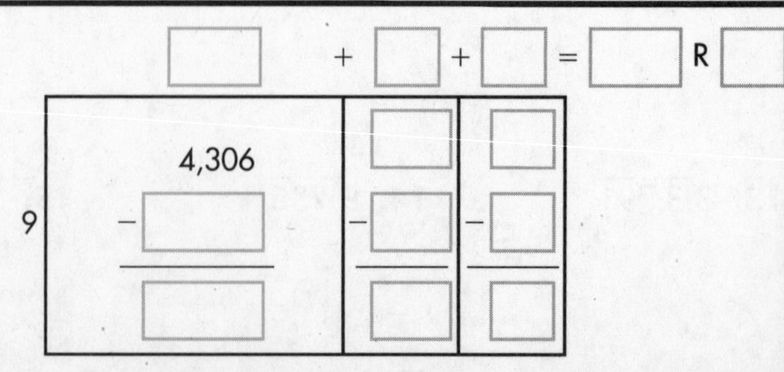

Name ____________________

Lesson 5-8
Divide with 1-Digit Numbers

I can ...
use place value and sharing to divide.

Content Standards 4.C.3, 4.AT.2
Process Standards PS.2, PS.3, PS.4, PS.6

Solve & Share Sara is packing T-shirts and shorts into bins to store for the winter. There are 42 items to pack. She packs the same number of items into 3 bins. How many items does Sara pack in each bin? ***Solve this problem using any strategy you choose.***

Be precise and use math symbols, numbers, and labels to help you solve a problem. *Show your work in the space below!*

Look Back! Construct Arguments Your classmate solved the same problem and said each bin would have 10 items and there would be 2 items left over. Do you agree or disagree? If you disagree, what did your classmate do wrong?

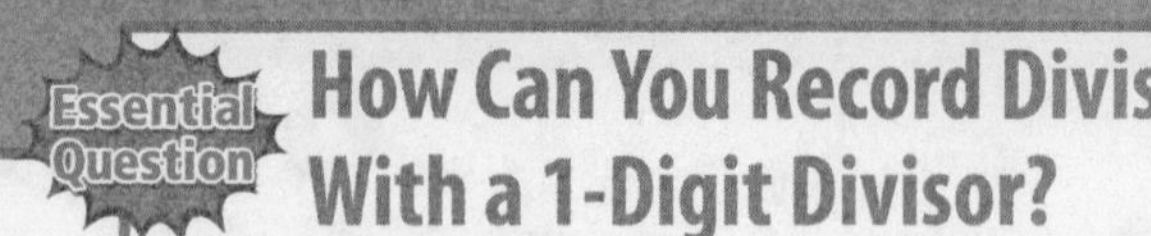

How Can You Record Division With a 1-Digit Divisor?

A

A factory shipped 477 watches in 3 boxes. Each box had the same number of watches. How many watches were in each box?

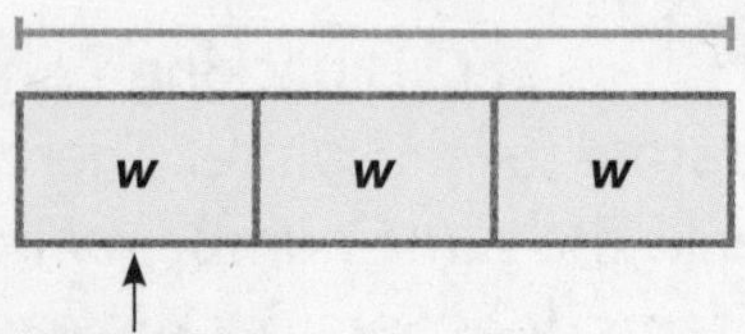

Divide 4 hundreds, 7 tens, and 7 ones among 3 groups. Start dividing with the hundreds.

Write an equation:

$477 \div 3 = w$

Estimate: $450 \div 3 = 150$

B

Step 1

Divide the hundreds.

$$\begin{array}{r} 1 \\ 3\overline{)477} \\ -3 \\ \hline 17 \end{array}$$

4 hundreds ÷ 3

Each group gets 1 hundred.

1 hundred is left.

Unbundle 1 hundred.
10 tens + 7 tens = 17 tens

3 groups

1 H
1 H
1 H

C

Step 2

Divide the tens.

$$\begin{array}{r} 15 \\ 3\overline{)477} \\ -3 \\ \hline 17 \\ -15 \\ \hline 27 \end{array}$$

17 tens ÷ 3

Each group gets 5 tens.

2 tens are left.

Unbundle 2 tens.
20 ones + 7 ones = 27 ones

3 groups

1 H + 5 T
1 H + 5 T
1 H + 5 T

D

Step 3

Divide the ones.

$$\begin{array}{r} 159 \\ 3\overline{)477} \\ -3 \\ \hline 17 \\ -15 \\ \hline 27 \\ -27 \\ \hline 0 \end{array}$$

$w = 159$

27 ones ÷ 3

Each group gets 9 ones.

3 groups

1 H + 5 T + 9
1 H + 5 T + 9
1 H + 5 T + 9

There were 159 watches in each box.

Convince Me! **Reasoning** How can you use the relationship between multiplication and division to check your answer?

Name ____________________

Practice Buddy Tools Assessment

Another Example!

Find 257 ÷ 5.

Estimate: 250 ÷ 5 = 50

257 ÷ 5 = 51 R2

```
   51 R2
5)257
 - 25       25 tens ÷ 5
            Each group gets 5 tens.
     7      7 ones ÷ 5
   - 5      Each group gets 1 one.
     2      2 ones are left.
```

5 groups: 5 T + 1 | 5 T + 1 | 5 T + 1 | 5 T + 1 | 5 T + 1

Guided Practice*

Do You Understand?

1. **Construct Arguments** Explain why 25 tens are divided by 5 in the problem above.

2. Tori bought some patio bricks and paid $232. If each brick costs $2, how many patio bricks did Tori buy?

Do You Know How?

For **3–4**, complete each calculation.

3. 5)8 2 — quotient: □6 R□; − 5; □□; − □□; □

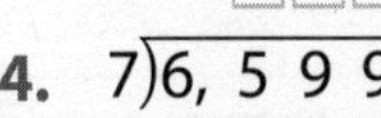

4. 7)6, 5 9 9 — quotient: □□□ R□; − □□; □□; − □□; □□; − □□; □

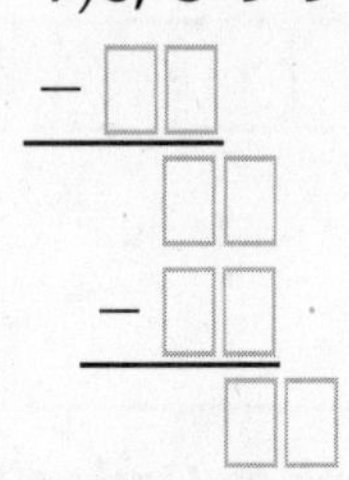

Independent Practice

Leveled Practice For **5–12**, find each quotient.

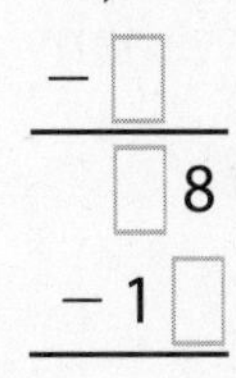

5. 3)7 8 — quotient: □6; − □; □8; − 1□; 0

6. 3)8 6 — quotient: 2□ R□; − □; □□; − □□; □

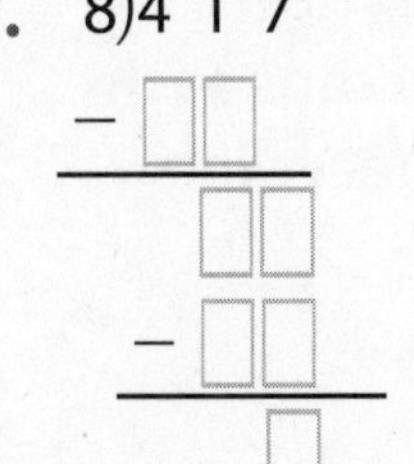

7. 8)4 1 7 — quotient: 5□ R□; − □□; □□; − □□; □

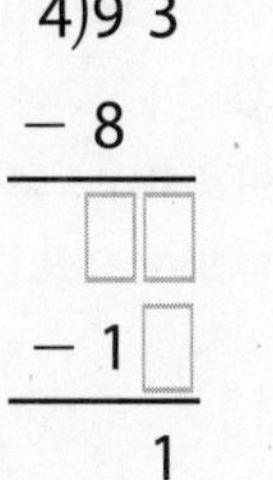

8. 4)9 3 — quotient: □□ R□; − 8; □□; − 1□; 1

9. 8)526

10. 7)88

11. 3)761

12. 6)96

*For another example, see Set F on page 317.

Problem Solving

13. Reasoning Some of the tallest selenite crystals in a cave in Chihuahua, Mexico are 50 feet tall. Nathan is 4 feet tall. About how many times as tall as Nathan are the tallest crystals?

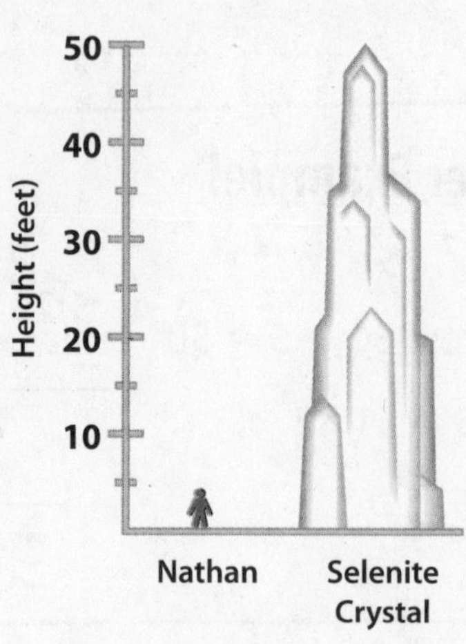

14. Model with Math The Galveston-Port Bolivar Ferry takes cars across Galveston Bay. One day, the ferry transported a total of 685 cars over a 5-hour period. The ferry took the same number of cars each hour. How many cars did it take each hour?

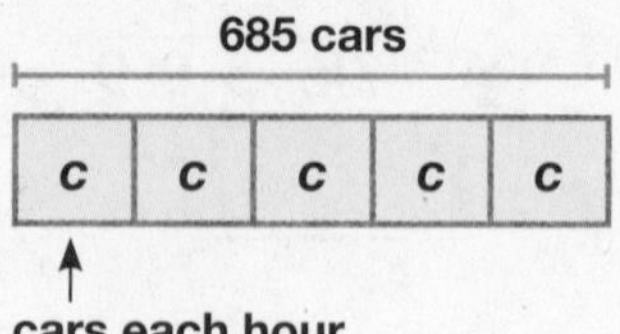

15. Zelda has a piece of fabric that is 74 inches long. She wants to divide it into 2 equal pieces. What is the length of each piece?

16. Higher Order Thinking Maggie is making trail mix. She makes 4 batches of the recipe shown. She divides it into 3 equal-sized bags. How many ounces are in each bag?

DATA

Tasty Trail Mix	
Granola	8 oz
Nuts	5 oz
Raisins	2 oz
Cranberries	3 oz

Assessment — ISTEP+ Ready

17. In one week, the Green Recycling Center received 784 aluminum cans. They received the same number of cans each day. How many cans did the recycling center receive each day?

Ⓐ 112 cans
Ⓑ 114 cans
Ⓒ 121 cans
Ⓓ 122 cans

18. Every year, the city of San Marcos holds a Cinco de Mayo festival. If 60 students perform in 5 equal groups, how many students are in each group?

Ⓐ 10 students
Ⓑ 12 students
Ⓒ 25 students
Ⓓ 55 students

Name ____________________

Help Practice Buddy Tools Games

Homework & Practice 5-8

Divide with 1-Digit Numbers

Another Look!

Find 957 ÷ 3.

Estimate: 960 ÷ 3 = 320

Step 1

Divide the hundreds.

$$\begin{array}{r} 3 \\ 3\overline{)957} \\ -9 \\ \hline 0 \end{array}$$

9 hundreds ÷ 3
Each group gets 3 hundreds.
0 hundreds left.

3 H
3 H
3 H

Step 2

Divide the tens.

$$\begin{array}{r} 31 \\ 3\overline{)957} \\ -9 \\ \hline 05 \\ -3 \\ \hline 2 \end{array}$$

5 tens ÷ 3
Each group gets 1 ten.
2 tens are left.

Unbundle 2 tens.
20 ones + 7 ones = 27 ones

3 H + 1 T
3 H + 1 T
3 H + 1 T

Step 3

Divide the ones.

$$\begin{array}{r} 319 \\ 3\overline{)957} \\ -9 \\ \hline 05 \\ -3 \\ \hline 27 \\ -27 \\ \hline 0 \end{array}$$

27 ones ÷ 3
Each group gets 9 ones.

3 H + 1 T + 9
3 H + 1 T + 9
3 H + 1 T + 9

957 ÷ 3 = 319.

319 is close to the estimate of 320.

The answer is reasonable.

For **1–8**, find each quotient.

1. 4)3 3 4 → 8 3 R☐
− ☐☐
☐☐
− 1 2
☐

2. 6)1 4 8 → ☐☐ R4
− ☐☐
☐☐
− ☐4
☐

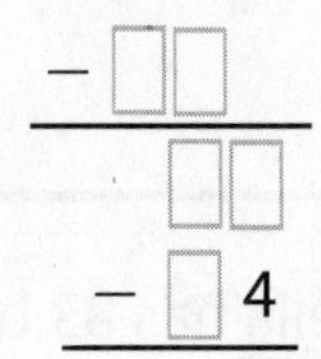
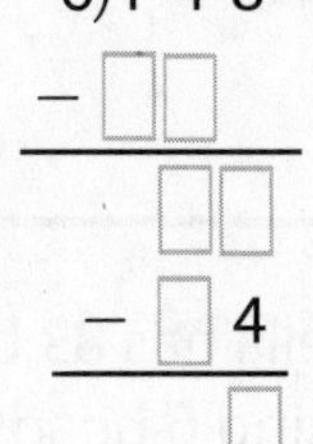

3. 7)9 4 8 → ☐ 3 ☐ R3
− ☐
☐☐
− ☐☐
☐☐
− ☐☐
☐

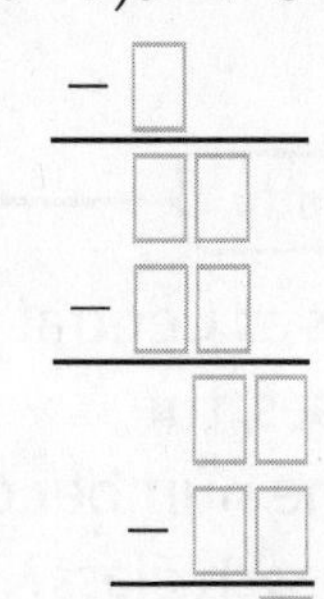

4. 4)1 7 9 → 4 ☐ R3
− ☐☐
☐☐
− ☐☐
☐

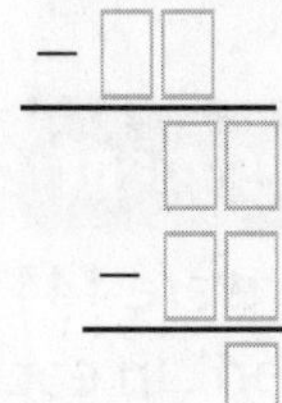

5. 5)125

6. 8)418

7. 2)587

8. 8)747

9. Reasoning Using hundreds, tens, and ones, what are three different ways the number 352 can be represented other than the way shown at the right?

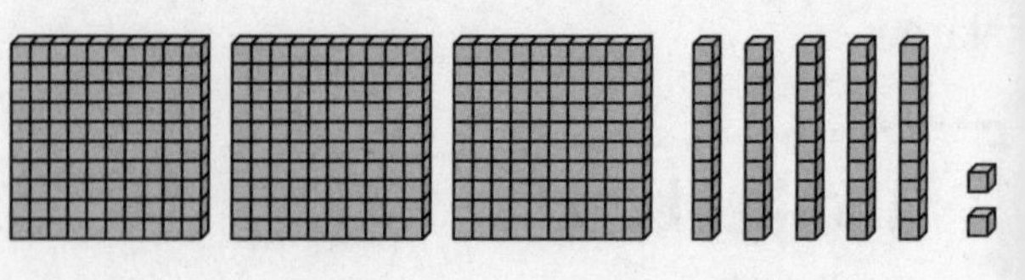

10. A toy store received a shipment of 17 cases of teddy bears. Use compatible numbers to estimate the total number of teddy bears in the shipment.

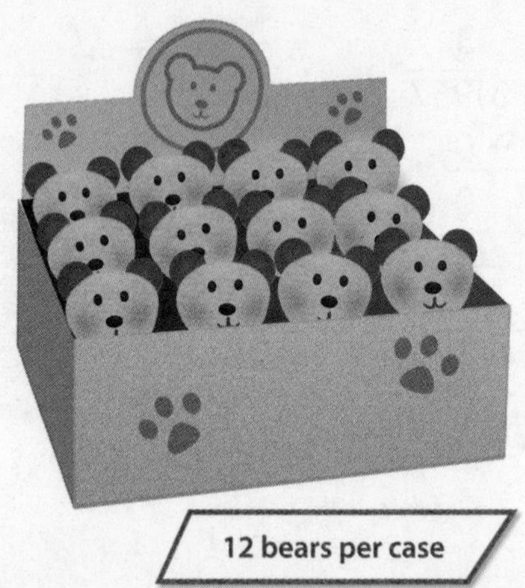

11. How many bears are in the shipment?

12. Algebra What is the unknown number in the equation?

$$5 \times n = 3{,}000$$

13. Higher Order Thinking Tammy invited 144 guests to her wedding. Tammy is renting tables that seat 8 guests at each table. If each table costs $5 to rent, how much will Tammy spend to rent the tables?

14. There are 144 fourth-graders at Central School. In each of the 6 classes, the number of girls is equal to the number of boys. How many girls are in each class?

Ⓐ 9 girls
Ⓑ 11 girls
Ⓒ 12 girls
Ⓓ 24 girls

15. Celia has 83 beads. She makes bracelets using 6 beads for each bracelet. How many beads does Celia have left over?

Ⓐ 13 beads
Ⓑ 5 beads
Ⓒ 3 beads
Ⓓ 0 beads

Name ______________________________

Lesson 5-9
Continue to Divide with 1-Digit Numbers

I can ...
follow a series of steps that breaks the division into simpler calculations.

Content Standard 4.C.3
Process Standards PS.2, PS.3, PS.7

Solve & Share A high school football stadium has 6 sections. Each section seats the same number of people. A total of 1,950 people can be seated in the stadium. About how many people can be seated in each section? Will your estimate be greater than or less than the actual answer? ***Solve this problem using any strategy you choose.***

You can use reasoning. What does the word "about" in the problem tell you? *Show your work in the space below!*

Look Back! **Look for Relationships** How can you use a pattern to solve the problem?

Essential Question How Can You Find Larger Quotients?

A

In all, 4,729 hot dogs were sold at a football game. If there are 8 hot dogs in a package, how many packages of hot dogs were sold?

There is more than one way to represent this problem.

4,729 hot dogs sold

Draw a bar diagram:

Write an equation:

$4{,}729 \div 8 = p$

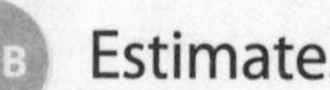

B Estimate.

Decide where to start.

$500 \times 8 = 4{,}000$

The answer is more than 500 packages.

$600 \times 8 = 4{,}800$

The answer is less than, but close to, 600 packages.

Start dividing in the hundreds.

C Divide.

$$\begin{array}{r} 591 \text{ R1} \\ 8\overline{)4{,}729} \\ -\,40 \\ \hline 72 \\ -\,72 \\ \hline 09 \\ -\,8 \\ \hline 1 \end{array}$$

47 hundreds ÷ 8 is about 5 hundreds.

$8 \times 5 = 40$

72 tens ÷ 8 is 9 tens.

$8 \times 9 = 72$

9 ones ÷ 8 is about 1 one.

$8 \times 1 = 8$

$p = 591$ R1

There were 591 packages of hot dogs sold, and 1 hot dog was sold from another package.

Convince Me! Reasoning Use estimation to decide which of the division problems have a quotient between 300 and 400. Tell how you decided.

$4\overline{)1{,}174}$ $5\overline{)1{,}988}$ $6\overline{)2{,}146}$ $7\overline{)2{,}887}$

Name ____________________

Guided Practice*

Do You Understand?

1. **Reasoning** Your estimate can help you determine whether the quotient will have 2 or 3 digits. Does an estimate help you determine if there is going to be a remainder? Explain.

2. **Critique Reasoning** Vickie's estimated quotient was 80. The actual quotient she calculated was 48. Is her actual quotient reasonable? Explain.

Do You Know How?

For **3–6**, divide. Start by estimating.

3. $9\overline{)2{,}871}$ **4.** $4\overline{)468}$

5. $9\overline{)691}$ **6.** $4\overline{)1{,}140}$

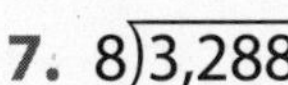

Independent Practice

For **7–10**, divide. Start by estimating.

7. $8\overline{)3{,}288}$ **8.** $5\overline{)247}$ **9.** $6\overline{)1{,}380}$ **10.** $5\overline{)3{,}980}$

For **11–18**, estimate to decide if the answers are reasonable. If the answer is not reasonable, find the correct answer.

11. $6\overline{)367}$ = 61 R1 **12.** $3\overline{)3{,}582}$ = 911 R6 **13.** $5\overline{)247}$ = 49 R2 **14.** $6\overline{)999}$ = 166 R3

15. $9\overline{)1{,}745}$ = 93 R8 **16.** $7\overline{)375}$ = 53 R4 **17.** $8\overline{)1{,}535}$ = 91 R7 **18.** $9\overline{)8{,}772}$ = 974 R6

*For another example, see Set G on page 318.

Problem Solving

19. A family of four drove from San Francisco to New York. They drove the same number of miles each day for 6 days. How many miles did they drive each day? How can you interpret the remainder?

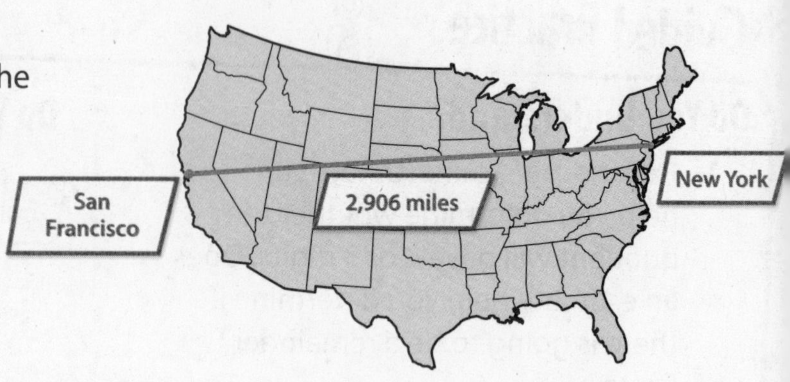

20. Reasoning Without dividing, how can you tell if the quotient for 5,873 ÷ 8 is greater than 700? Explain whether the quotient is less than 800.

21. A square dance set is made up of 4 couples (8 dancers). There are 150 people at a square dance. What is the greatest number of sets possible at the dance?

22. Higher Order Thinking Is rounding or using compatible numbers a more useful method when finding quotients in division problems? Explain.

23. Ron's Tires has 1,767 tires for heavy-duty trucks. Each heavy-duty truck needs 6 tires. How many heavy-duty trucks can get all new tires at Ron's?

24. Use each number in the box once to complete the division problem.

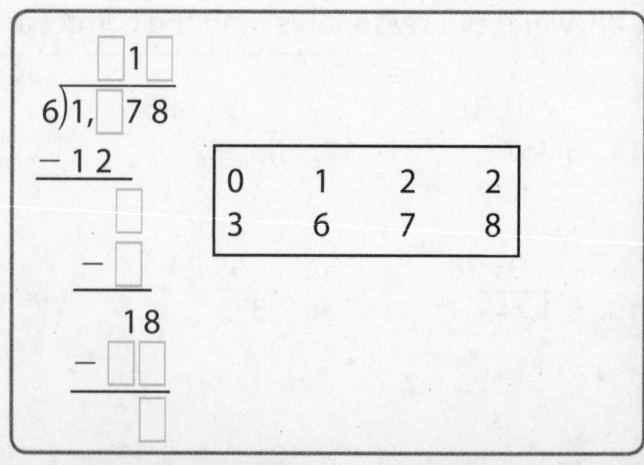

Name ________________________

Help Practice Buddy Tools Games

Homework & Practice 5-9

Continue to Divide with 1-Digit Numbers

Another Look!

Use the same steps for dividing a 4-digit number that you used for dividing 3-digit numbers.

Find 5,490 ÷ 6.

Estimate first. You can use compatible numbers to divide mentally.

54 is a multiple of 6.

5,400 is close to 5,490, and 5,400 ÷ 6 is easy to divide.

5,400 ÷ 6 = 900

Divide to find the actual quotient.

```
   915
6)5,490
 - 54
    09
   - 6
    30
  - 30
     0
```

Compare. Is the estimate close to the quotient?

The estimate of 900 is close to the actual quotient of 915, so the answer is reasonable.

For **1–8**, estimate first. Then find each quotient.

1. Divide 4,318 ÷ 7.

Estimate: ________ ÷ ____ = ________

4,318 ÷ 7 = ________

2. Divide 4,826 ÷ 5.

Estimate: ________ ÷ ____ = ________

4,826 ÷ 5 = ________

3. 8)4,377

4. 9)7,192

5. 6)2,750

6. 4)6,208

7. 7)2,025

8. 5)9,490

9. **Math and Science** Sound travels in waves. In dry air at 20° Celsius, sound travels about 343 meters in one second. How many meters will sound travel in 7 seconds?

10. **Construct Arguments** Lilly estimated a quotient of 120 and found an actual quotient of 83. What should she do next? Explain.

11. At the airport, there are a total of 1,160 seats in the waiting areas. There are 8 separate, same size, waiting areas. How many seats are in each waiting area?

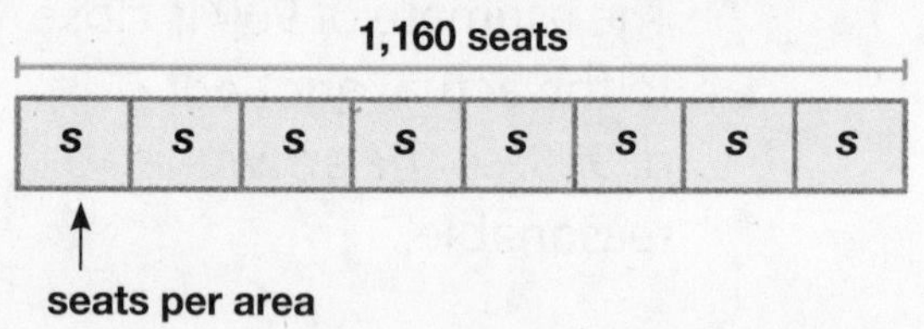

12. A fence around the school football field is 1,666 feet long. Seven teams of students will paint the fence. Each team will paint an equal length of the fence. What length of the fence will each team paint?

13. **Higher Order Thinking** Mr. Conners put a fence around the outside of his rectangular yard shown at the right. He put a fence post every 6 feet. How many fence posts did he use?

330 ft

102 ft 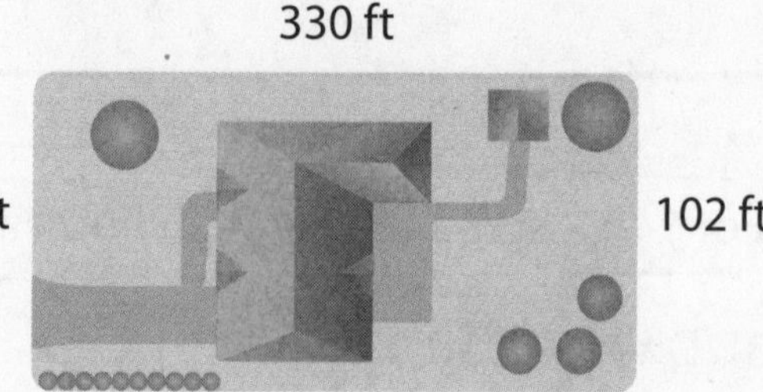 102 ft

330 ft

Assessment ISTEP+ Ready

14. Use each number in the box once to complete the division.

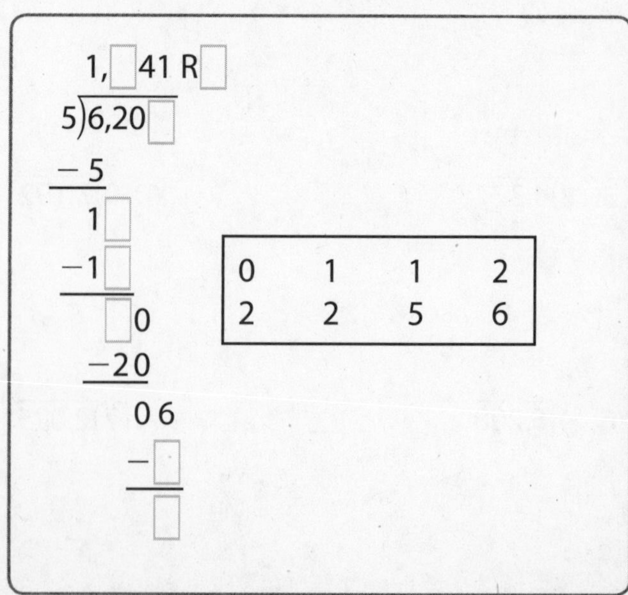

Name ________________________________

Problem Solving

Lesson 5-10

Model with Math

I can ...
use a drawing, diagram, or table to model a problem.

Process Standards PS.4 Also PS.1, PS.2, PS.6, PS.7, PS.8
Content Standard 4.C.3

Solve & Share

Allen set a goal to do at least 120 minutes of outdoor activities a day, Monday through Friday. He made a list of each activity and the amount of time he spends doing it every week. The same amount of time is spent every day doing the activities. Is Allen spending enough time each day on outdoor activities to meet his goal? What math can you use to solve this problem?

DATA

Activity	Weekly Time in Minutes
Soccer	200
Bicycling	150
Walking	300
Running	75

Thinking Habits

Be a good thinker!
These questions can help you.

- How can I use math I know to help solve this problem?
- Can I use pictures, objects, or an equation to represent this problem?
- How can I use numbers, words, and symbols to solve the problem?

Look Back! Model with Math What hidden question do you have to answer before you can determine if Allen met his goal? Explain.

Essential Question

How Can You Apply Math You Know to Solve Problems?

A

A class is making decorations using same-size straws. They use the straws to make triangles, squares, pentagons, and hexagons. One package of straws is used for each group of polygons with the same number of sides. How many decorations can the class make?

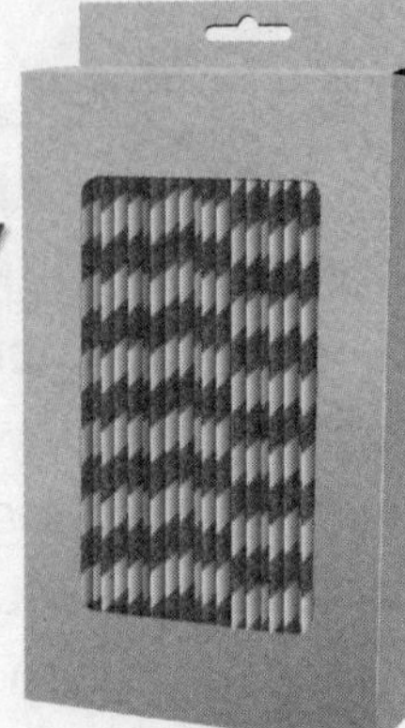

What math can you use to solve the problem?

I need to divide to find how many decorations can be made from one box of straws.

B

How can I model with math?

I can

- use previously learned concepts and skills.
- find and answer any hidden questions.
- decide if my results make sense.

C

Here's my thinking.

Each polygon has a different number of sides.

I will divide 1,500 straws by the number of sides for each polygon:

$1,500 \div 3 = 500$ triangles $\quad 1,500 \div 4 = 375$ squares

$1,500 \div 5 = 300$ pentagons $\quad 1,500 \div 6 = 250$ hexagons

I will add all the decorations together:

$500 + 375 + 300 + 250 = 1,425$

The class can make 1,425 decorations.

Convince Me! **Reasoning** The class made 200 octagon-shaped decorations. How many straws did they use?

Name ____________________

Practice Buddy Tools Assessment

Guided Practice*

Model with Math

Miguel is going camping with 3 friends. He packed sandwiches for everyone to share equally. How many sandwiches did Miguel pack for each camper?

1. What hidden question do you need to solve first? Explain how it relates to the solution.

2. Complete the bar diagram. Write and solve an equation to find the number of sandwiches, s, for each camper.

sandwiches

You can use a bar diagram and write an equation to model with math.

Independent Practice

Model with Math

Jodi delivers 54 newspapers on Saturday and 78 newspapers on Sunday. She makes bundles of 6 newspapers for each of her delivery routes. How many delivery routes does Jodi have on Saturday and Sunday?

3. Explain how you could use a picture to represent the problem and show the relationships.

4. Write and solve equations to represent the problem. Explain how you can check that your solution is reasonable.

*For another example, see Set H on page 318.

Problem Solving

Performance Assessment ISTEP+ Ready

Dog Grooming

Patricia and Antonio own a dog grooming business. To attract new customers, they offered free dog baths with the purchase of a grooming service. During the first 6 days of the promotion, they bathed 26 beagles, 12 boxers, 17 pugs, and 5 golden retrievers. Patricia and Antonio each bathed the same number of dogs each day.

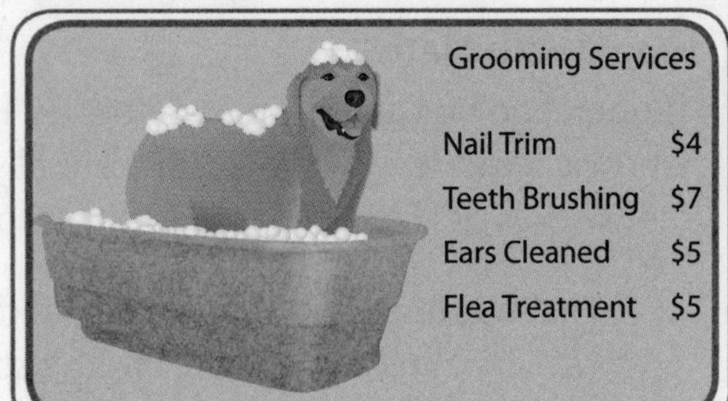

Grooming Services
Nail Trim $4
Teeth Brushing $7
Ears Cleaned $5
Flea Treatment $5

5. **Make Sense and Persevere** What are the quantities given in the problem?

6. **Reasoning** What do you need to know to determine how many dogs Patricia bathed each day?

7. **Model with Math** Draw a bar diagram. Write and solve an equation to find how many dogs were bathed in all.

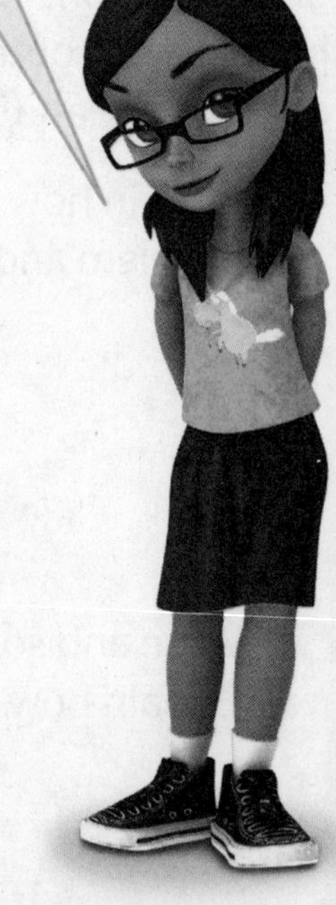

You model with math when you use a picture or object to represent the problem.

8. **Be Precise** How many dogs were bathed each day? Show your work.

9. **Use Structure** Use what you already know to find how many dogs Patricia bathed each day. Explain how you were able to find the solution.

Name ______________________

Homework & Practice 5-10
Model with Math

Another Look!

Molly is making tissue-paper flowers. She has 240 sheets of pink tissue paper and 260 sheets of yellow tissue paper. How many flowers will Molly be able to make with all her tissue paper?

7 sheets of any color tissue paper to make each flower

How you can model with math?

- I can use pictures, objects, and equations to show how to solve this problem.
- I can improve my math model if needed.

Find the hidden question to solve the problem.

How much tissue paper does Molly have in all?

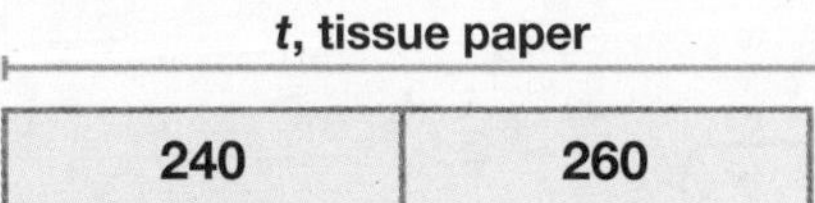

$240 + 260 = t$
$t = 500$
Molly has 500 sheets of tissue paper.

Answer the original question.

How many flowers will Molly be able to make?

Find $500 \div 7$.

$500 \div 7 = 71$ R3

Molly can make 71 tissue-paper flowers.

Model with Math
A school baseball team raised $810 for new uniforms. Each player on the team sold one book of tickets. There were 10 tickets in a book and each ticket cost $3. How many tickets were sold?

1. What extra information in the problem is **NOT** needed?

2. What equation can you write and solve to find the cost of each book of tickets sold?

3. How many tickets were sold? Explain.

4. How many players are on the baseball team?

Performance Assessment — ISTEP+ Ready

Yoga

Regina takes yoga classes 2 days a week at the community center. The cost for the classes is $72, and Regina pays an additional one-time fee of $12 to rent the yoga equipment used in class. The classes run for 6 weeks. The local gym offers the same yoga program, including equipment, for $8 a class. Is Regina paying more or less than what the local gym charges for yoga classes?

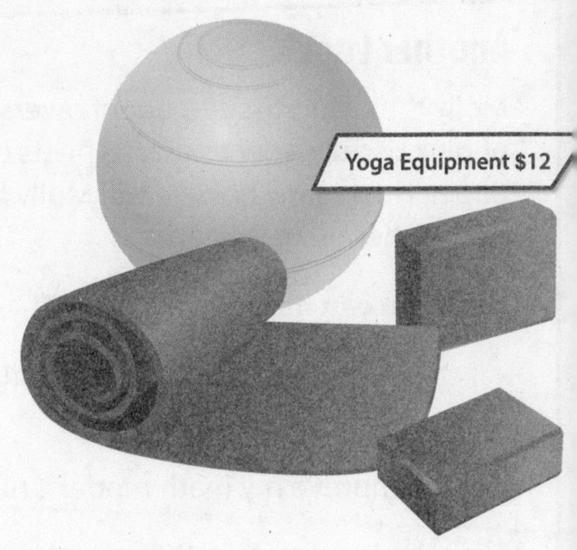

5. **Reasoning** What are the quantities given in the problem, and how are they related?

6. **Make Sense and Persevere** What is a good plan for solving the problem? Explain your strategy.

When you model with math, you use equations to model the problem.

7. **Be Precise** Is Regina paying more or less for yoga classes at the community center than what the local gym charges for the same program? Show how you calculated accurately.

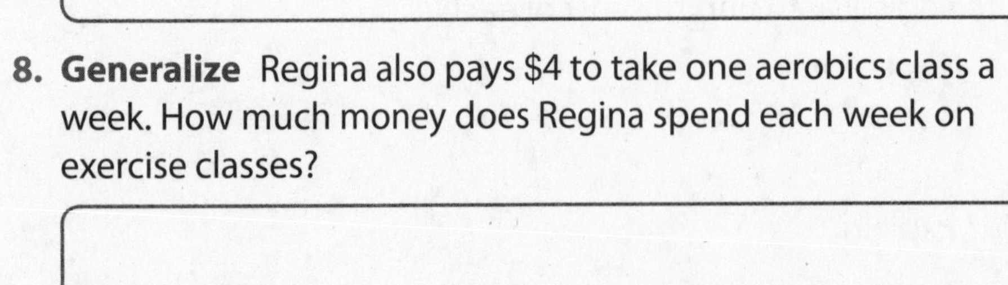

8. **Generalize** Regina also pays $4 to take one aerobics class a week. How much money does Regina spend each week on exercise classes?

Name ____________________

Fluency Practice Activity

Shade a path from **START** to **FINISH**. Follow the sums and differences that are between 1,000 and 1,200. You can only move up, down, right, or left.

I can ...
add and subtract whole numbers with regrouping.

Start				
314 + 707	7,020 − 5,001	686 + 304	1,064 − 145	1,201 + 289
4,300 − 3,200	1,220 + 99	4,054 − 3,913	909 + 402	1,509 − 519
999 + 200	3,099 − 899	484 + 750	1,580 − 670	1,010 + 1,101
3,455 − 2,305	807 + 499	3,704 − 2,544	725 + 460	1,388 − 209
623 + 500	2,010 − 1,009	800 + 350	1,577 − 368	1,050 + 99
				Finish

TOPIC 5 Vocabulary Review

Glossary

Word List

- dividend
- divisible
- division
- divisor
- equation
- partial quotients
- quotient
- remainder

Understand Vocabulary

Choose the best term from the box. Write it on the blank.

1. The answer to a division problem is called the ________________.

2. The number to be divided in a division problem is called the ________________.

3. A way to divide that finds quotients in parts until only a remainder, if any, is left is called using ________________.

4. The number by which another number is divided is called the ________________.

5. The operation that tells how many equal groups there are or how many are in each group is called ________________.

For each of these terms, give an example and a non-example.

	Example	Non-example
6. equation	________________	________________
7. remainder	________________	________________
8. divisible numbers	________________	________________

Use Vocabulary in Writing

9. Megan made 21 loom bracelets to share equally among her 7 friends. How many bracelets will each friend receive? Write and solve an equation. Use at least 3 terms from the Word List to describe your equation.

Name ______________________________

Set A pages 253–258

A school district shares 2,700 chairs equally among 3 school buildings.

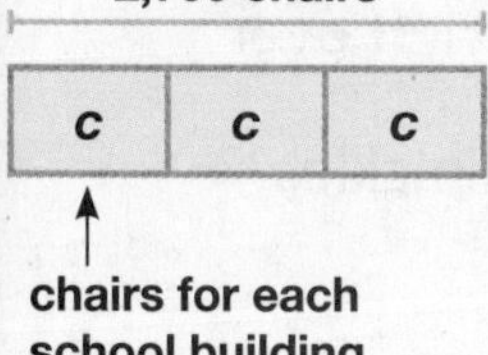

Find $2{,}700 \div 3 = c$.

The basic fact is $27 \div 3 = 9$.

27 hundreds $\div\ 3 = 9$ hundreds, or 900.

So, $2{,}700 \div 3 = 900$ chairs.

Remember you can use basic division facts and patterns to divide mentally.

1. $250 \div 5$
2. $810 \div 9$
3. $3{,}200 \div 4$
4. $4{,}200 \div 7$
5. $1{,}000 \div 2$
6. $240 \div 4$
7. $450 \div 5$
8. $720 \div 9$
9. $3{,}600 \div 4$
10. $4{,}900 \div 7$
11. $2{,}000 \div 2$
12. $280 \div 4$
13. $2{,}100 \div 7$
14. $560 \div 8$

Set B pages 259–270

Use multiplication to estimate $420 \div 8$.

8 times what number is about 420?

$8 \times 5 = 40$,
so, $8 \times 50 = 400$.

So, $420 \div 8$ is about 50.

Use compatible numbers to estimate $1{,}519 \div 7$.

What number close to 1,519 is easily divided by 7?

Try division facts to help find compatible numbers for 1,519

1,519 is close to 1,400.

$14 \div 7 = 2$,
so $1{,}400 \div 7 = 200$.

So, $1{,}519 \div 7$ is about 200.

Remember basic facts can help you find a number that is easily divided by the divisor.

Estimate each quotient.

1. $718 \div 8$
2. $156 \div 4$
3. $482 \div 8$
4. $174 \div 3$
5. $843 \div 7$
6. $321 \div 2$
7. $428 \div 6$
8. $811 \div 9$
9. $5{,}616 \div 8$
10. $7{,}224 \div 8$
11. $6{,}324 \div 9$
12. $3{,}627 \div 9$
13. $331 \div 4$
14. $1{,}222 \div 6$
15. $2{,}511 \div 5$
16. $362 \div 6$
17. $4{,}940 \div 7$
18. $9{,}312 \div 3$

Set C pages 271–276

Tom is putting 14 apples into bags. Each bag holds 4 apples. How many bags can Tom fill? Will any apples be left over?

Use a model to represent $14 \div 4$.

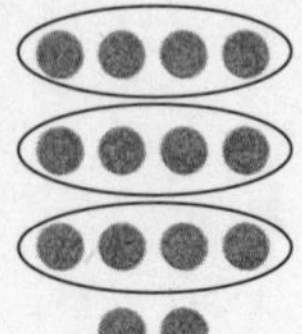

$14 \div 4 = 3$ R2

Tom can fill 3 bags. There will be 2 apples left over.

Remember to make sure the remainder is less than the divisor.

1. 22 pickles
3 pickles on each plate
$22 \div 3 =$ ____ with ____ left over

How many plates have 3 pickles?

____

2. 19 stamps
2 stamps on each envelope
$19 \div 2 =$ ____ with ____ left over

How many stamps are not on an envelope?

____

Set D pages 277–282

Margaret packed 68 books equally into 2 boxes. How many books did Margaret pack in each box?

Find $68 \div 2$.

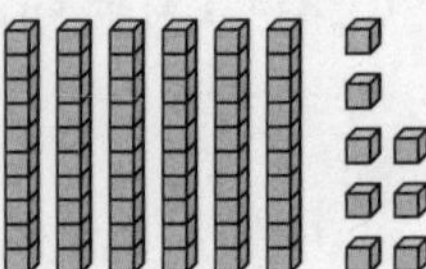

68 books

Divide the tens into two equal groups.
Then divide the ones into two equal groups.

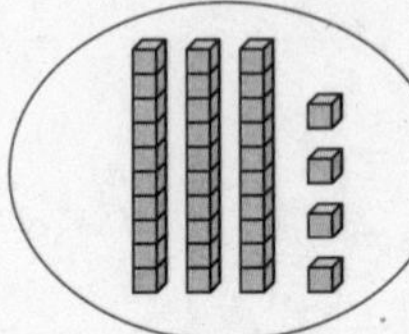

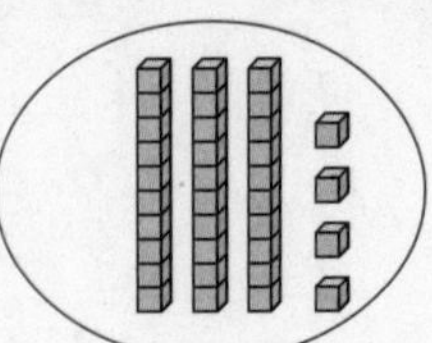

$68 \div 2 = 34$, because $2 \times 34 = 68$.

Margaret packed 34 books in each box.

Remember to check if your answer is reasonable.

Tell how many are in each group and how many are left over.

1. 138 books; 5 stacks

2. 55 shells; 3 jars

3. 217 pens; 7 cases

4. 154 shoes; 4 boxes

5. 195 seeds; 6 planters

6. 110 books; 6 shelves

Name ______________________________

TOPIC 5

Reteaching
Continued

Set E pages 283–294

Find $357 \div 7$.

Use a model. Divide by finding partial quotients.

	50	+ 1 = 51
7	$357 - 350 = 7$	$7 - 7 = 0$

$$\begin{array}{r} 1 \\ 50 \\ 7\overline{)357} \\ -350 \\ \hline 7 \\ -7 \\ \hline 0 \end{array} \quad 1 + 50 = 51$$

Remember to add the partial quotients to find the actual quotient.

Use partial quotients to solve.

1. There are 81 chairs in 3 equal groups. How many chairs are in each group?

2. There are 174 games scheduled for 6 different leagues. Each league has the same number of games scheduled. How many games does each league have scheduled?

3. There were 1,278 people at the last basketball game. The stands were divided into 6 sections. The same number of people sat in each section. How many people sat in each section?

Set F pages 295–300

Find $566 \div 6$.
Estimate $600 \div 6 = 100$.

$$\begin{array}{r} 94 \text{ R2} \\ 6\overline{)566} \\ -54 \\ \hline 26 \\ -24 \\ \hline 2 \end{array}$$

56 tens ÷ 6
Each group gets 9 tens.
2 tens are left.
Unbundle 2 tens.
20 ones + 6 ones = 26 ones
26 ÷ 6
Each group gets 4 ones.
2 ones are left.

94 R2 is close to 100, so the answer is reasonable.

Remember to estimate the quotient to check if your answer is reasonable.

1. $710 \div 9$
2. $657 \div 5$
3. $398 \div 8$
4. $429 \div 2$
5. $470 \div 6$
6. $255 \div 4$

Set G pages 301–306

Find 8,951 ÷ 8.
Estimate: 8,800 ÷ 8 = 1,100.

1,118 R7	
8)8,951	8 thousands ÷ 8 is 1 thousand.
− 8	8 × 1 = 8
9	9 hundreds ÷ 8 is about 1 hundred.
− 8	8 × 1 = 8
15	15 tens ÷ 8 is about 1 ten.
− 8	8 × 1 = 8
71	71 ones ÷ 8 is about 8 ones.
− 64	8 × 8 = 64
7	

Remember you can use your estimate to check if your answer is reasonable.

1. 4,649 ÷ 4
2. 2,843 ÷ 3
3. 8,478 ÷ 6
4. 6,399 ÷ 9
5. 379 ÷ 2
6. 3,812 ÷ 5
7. 4,793 ÷ 5
8. 5,957 ÷ 7
9. 9,579 ÷ 4
10. 3,668 ÷ 6

Set H pages 307–312

Think about these questions to help you **model with math**.

Thinking Habits

- How can I use math I know to help solve this problem?
- Can I use pictures, objects, or an equation to represent the problem?
- How can I use numbers, words, and symbols to solve the problem?

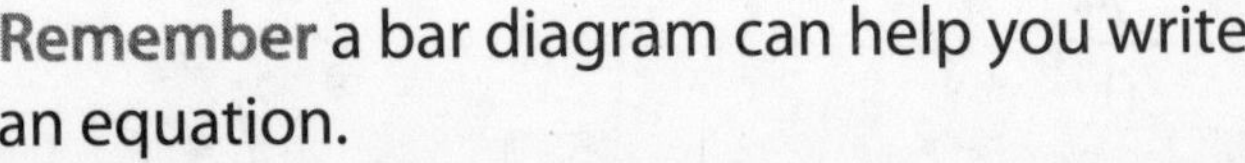

Remember a bar diagram can help you write an equation.

A paint supplier delivered 1,345 cans of paint to 5 different hardware stores. Each store got the same number of paint cans. How many cans of paint were delivered to each store?

1. How can you use pictures, a bar diagram, and an equation to find the number of paint cans delivered to each store?

2. How can you decide if your answer makes sense?

Name ____________________

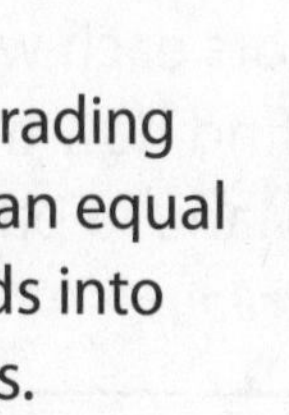

1. Robert earned $184 mowing 8 lawns. He earned the same amount for mowing each lawn. Select all the equations that show reasonable estimates for the amount Robert earned mowing each lawn.

   ☐ $160 ÷ 8 = $20
   ☐ $200 ÷ 5 = $40
   ☐ $180 ÷ 9 = $20
   ☐ $150 ÷ 5 = $30
   ☐ $180 ÷ 6 = $30

2. Mr. Dermot saves an equal amount of money each month for 6 months. He is saving to buy a motorcycle that costs $2,400. Draw a bar diagram. Write and solve an equation to find how much money Mr. Dermot needs to save each month to buy the motorcycle.

3. Mrs. Bollis has 26 yards of fabric to make costumes. Each costume requires 3 yards of fabric. How many costumes can Mrs. Bollis make? How many yards will she have left?

4. Trace has 453 trading cards. He puts an equal number of cards into each of 3 books.

Part A

Write an equation to show the number of cards Trace put in each book.

Part B

Complete the model. How many trading cards did Trace put in each book?

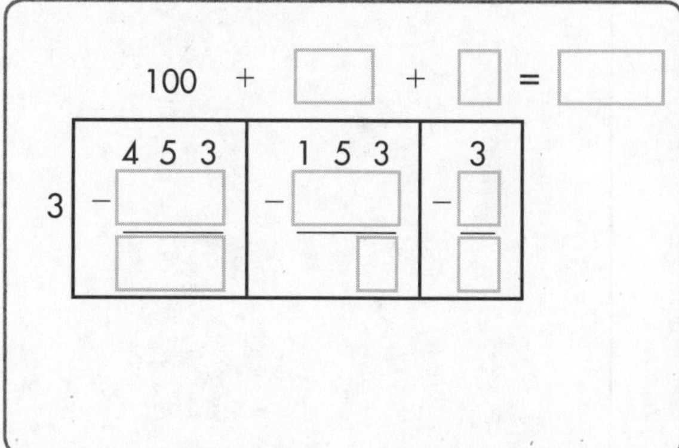

5. A school has $3,664 for scholarships. The scholarship money was awarded equally to 8 students. How much money did each student receive?

   Ⓐ $358
   Ⓑ $450
   Ⓒ $458
   Ⓓ $485

6. Marla will paint 48 pots. She plans to paint 9 pots each week. Draw an array to find how many weeks it will take Marla to paint all of the pots. Explain.

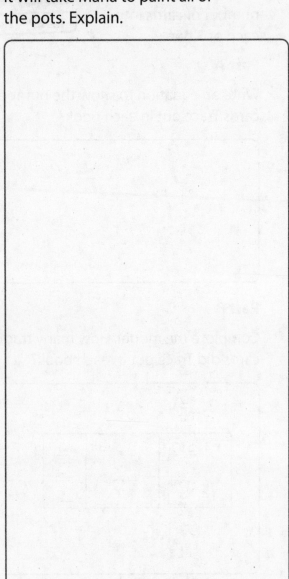

7. Draw lines to match the expression to the estimated quotient.

330 ÷ 4	About 400
1,199 ÷ 3	About 60
614 ÷ 6	About 80
475 ÷ 8	About 100

8. There are 4,800 plastic spoons in a case. There are 6 boxes of spoons in each case. How many spoons are in each box?

9. Choose Yes or No to tell if the remainder is 5.

9a. 59 ÷ 9 = 6 R? ○ Yes ○ No

9b. 352 ÷ 6 = 58 R? ○ Yes ○ No

9c. 1,486 ÷ 7 = 212 R? ○ Yes ○ No

9d. 2,957 ÷ 8 = 369 R? ○ Yes ○ No

10. Olivia has 36 daisies and 6 vases. She puts the same number of daisies in each vase. Which equation shows how to find the number, n, of daisies Olivia puts in each vase?

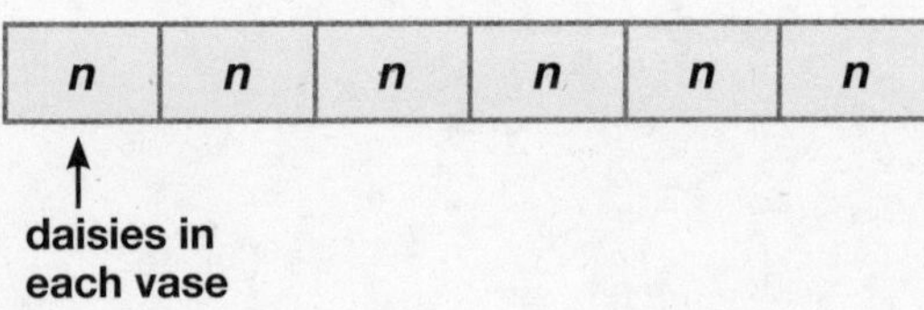

Ⓐ $36 \div 6 = n$

Ⓑ $36 \times 6 = n$

Ⓒ $36 + 6 = n$

Ⓓ $36 - 6 = n$

11. The distance from Mac's house to school is 575 yards. Mac's goal is to walk to school in 5 minutes. How many yards does Mac need to walk each minute to meet his goal?

Name ______________________________

12. There are 472 students in 6 different grades. Each grade has about the same number of students. Select all the statements that are reasonable estimates for the number of students in each grade.

- ☐ 50 students, because $472 \div 6$ is about $450 \div 5$.
- ☐ 80 students, because $472 \div 6$ is about $480 \div 6$.
- ☐ 100 students, because $472 \div 6$ is about $500 \div 5$.
- ☐ 150 students, because $472 \div 6$ is about $450 \div 3$.
- ☐ 200 students, because $472 \div 6$ is about $1{,}200 \div 6 = 200$.

13. Use an algorithm to find the quotient. Choose numbers from the box to complete the calculations. Use each number once.

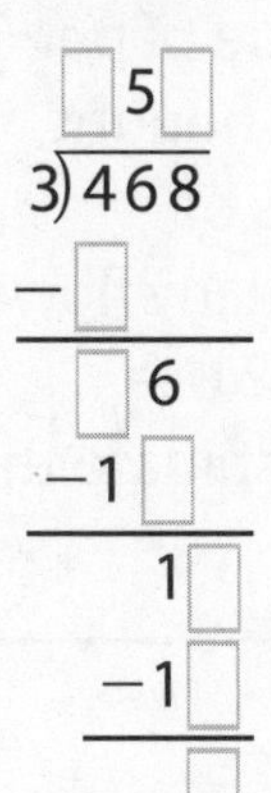

0	1
1	3
5	6
8	8

14. Carla needs 1,600 beads to make 8 necklaces. She divides the beads equally. How many beads does Carla use for each necklace? What basic fact did you use?

15. The fourth graders are going to the science museum.

DATA

Group	Number of People
Mr. Vorel's Class	30
Ms. Cahill's Class	32
Mrs. Winter's Class	29
Miss Meyer's Class	28
Teachers and Chaperones	9

Groups of 8 people can see a special exhibit on space travel. How many groups will be needed so everyone can see the exhibit?

16. Albert was asked to find the quotient for $63 \div 3$. He drew an array and used the Distributive Property to find the quotient. Show Albert's work.

17. The Pizza Stand gives patrons a free pizza when they collect 8 coupons. How many free pizzas can Mrs. Fowler get if she has 78 coupons? How many more coupons does she need for the next free pizza?

18. Estimate $257 \div 5$. Explain how you can use multiplication to estimate the quotient.

19. Alex has 128 photos of his friends to display equally in 4 photo albums. Which equation can you use to find how many photos will be in each album?

Ⓐ $128 - 4 = p$

Ⓑ $128 + 4 = p$

Ⓒ $128 \div 4 = p$

Ⓓ $128 \times 4 = p$

20. Draw a picture to explain why $657 \div 5 = 131$ R2.

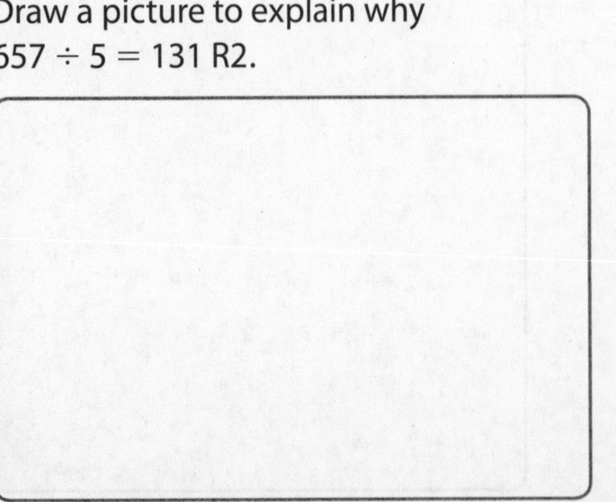

21. The 6 fourth-grade classes at West Elementary donated a total of $1,792 to restore a wildlife habitat. Write and solve an equation that shows one way to estimate the amount donated by each class.

22. Draw lines to match the equation to the correct missing number.

4,__00 ÷ 6 = 800	6
675 ÷ __ = 135	3
360 ÷ 6 = __0	8
98 ÷ 5 = 19 R__	5

23. Holly uses 7 sheets of tissue paper to make one flower. If she bought a package with 500 sheets of tissue paper, about how many flowers will Holly be able to make? Use compatible numbers to estimate the number of flowers.

Name ______________________________

TOPIC 5

Performance Assessment

ISTEP+ Ready

Saving What You Earn

Trista's older brother Ryan got a job. Ryan would like to buy the items shown with his earnings. Ryan earns $8 for each hour he works.

1. Ryan is curious and wants to know the amount of time it will take him to earn enough money to buy the items shown.

$480

$341

Game Box
BASKETBALL HEAT

$44

Part A

How many hours does Ryan need to work to earn enough money to buy the computer? Use place value and mental math to solve.

Part B

How many hours does Ryan need to work to buy the video game? Use a model to show how to find the quotient. Explain how to interpret the remainder.

Part C

How many hours will Ryan need to work to earn enough money to buy the smart phone? Use partial quotients to divide.

2. Ryan gets a raise. He now earns $9 an hour. Ryan decides to start saving for a car. He works 9 hours a week.

Used car: $2,793
Taxes, title, and plates: $235

Part A

How many hours does Ryan need to work to earn enough money to buy the car, as well as pay for the taxes, title, and plates as shown? Draw bar diagrams to help write and solve equations.

Part B

About how many weeks will Ryan need to work to buy the car and pay for the taxes, title, and plates? Explain.

Part C

How many actual weeks does Ryan need to work to buy the car and pay for the taxes, title, and plates? Show your computations. Explain why your solution is reasonable.

Use Operations with Whole Numbers to Solve Problems

Essential Questions: How is comparing with multiplication different from comparing with addition? How can you use equations to solve multi-step problems?

It takes a lot of energy to power a neighborhood. Renewable energy can lower the pollution produced by powering these homes!

Some homes use solar power for energy. This type of renewable energy uses sunlight and is good for the environment!

Some of the energy is stored for nighttime or when it is cloudy. Here is a project on energy and multiplication.

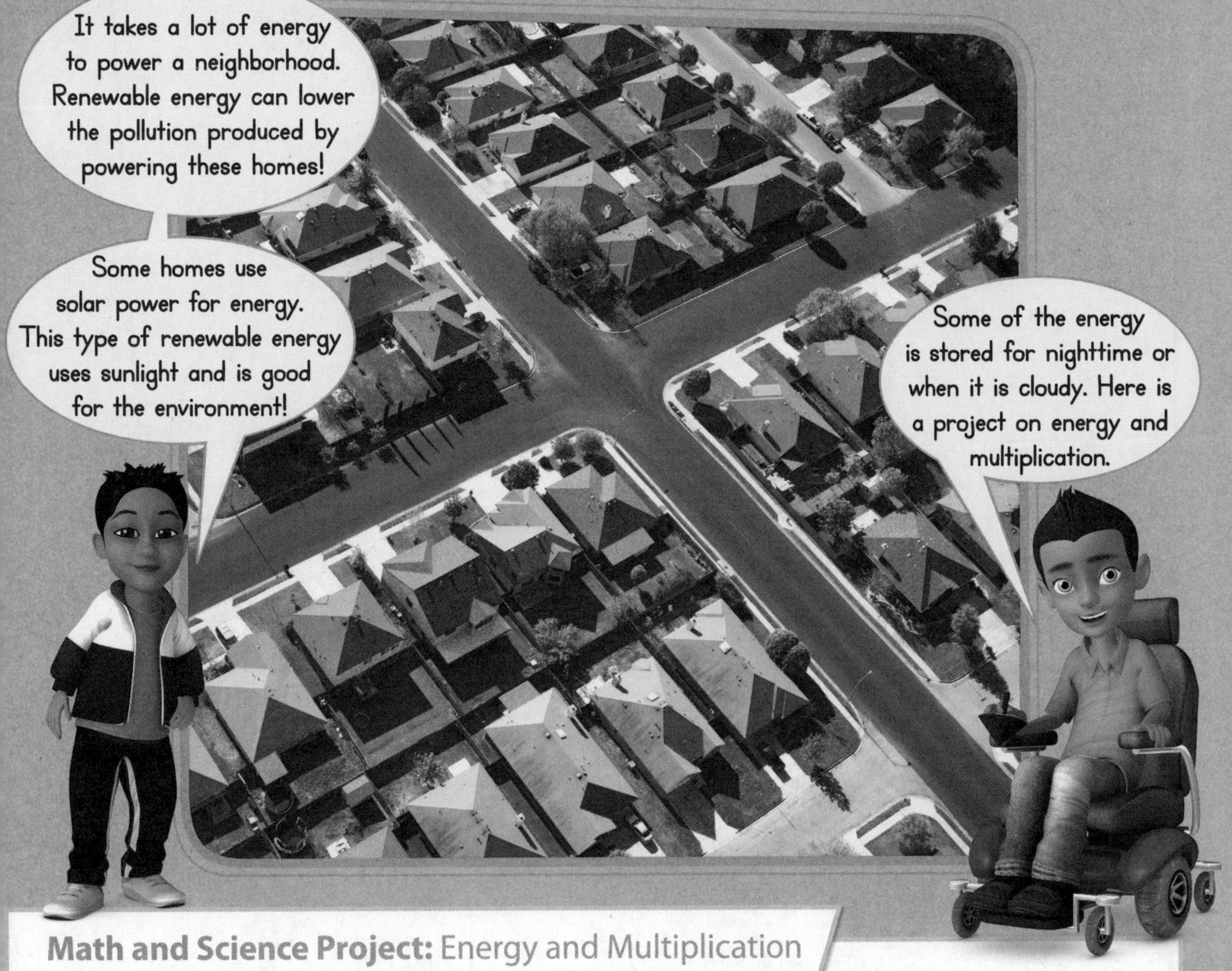

Math and Science Project: Energy and Multiplication

Do Research Use the Internet or other sources to find and describe 3 examples of renewable energy.

Journal: Write a Report Include what you found. Also in your report:

- Solar panels are made up of smaller modules or sections called cells. Find a picture of a solar panel. How many cells are in 6 solar panels? How many cells are in 9 solar panels? How many more cells are in the 9 solar panels than the 6 solar panels?
- Find examples of other items that use solar power.

Name ___________________________

Review What You Know

Vocabulary

Choose the best term from the box. Write it on the blank.

- Associative Property of Multiplication
- Commutative Property of Multiplication
- compatible numbers
- Distributive Property

1. The ___________________ ___________________ says that factors can be multiplied in any order and the product remains the same.

2. Breaking apart a multiplication problem into the sum or difference of two simpler multiplication problems is an example of using the ___________________.

3. According to the ___________________, factors can be regrouped and the product remains the same.

Dividing by 1-Digit Numbers

Estimate each quotient.

4. 16 ÷ 3 **5.** 25 ÷ 4 **6.** 155 ÷ 4

7. 304 ÷ 3 **8.** 1,283 ÷ 6 **9.** 1,999 ÷ 4

Multiplying by 1-Digit Numbers

Find each product.

10. 53 × 9 **11.** 1,127 × 7 **12.** 2,769 × 5

13. 3 × 215 **14.** 914 × 5 **15.** 1,238 × 5

Problem Solving

16. Construct Arguments Explain why the array represents 3 × 21.

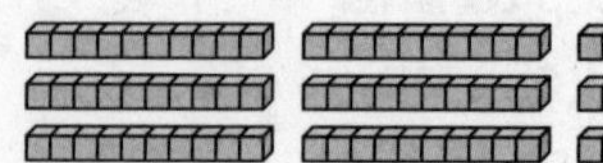

17. James multiplies 38 by 55. He finds three of the four partial products: 40, 150, and 400. Which partial product is James missing? What is the solution?

Name ______________________________

Solve

Lesson 6-1

Solve Comparison Situations

I can ...

use multiplication or addition to compare one quantity to another.

Content Standards 4.AT.3, 4.AT.4
Process Standards PS.1, PS.2, PS.3, PS.4, PS.5

Solve & Share

Sarah is making a square pillow with edges that each measure 18 inches long. She needs a strip of fabric 4 times as long as one edge of the pillow to make a border around the pillow. How long does the strip of fabric need to be? ***Solve this problem any way you choose.***

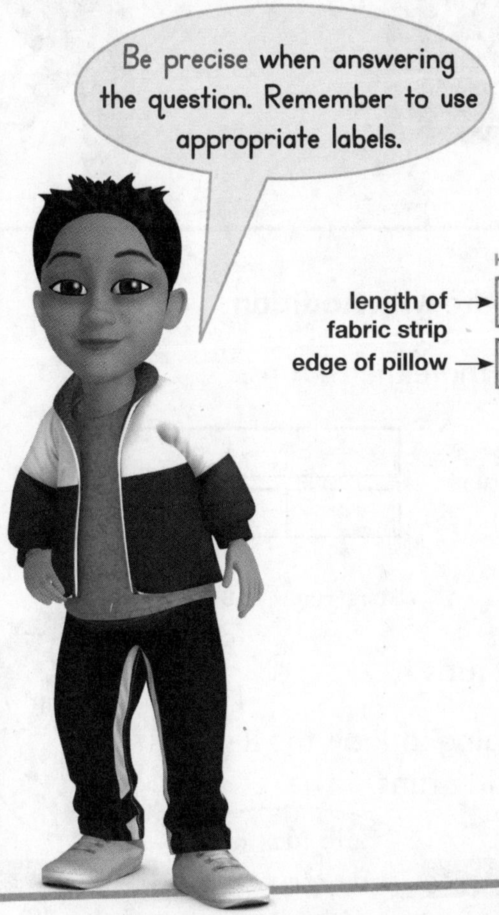

Be precise when answering the question. Remember to use appropriate labels.

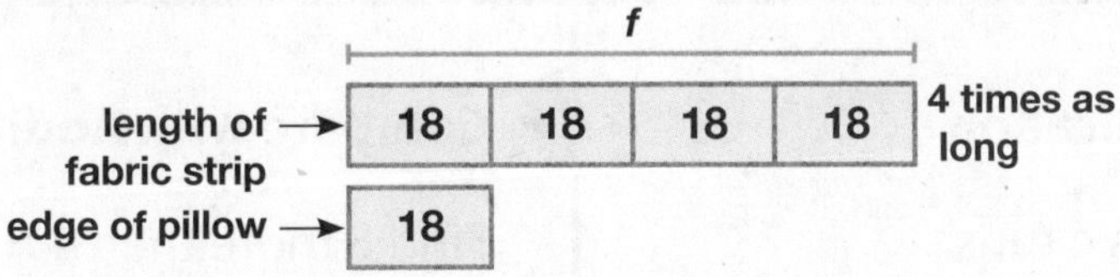

f

length of fabric strip → | 18 | 18 | 18 | 18 | 4 times as long

edge of pillow → | 18 |

Look Back! Use Appropriate Tools How does the bar diagram help you write and solve an equation for the problem?

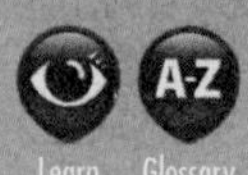

How Is Comparing with Multiplication Different from Comparing with Addition?

A

Max said the Rangers scored 3 times as many runs as the Stars. Jody said the Rangers scored 8 more runs than the Stars. Could both Max and Jody be correct?

You can use multiplication and addition to compare the number of runs made by each team.

B

Compare with Multiplication

Find 3 times as many as 4 runs.

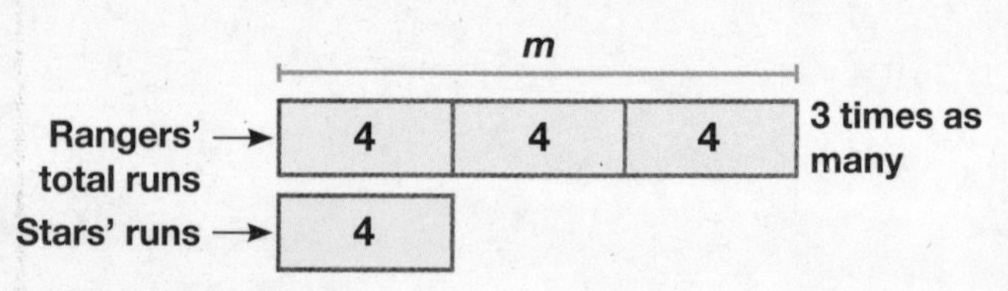

$m = 3 \times 4$

$m = 12$ runs

According to Max, the Rangers scored 12 runs.

C

Compare with Addition

Find 8 more than 4 runs.

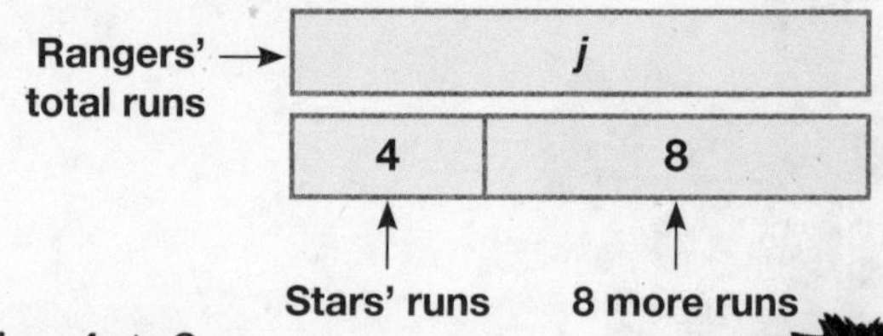

$j = 4 + 8$

$j = 12$ runs

According to Jody, the Rangers scored 12 runs.

Both Max and Jody are correct.

Convince Me! **Make Sense and Persevere** Describe when you would use multiplication and when you would use addition to make a comparison.

Name ____________________

Guided Practice*

Do You Understand?

1. **Reasoning** Use the information from the previous page. If the Rangers scored 5 times as many runs as the Stars, how many runs would the Rangers have scored?

   a. Compare using multiplication. Write and solve an equation.

   b. What is another way to compare the runs for the two teams?

Do You Know How?

For **2–3**, complete the comparison sentence. Find the value of the variable that makes the sentence true.

2. Sam has 4 times as many hats as Olga. Olga has 21 hats. How many hats does Sam have?

   h is ____ times as many as ____.
   h = ____

3. There are 128 more trees in the park than at Ty's house. There are 3 trees at Ty's house. How many trees are in the park?

   ____ more than ____ is *t*. *t* = ____

Independent Practice

Use *times as many as* or *more than* to compare the amounts.

For **4–9**, complete the comparison sentence. For **4–7**, find the value of the variable that makes the sentence true.

4. Katy has 6 times as many nickels as Shaun. Shaun has 18 nickels. How many nickels, *n*, does Katy have?

   n is 6 ____________ 18.
   n = ____

5. Kyle has watched 238 movies. Jason has watched 49 more movies than Kyle. How many movies, *m*, has Jason watched?

   m is 49 ____________ 238.
   m = ____

6. Amber tied 89 knots in a rope. Hunter tied 3 times as many knots in a rope as Amber. How many knots, *k*, did Hunter tie in a rope?

   k is 3 ____________ 89.
   k = ____

7. Tia sells 292 newspapers. Tess sells 117 more newspapers than Tia. How many newspapers, *n*, does Tess sell?

   n is 117 ____________ 292.
   n = ____

8. Trent has 48 markers. Sharon has 8 markers.

   Trent has ____ times as many markers as Sharon.

9. Lucy has 317 bottles. Craig has 82 bottles.

   Lucy has ____ more bottles than Craig.

*For another example, see Set A on page 359.

Problem Solving

10. **Model with Math** Roger swam 19 laps in the pool. Anna Maria swam 4 times as many laps as Roger. How many laps did Anna Maria swim? Draw a bar diagram and write an equation to solve the problem.

11. **Critique Reasoning** Nina says the equation $600 = 12 \times 50$ means 600 is 12 times as many as 50. Julio says the equation means 600 is 50 times as many as 12. Who is correct? Explain.

12. **Vocabulary** The amount that is left after dividing a number into equal parts is called the ________.

$13 \div 4 =$ ____

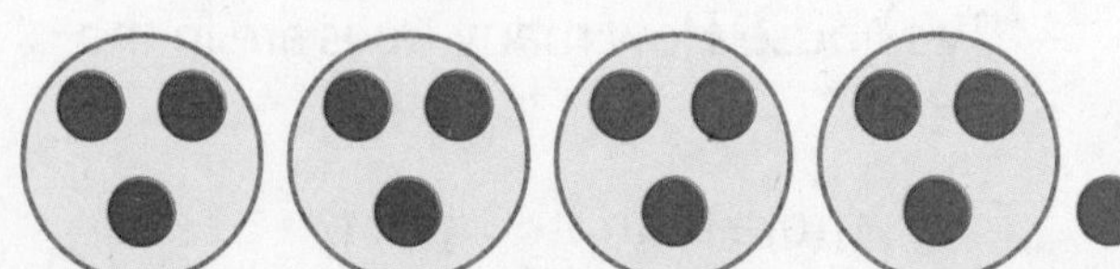

13. **Higher Order Thinking** A shirt is on sale for *d* dollars. The regular price is 4 times as much. Todd has enough money to buy 2 shirts at the regular price. How many shirts can Todd buy at the sale price? Explain.

Assessment ISTEP+ Ready

14. Select all the sentences that involve a comparison using multiplication.

- ☐ *k* is 26 times as many as 7.
- ☐ 18 more than 314 is *u*.
- ☐ Tom ran 4 miles. Cindy ran 2 more miles than Tom. How many miles did Cindy run?
- ☐ Yuhan has 2 dogs and Jon has 3 times as many dogs. How many dogs does Jon have?
- ☐ Kris has 14 times as many pairs of shoes as her brother. Her brother has 8 pairs of shoes.

15. Select all the sentences that can be represented by the equation $52 \times 13 = w$.

- ☐ 13 more than 52 is *w*.
- ☐ 52 times as much as 13 is *w*.
- ☐ Henry sang 52 songs during practice. He sang 13 times as many as Joe. How many songs did Joe sing?
- ☐ Greg carried 13 buckets of water to his sister's baby pool. His mother carried 52 times as many. How many buckets did Greg's mother carry?
- ☐ Tom has 52 pens. Joan has 13 fewer.

Name ______________________________

Homework & Practice 6-1

Solve Comparison Situations

Another Look!

Write an equation to represent each comparison problem. Find the value of the variable that makes the equation true.

Addition

The Tigers practice 26 hours a week more than the Bucks. The Bucks practice 13 hours a week. How many hours a week do the Tigers practice?

$13 + 26 = h$

$h = 39$ hours

The Tigers practice 39 hours each week.

Multiplication

The Tigers practice 3 times as many hours a week as the Bucks. The Bucks practice 13 hours a week. How many hours a week do the Tigers practice?

$3 \times 13 = h$

$h = 39$ hours

The Tigers practice 39 hours each week.

For **1–6**, complete the comparison sentence. For **1–4**, find the value of the variable that makes the sentence true.

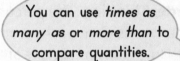

You can use *times as many as* or *more than* to compare quantities.

1. Jessica has 7 times as many paint brushes as Mike. Mike has 14 paint brushes. How many paint brushes, p, does Jessica have?

   p is 7 ______________ 14.
   $p =$ _____

2. Karin has 461 songs downloaded. Joe has 123 more songs downloaded than Karin. How many songs, s, does Joe have?

   s is 123 ______________ 461.
   $s =$ _____

3. David collected 617 cards. Sam collected 3 times as many cards as David. How many cards, c, does Sam have?

   c is 3 ______________ 617.
   $c =$ _____

4. Brandon bought 192 balloons. Adam bought 118 more balloons than Brandon. How many balloons, b, did Adam buy?

   b is 118 ______________ 192.
   $b =$ _____

5. Tammy worked 618 hours last year. Louie worked 487 hours last year.

   Tammy worked _____ more hours last year than Louie.

6. Stella saved $81. Her sister saved $9.

   Stella saved _____ times as much as her sister.

7. **Algebra** Martin has 12 times as many baseball cards as Josie. Josie has 29 more cards than Kal. How many baseball cards does Martin have? Write and solve equations.

8. Matt has 14 times as many cards as Kal. How many cards does Matt have?

Kal has 28 baseball cards.

For **9–10**, use the table at the right.

9. A marching band has 3 times as many trumpet players as tuba players. How many trumpet players are there? Write and solve an equation.

	t			
trumpets	16	16	16	3 times as many
tubas	16			

Brass Section

DATA	
Trombones	18
French horns	12
Trumpets	t
Tubas	16

10. **Higher Order Thinking** The percussion section has four times as many musicians as the trombones and French horns combined. How many musicians are in the percussion section? Write and solve equations.

Assessment ISTEP+ Ready

11. Select all the sentences that show a comparison using addition.

- ☐ j is 60 more than 17.
- ☐ 8 times as many as 50 is w.
- ☐ A watermelon costs $4 more than a bag of apples. A bag of apples costs $5. How much does a watermelon cost?
- ☐ Sharif has 8 yen in his money collection. He has twice as many pesos. How many pesos does Sharif have?
- ☐ 12 more than 20 is j.

12. Select all the sentences that can be represented by the equation $14 \times 82 = v$.

- ☐ 82 more than 14 is v.
- ☐ 14 times as many as 82 is v.
- ☐ Linda had 82 violets and Carrie had 14 times as many. How many violets did Carrie have?
- ☐ Ben takes 82 pictures. Ella takes 14 more. How many pictures does Ella take?
- ☐ 14 less than 82 is v.

Name ________________________________ Solve

Solve & Share

The students in Ms. Chang's fourth-grade class plant a tree every year. The diagram shows the current heights of this year's tree and last year's tree. Complete the sentences and equation to show a way to compare the heights of the trees.

Lesson 6-2

Continue to Solve Comparison Situations

I can ...

use multiplication or division to compare one quantity to another.

Content Standards 4.AT.3, 4.AT.4
Process Standards PS.1, PS.2, PS.3, PS.4

This year's tree is ________ inches tall.

Last year's tree is ________ times as tall as this year's tree. ________ × ________ = 36

Last Year's Tree
36 inches
This Year's Tree
6 inches
You can model with math and use equations to compare the heights of the two trees.

Look Back! Reasoning Compare the heights of the 2 trees using addition.

Essential Question

How Can You Solve a Comparison Problem Involving Multiplication as Comparison?

A

Calvin's sister travels 4 times as far to college as he travels. How far does Calvin travel to college?

Calvin's sister travels 192 miles to college

	192 miles				
Calvin's sister	*m*	*m*	*m*	*m*	4 times as far
Calvin	*m*				

Multiplication and division have an inverse relationship.

B The number of miles Calvin's sister travels, or 192 miles, is 4 times as far as Calvin travels.

Write a multiplication equation to find the number of miles Calvin travels to college.

$$192 = 4 \times m$$

What number times 4 equals 192?

C If $192 = 4 \times m$, then $m = 192 \div 4$.

$$\begin{array}{r} 48 \\ 4\overline{)192} \\ -16 \\ \hline 32 \\ -32 \\ \hline 0 \end{array}$$

	40	8
4	160	32

192

$m = 48$ miles

Calvin travels 48 miles to college.

Convince Me! **Make Sense and Persevere** When do you use division to make a comparison?

Name ____________________

Practice Buddy Tools Assessment

Guided Practice*

Do You Understand?

1. **Reasoning** Calvin's sister travels 3 times as far to college as his friend travels to college. Write and solve a related multiplication and division equation to find how far Calvin's friend travels to college.

Do You Know How?

2. Complete the comparison sentence. Find the value of the variable that makes the sentence true.

If $3 \times m = 48$, then $m = 48 \div 3$.

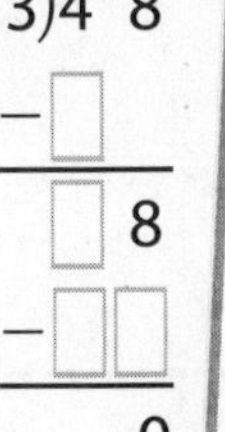

____ times as many as ____ is ____.

$m =$ ____

Independent Practice

For **3–8**, complete the comparison sentence. Find the value of the variable that makes the sentence true.

3. Connor has 77 magazines. That is 7 times as many magazines as Kristen has. How many magazines, n, does Kristen have?

   n ____________ 7 is 77.

   $n =$ ____ $\div 7$

   $n =$ ____

4. Eric completed 75 math problems. That is 5 times as many math problems as Katie completed. How many math problems, m, did Katie complete?

   75 is 5 ____________ m.

   ____ $\div 5 = m$

   $m =$ ____

5. Clare counted 117 different colors at the paint store. That is 9 times as many as the number James counted. How many different colors, c, did James count?

   117 is 9 ____________ c.

   ____ $\div$ ____ $= c$

   $c =$ ____

6. Alisa has 153 dominoes. That is 3 times as many dominoes as Stan has. How many dominoes, d, does Stan have?

   153 is 3 ____________ d.

   ____ $\div$ ____ $= d$

   $d =$ ____

7. Justin practiced piano for h hours. His sister practiced for 12 hours, which was 3 times as many hours as Justin practiced. Write and solve an equation to find how many hours Justin practiced piano.

8. Mary practiced violin for 2 hours and her brother practiced trombone t times as long or 8 hours. Write and solve an equation to find how many times as long Mary's brother practiced trombone.

*For another example, see Set B on page 359.

Problem Solving

9. **Model with Math** Dave is making soup that includes 12 cups of water and 3 cups of broth. How many times as much water as broth will be in the soup? Draw a bar diagram and write and solve an equation.

10. **Construct Arguments** Trevor wants to buy three light fixtures that cost $168 each. He has $500. Does he have enough money to buy the three light fixtures? Use a comparison sentence to explain your reasoning.

11. Miranda has 4 times as many leaves in her collection as Joy. Joy has 13 more leaves than Armani. Armani has 10 leaves in his collection. How many leaves does Miranda have in her collection? Explain.

12. **Higher Order Thinking** Jordan needs $9,240 for her first year of college tuition. Each of her two grandfathers said they would match what she saves. She has 8 years before she goes to college. How much does Jordan need to save on her own each year to have enough for her first year with the help from her two grandfathers?

Some problems require more than one operation.

Assessment ISTEP+ Ready

13. Tina walked 20 miles for a fundraiser. Lia walked *m* miles. Tina walked 4 times as far as Lia. Which equation can be used to find *m*, the number of miles Lia walked?

Ⓐ $m = 4 \times 20$

Ⓑ $20 = 4 \times m$

Ⓒ $20 = m \div 4$

Ⓓ $m = 20 + 4$

14. Jason and Raul kept a reading log for the year. Jason read 7 books and Raul read 35. How many times as many books as Jason did Raul read?

Ⓐ 3 times

Ⓑ 4 times

Ⓒ 5 times

Ⓓ 6 times

Name ______________________

Help Practice Buddy Tools Games

Homework & Practice 6-2

Continue to Solve Comparison Situations

Another Look!

Darrell has 3 cousins. Robert has 42 cousins. How many times as many cousins does Robert have as Darrell?

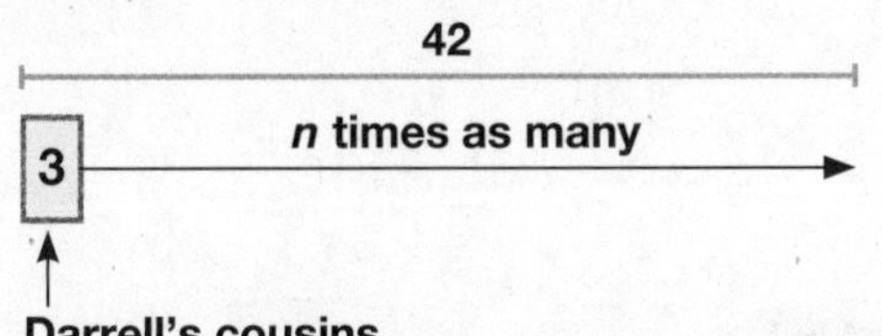

Since you know the original amount and the total, you need to divide to find how many times as many.

Write a multiplication equation to compare the numbers of cousins.

Robert's cousins = n times as many × Darrell's cousins

$42 = n \times 3$

What number times 3 equals 42?

Write and solve a related division equation.

If $42 = n \times 3$, then $n = 42 \div 3$.

$n = 14$

$$\begin{array}{r} 14 \\ 3\overline{)42} \\ -3 \\ \hline 12 \\ -12 \\ \hline 0 \end{array}$$

Robert has 14 times as many cousins as Darrell.

For **1–4**, complete the comparison sentence. Find the value of the variable that makes the sentence true.

1. There are 51 families in Oakville who have a pool. That is 3 times as many families with a pool than in Elmburg. How many families in Elmburg have a pool?

51 is 3 ______________ n.

$n =$ ____ $\div$ ____

$n =$ ____

2. Gilbert walked 288 minutes. That is 4 times as many minutes as Eileen walked. How many minutes, m, did Eileen walk?

288 is 4 ______________ m.

____ $\div$ ____ $= m$

$m =$ ____

3. Marcy picked 3 times as many ounces of kale as Phil picked. Phil picked 42 ounces of kale. How many ounces of kale, k, did Marcy pick?

3 ______________ 42 is k.

$k =$ ____ $\times$ ____

$k =$ ____

4. Jennifer feeds 5 times as many fish as Tony. Tony feeds 56 fish. How many fish, f, does Jennifer feed?

5 ______________ 56 is f.

$5 \times$ ____

$f =$ ____

5. Algebra How many times as much does the yellow T-shirt cost as the blue T-shirt? Draw a bar diagram and write and solve an equation.

6. Algebra Mason is 9 years old. His mother's age is 4 times Mason's age. How old is Mason's mother? Draw a bar diagram and write and solve an equation.

You can multiply to find Mason's mother's age.

7. Critique Reasoning Hilary walked 654 feet in 3 minutes. She says she walked about 200 feet per minute. Is Hilary's estimate reasonable? Explain.

8. Higher Order Thinking The value of n is both 5 times as much as the value of m and 36 more than the value of m. What are the values of n and m? Explain.

ISTEP+ Ready

9. Debbie has 8 quarters and 24 pennies in her piggy bank. She has n times as many pennies as quarters. Which equation can be used to find n?

Ⓐ $n = 8 \times 24$

Ⓑ $24 = 4 + n$

Ⓒ $24 = n \div 8$

Ⓓ $24 = n \times 8$

10. Marcus plays basketball 42 hours a week. This is 6 times as many hours as he plays chess. How hours a week does Marcus play chess?

Ⓐ 6 hours

Ⓑ 7 hours

Ⓒ 8 hours

Ⓓ 9 hours

Name ____________________

Lesson 6-3
Solve Multi-Step Problems

Solve & Share

Three girls and four boys went to an amusement park. The total cost for the group was $189. What was the cost of admission for each person? ***Solve this problem any way you choose.***

I can ...
solve multi-step problems by finding and solving the hidden question first.

Content Standards 4.AT.3, 4.AT.4
Process Standards PS.1, PS.4, PS.7, PS.8

You can make sense and persevere by finding and answering the hidden question.

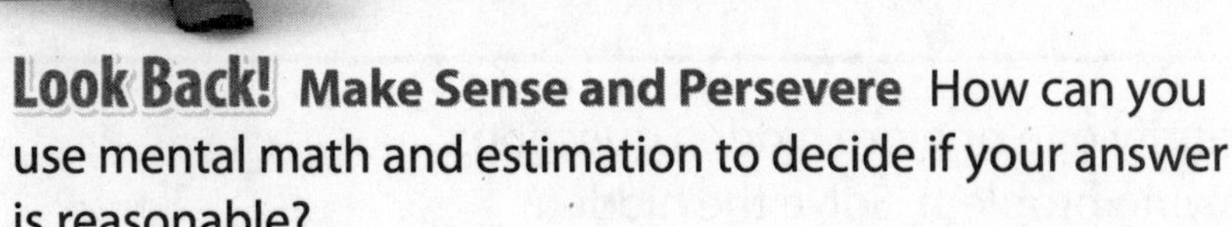

Look Back! Make Sense and Persevere How can you use mental math and estimation to decide if your answer is reasonable?

How Can You Use Diagrams and Equations to Solve Multi-Step Problems?

A

Last year, 18 people went on a family camping trip. How many more people went this year than last year?

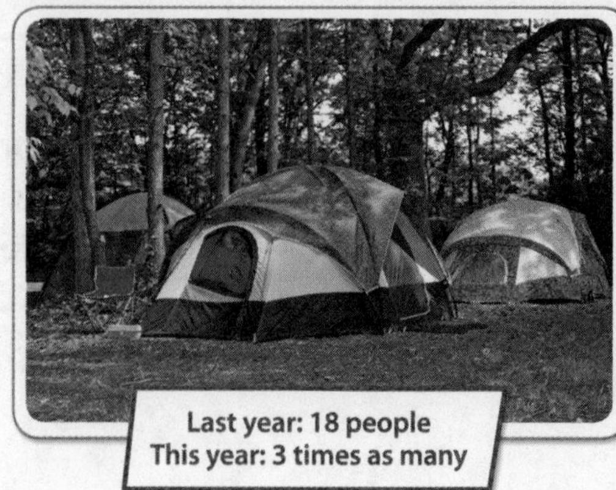

Last year: 18 people
This year: 3 times as many

You can use bar diagrams to help you make sense and persevere in solving multi-step problems.

B

Step 1

Find the hidden question and use a bar diagram and equation to answer it.

Hidden Question: How many people went on the family camping trip this year?

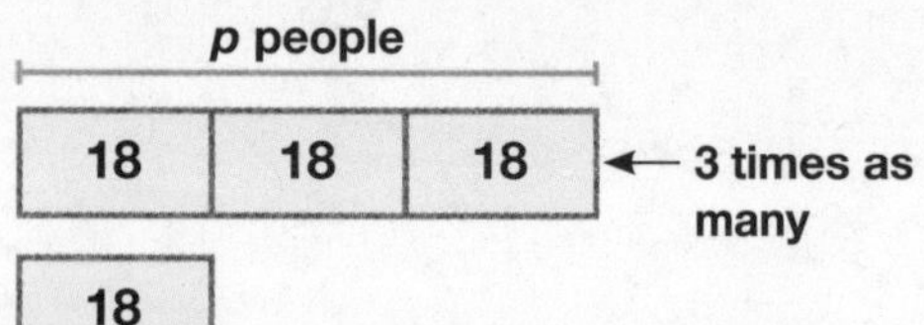

$3 \times 18 = p$
$p = 54$

This year, 54 people went on the camping trip.

C

Step 2

Use the answer to the hidden question to answer the original question.

Original Question: How many more people went this year than last year?

54 people

18	*m*

$54 - 18 = m$
$m = 36$

36 more people went this year than last year.

Convince Me! **Use Structure** Identify one or more hidden questions that need to be solved for the following problem. Solve the hidden questions and answer the problem. Suppose 18 more people are going on the camping trip next year than this year. How many times as many people are going on the camping trip next year than went last year?

Name ____________________

Guided Practice*

Do You Understand?

1. In the problem on the previous page, suppose there were 4 large tents for the people to stay in for this year's trip. The planners tried to put the same number of people in each tent. How many people were in each tent?

Do You Know How?

2. **Make Sense and Persevere** How can you decide if your answer to Exercise 1 is reasonable?

Independent Practice

For **3–8**, write the hidden question, then draw bar diagrams and write equations to solve each problem. Use estimation to decide if your answer is reasonable.

3. Martin raked 3 lawns last week and 4 lawns this week and earned \$168. He earned the same amount raking each lawn. How much did Martin earn raking each lawn?

4. There are 24 students in a class. All of the students, except 2, went bowling. What is the total cost if each student who went bowling paid \$5?

5. Rosie sold 19 calendars. Suzy sold 26. Juan sold 4 times as many calendars as Rosie and Suzy combined. How many calendars did Juan sell?

6. Marcus sold 6 pizzas. Sue sold 4 pizzas. If each pizza costs \$10, how much did Marcus and Sue earn?

7. Bella baked 3 batches of 24 homemade dog treats. She packed 12 bags with an equal number of treats. How many treats were in each bag?

8. Eight toymakers each carved 25 blocks and 15 cars. How many toys did they carve in all?

For another example, see Set C on page 359.

Problem Solving

9. **Model with Math** Kendra is using 27 blue patches and some white patches to make a quilt. The quilt has a total area of 540 square inches. Each patch has an area of 5 square inches. How much of the area of the quilt is white? Explain.

10. **Model with Math** A ticket to a movie theatre for a student is $7. The cost for an adult is $2 more than for a student. How much would it cost 13 adults and 11 students for tickets to the movie theatre?

For **11–12**, use the table at the right.

11. **Number Sense** Brendan, Zach, and their father have $30 to spend at the county fair. Brendan and Zach qualify for a child's admission. How many times can all 3 go on the boat rides? Explain.

DATA

County Fair

Kind of Ticket	Adult	Child
Admission	$8	$4
Boat Rides	$2	$1

12. **Higher Order Thinking** How much does it cost for 1 adult and 4 children to go to the fair and take a boat ride? Explain.

13. The third-grade class collected 148 books to donate to the library. The fourth-grade class collected 175 books. The students need to pack the books into boxes with 9 books in each box. How many boxes do they need to hold all the books? Complete the bar diagram and equation.

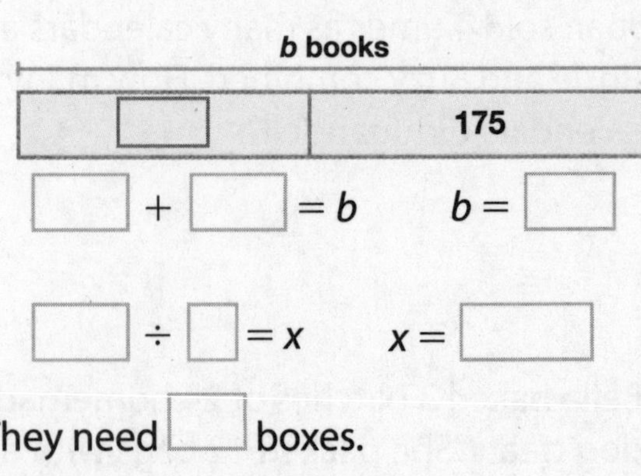

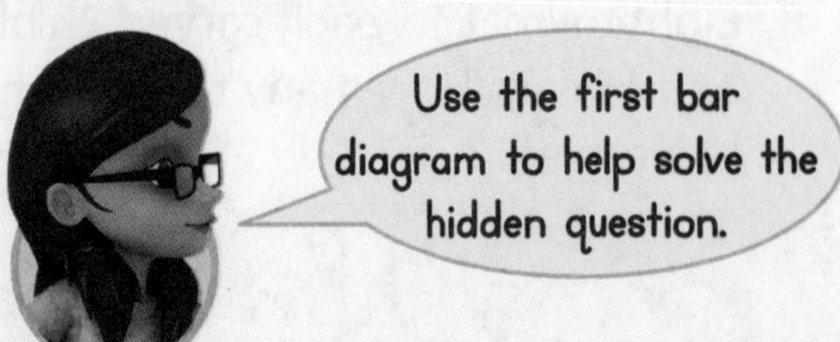

Use the first bar diagram to help solve the hidden question.

Name ______________________

Homework & Practice 6-3

Solve Multi-Step Problems

Another Look!

A family brought 160 one-pint servings of lemonade to a community picnic. Family members drank 98 servings. How many whole gallons of lemonade did the family have left?

Use diagrams and equations to help answer the hidden question and the original question.

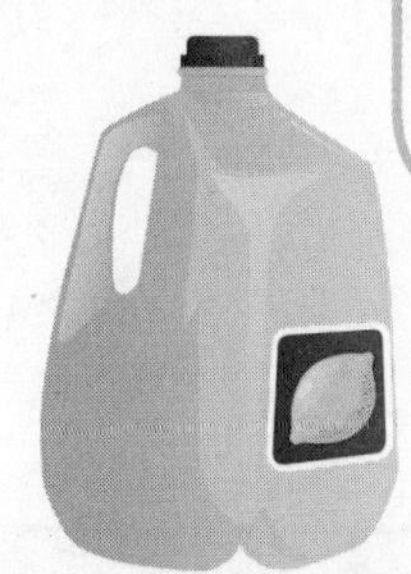

1 gallon = 8 one-pint servings

Find the hidden question and use a diagram and equation to answer it.

Hidden Question: How many one-pint servings of lemonade did the family have left?

160 servings

98	s

$160 - 98 = s$
$s = 62$

The family had 62 one-pint servings left.

Use the answer to the hidden question to answer the original question.

Original Question: How many whole gallons of lemonade did the family have left?

$62 \div 8 = g$
$g = 7 \text{ R6}$

The family had 7 whole gallons of lemonade left.

For **1–2**, draw bar diagrams and write equations to solve each problem.

1. Kareem has 216 role-playing game cards. His goal is to collect all 15 sets of cards. There are 72 cards in a set. How many more cards does Kareem need to reach his goal?

2. Nicole has $9 to spend on cards. She finds friends with the same amount of money to split the cost of a set. One set costs $27. Each friend gets the same number of cards. How many cards does each friend get?

3. **Math and Science** A power plant has 4 tons of coal. A ton of coal produces 2,460 kilowatt hours of electricity. Is this enough to power 9 light bulbs for a year? Explain.

It takes 876 kilowatt hours of electricity to power a 100-watt light bulb for a year.

4. **Generalize** Tina practiced piano for 15 hours last month and 45 hours this month.

   a. Use multiplication to write a statement comparing the hours Tina practiced during the two months.

   b. Use addition to write a statement comparing the hours Tina practiced during the two months.

5. **Higher Order Thinking** Jenny washed dishes 4 times as many times as her brother last month. Her brother washed dishes 8 times. Jenny said she could multiply 3 times 8 to find how many more times she washed dishes than her brother. Is Jenny correct? Explain.

6. Raj collected 17 leaves during the field trip. His goal is to collect 5 times as many leaves. How many more leaves does Raj need? Complete each bar diagram and equation.

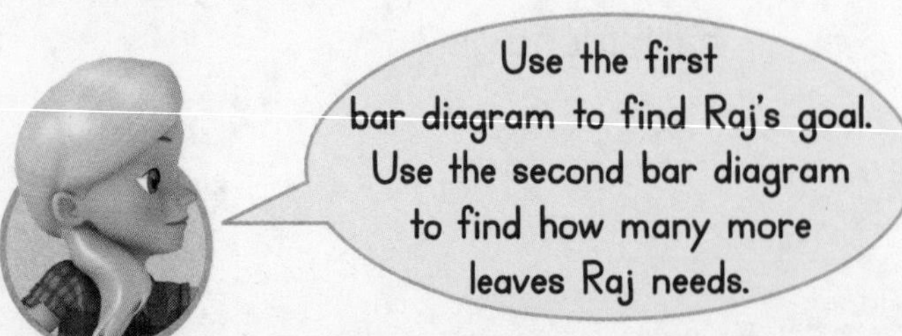

Use the first bar diagram to find Raj's goal. Use the second bar diagram to find how many more leaves Raj needs.

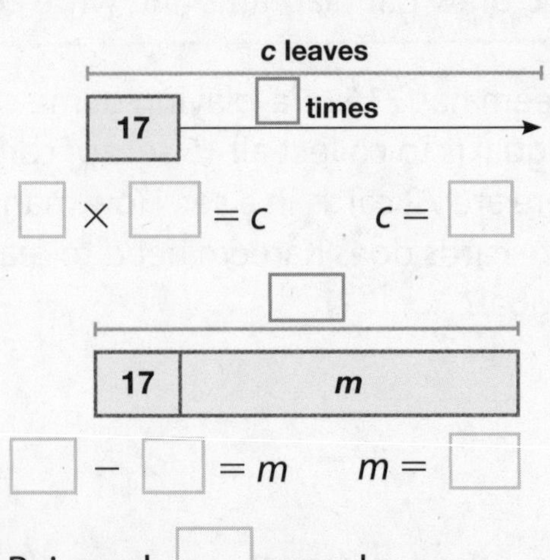

Raj needs ☐ more leaves.

Name ______________________

Lesson 6-4
Solve More Multi-Step Problems

I can ...
solve multi-step problems by finding and solving hidden questions first.

Content Standards 4.AT.3, 4.AT.4
Process Standards PS.1, PS.3, PS.4

Solve & Share

A tree farm is going out of business. It has 45 maple trees and 27 pine trees left for sale. How much money would the owners make if they sell all the trees? ***Solve this problem any way you choose.***

You can make sense and persevere by finding and solving the hidden questions.

Look Back! Make Sense and Persevere What hidden questions did you need to answer before you could answer the question above?

How Can You Use Equations to Solve More Multi-Step Problems?

A

The students in the fourth and fifth grades are going to a concert. There are 178 students. How many rows are needed for the fourth graders?

Each row has 8 seats.
The fifth-grade students fill 12 rows.

To find how many fourth graders there are, you need to know how many fifth graders there are.

To find the number of rows, you need to know how many fourth graders there are.

B

Step 1

Find and solve the first hidden question.

Hidden Question: How many fifth graders are there?

$12 \times 8 = s$
$s = 96$

There are 96 fifth graders.

C

Step 2

Find and solve the second hidden question.

Hidden Question: How many fourth graders are there?

$178 - 96 = f$
$f = 82$

There are 82 fourth graders.

D

Step 3

Answer the original question.

Original Question: How many rows are needed for the fourth graders?

$82 \div 8 = r$
$r = 10 \text{ R}2$

There will be 10 rows with 2 fourth graders left over. So, 11 rows are needed.

Convince Me! Make Sense and Persevere Does the answer of 11 rows make sense for the problem above? Explain.

Name ______________________________

Guided Practice*

Do You Understand?

1. Construct Arguments On the previous page, suppose there were only 11 rows of fifth graders, but the same total number of students. Do you need to solve the whole problem again to find how many rows are needed for the fourth graders? Explain.

Do You Know How?

2. Show another way to solve the problem on the previous page.

Independent Practice

For **3–4**, solve each multi-step problem. Write equations to show each step. Use estimation to decide if your answer is reasonable.

3. Vanya bought 5 medium packages of buttons and 3 small packages of buttons. What was the total number of buttons Vanya bought?

DATA

Number of Items in Package

Item	Small	Medium	Large
Beads	32	64	96
Buttons	18	38	56

4. Vance bought 2 packages of large beads and 1 package of medium beads. He bought 2 packages of large buttons and 2 packages of medium buttons. How many more beads than buttons did Vance buy?

*For another example, see Set D on page 360.

Problem Solving

5. **Math and Science** How much more does it cost to generate 9 megawatt hours of electricity with conventional coal than with wind energy?

It costs $87 to generate 1 megawatt hour of electricity with wind energy.

It costs $105 to generate 1 megawatt hour of electricity with conventional coal.

6. **Model with Math** Bert has $50 to spend at the book store. He buys 2 magazines for $6 each. How many $9 books can Bert buy? Write equations to show each step. Explain how to interpret the remainder.

7. **Higher Order Thinking** Show two different ways to find the answer to the problem.

   Dog and cat food are sold in 20-pound bags. There are 14 bags of dog food and 12 bags of cat food on the store shelves. How many pounds of dog and cat food are on the shelves?

Assessment ISTEP+ Ready

8. Chris needs $858 to buy a computer. She has already saved $575. She gets $15 an hour for babysitting and will babysit 12 hours in the next month. She can save $8 a week from her allowance. How many weeks of allowance will it take Chris to save enough to buy the computer?

Part A

Write and solve an equation that can be used to answer each hidden question.

Part B

Write and solve an equation that can be used to answer the original question.

Name ______________________________

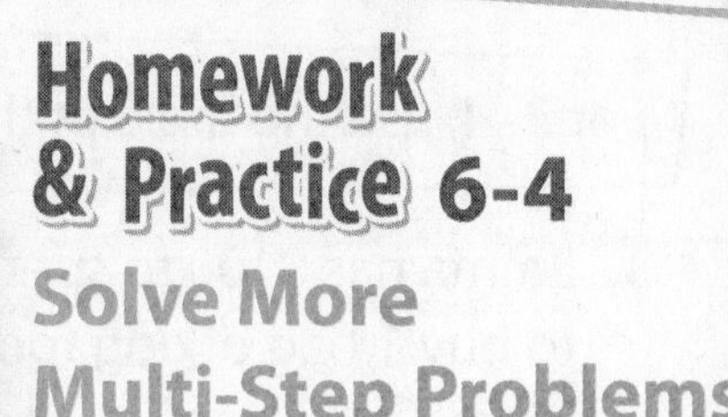

Homework & Practice 6-4

Solve More Multi-Step Problems

Another Look!

There are 84 students in the band. The boys and girls are in separate rows. There are 6 students in each row. There are 8 rows of boys. How many rows of girls are there?

You have to answer the hidden questions before you can answer the question that is asked.

Step 1

Hidden Question: How many boys are in the band?

$8 \times 6 = b$
$b = 48$

There are 48 boys in the band.

Step 2

Hidden Question: How many girls are in the band?

$84 - 48 = g$
$g = 36$

There are 36 girls in the band.

Step 3

Original Question: How many rows of girls are in the band?

$36 \div 6 = r$
$r = 6$

There are 6 rows of girls.

For **1–2**, solve each multi-step problem. Write equations to show each step.

1. Friday night, a pizza parlor sold 5 large pizzas and some medium pizzas. The pizza parlor made a total of $291. How many medium pizzas were sold?

2. What is the area of the giant American flag shown? All stripes are the same height.

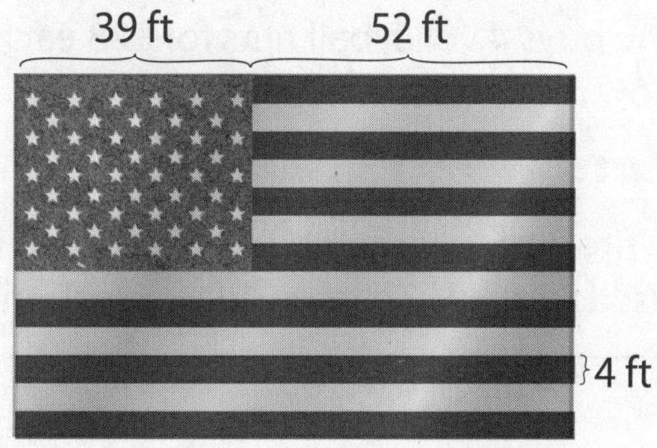

For **3–4**, use the table at the right.

3. Emma has $100 to spend at the pet store. She needs to buy 1 bag of dog food and 2 chew toys. Will Emma have enough money left over to buy 3 times as many catnip toys as chew toys? Explain.

DATA

Barky's Pet Store

Product	Cost
Bag of Dog Food	$35
Bag of Cat Food	$18
Chew Toy	$12
Catnip Toy	$9

4. A-Z **Vocabulary** Define *partial products*. What partial products can you use to find how much 6 bags of cat food will cost?

5. Higher Order Thinking Maurice and Trina both solve the problem at the right. Maurice plans to add first and then multiply. Trina plans to multiply first and then add. Who is correct? Use a property of operations to justify your answer.

A large wind turbine can power 598 homes. A company had 4 turbines and then built 5 more. How many homes can the company power with its wind turbines?

Assessment ISTEP+ Ready

6. The gym teacher has $250 to spend on volleyball equipment. She buys 4 volleyball nets for $28 each. Volleyballs cost $7 each. How many volleyballs can she buy?

Part A

Write and solve an equation that can be used to answer each hidden question.

Part B

Write and solve an equation that can be used to answer the original question.

Name ______________________________

Problem Solving

Lesson 6-5

Make Sense and Persevere

I can ...
make sense of problems and keep working if I get stuck.

Process Standards PS.1 Also PS.2, PS.4, PS.6
Content Standards 4.AT.3, 4.AT.4

Solve & Share Ms. Valenzuela had her students design a snake house for the zoo. In the design shown, the anaconda has 538 more square feet than the python. The python has twice as many square feet as the rattlesnake. How much area does each snake have? ***Solve this problem any way you choose.***

Thinking Habits

Be a good thinker!
These questions can help you.

- What do I need to find?
- What do I know?
- What's my plan for solving the problem?
- What else can I try if I get stuck?
- How can I check that my solution makes sense?

Look Back! Make Sense and Persevere How can you check that your solution makes sense?

Learn
Glossary

Essential Question

How Do You Make Sense of a Multi-Step Problem and Persevere in Solving It?

A

Bryan and Alex have to buy their own instruments for the band. Alex made $1,025 from a fundraiser. He has a part-time job that pays $8 an hour. How many hours does Alex need to work to have enough money to buy his instrument?

Bryan's trumpet costs $159.
Alex's tuba costs 9 times as much as Bryan's trumpet.

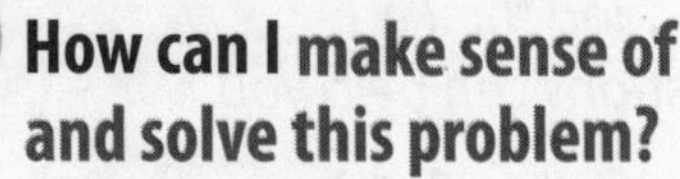

What do you need to do to solve this problem?

I need to determine how much Alex's tuba costs and how much Alex needs to earn to buy the tuba.

Here's my thinking.

B

How can I make sense of and solve this problem?

I can

- identify the quantities given.
- understand how the quantities are related.
- choose and implement an appropriate strategy.
- check to be sure my work and answer make sense.

C

Use the cost of the trumpet to find the cost of the tuba.

$\$159 \times 9 = \$1,431$ Alex's tuba costs $1,431.

Find how much more money Alex needs to earn.

$\$1,431 - \$1,025 = \$406$ Alex needs to earn $406.

Find how many hours Alex needs to work.

$\$406 \div 8 = 50 \text{ R}6$

Alex will not have enough money by working 50 hours, so he needs to work 51 hours.

Convince Me! **Make Sense and Persevere** How can you check to make sure the work and answer given above make sense?

Name ______________________________________

Guided Practice*

Make Sense and Persevere

In the problem on the previous page, suppose Alex wanted to know how many weeks it would take him to work 51 hours. Alex works 3 hours a day and 4 days a week.

1. What are you asked to find?

2. What is a good plan for solving the problem?

3. Does your answer make sense? Explain.

Think about this question to help you persevere in solving the problem. What's a good plan for solving the problem?

Independent Practice

Make Sense and Persevere

The high school tennis team is selling tennis balls to raise $500 for new equipment. They sell the balls for $2 each.

4. How many cases of tennis balls does the tennis team have to sell in order to raise enough money for the new equipment?

5. Write and solve the hidden questions you need to answer before finding the answer to Exercise 4.

A case has 24 packages.
Each package has 3 tennis balls.

*For another example, see Set E on page 360.

Problem Solving

Performance Assessment ISTEP+ Ready

Designing a Flag

Rainey's group designed the flag shown for a class project. They used 234 square inches of green fabric. After making one flag, Rainey's group has 35 square inches of yellow fabric left. How can Rainey's group determine the total area of the flag?

Twice as much green as orange

3 times as much green as yellow

6. **Make Sense and Persevere** What hidden question(s) do you need to answer first?

7. **Model with Math** How can you use bar diagrams and equations to represent the hidden question(s) and show the relationships?

When you make sense of a problem, you check that your solution makes sense.

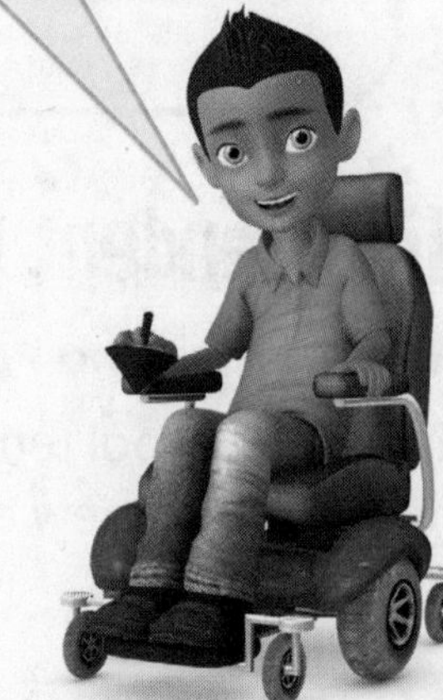

8. **Be Precise** Use your drawings and equations to find the total area of the flag.

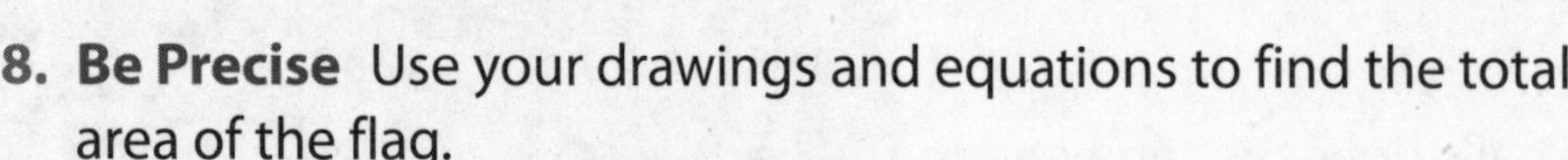

9. **Make Sense and Persevere** What information was not needed to solve the problem?

Name ____________________

Homework & Practice 6-5
Make Sense and Persevere

Another Look!

A museum director would like to display butterflies and dragonflies in 5 cases with about the same number of insects in each case. How many insects should go in each case?

Identify the hidden questions and choose a strategy to solve.

- How many butterflies are there?
- How many insects are there?

36 dragonflies

3 times as many butterflies as dragonflies

Understand how the quantities are related to solve the original question.

There are 3 times as many butterflies as dragonflies.

$$3 \times 36 = 108 \text{ butterflies}$$

You can make sense of problems by finding the hidden questions.

The sum of dragonflies and butterflies is used to find the number of insects that should go in each of the 5 cases.

$$36 + 108 = 144 \text{ insects}$$

$$144 \div 5 = 28 \text{ R4}$$

28 insects should go in one display case and 29 insects should go in each of the other 4 cases.

Make Sense and Persevere

The diagram shows how many laps three friends swim each week. How can you determine the number of miles Ariel swam?

MacKenzie: 28 laps
June: 3 times as many laps as MacKenzie
Ariel: 20 more laps than June

8 laps equal a mile

1. Write and solve the hidden question(s) you need to answer before you answer the original question.

2. Use your answers to the hidden question(s) and an equation to determine how many miles Ariel swam.

Selling Potatoes

Ms. Sacksteader owns a grocery store. She buys 272 pounds of potatoes for $99. She wants to sell them for twice as much. She makes 9 bags containing 10 pounds each and puts the rest in 5-pound bags. Her family will eat any of the leftover potatoes. Ms. Sacksteader wants to know how many 5-pound bags of potatoes she can sell.

Each 5-pound bag of potatoes sells for $4.

3. **Make Sense and Persevere** What hidden question do you need to answer first?

4. **Reasoning** How does the answer to the hidden question relate to the original question?

5. **Model with Math** How can you use an equation to represent and find how many 5-pound bags of potatoes Ms. Sacksteader can sell?

6. **Be Precise** How much money will Ms. Sacksteader make for the 5-pound bags? Write and solve an equation to show you computed accurately.

Name ______________________________

TOPIC 6

Fluency Practice Activity

I can ...
subtract multi-digit whole numbers.

Find a Match

Work with a partner. Point to a clue.

Read the clue.

Look below the clues to find a match. Write the clue letter in the box next to the match.

Find a match for every clue.

Clues

A The difference is exactly 528.

B The difference is between 550 and 560.

C The difference is between 800 and 900.

D The difference is exactly 614.

E The difference is between 100 and 105.

F The difference is between 470 and 480.

G The difference is exactly 392.

H The difference is between 70 and 80.

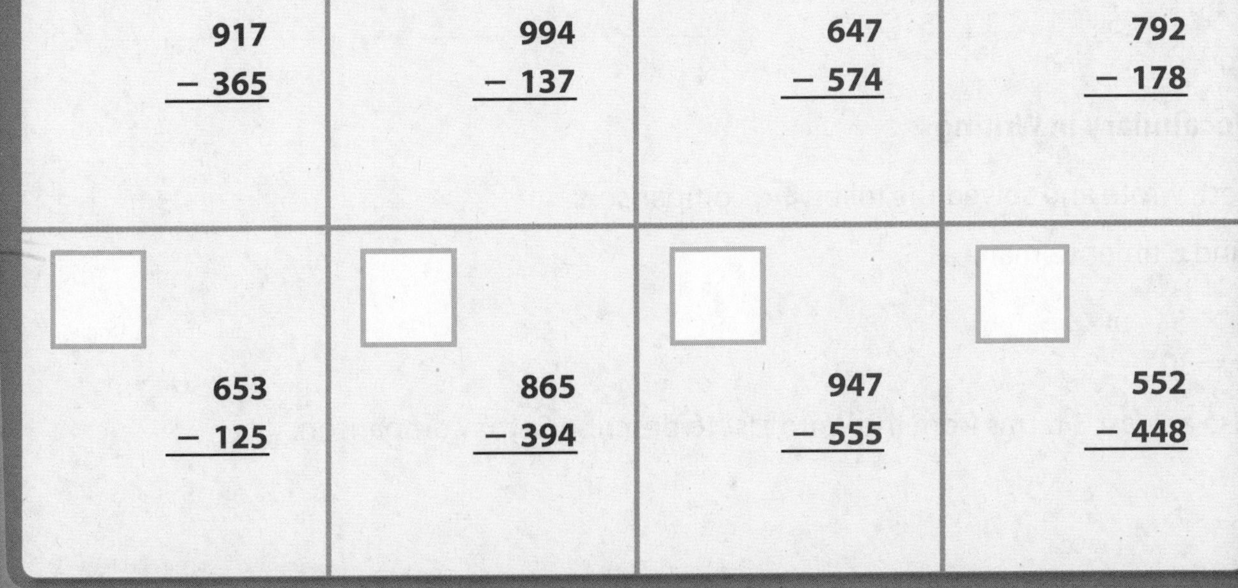

☐ 917 − 365	☐ 994 − 137	☐ 647 − 574	☐ 792 − 178
☐ 653 − 125	☐ 865 − 394	☐ 947 − 555	☐ 552 − 448

TOPIC 6 Vocabulary Review

A-Z Glossary

Word List

- addition comparison
- Associative Property of Multiplication
- Commutative Property of Multiplication
- Distributive Property
- equation
- multiplication comparison
- product
- variable

Understand Vocabulary

Write T for *true* and F for *false*.

1. ______ Addition comparison is used when you can multiply to find how one quantity is related to another.

2. ______ Multiplication comparison is used when one quantity is x times more than another quantity or you can show the comparison with equal groups.

3. ______ A number sentence that uses an equal sign to show that two expressions have the same value is called an equation.

4. ______ The answer to a subtraction problem is called the product.

5. ______ A symbol or letter that stands for a number is called a variable.

Label each example of a property with a term from the Word List.

6. $(3 \times 4) \times 5 = 3 \times (4 \times 5)$ ______

7. $3 \times (4 + 5) = (3 \times 4) + (3 \times 5)$ ______

8. $3 \times 4 \times 5 = 4 \times 3 \times 5$ ______

Use Vocabulary in Writing

9. Seth wrote and solved the following comparison:

   Find 6 times as many as 5.

   $6 \times 5 = n$
   $n = 30$

   Use at least 3 terms from the Word List to describe Seth's comparison.

Name ____

TOPIC 6

Reteaching

Set A pages 327–332

Write a comparison sentence for each equation.

$27 = 9 \times 3$

27 is 9 times as many as 3.

$27 = 6 + 21$

27 is 6 more than 21.

Remember when you add or multiply you can change the order of the numbers.

Write and solve an equation to match each comparison sentence.

1. *y* is 9 times as many as 4.

2. *x* is 21 more than 21.

Set B pages 333–338

There are 30 apples and 6 bananas in a basket. How many times as many apples as bananas are in the basket?

30	÷	x	=	6
↑		↑		↑
number of apples		How many times as many?		number of bananas

Since $6 \times 5 = 30$, there are 5 times as many apples as bananas in the basket.

Remember you can write equations to help solve problems.

1. Macon has 32 rocks in his collection. He has 4 times as many rocks as his brother. How many rocks does Macon's brother have?

2. Pam has 24 pencils and 6 erasers. How many times as many pencils as erasers does Pam have?

Set C pages 339–344

There are 13 girls and 14 boys that will form volleyball teams. Each team needs 6 players. Extra players will be alternates. How many teams can be formed? How many players will be alternates?

Step 1

$13 + 14 = 27$ Find the total number of players.

Step 2

$$\begin{array}{r} 4\text{ R3} \\ 6\overline{)27} \\ -24 \\ \hline 3 \end{array}$$

Divide 27 by 6 to find the number of teams.

There will be 4 teams with 3 alternates.

Remember to answer the hidden question and use the answer to solve the problem.

1. Three friends ordered 2 pizzas. Each pizza was cut into 8 slices. If each person ate the same number of slices, how many slices did each person eat?

2. Mark spent \$79 on 3 shirts and a package of socks. If each shirt cost \$24, how much did the package of socks cost?

Set D pages 345–350

To solve a multi-step problem, first find and answer any hidden questions.

At a restaurant, a children's meal costs \$5 and an adult meal costs \$9. If 11 children and 16 adults purchase meals, how much did the meals cost?

How much did the children's meals cost?
$\$5 \times 11 = c$
$c = \$55$

How much did the adults' meals cost?
$\$9 \times 16 = a$
$a = \$144$

How much did all the meals cost?
$\$55 + \$144 = t$
$t = \$199$

Remember to first find and answer any hidden questions.

1. There are 64 singers in the choir. The tenors and sopranos are in separate rows. There are 8 singers in each row. There are 4 rows of tenors. How many rows of sopranos are there?

2. Samantha has \$600 saved for a trip. She buys an airline ticket for \$120 and reserves a hotel room for \$55 each night for 4 nights. If Samantha's trip lasts for 5 days and she spends the same amount each day, how much can Samantha spend each day?

Set E pages 351–356

Think about these questions to help you **make sense** of the problem.

Thinking Habits

- What do I need to find?
- What do I know?
- What's my plan for solving the problem?
- What else can I try if I get stuck?
- How can I check that my solution makes sense?

Remember to make sense of the problem before starting to solve the problem.

At a local shelter, large dogs can be adopted for \$10 each. Small dogs can be adopted for \$5 each. There are 17 large dogs available for adoption. If all the dogs are adopted, the shelter will make \$215.

1. Describe a strategy to find the number of small dogs at the shelter.

2. How many small dogs are at the shelter?

Name ____________________

1. Jason and his 3 brothers want to buy a gift for their mother. They have \$314 saved. Each of them will save \$17 a week until they have at least \$515 for her gift. How much money will they save after 3 weeks? Will they have enough money to buy the gift?

Part A

What are the hidden questions?

Part B

Write an equation that can be used to answer each hidden question. Then solve.

Part C

Write and solve an equation to find how much money they will save after 3 weeks. Will they have enough to buy the gift? Explain.

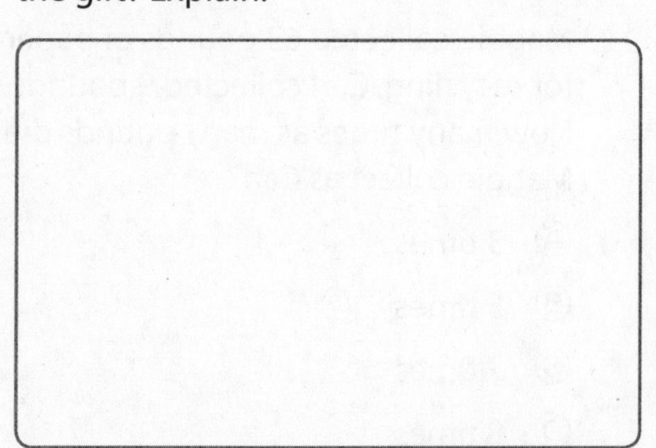

2. A kangaroo can jump 6 times the length of its body. For a kangaroo that is 5 feet long, select all the equations that can find how many feet, f, the kangaroo can jump.

- ☐ $f \div 6 = 5$
- ☐ $6 \times f = 5$
- ☐ $5 \times f = 6$
- ☐ $6 \times 5 = f$
- ☐ $6 - f = 5$

3. Mitchell wants to beat the record for the most points scored in a season. This season, he has scored 51 points. If he scores 27 points at each of the next 7 games, he will break the record by 1 point. How many total points will break the record by 1 point?

***p* points needed**

27	27	27	27	27	27	27

☐ $\times 27 = p$ $p =$ ☐

m

☐ $+ 51 = m$ $m =$ ☐

Mitchell will break the record by 1 point if he scores a total of ☐ points.

4. Select all the sentences that describe a comparison using multiplication.

- ☐ 9 is 3 times as many as p.
- ☐ 27 more than r is 41.
- ☐ A bus can travel 3 times as fast as a boat.
- ☐ It costs d dollars for 9 packages.
- ☐ There are 4 times as many girls as boys.

5. Choose the correct word from the box to complete each statement.

more than	times as many as

45 is 9 [ ] 5.

120 is 68 [ ] 52.

86 is 12 [ ] 74.

33 is 3 [ ] 11.

6. Miguel wrote a list of expressions and a list of solutions. Draw lines to match the expression with the correct solution.

Expression	Solution
4 times as many as 8	85
48 is 3 times as many as t	6
5×17	32
35 times as many as p is 210	16

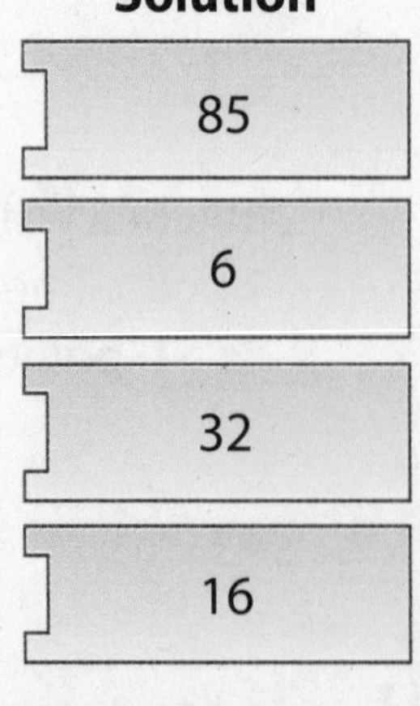

7. Darcy ordered 7 boxes of red balloons and 2 boxes of blue balloons for a party. She ordered a total of 1,125 balloons. Which equation does **NOT** tell how many balloons are in each box?

Ⓐ $b \times (7 + 2) = 1{,}125$

Ⓑ $1{,}125 \div 9 = b$

Ⓒ $9 \times b = 1{,}125$

Ⓓ $1{,}125 \times 9 = b$

8. Choose Yes or No to tell if 9 will make each sentence true.

8a. $18 \times$ __ $= 162$	○ Yes	○ No
8b. $20 \times$ __ $= 189$	○ Yes	○ No
8c. __ times as many as 16 is 145.	○ Yes	○ No
8d. 315 is the product of __ times 35.	○ Yes	○ No

9. Select all the expressions that are equal to the product of 14 and 9.

- ☐ $(2 \times 7) + 9$
- ☐ 9 times as many as 14
- ☐ 14×9
- ☐ 14 more than 9
- ☐ 9 less than 14

10. Maggie collected 63 pounds of paper for recycling. Carl collected 9 pounds. How many times as many pounds did Maggie collect as Carl?

Ⓐ 3 times

Ⓑ 5 times

Ⓒ 7 times

Ⓓ 8 times

Name ______________________________

Ski Jumping

Jackie did some research on ski jumping after she watched the Winter Olympics. Jump distances usually describe ski jumps. The **Ski Jump Diagram** illustrates a ski jump. The **Ski Jumping** table provides the distances for an intermediate and an advanced jump.

Ski Jump Diagram

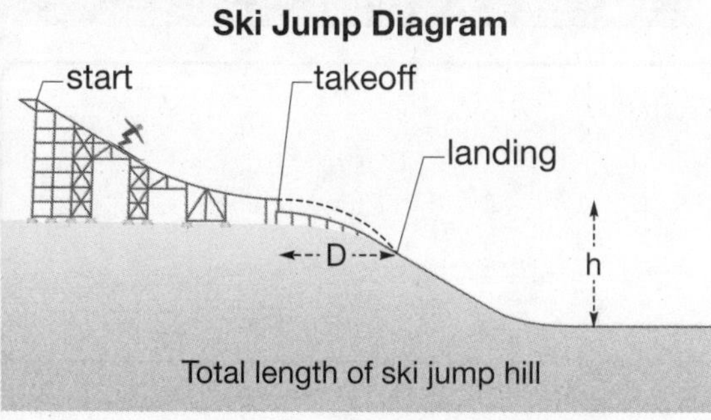

Ski Jumping

Feature	Distance: Intermediate	Distance: Advanced
Jump distance	297 feet	408 feet
Total length	3 times the jump distance	3 times the jump distance
Height	38 feet more than the jump distance	48 feet more than the jump distance

1. Jackie wants to find the total length of the ski jump hill and the height of the intermediate jump.

Part A

What is the total length of the ski jump hill on an intermediate jump? Draw a bar diagram and write and solve an equation to represent the problem. Does this situation use addition or multiplication to compare?

Part B

What is the height of an intermediate jump? Write and solve an equation. Does this situation use addition or multiplication to compare?

2. Use the **Beginner Jump** information to find how much longer the total length of the ski jump hill for an advanced jump is than a beginner jump.

Beginner Jump

The advanced jump distance is 8 times the beginner jump distance.

The total length of a beginner jump hill is 3 times the beginner jump distance.

Part A

What are the hidden questions you need to answer to solve the problem?

Part B

How much longer is the total length of an advanced jump hill than a beginner jump hill? Write equations and explain how to solve the hidden questions and the original question.

Part C

Is the answer you found in Part B reasonable? Explain.

3. How much greater is the height of an advanced jump than an intermediate jump? Explain.

Factors and Multiples

Essential Questions: How can you use arrays or multiplication to find the factors of a number? How can you identify prime and composite numbers? How can you find multiples of a number?

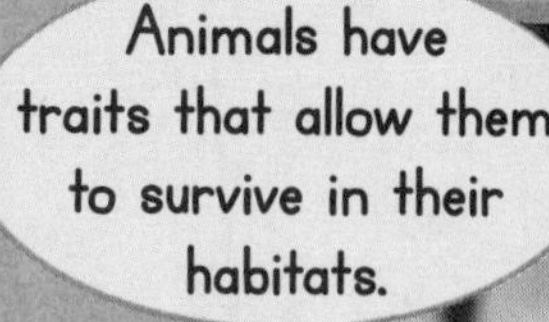

Animals have traits that allow them to survive in their habitats.

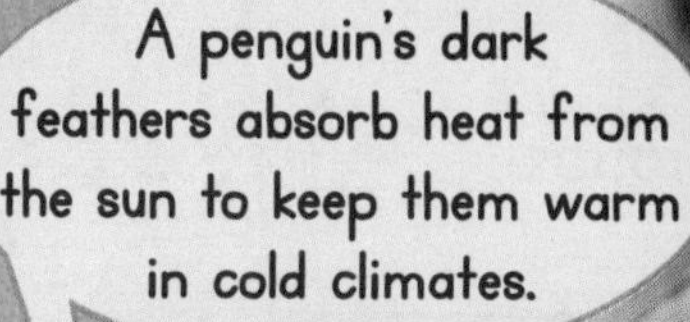

A penguin's dark feathers absorb heat from the sun to keep them warm in cold climates.

Penguins live in some of the coldest places on Earth! Here is a project on the animal kingdom and multiples.

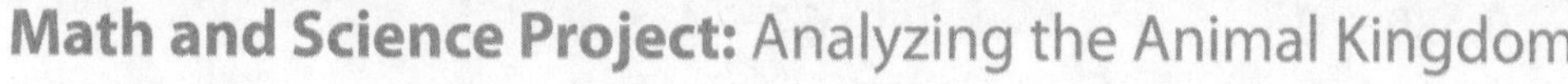

Math and Science Project: Analyzing the Animal Kingdom

Do Research As a defense against the cold, emperor penguins huddle together in large groups. Use the Internet or other sources to research how this helps them protect each other and their chicks.

Journal: Write a Report Include what you found. Also in your report:

- Suppose 64 penguins form a huddle to keep warm. Use a grid to draw all the possible arrays for 64.
- If a huddle of 72 penguins breaks apart, how many different ways can the penguins form equal groups? Is 72 prime or composite? Write the factor pairs of 72 to show all the ways the penguins can form equal groups.

Name ______________________

Review What You Know

Vocabulary

Choose the best term from the box. Write it on the blank.

- dividend
- divisor
- product
- quotient

1. The ______________ is the answer to a division problem.

2. The number being divided is the ______________.

3. The ______________ is the number that tells into how many groups something is being divided.

Multiplication

Find each product.

4. 8 × 4
5. 17 × 6
6. 304 × 9
7. 555 × 5
8. 22 × 26
9. 33 × 11
10. 56 × 70
11. 36 × 91
12. 27 × 48
13. 56 × 13
14. 12 × 19
15. 36 × 16

Division

Find each quotient.

16. 27 ÷ 3
17. 56 ÷ 8
18. 36 ÷ 4
19. 72 ÷ 9
20. 39 ÷ 3
21. 64 ÷ 4
22. 105 ÷ 5
23. 824 ÷ 4
24. 942 ÷ 3
25. 9,156 ÷ 3
26. 2,156 ÷ 4
27. 4,136 ÷ 8

Problem Solving

28. **Model with Math** Cecilia bought 2 sandwiches last week and 4 sandwiches this week. She spent a total of $42. If each sandwich costs the same amount, how much did Cecilia spend on each sandwich? Write and solve equations.

A-Z Glossary

My Word Cards

Use the examples for each word on the front of the card to help complete the definitions on the back.

$7 \times 3 = 21$

factors

0, 4, 8, 12, and 16 are some of the multiples of 4.

The factor pairs for 12 are:
1 and 12
2 and 6
3 and 4

All even numbers end in 0, 2, 4, 6, or 8.

13

factors: 1, 13

composite number

14

factors: 1, 2, 7, 14

My Word Cards

Complete each definition. Extend learning by writing your own definitions.

The product of a given number and any other whole number is called a

________________________.

The numbers that are multiplied together to give a product are called

________________________.

To ________________ means to make a general statement.

____________________ are two numbers that when multiplied together give a certain product.

A ____________________ is a whole number greater than 1 with more than two factors.

A ____________________ is a whole number greater than 1 that has exactly two factors, itself and 1.

Name ____________________

Solve

Lesson 7-1
Understand Factors

I can …
find the factors of a whole number.

Content Standard 4.NS.8
Process Standards PS.2, PS.3, PS.5, PS.7

Solve & Share

Fourth-graders at Ames School have 24 carpet squares. What are all the different ways they can organize the carpet squares into a rectangular array? ***Solve this problem any way you choose.***

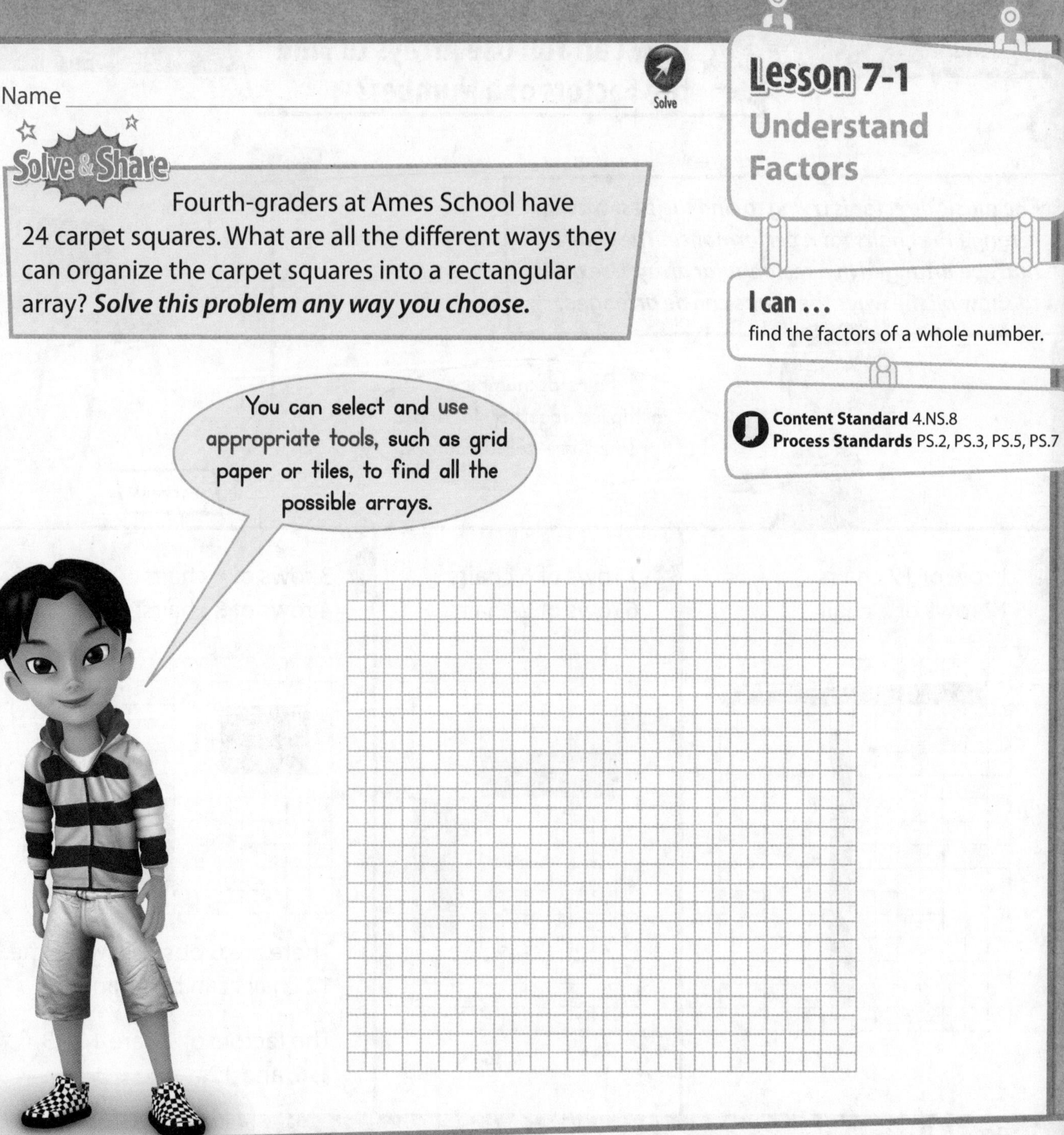

You can select and use appropriate tools, such as grid paper or tiles, to find all the possible arrays.

Look Back! Look for Relationships What patterns do you see in the arrays?

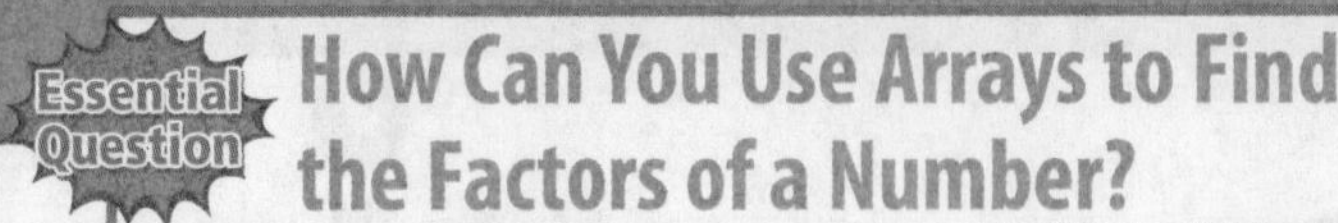

How Can You Use Arrays to Find the Factors of a Number?

A

The music director is trying to find the best way to arrange the chairs for a performance. The chairs must be arranged in a rectangular array. Use grids to show all the ways the chairs can be arranged.

Pairs of numbers multiplied together to find a product are called factors.

12 chairs

B

1 row of 12 chairs
12 rows of 1 chair

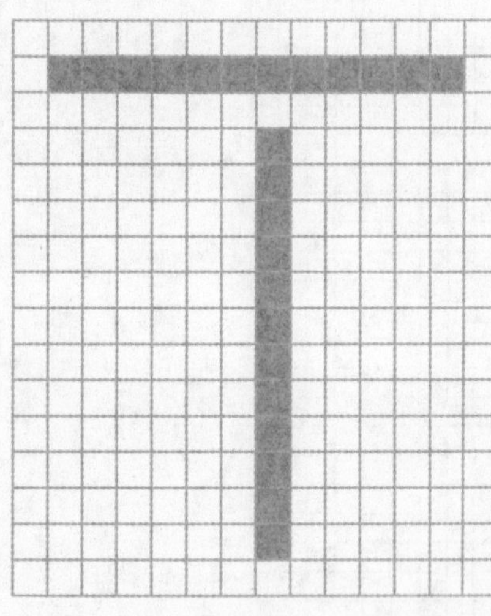

C

2 rows of 6 chairs
6 rows of 2 chairs

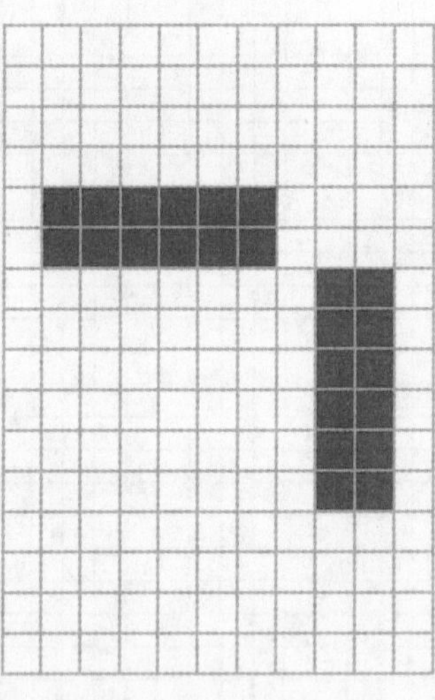

D

3 rows of 4 chairs
4 rows of 3 chairs

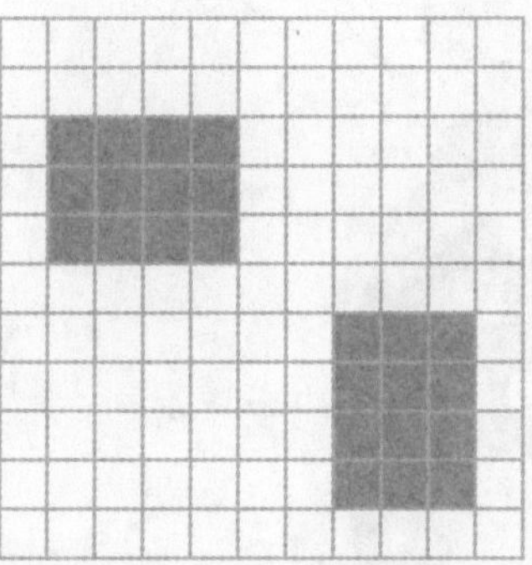

There are 6 possible ways the 12 chairs can be arranged.

The factors of 12 are 1, 2, 3, 4, 6, and 12.

Convince Me! **Critique Reasoning** Blake says, "Every number can be shown with at least two arrays." Do you agree? Explain.

Name ____________________

Guided Practice*

Do You Understand?

1. Reasoning How are the lengths of the sides of the arrays shown on the grids on the previous page related to the factors of 12?

2. What are the lengths of the sides of the arrays that show how 5 chairs can be arranged?

Do You Know How?

For **3–4**, use grids to find all the possible arrays for each number.

3. 6

4. 16

For **5–6**, use grids to find the factors of each number.

5. 45

6. 30

Independent Practice

For **7–8**, use the grids to find all the possible the arrays for each number. Use the arrays to help write the factors.

7. 9

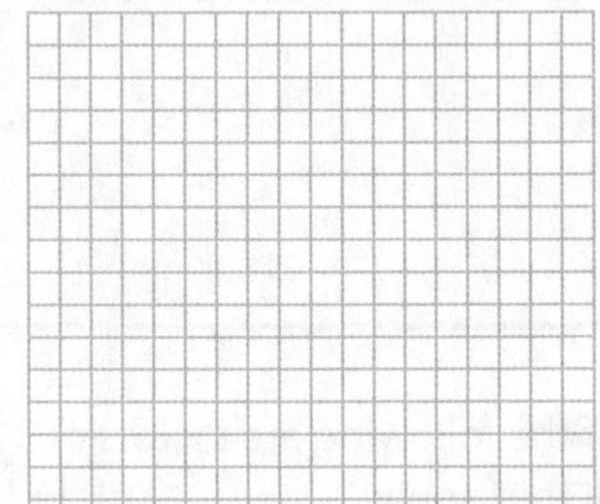

8. 14

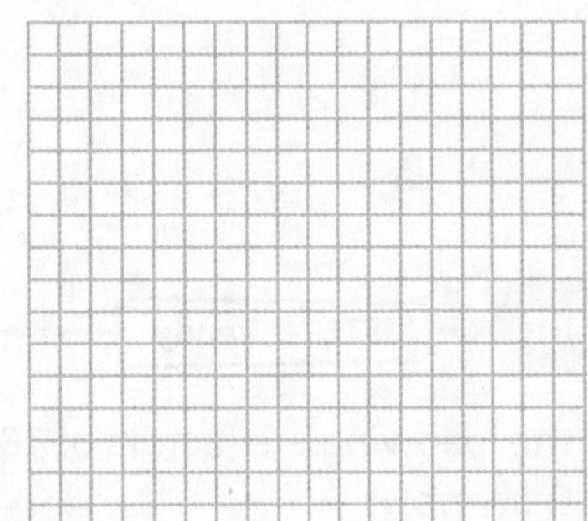

For **9–14**, use grids to find the factors for each number.

9. 5

10. 25

11. 8

12. 36

13. 23

14. 27

*For another example, see Set A on page 401.

Problem Solving

15. **Reasoning** Use the grid to find two numbers that have 2 and 3 as factors.

Draw arrays with side lengths that have 2 or 3 as factors.

16. The dwarf planet Pluto takes about 90,403 days to orbit the sun. Write this number in expanded form and using number names.

17. David makes 17 dollars in an hour and works 25 hours each week. Linda makes 25 dollars in an hour and works 17 hours each week. How much do David and Linda make together each week? What property of multiplication does this represent?

18. What do you notice about the number of possible arrays and the number of factors of 22?

19. **Higher Order Thinking** Jane says 5 is a factor of every whole number that has a 5 in the ones place. Fred says 5 is a factor of every whole number that has a 0 in the ones place. Who is correct? Explain.

Assessment ISTEP+ Ready

20. Which of the following are factors of 18? Select all that apply.

- ☐ 1
- ☐ 2
- ☐ 4
- ☐ 6
- ☐ 23

21. Which of the following are factors of 31? Select all that apply.

- ☐ 1
- ☐ 3
- ☐ 7
- ☐ 31
- ☐ 62

Name ____________________

Homework & Practice 7-1

Understand Factors

Another Look!

Mark is rearranging 15 desks in his classroom. Use the grid to show all the ways the desks could be arranged in a rectangular array. What are the factors of 15?

A grid can help you find the factors of a number.

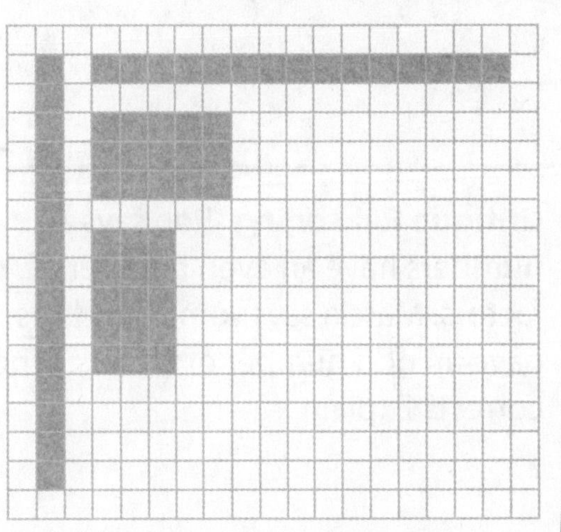

Mark can arrange the desks in 4 different ways.

The factors of 15 are 1, 3, 5, and 15.

For **1–2**, find all the possible arrays for each number. Use the arrays to help write the factors.

1. 13

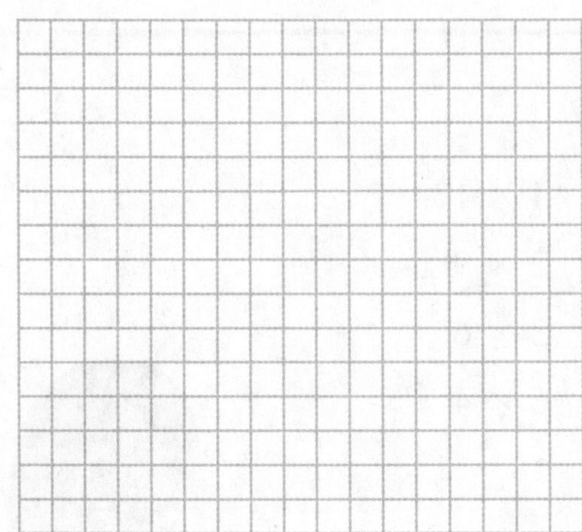

2. 10

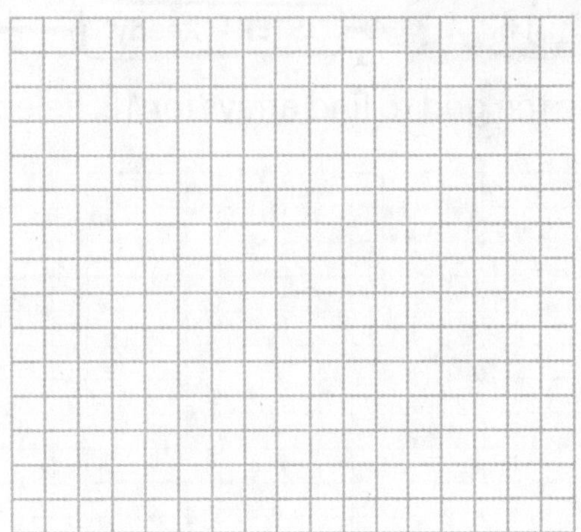

For **3–8**, use grids to find the factors of each number.

3. 17

4. 37

5. 42

6. 29

7. 33

8. 48

9. **Math and Science** Solar panels use the sun's energy to generate power. A town wants to install 28 solar panels in an array. What are all the possible ways the panels could be installed?

10. Use grids to draw all the possible arrays for 5, 7, and 11. What do you notice about the arrays for these numbers?

11. **Critique Reasoning** Rob says all numbers have an even number of factors. Marcia says some numbers have an odd number of factors. Who is correct? Explain.

12. **Higher Order Thinking** Find all the factors of 38, 39, and 40. Do they have any factors in common? Explain how you can tell if some numbers have factors in common without finding the factors.

13. Use the grid to find arrays for 18. Select all that apply.

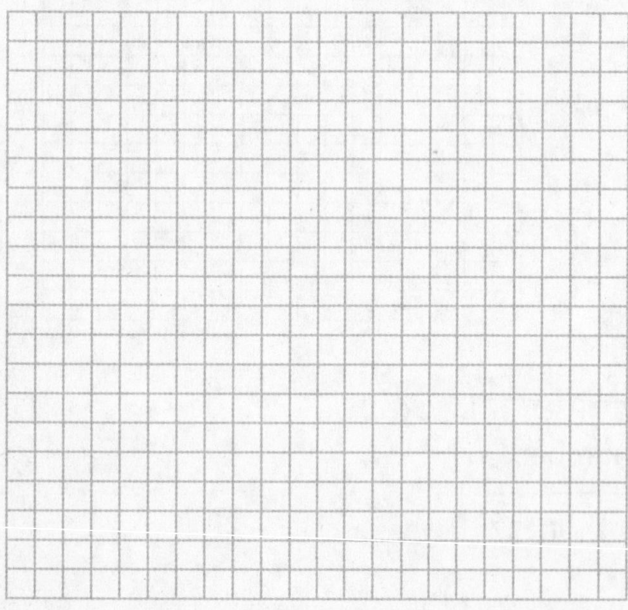

- ☐ 1×18
- ☐ 2×9
- ☐ 3×6
- ☐ 6×4
- ☐ 18×1

What number is a factor of every even number?

Name ______________________

Lesson 7-2
Factors

I can ...
use multiplication to find the factor pairs for a whole number.

Content Standard 4.NS.8
Process Standards PS.2, PS.3, PS.4, PS.5

Solve & Share Jared has 20 flowers. He wants to plant all of the flowers in equal rows in his garden. What are the different ways Jared can arrange the flowers in equal rows? ***Solve this problem any way you choose.***

You can select and use appropriate tools, such as counters or grid paper, to find the different ways Jared can plant his flowers.

Look Back! Make Sense and Persevere How can you check you have found all the different ways Jared can plant his flowers?

How Can You Use Multiplication to Find the Factors of a Number?

A

Jean wants to arrange her action figures in equal-size groups. What are all the ways Jean can arrange her action figures?

Jean can think of all the factor pairs of 16. Factor pairs are two numbers that when multiplied give you a certain product.

16 action figures

B

1 group of 16

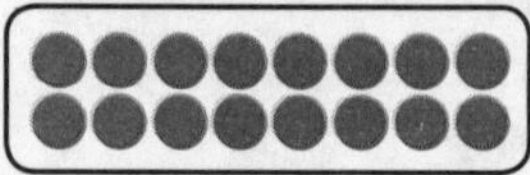

16 groups of 1

Jean can arrange 1 group of 16 figures or 16 groups of 1 figure.

So, 1 and 16 are factors of 16.

C

8 groups of 2

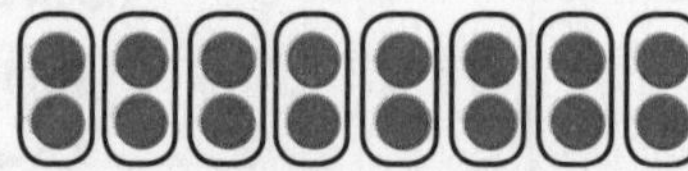

2 groups of 8

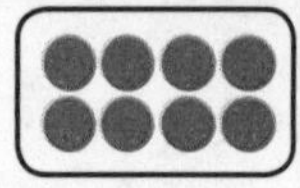

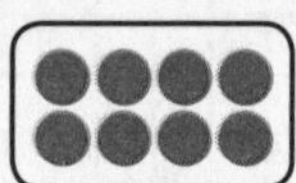

Jean can arrange 8 groups of 2 figures or 2 groups of 8 figures.

So, 2 and 8 are factors of 16.

D

4 groups of 4

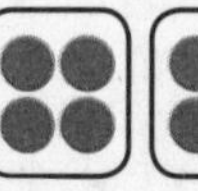

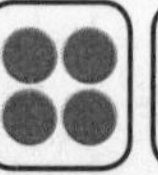

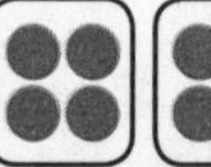

Jean can arrange 4 groups of 4 figures. 4 is a factor of 16.

The factor pairs for 16 are 1 and 16, 2 and 8, and 4 and 4.

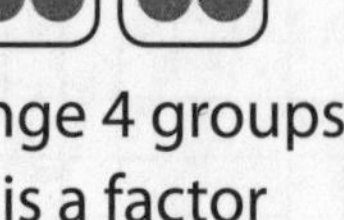

A whole number is a multiple of each of its factors. 16 is a multiple of 1, 2, 4, 8, and 16.

Convince Me! Construct Arguments How do you know there are no other factors for 16 other than 1, 2, 4, 8, and 16? Explain.

Name ___

Guided Practice*

Do You Understand?

1. Jean bought 7 more action figures. What are the different equal-size groups she can make now?

2. **Reasoning** What factor besides 1 does every even number have?

Do You Know How?

For **3–6**, write the factors of each number. Use counters to help.

3. 2
4. 20
5. 28
6. 54

Independent Practice

Remember, the factors of a number always include 1 and the number.

Leveled Practice For **7–12**, write the factor pairs for each number.

7. 34
   ___ and 34
   2 and ___

8. 39
   1 and ___
   ___ and 13

9. 61
   1 and ___

10. 14
    ___ and ___
    ___ and ___

11. 22
    ___ and ___
    ___ and ___

12. 51
    ___ and ___
    ___ and ___

For **13–21**, write the factors of each number. Use counters to help as needed.

13. 6
14. 32
15. 83
16. 11
17. 49
18. 25
19. 30
20. 63
21. 19

For another example, see Set B on page 401.

Problem Solving

22. Irene wants to list the factors for 88. She writes 2, 4, 8, 11, 22, 44, and 88. Is Irene correct? Explain.

23. **Math and Science** The roots of a plant are often the largest part of the plant. Winter rye can grow combined root tissue well over 984,000 feet in length. Write this number in expanded form.

24. A restaurant receives a shipment of 5,000 ketchup packets. In one week, they use 1,824 packets. The next week, they use 2,352 packets. How many ketchup packets does the restaurant have left?

25. Any number that has 9 as a factor also has 3 as a factor. Why is this?

26. **Higher Order Thinking** A mother manatee, pictured to the right, is three times as long as her baby manatee.

    a. How long is her baby manatee? Write and solve an equation.

    b. If a blue whale is 9 times as long as the manatee shown, how much longer is a blue whale than the manatee? Write and solve equations.

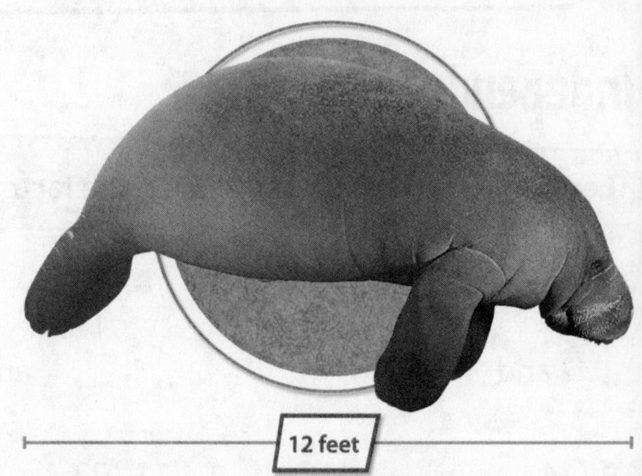

Assessment ISTEP+ Ready

27. Which lists all the factors of 38?

    Ⓐ 1, 38

    Ⓑ 1, 2, 14, 38

    Ⓒ 1, 2, 38

    Ⓓ 1, 2, 19, 38

28. A store manager wants to display 45 cans of soup in an array. Which of the following shows 3 ways the cans could be displayed?

    Ⓐ $1 \times 9, 9 \times 5, 3 \times 15$

    Ⓑ $15 \times 3, 9 \times 1, 5 \times 9$

    Ⓒ $5 \times 9, 3 \times 15, 9 \times 5$

    Ⓓ $45 \times 1, 15 \times 1, 9 \times 1$

Name ______________________

Homework & Practice 7-2

Factors

Another Look!

Find the factors and factor pairs for 8.

1 group of 8 or 8 groups of 1

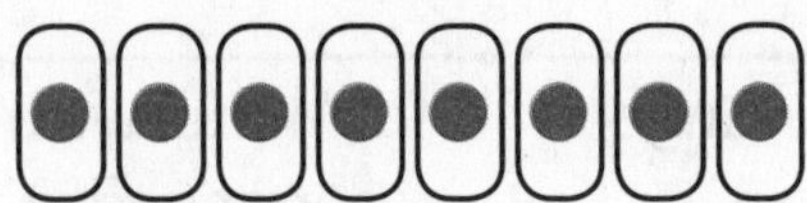

2 groups of 4 or 4 groups of 2

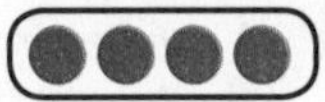

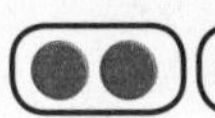

The factor pairs are 1 and 8, 2 and 4

The factors of 8 are 1, 2, 4, and 8.

When multiplying two numbers, both numbers are factors of the product.

For **1–6**, write the factor pairs for each number.

1. 75
1 and ____
____ and 25
____ and 15

2. 28
____ and 28
____ and 14
4 and ____

3. 46
____ and 46
____ and 23

4. 47

5. 77

6. 23

For **7–15**, write the factors of each number. Use counters to help as needed.

7. 74

8. 58

9. 44

10. 72

11. 57

12. 10

13. 7

14. 60

15. 66

16. Mr. Matthews purchases 22 boxes of pencils for 5 fourth-grade classes. Each box contains 45 pencils. How many pencils will each class receive?

17. Damita wants to read a 257-page book in one week. She plans to read 36 pages each day. Will she reach her goal? Explain.

18. Algebra Crystal has 81 buttons arranged equally in 3 rows. Write and solve an equation to find the number of buttons in each row.

19. Model with Math Sal has 13 stamps arranged in an array. Describe Sal's array.

20. As part of her science project, Shay is making a model of a wind farm. She wants to put 24 turbines in her model. What arrays can Shay make using 24 turbines?

21. Mrs. Fisher has 91 watches on display at her store. She says she can arrange them into rows and columns without any watches left over. Mr. Fisher says she can only make 1 row with all 91 watches. Who is correct? Explain.

22. Higher Order Thinking Mr. Deets is making an array to display 9 pictures. For each pair of different factors, there are two arrays he can make. How many different arrays can Mr. Deets make? Is the number of arrays odd or even? Explain.

23. Which lists the factors of 62?

Ⓐ 1, 62

Ⓑ 1, 2, 30, 62

Ⓒ 1, 2, 31, 62

Ⓓ 1, 2, 3, 21, 31, 62

24. Dana has 39 coins. She wants to display them in an array. Which of the following describes the arrays Dana can make?

Ⓐ 1×39

Ⓑ $3 \times 13, 13 \times 3$

Ⓒ $1 \times 39, 3 \times 13$

Ⓓ $1 \times 39, 39 \times 1, 3 \times 13, 13 \times 3$

Name ______________________

Problem Solving

Lesson 7-3
Repeated Reasoning

I can . . .
use repeated reasoning to generalize how to solve similar problems.

Process Standards PS.8 Also PS.2, PS.3, PS.4, PS.7
Content Standard 4.NS.8

A closet company sells wooden storage cubicles. Jane bought 24 cubicles. She wants to arrange them in a rectangular array. What are all of the different ways Jane can arrange them, using all of her cubicles? Explain how you know you found them all.

DATA

These cubicles are arranged in an array.	These cubicles are not arranged in an array.
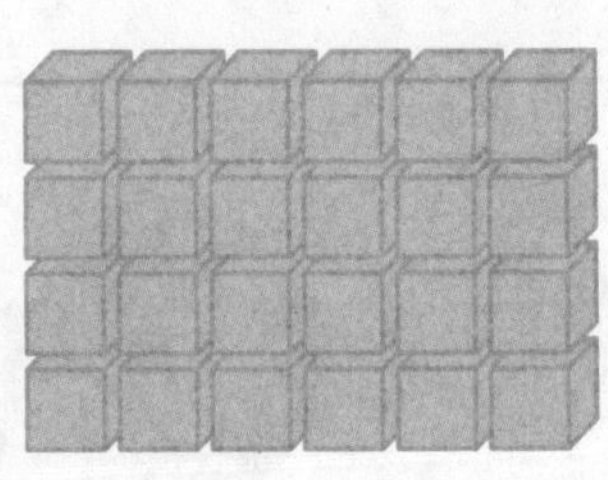	

Thinking Habits

Be a good thinker!
These questions can help you.

- Are any calculations repeated?
- Can I generalize from examples?
- What shortcuts do I notice?

Look Back! Generalize Do you need to try all numbers from 1 to 24 to be sure you have all the factor pairs for 24? Explain.

How Can You Use Repeated Reasoning to Find All the Factors for a Number?

A

A new city park is opening. The gardener needs to select 15 trees from a nursery and plant the trees in a rectangular array. What are all the different ways the gardener can plant the trees?

Select 15 trees to plant

Can you look for a general method to solve this problem?

I can find all the possible factors of 15 that can be arranged in a rectangular array.

Here's my thinking.

B

How can I make a generalization from repeated reasoning?

I can

- look for things that repeat in a problem.
- look for shortcuts.
- generalize from the example.

C

To find all of the factors of 15, I divide 15 by divisors starting with 1. Then I use the Commutative Property to write two multiplication equations.

$1 \times 15 = 15$ and $15 \times 1 = 15$
2 is not a factor
$3 \times 5 = 15$ and $5 \times 3 = 15$
4 is not a factor
$5 \times 3 = 15$ and $3 \times 5 = 15$

I already found the factor paired with 5, 3×5 and 5×3.

When factor pairs start repeating, you can make a general statement, or generalize, that all the factors of a number are found.

The gardener has 4 different ways to plant the trees: 1×15, 15×1, 5×3, and 3×5 arrays.

Convince Me! **Construct Arguments** The diagram shows all the factor pairs of 24. Use the diagram to justify the conclusion that when factor pairs start repeating, you know you have found all the factors of a number.

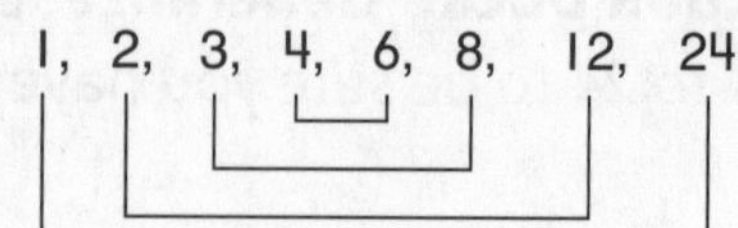

Name ____

Practice Buddy Tools Assessment

Guided Practice*

Generalize

Ms. Maribel wants to arrange the 20 desks in her classroom into rows with the same number of desks in each row. She wants at least 2, but not more than 8 rows.

When you generalize, you find general methods and shortcuts to help solve a problem.

1. What are the factor pairs for 20? Explain how you know you have found them all.

2. Find the ways Ms. Maribel can arrange the desks.

Independent Practice

Generalize

Kevin invited 15 friends to his birthday party. They played a game where everyone had to separate into groups. Each group had the same number of children. The game could not be played with all 16 children in one group and each group had to have more than 1 child.

3. List the factor pairs of 16 and then find the different ways Kevin and his friends could divide into groups.

4. Why does 16 have an odd number of factors?

5. Can you stop checking for factor pairs when you find a pair that repeats? Explain.

*For another example, see Set C on page 401.

Problem Solving

Performance Assessment

ISTEP+ Ready

Store Displays

A pet store needs 3 displays with the products shown. The boxes of kitty litter need to be stacked with the same number of boxes in each row. There needs to be at least 3 rows with at least 3 boxes in each row. What are all the ways the boxes of kitty litter could be stacked?

50 fish bowls

48 boxes of kitty litter

88 bags of dog food

6. **Make Sense and Persevere** What quantities are given in the problem and what do the numbers mean?

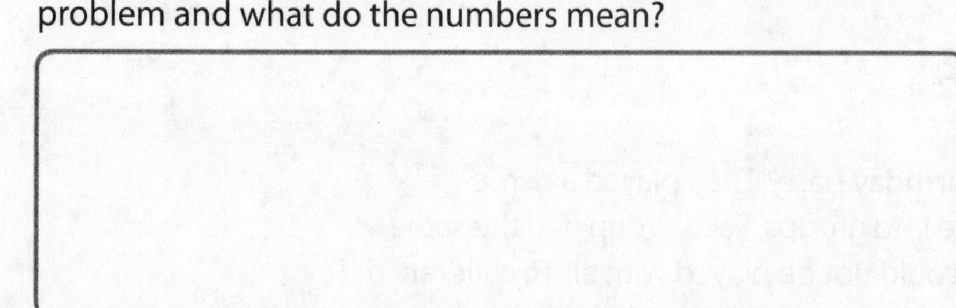

When you notice repetition in calculations, you can generalize to help solve problems.

7. **Reasoning** What are the factor pairs for 48?

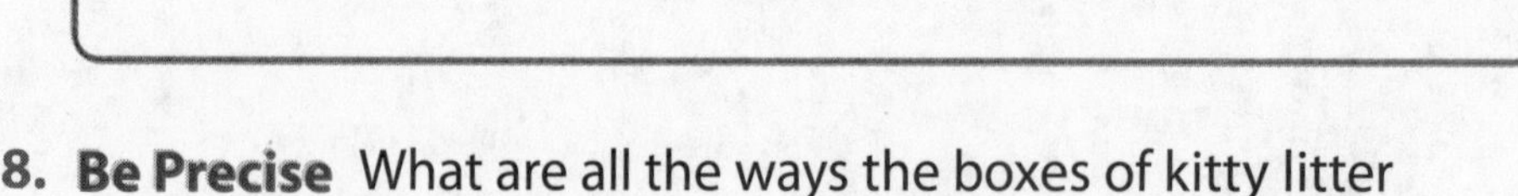

8. **Be Precise** What are all the ways the boxes of kitty litter can be stacked with at least 3 rows with at least 3 boxes in each row?

Name ______________________

Homework & Practice 7-3
Repeated Reasoning

Another Look!

Silvia has 45 cans of paint to put on shelves. Each shelf can hold up to 15 cans of paint. Each row must have the same number of cans on the shelf. How many different ways might Sylvia put the cans on the shelves?

Tell how you can generalize to find how many different ways Silvia can put the cans of paint on the shelves.

- I can look for things that repeat in a problem.
- I can look for shortcuts.
- I can generalize from an example.

Find the factors of 45.

1 × **45** = 45 and **45** × **1** = 45
3 × **15** = 45 and **15** × **3** = 45
5 × **9** = 45 and **9** × **5** = 45
2, **4**, **6**, **7**, and **8** are not factors.

The factors of 45 are **1**, **3**, **5**, **9**, **15**, and **45**.

Silvia can put the cans of paint on 5 shelves with 9 cans on each shelf or 3 shelves with 15 cans on each shelf.

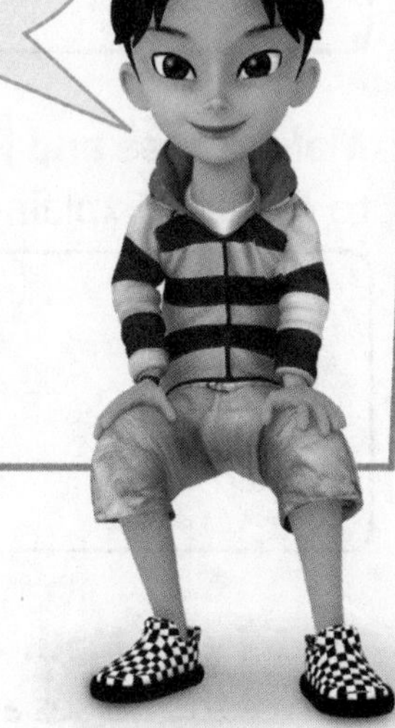

When you generalize, you look for steps that repeat.

Generalize

An auditorium has rows of seats with 8 seats in each row. Kayla knows there are at least 70 seats but fewer than 150 seats in the auditorium. How many rows of seats can there be in the auditorium? Use Exercises 1–3 to answer the question.

1. Explain how you would find the least possible number of rows in the auditorium.

2. How would you find all the possible numbers of rows, without having to check if 8 is a factor of every number between 70 and 150?

3. Name all the possible numbers of rows in the auditorium.

Performance Assessment — ISTEP+ Ready

County Fair

At the county fair, animals are judged for the quality of their breeding and health. The animal pens are arranged in an array, with one animal in each pen. A barn can hold at most 10 rows of pens and at most 6 pens in each row, with room for people to walk around them. What different ways can the planners of the county fair arrange the pens for the horses and cows in the same barn?

4. Reasoning How do the quantities given in the problem relate to each other?

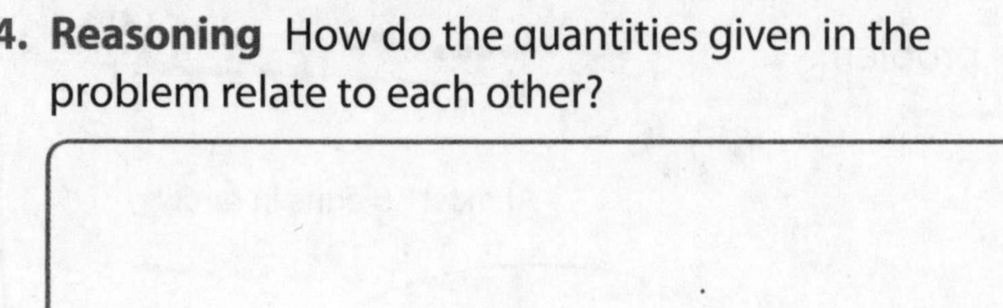

5. Make Sense and Persevere What steps do you need to do first? Explain.

When you generalize, you find an efficient method for solving a problem, which can be used to solve similar problems.

6. Model with Math What are all the factor pairs for the sum of the horses and cows? Represent the factors with a diagram to show how you found all the factor pairs.

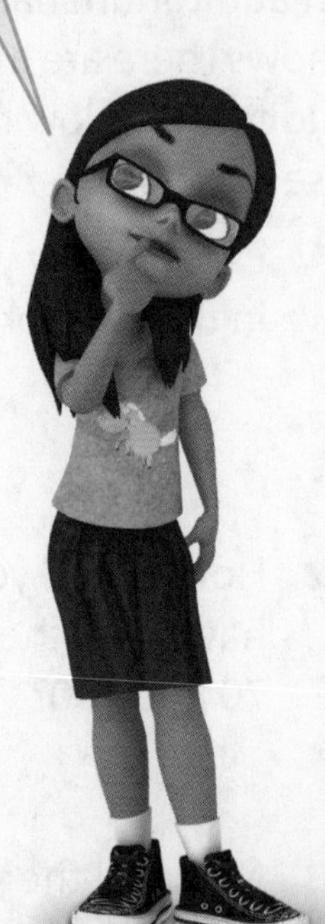

7. Be Precise What are all the different ways the planners can arrange the pens for the horses and cows in the barn?

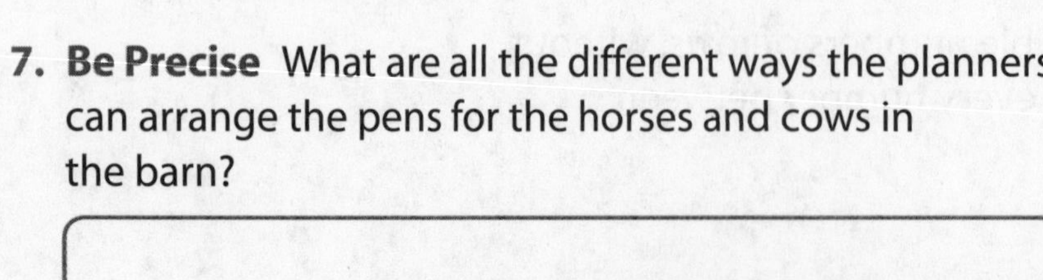

Name ______________________________

Lesson 7-4
Prime and Composite Numbers

I can ...
use factors to determine if a whole number is prime or composite.

Content Standard Extends 4.NS.8
Process Standards PS.2, PS.7, PS.8

Solve & Share Max has 2 red tiles, 3 blue tiles, 4 yellow tiles, and 8 green tiles. How many different arrays can Max make with each color of tile? Explain how you know you found all the arrays. ***Solve this problem any way you choose.***

You can use reasoning. Find the factors of each number of tiles to help find the number of arrays.

Look Back! Generalize What do you notice about the factors of each number of color tiles and the number of arrays?

How Can You Identify Prime and Composite Numbers?

A

The data table lists the factors for 2, 3, 4, 5, and 6. What do you notice about the factors for 5? What do you notice about the factors for 6?

DATA

Number	Factors
2	1, 2
3	1, 3
4	1, 2, 4
5	1, 5
6	1, 2, 3, 6

A prime number is a whole number greater than 1 that has exactly two factors, 1 and itself.

A composite number is a whole number greater than 1 that has more than 2 factors.

B

Prime Numbers

5 is a prime number.
It has only 2 factors, 1 and itself.

$1 \times 5 = 5$

$5 \times 1 = 5$

The number 1 is a special number. It is neither prime nor composite.

C

Composite Numbers

6 is a composite number.
The factors for 6 are 1, 2, 3, and 6.

$1 \times 6 = 6$

$6 \times 1 = 6$

$2 \times 3 = 6$

$3 \times 2 = 6$

Convince Me! **Generalize** Can a number be both prime and composite? Explain.

Name

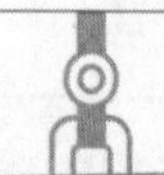

Guided Practice*

Do You Understand?

1. What is the only even prime number?

2. **Construct Arguments** Write an odd number that is not prime. What makes it a composite number?

3. Roger has 47 cars. Can he group the cars in more than 2 ways?

Do You Know How?

For **4–9**, tell whether each number is prime or composite.

4. 32 **5.** 51

6. 17 **7.** 21

8. 95 **9.** 29

A number is composite if it has more than 2 factors.

Independent Practice

Leveled Practice For **10–19**, tell whether each number is prime or composite.

10. 6

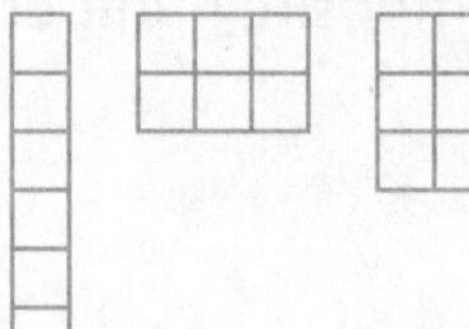

11. 10

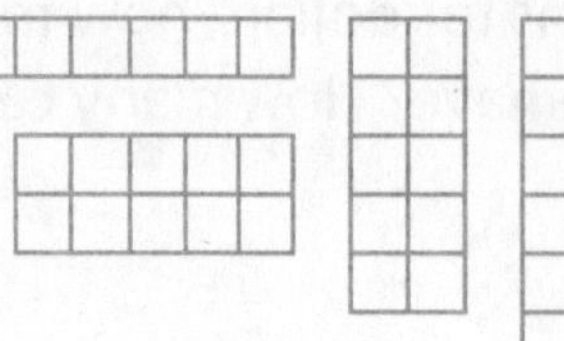

12. 12 **13.** 97 **14.** 90 **15.** 31

16. 11 **17.** 44 **18.** 3 **19.** 59

*For another example, see Set D on page 402.

Problem Solving

For **20–21**, use the graph at the right.

20. Which type of flower received a prime number of votes?

21. How many votes are represented by the picture graph?

Favorite Flowers	
Daffodils	🌼🌼◐
Daisies	✿✿✿
Tulips	🌷🌷🌷🌷🌷

Key: Each flower icon equals 2 votes.

22. Critique Reasoning Maria says every number in the nineties is composite. Jackie says one number in the nineties is prime. Who is correct? Explain your answer.

23. Critique Reasoning Greta says the product of two prime numbers must also be prime. Joan disagreed. Who is correct?

24. Janelle has 342 pennies, 62 nickels, and 12 dimes. If Janelle exchanges her coins for dollars, how many dollars will she have? How many cents will remain?

25. Higher Order Thinking Why is 1 neither a prime number nor a composite number?

Assessment ISTEP+ Ready

26. Select all the numbers that are prime.

- ☐ 17
- ☐ 37
- ☐ 52
- ☐ 63
- ☐ 89

27. Select all the numbers that are composite.

- ☐ 39
- ☐ 45
- ☐ 54
- ☐ 61
- ☐ 92

Name ______________________________

Homework & Practice 7-4
Prime and Composite Numbers

Another Look!

You can look for factors to help you tell whether a number is prime or composite.

Is 15 a prime or a composite number? Find all the factors of 15.

Factors of 15: 1, 3, 5, 15

15 is a composite number because it has more than two factors.

Is 29 a prime or a composite number? Find all the factors of 29.

Factors of 29: 1, 29

29 is a prime number because it only has two factors, 1 and the number itself.

For **1–4**, use or draw arrays to tell whether each number is prime or composite.

1. 7

2. 9

3. 8

4. 4

For **5–16**, tell whether each number is prime or composite.

5. 81 **6.** 43 **7.** 72 **8.** 93

9. 53 **10.** 87 **11.** 13 **12.** 27

13. 88 **14.** 19 **15.** 69 **16.** 79

17. **Use Structure** Create a list of prime numbers from 1 to 100.

- Write all the numbers from 1 to 100.
- Draw a triangle around 1; it is neither prime nor composite.
- Circle 2 and cross out all other multiples of 2.
- Circle 3 and cross out all other multiples of 3.
- Circle 5 and cross out all other multiples of 5.
- Continue in the same way. The circled numbers are prime.

1	2	3	4	5
6	7	8	9	10
11	12	13	14	15
16	17	18	19	20
21	22	23	24	25
26	27	28	29	30
31	32	33	34	35
36	37	38	39	40

How many prime numbers are between 1 and 100?

18. **Number Sense** Are all odd numbers prime numbers? Explain.

19. **Math and Science** Some plants have thorns for protection. Ben is a florist and cuts thorns from flowers. On Monday, he cut 267 thorns. On Tuesday, he cut 381 thorns. On Wednesday, he cut 522 thorns. How many thorns did Ben cut?

20. A-Z **Vocabulary** Use *prime* and *composite* to complete the definitions.

A __________ number is a whole number greater than 1 that has more than 2 factors. A ______ number is a whole number greater than 1 that has exactly two factors, 1 and itself.

21. **Higher Order Thinking** Larry says all numbers that have a 2 in the ones place are composite numbers. Explain if Larry is correct or incorrect.

Assessment ISTEP+ Ready

22. Which of the following digits might composite numbers greater than 10 have in the ones place? Select all that apply.

- ☐ 1
- ☐ 2
- ☐ 3
- ☐ 4
- ☐ 5

23. Which of the following digits might prime numbers greater than 10 have in the ones place? Select all that apply.

- ☐ 0
- ☐ 2
- ☐ 3
- ☐ 7
- ☐ 9

Name ______________________________

Lesson 7-5
Multiples

I can ...
use multiplication to find multiples of a number.

Content Standard 4.NS.8
Process Standards PS.2, PS.3, PS.4, PS.7, PS.8

Solve & Share

There are 9 players on the golf practice range. If each player practices with the same number of golf balls, how many balls might be in play at the same time? ***Solve this problem any way you choose.***

You can use reasoning. What do you notice about the number of balls in play?

Golf Balls in Play

Balls per Player	Balls in Play
1	1 × 9 = 9 balls in play
2	2 × 9 = 18 balls in play
3	3 × 9 = 27 balls in play
4	
5	

Look Back! Generalize Can you show all of the answers for the problem? Explain.

How Can You Find Multiples of a Number?

A

It takes 8 minutes for Car A to make one full turn on the Ferris wheel. If the Ferris wheel continues to turn at the same speed for the next hour, at what times during the hour will Car A return to the starting point?

A multiple is the product of a given factor and a whole number.

B

Step 1

One full turn takes 8 minutes.

$1 \times 8 = 8$

8 is a multiple of 1 and 8 because $1 \times 8 = 8$.

Car A is back at the starting point after 8 minutes.

C

Step 2

Two full turns take 16 minutes.

$2 \times 8 = 16$

Car A is back at the starting point after another 8 minutes.

2 and 8 are *factors* of 16. 16 is a *multiple* of 2 and 8.

D

Step 3

Car A is at the starting point every 8 minutes after that:

$3 \times 8 = 24$
$4 \times 8 = 32$
$5 \times 8 = 40$
$6 \times 8 = 48$
$7 \times 8 = 56$

During the hour, Car A returns to the starting point after 8, 16, 24, 32, 40, 48, and 56 minutes.

Convince Me! Reasoning What is the next multiple after 56? Explain why it is **NOT** used.

Name ______________________________

Practice Buddy Tools Assessment

Guided Practice*

Do You Understand?

1. **Look for Relationships** If the Ferris wheel in the example on the previous page turns at the same speed, will Car A return to the starting point at 75 minutes? Explain.

2. Suppose the Ferris wheel speeds up so it makes one full turn every 6 minutes. When will Car A return to the starting point if the Ferris wheel continues to turn for one half hour?

Do You Know How?

For **3–6**, write five multiples of each number.

3. 2 **4.** 9

5. 3 **6.** 10

For **7–10**, tell whether the first number is a multiple of the second number.

7. 14, 2 **8.** 3, 18

9. 56, 9 **10.** 42, 7

Independent Practice

You can skip count to find multiples of numbers.

For **11–18**, write five multiples of each number.

11. 7 **12.** 4 **13.** 6 **14.** 5

15. 11 **16.** 1 **17.** 20 **18.** 15

For **19–26**, tell whether the first number is a multiple of the second number.

19. 44, 6 **20.** 25, 5 **21.** 30, 6 **22.** 54, 9

23. 28, 3 **24.** 45, 5 **25.** 64, 7 **26.** 48, 8

*For another example, see Set E on page 402.

Problem Solving

27. Name three numbers that are a multiple of 2 and a multiple of 5.

28. Critique Reasoning Lindsay says all numbers that are multiples of 4 have 2 as a factor. Is Lindsay correct? Explain.

29. Model with Math Lisa made a Venn diagram showing five multiples of 3 and five multiples of 4. What does the shaded section in her diagram show?

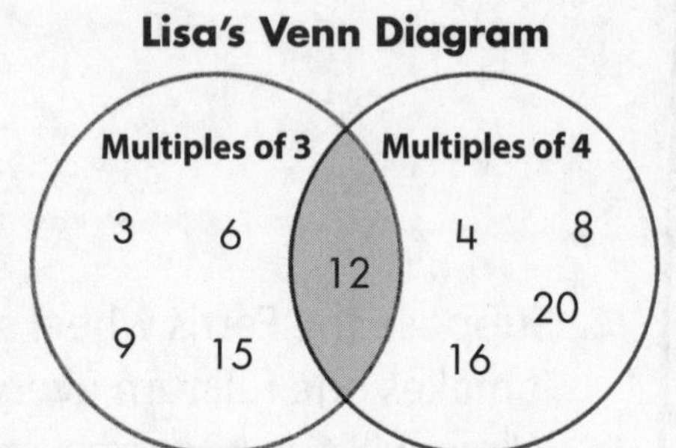

Venn diagrams are used to compare data about two or more groups.

30. Describe how 20,000 and 2,000 are related.

31. Higher Order Thinking Isabel wrote this mystery problem: The quotient is a multiple of 6. The dividend is a multiple of 9. The divisor is a factor of 12. Find one possible solution to Isabel's mystery problem.

Assessment ISTEP+ Ready

32. Latifa and John played a game of multiples. Each player picks a number card and says a multiple of that number. Latifa picked a 9. Write all the multiples of 9 from the box.

Multiples of 9
9 17 29 36 45 51

33. A roller-coaster ride completes a full loop every 3 minutes. Seth listed multiples of 3 to determine when the ride would be back at its starting point. Write all the multiples of 3 from the box.

Multiples of 3
9 11 12 13 19 33

Name ______________________________

Homework & Practice 7-5
Multiples

Another Look!

What are some multiples of 7?

Step 1 Find the column (or row) for 7.

Step 2 All the numbers in that column (or row) are multiples of 7.

In the chart, the multiples of 7 are 7, 14, 21, 28, 35, 42, 49, 56, and 63.

7, 14, 21, 28, 35, 42, 49, 56, and 63 are multiples of 7 because $1 \times 7 = 7$, $2 \times 7 = 14$, $3 \times 7 = 21$, and so on.

×	1	2	3	4	5	6	7	8	9
1	1	2	3	4	5	6	7	8	9
2	2	4	6	8	10	12	14	16	18
3	3	6	9	12	15	18	21	24	27
4	4	8	12	16	20	24	28	32	36
5	5	10	15	20	25	30	35	40	45
6	6	12	18	24	30	36	42	48	54
7	7	14	21	28	35	42	49	56	63
8	8	16	24	32	40	48	56	64	72
9	9	18	27	36	45	54	63	72	81

You can use a multiplication chart to find multiples.

For **1–8**, write five multiples of each number.

1. 12 **2.** 18 **3.** 40 **4.** 16

5. 100 **6.** 25 **7.** 50 **8.** 63

For **9–20**, tell whether the first number is a multiple of the second number.

9. 21, 7 **10.** 28, 3 **11.** 17, 3 **12.** 20, 4

13. 55, 5 **14.** 15, 5 **15.** 26, 4 **16.** 32, 8

17. 48, 7 **18.** 60, 2 **19.** 79, 4 **20.** 81, 3

21. Is 6 a multiple or a factor of 12?

22. Is 8 a multiple or a factor of 4?

23. **Reasoning** What number has factors of 2 and 3 and 12 and 18 as multiples?

24. **Look for Relationships** What numbers have 12, 24, and 36 as multiples?

Make a list of the numbers that can be divided evenly by 2 and 3.
Make a list of the numbers that divide evenly into 12, 24, and 36.

For **25** and **26**, use the table at the right.

25. Paulo's family arrived at the reunion at 8:30 A.M. How long do they have before the trip to Scenic Lake Park?

26. How much longer is dinner than the slide show?

DATA

Suarez Family Reunion Schedule	
Trip to Scenic Lake Park	10:15 A.M. to 2:30 P.M.
Slide show	4:15 P.M. to 5:10 P.M.
Dinner	5:30 P.M. to 7:00 P.M.
Campfire	7:55 P.M. to 9:30 P.M.

27. Carmen listed the multiples of 24 as 1, 2, 3, 4, 6, 8, 12, and 24. Is she correct? Explain why or why not.

28. **Higher Order Thinking** What is the least multiple 6 and 8 have in common? Explain.

Assessment ISTEP+ Ready

29. Which numbers are **NOT** multiples of 6? Write all the numbers that are **NOT** multiples of 6 from the box.

NOT Multiples of 6
1 2 6 16 26 36

30. Which multiples do 3 and 5 have in common? Write all the common multiples of 3 and 5 from the box.

Common Multiples of 3 and 5
3 5 15 30 33 35

Name ____________________

Fluency Practice Activity

Shade a path from **START** to **FINISH**. Follow the sums and differences that are correct. You can only move up, down, right, or left.

I can ...
add and subtract multi-digit whole numbers.

Start

573 + 417 = 990	685 − 559 = 137	808 + 123 = 921	609 − 541 = 48	501 + 469 = 170
491 − 188 = 303	347 + 607 = 954	948 − 558 = 410	505 + 125 = 620	987 − 696 = 311
764 + 346 = 1,000	994 − 405 = 589	874 + 721 = 1,595	894 − 455 = 449	369 + 290 = 669
668 − 485 = 253	762 + 901 = 2,663	941 − 725 = 216	640 + 89 = 729	537 − 271 = 806
119 + 679 = 698	977 − 239 = 642	987 + 111 = 998	812 − 99 = 713	335 + 25 = 360

Finish

Word List

- array
- composite number
- factor
- factor pairs
- generalization
- multiple
- prime number
- whole number

Understand Vocabulary

1. Cross out the numbers that are **NOT** factors of 16.

1 2 3 4 8

2. Cross out the numbers that are **NOT** multiples of 3.

3 6 9 13 23

3. Cross out the numbers that are **NOT** whole numbers.

$\frac{1}{4}$ $\frac{1}{2}$ 7 $17\frac{1}{5}$ 6,219

4. Cross out the numbers that are **NOT** factor pairs for 24.

1 and 24 2 and 12 3 and 6 4 and 8 4 and 6

Label each example with a term from the Word List.

5. 13 ________________

6. 12 ________________

7. ●●● ________________

8. When factor pairs begin repeating, I have found all the pairs for a number. ________________

Use Vocabulary in Writing

9. Marisol says 23 is both a prime and a composite number because 2 and 3 are both prime. Use at least 3 terms from the Word List to explain the error in Marisol's reasoning.

Name ____________________

Reteaching

Set A pages 369–374

Draw arrays to find all the factors of 8.

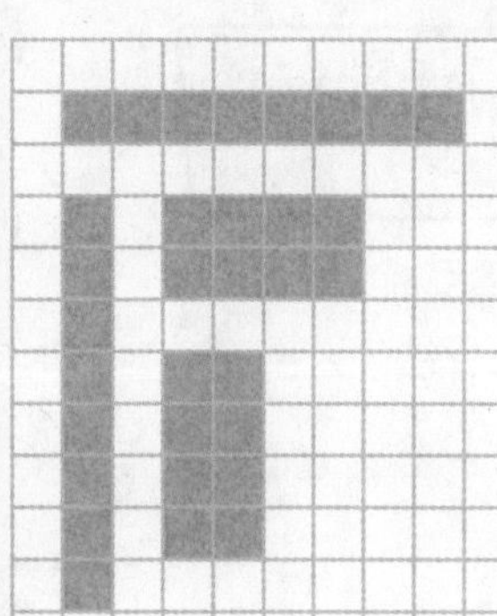

1 row of 8
8 rows of 1

2 rows of 4
4 rows of 2

The factors of 8 are 1, 2, 4, and 8.

Remember that 1 is a factor of every number.

Use grid paper to find the factors of each number.

1. 26
2. 9
3. 37
4. 24
5. 19

Set B pages 375–380

Find the factor pairs for 12.

1 and 12

2 and 6

3 and 4

The factors of 12 are 1, 2, 3, 4, 6, and 12.

Remember you can use counters or grids to make arrays and find the factors of a number.

Find the factors of each number.

1. 45
2. 40
3. 56
4. 63

Set C pages 381–386

Think about these questions to help you use **repeated reasoning.**

Thinking Habits

- Are any calculations repeated?
- Can I generalize from examples?
- What shortcuts do I notice?

Remember to look for repeating factors when dividing to find the factor pairs of a number.

A valet has 34 cars to park in a rectangular array.

1. What are the different ways the valet could park the cars?

2. How do you know when you can stop looking for factors of a number?

Set D pages 387–392

Is 49 prime or composite?

To determine if 49 is prime or composite, find whether 49 has factors other than 1 and 49.

49 is composite because it is divisible by 7.

$49 = 7 \times 7$

Remember you can use an array to determine if a number is prime or composite.

Tell whether each number is prime or composite.

1. 13
2. 25
3. 55
4. 2
5. 29
6. 23
7. 64
8. 99
9. 5
10. 21

Set E pages 393–398

Find five multiples of 7.

Use multiplication.

$7 \times 1 = 7$

$7 \times 2 = 14$

$7 \times 3 = 21$

$7 \times 4 = 28$

$7 \times 5 = 35$

You can skip count to find multiples of a number.

Remember that to find multiples of a number, multiply the number by any whole number.

Find five multiples of each number.

1. 3
2. 6
3. 4
4. 9

Tell whether the first number is a multiple of the second number.

5. 22, 2
6. 29, 3
7. 25, 5
8. 40, 8

Name ____________________

TOPIC 7

Assessment

ISTEP+ Ready

1. Courtney has 36 photos to arrange on a gallery wall.

Part A

How many arrays can Courtney make with the 36 photos? List all the possible arrays.

Part B

How many factors are there for 36? Write them. What do you notice about the number of factors of 36 and the number of arrays Courtney can make with the photos?

Part C

Write all the factor pairs for 36. Is 36 prime or composite? Explain.

2. Peter wrote 4 sets of numbers. Which sets show only multiples of 6?

2a. 6, 12, 18, 24 ○ Yes ○ No

2b. 6, 16, 26, 36 ○ Yes ○ No

2c. 1, 2, 3, 6 ○ Yes ○ No

2d. 6, 60, 66, 600 ○ Yes ○ No

3. Which statement is true?

Ⓐ The only factors of 3 are 3 and 1.

Ⓑ The only factors of 4 are 4 and 1.

Ⓒ The only factors of 6 are 6 and 1.

Ⓓ The only factors of 8 are 8 and 1.

4. Choose the correct word from the box to complete each statement.

Prime Composite

19 is a ______ number.

12 is a ______ number.

33 is a ______ number.

17 is a ______ number.

5. The dividend is a multiple of 4. The divisor is a factor of 12. The quotient is a factor of 18. Choose numbers from the box to find one possible solution.

______ ÷ ______ = ______

Dividend Divisor Quotient

2 3 4 6 8 9 12 36

6. Write 3 multiples and 3 factors for 24.

7. Corky wrote a list of factors and a list of multiples. Draw lines to match the factors with the multiples.

Factors	Multiples
9	25
7	6
5	27
2	49

8. Select all the true statements.

- ☐ A composite number has at least 3 factors.
- ☐ All prime numbers are odd.
- ☐ 99 is a prime number.
- ☐ 2 is the smallest prime number.
- ☐ All even numbers greater than 2 are composite.
- ☐ All prime numbers have 2 factors.

9. Martika says factors and multiples are related. Use the equation $6 \times 7 = 42$ to describe the relationship between factors and multiples.

10. Which lists all the factors of 25?

Ⓐ 1, 25
Ⓑ 1, 5, 25
Ⓒ 1, 10, 25
Ⓓ 1, 25, 50

11. Carter lives on a street where all the house numbers are multiples of 6. Name two possible house numbers between 601 and 650. Explain.

12. Write each number in the correct answer space to show factors of 27 and 35.

Factors of 27	Factors of 35

3 5 7 9 27 35

13. Javier says all odd numbers greater than 2 and less than 20 are prime. Find an odd number greater than 2 and less than 20 that is **NOT** prime. Explain why the number is not prime.

Name ____________________

Arranging Cars to Sell

Ms. Ortiz owns a car dealership. The dealership has the inventory of cars listed in the **Ortiz Car Dealership** table.

Ortiz Car Dealership

Type of Vehicle	Number Dealership Has
Compact	40
Sedan	36
SUV	23
Truck	15

1. Ms. Ortiz wants to arrange all of the trucks in the front lot. She would like to have same number of trucks in each row.

Part A

How many different ways can the trucks be arranged in the front lot if the same number of trucks are parked in each row?

Part B

What are all the ways the trucks can be arranged? Draw and label the different arrays.

Part C

Ms. Ortiz would like the arrangement to have more than 2 rows of trucks but less than 6 rows. What are the ways the trucks can be arranged? Explain.

2. As Ms. Ortiz sells sedans, those sedans remaining are parked in different arrangements.

Complete the **Arranging Sedans** table to find the number of ways Ms. Ortiz can arrange each number of sedans in the front lot so there are at least 2 rows and more than one sedan in each row.

Arranging Sedans

Sedans Sold	Number Left	Number of Arrangements	Arrangements
1			
2			
3			
4			
5			
6			
7			

Glossary

acute angle An angle that is open less than a right angle.

acute triangle A triangle that has three acute angles.

addends The numbers that are added together to find a sum.
Example: $2 + 7 = 9$
Addends

algorithm A set of steps used to solve a math problem.

angle A figure formed by two rays that have the same endpoint.

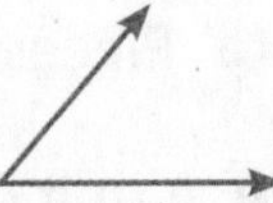

angle measure The number of degrees in an angle.

area The number of square units needed to cover a region.

array A way of displaying objects in rows and columns.

Associative Property of Addition Addends can be regrouped and the sum remains the same.

Associative Property of Multiplication Factors can be regrouped and the product stays the same.

bar diagram A tool used to help understand and solve word problems.

bar graph A graph using bars to show data.

benchmark fraction A known fraction that is commonly used for estimating. *Examples:* $\frac{1}{4}$, $\frac{1}{3}$, $\frac{1}{2}$, $\frac{2}{3}$, and $\frac{3}{4}$.

billions A period of three places to the left of the millions period.

breaking apart Mental math method used to rewrite a number as the sum of numbers to form an easier problem.

capacity The amount a container can hold, measured in liquid units.

center A point within a circle that is the same distance from all points on a circle.

centimeter (cm) A metric unit used to measure length. 100 centimeters = 1 meter

century A unit of time equal to 100 years.

circle A closed plane figure in which all the points are the same distance from a point called the center.

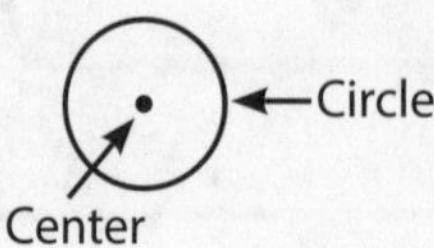

common denominator A number that is the denominator of two or more fractions.

common factor A number that is a factor of two or more given numbers.

Commutative Property of Addition Numbers can be added in any order and the sum remains the same.

Commutative Property of Multiplication Factors can be multiplied in any order and the product stays the same.

compare Decide if one number is greater than, less than, or equal to another number.

compatible numbers Numbers that are easy to compute mentally.

compensation Choosing numbers close to the numbers in a problem to make the computation easier, and then adjusting the answer for the numbers chosen.

compose To combine parts.

composite number A whole number greater than 1 with more than two factors.

conjecture Statement that is believed to be true but has not been proven.

coordinate grid A grid used to show ordered pairs.

counting on Counting up from the lesser number to the greater number to find the difference of two numbers.

cube A solid figure with six identical squares as its faces.

cubic unit The volume of a cube that measures 1 unit on each edge.

cup (c) A customary unit of capacity. 1 cup = 8 fluid ounces

customary units of measure Units of measure that are used in the United States.

data Pieces of collected information.

day A unit of time equal to 24 hours.

decade A unit of time equal to 10 years.

decimal A number with one or more digits to the right of the decimal point.

decimal point A dot used to separate dollars from cents in money or to separate ones from tenths in a number.

decimeter (dm) A metric unit of length equal to 10 centimeters.

decompose To break into parts.

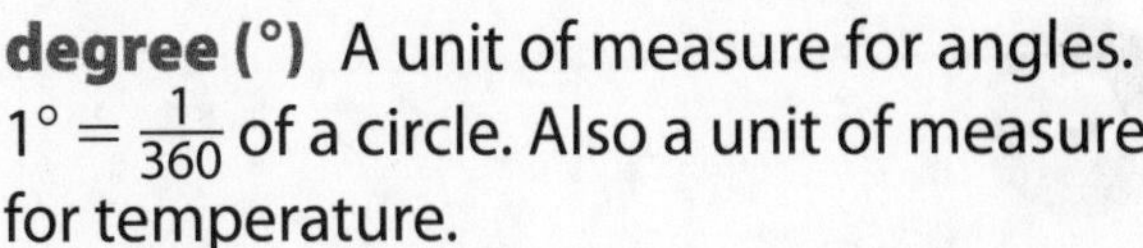

degree (°) A unit of measure for angles. $1° = \frac{1}{360}$ of a circle. Also a unit of measure for temperature.

denominator The number below the fraction bar in a fraction that represents the total number of equal parts in one whole.

difference The answer when subtracting two numbers.

digits The symbols used to write a number: 0, 1, 2, 3, 4, 5, 6, 7, 8, and 9.

Distributive Property Multiplying a sum (or difference) by a number is the same as multiplying each number in the sum (or difference) by that number and adding (or subtracting) the products.
Example: $(3 \times 21) = (3 \times 20) + (3 \times 1)$

divide An operation to find the number in each group or the number of equal groups.

dividend The number to be divided.

divisibility rules The rules that state when a number is divisible by another number.

divisible Can be divided by another number without leaving a remainder.
Example: 10 is divisible by 2

divisor The number by which another number is divided.
Example: $32 \div 4 = 8$
↑ Divisor

dot plot A type of line plot that uses dots to indicate the number of times a response occurred.

elapsed time The amount of time between the beginning of an event and the end of the event.

equation A number sentence that uses the equal sign (=) to show that two expressions have the same value.
Example: $9 + 3 = 12$

equilateral triangle A triangle with three sides that are the same length.

equivalent Numbers that name the same amount.

equivalent fractions Fractions that name the same region, part of a set, or part of a segment.

estimate To give an approximate value rather than an exact answer.

expanded form A number written as the sum of the values of its digits.
Example: $2{,}476 = 2{,}000 + 400 + 70 + 6$

expression A mathematical phrase.
Examples: $x - 3$ or $2 + 7$

fact family A group of related facts using the same set of numbers.

factor pairs Numbers that when multiplied together give a certain product.

factors The numbers that are multiplied together to give a product.
Example: $3 \times 6 = 18$

fluid ounce (fl oz) A customary unit of capacity. 1 fluid ounce = 2 tablespoons; 8 fluid ounces = 1 cup

foot (ft) A customary unit of length. 1 foot = 12 inches

formula An equation that uses symbols to relate two or more quantities. *Example:* $A = \ell \times w$

fraction A symbol, such as $\frac{2}{3}$, $\frac{5}{1}$, or $\frac{8}{5}$, used to name a part of a whole, a part of a set, or a location on a number line.

frequency The number of times that a response occurs in a set of data.

frequency table A way to display data that shows how many times a response occurs in a set of data.

gallon (gal) A customary unit of capacity. 1 gallon = 4 quarts

generalize To make a general statement.

gram (g) A metric unit of mass. 1,000 grams = 1 kilogram

greater than symbol (>) A symbol that points away from a greater number or expression. *Example:* $450 > 449$

hexagon A polygon with 6 sides.

hour A unit of time equal to 60 minutes.

hundredth One part of 100 equal parts of a whole.

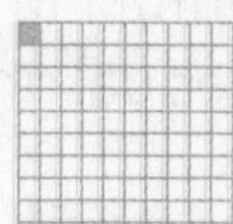

Identity Property of Addition The sum of any number and zero is that number.

Identity Property of Multiplication The product of any number and one is that number.

inch (in.) A customary unit of length. 12 inches = 1 foot

inequality A number sentence that uses the greater than sign (>) or the less than sign (<) to show that two expressions do not have the same value. *Example:* $5 > 3$

intersecting lines Lines that pass through the same point.

interval A number which is the difference between two consecutive numbers on the scale of a graph.

inverse operations Operations that undo each other.
Examples: Adding 6 and subtracting 6; Multiplying by 4 and dividing by 4.

isosceles triangle A triangle with at least two equal sides.

key Part of a graph that tells what each symbol stands for.

kilogram (kg) A metric unit of mass equal to 1,000 grams. 1 kilogram = 1,000 grams

kilometer (km) A metric unit of length equal to 1,000 meters. 1 kilometer = 1,000 meters

leap year A calendar occurrence that happens every four years when an extra day is added to February. Leap years have 366 days.

less than symbol (<) A symbol that points towards a lesser number or expression. *Example:* $305 < 320$

line A straight path of points that goes on and on in opposite directions.

line of symmetry A line on which a figure can be folded so both halves are the same.

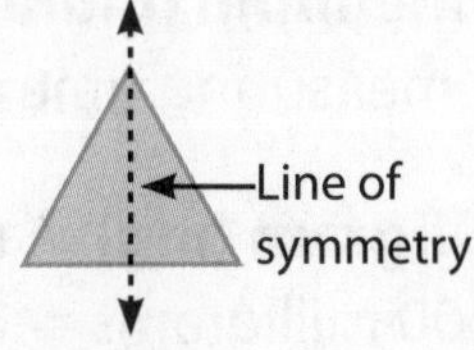

line plot A way to display data along a number line, where each dot represents one number in a set of data.

line segment A part of a line that has two endpoints.

line symmetric A figure that can be folded on a line to form two halves that fit exactly on top of each other.

liter (L) A metric unit of capacity. 1 liter = 1,000 milliliters

mass The amount of matter that something contains.

meter (m) A metric unit of length. 1 meter = 100 centimeters

metric units of measure Units of measure commonly used by scientists.

mile (mi) A customary unit of length. 1 mile = 5,280 feet

millennium (plural: millennia) A unit for measuring time equal to 1,000 years.

milligram (mg) A metric unit of mass. 1,000 milligrams = 1 gram

milliliter (mL) A metric unit of capacity. 1,000 milliliters = 1 liter

millimeter (mm) A metric unit of length. 1,000 millimeters = 1 meter

millions In a number, a period of three places to the left of the thousands period.

minute A unit of time equal to 60 seconds.

mixed number A number that has a whole number part and a fraction part.

month One of the 12 parts into which a year is divided.

multiple The product of a given whole number and any non-zero whole number.

number name A way to write a number in words. *Example:* Four thousand, six hundred thirty-two.

numerator In a fraction, the number above the fraction bar that represents the part of the whole.

numerical expression An expression that contains numbers and at least one operation. *Example:* $35 + 12$

obtuse angle An angle that is open more than a right angle but less than a straight angle.

obtuse triangle A triangle that has one obtuse angle.

octagon A polygon with 8 sides.

ounce (oz) A customary unit of weight. 16 ounces = 1 pound

outlier Any number in a data set that is very different from the rest of the numbers.

overestimate An estimate that is greater than the exact answer.

parallel lines
Lines that never intersect.

parallelogram
A quadrilateral that has two pairs of parallel sides.

partial products Products found by breaking one factor in a multiplication problem into ones, tens, hundreds, and so on and then multiplying each of these by the other factor.

partial quotients A way to divide that finds quotients in parts until only a remainder, if any, is left.

pentagon A plane figure with 5 sides.

perimeter The distance around a figure.

period In a number, a group of three digits, separated by commas, starting from the right.

perpendicular lines Intersecting lines that form right angles.

pint (pt) A customary unit of capacity.
1 pint = 2 cups

place value The value given to a place a digit has in a number.
Example: In 3,946, the 9 is in the hundreds place. So, the 9 has a value of 900.

point An exact location in space.

polygon A closed plane figure made up of line segments.

pound (lb) A customary unit of weight.
1 pound = 16 ounces

prime number A whole number greater than 1 that has exactly two factors, itself and 1.

product The answer to a multiplication problem.

protractor A tool used to measure and draw angles.

Q

quadrilateral A polygon with 4 sides.

quart (qt) A customary unit of capacity.
1 quart = 2 pints

quotient The answer to a division problem.

ray A part of a line that has one endpoint and continues on forever in one direction.

rectangle A quadrilateral that has four right angles.

rectangular prism A solid figure with 6 rectangular faces.

regroup To name a whole number in a different way. *Example:* 32 = 2 tens 12 ones

remainder The number that remains after the division is complete.

repeated addition A way to write a multiplication expression as an addition expression. *Example:* $3 \times 5 = 5 + 5 + 5$

repeating pattern Made up of shapes or numbers that form a part that repeats.

rhombus A quadrilateral that has opposite sides that are parallel and all of its sides are the same length.

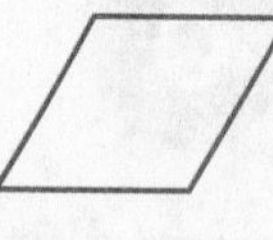

right angle An angle that forms a square corner.

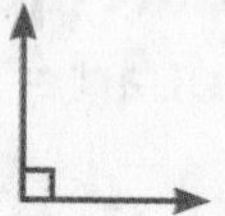

right triangle A triangle that has one right angle.

rounding A process that determines which multiple of 10, 100, 1,000, and so on a number is closest to.

rule A mathematical phrase that tells how numbers in a table are related.

scale Numbers that show the units used on a graph.

scalene triangle A triangle with no sides that are the same length.

second A unit of time. 60 seconds = 1 minute

sequence A set of numbers that follows a pattern.

side Each of the line segments of a polygon.

solid figure A figure with three dimensions that has length, width, and height.

solution The value of the variable that makes an equation true.

solve an equation Find a solution to an equation.

square A quadrilateral that has four right angles and all sides are the same length.

square unit A square with sides one unit long used to measure area.

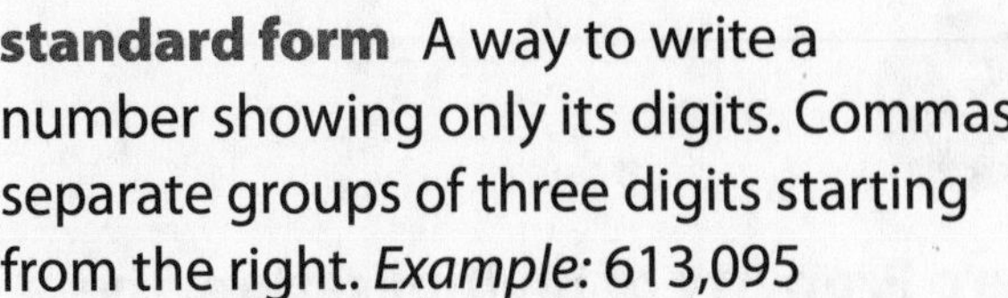

standard form A way to write a number showing only its digits. Commas separate groups of three digits starting from the right. *Example:* 613,095

straight angle An angle that forms a straight line.

sum The result of adding numbers together.

survey Collecting information by asking a number of people the same question and recording their answers.

tablespoon (tbsp) A customary unit of capacity. 1 tablespoon = 3 teaspoons

teaspoon (tsp) A customary unit of capacity. 3 teaspoons = 1 tablespoon

tenth One part of 10 equal parts of a whole.

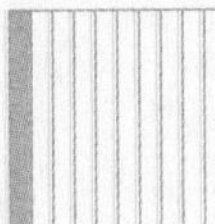

terms Numbers in a sequence or variables, such as x and y, in an expression.

ton (T) A customary unit of weight. 1 ton = 2,000 pounds

trapezoid A quadrilateral with only one pair of parallel sides.

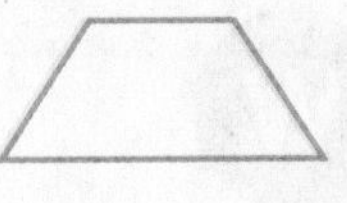

triangle A polygon with 3 sides.

underestimate An estimate that is less than the exact answer.

unit angle An angle that cuts off $\frac{1}{360}$ of a circle and measures 1°.

unit fraction A fraction with a numerator of 1. *Example:* $\frac{1}{2}$

unknown A symbol or letter, such as x, that represents a number in an expression or equation.

variable A symbol or letter that stands for a number.

vertex (plural: vertices) The point where two rays meet to form an angle.

volume The number of cubic units needed to fill a solid figure.

week A unit of time equal to 7 days.

weight A measure of how heavy an object is.

whole numbers The numbers 0, 1, 2, 3, 4, and so on.

yard (yd) A customary unit of length.
1 yard = 3 feet

year A unit of time equal to 365 days or 52 weeks or 12 months.

Zero Property of Multiplication The product of any number and zero is zero.
Examples: $3 \times 0 = 0$; $5 \times 0 = 0$

Photographs

Photo locators denoted as follows: Top (T), Center (C), Bottom (B), Left (L), Right (R), Background (Bkgd)

001 MarclSchauer/Shutterstock; **032** petr84/Fotolia; **043** forkArt Photography/Fotolia; **060** Alexey Usachev/Fotolia; **068** Digital Vision/Thinkstock; **091** John Hoffman/Shutterstock; **108** Stevanzz/Fotolia; **134CL** Andreanita/Fotolia; **134CR** Algre/Fotolia; **134L** EcoView/Fotolia; **134R** Eduardo Rivero/Fotolia; **138** Bork/Shutterstock; **152** Andrew Breeden/Fotolia; **167** Majeczka/Shutterstock; **204** Steve Byland/Shutterstock; **210** 2011/Photos To Go; **222** Rikke/Fotolia; **224** Fotolia; **236L** Neelsky/Shutterstock; **236R** Serg64/Shutterstock; **249** Mark McClare/Shutterstock; **325** ShutterStock; **340** Flashon Studio/Shutterstock; **344** Cbpix/Shutterstock; **348L** JackF/Fotolia; **348R** Smileus/Shutterstock; **365** ShutterStock; **378** Comstock Images/Jupiter Images; **382** Womue/Fotolia; **407** Kletr/Shutterstock; **414** Hamik/Fotolia; **461** Adrio/Fotolia; **468** Oleksii Sagitov/Shutterstock; **470** Africa Studio/Fotolia; **516** Werner Dreblow/Fotolia; **520** Image Source/Jupiter Images; **524C** Melinda Fawver/Shutterstock; **524L** Yaping/Shutterstock; **524R** Undy/Fotolia; **539** pk7comcastnet/Fotolia; **556** JLV Image Works/Fotolia; **587** NASA; **623** Bork/Shutterstock; **630** Hemera Technologies/ThinkStock; **648** Concept w/Fotolia; **651** StockPhotosArt/Fotolia; **669CL** Donfink/Fotolia; **669CR** Tim elliott/Fotolia; **669L** Proedding/Fotolia; **669R** Petergyure/Fotolia; **670** Redwood/Fotolia; **671** Katrina Brown/Fotolia; **690** CristinaMuraca/Shutterstock; **694** Duncan Noakes/Fotolia; **696** Viorel Sima/Shutterstock; **706** Sergio Martínez/Fotolia; **708** Pascal Rateau/Fotolia; **728B** LittleMiss/Shutterstock; **728T** Margouillat photo/Shutterstock; **729** luchschen/Shutterstock; **750** Justin Black/Shutterstock; **765** James Kingman/Shutterstock; **786** Tom Grundy/Shutterstock; **813** WitR/Shutterstock; **815** Dja65/Shutterstock; **822** Arina P Habich/Shutterstock; **842** Gary Blakeley/Fotolia; **863** EvrenKalinbacak/Shutterstock; **864B** Orhan Cam/Shutterstock; **864T** Thampapon/Shutterstock.

IN6 Szasz-Fabian Erika/Fotolia; **IN8** Zeng Wei Jun/Shutterstock; **IN54** speedygo/Shutterstock.

GRADE 4 LESSONS EXCLUSIVELY FOR INDIANA

VOLUME 1

You will use these lessons throughout the year.

VOLUME 2

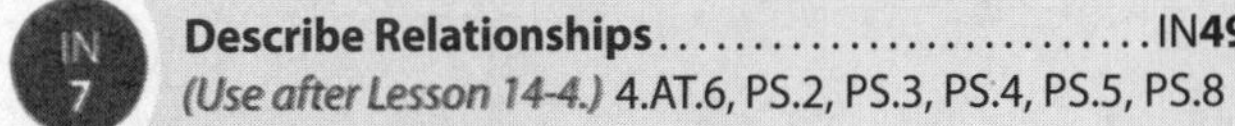

Name ________________________________

Indiana Lesson 1
Multiply Within 100

How could you use the drawing to find 3 × 14?

I can ...
fluently find products within 100.

Content Standard 4.C.4
Process Standards PS.1, PS.3, PS.4, PS.7, PS.8

You can construct an argument to explain how to use a strategy to find 3 × 14.

Look Back! Generalize What strategy could you use to find any product with 14 as a factor?

How Can You Multiply Fluently Within 100?

A

Stewart School had 4 tour groups at the museum. How many students from Stewart School were at the museum?

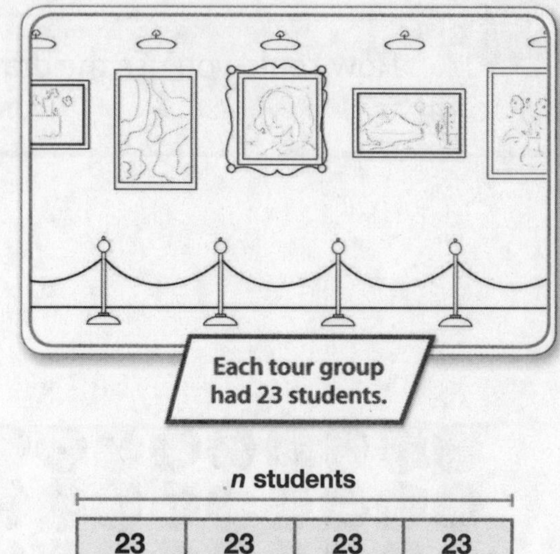

To find how many students are in 4 groups with 23 students in each group, multiply 4×23.

n students

23	23	23	23

B

One Way

One strategy is to use mental math and the Distributive Property.

$4 \times 23 = (4 \times 20) + (4 \times 3)$

$= 80 + 12$

$= 92$

	20	+ 3
4	$4 \times 20 = 80$	$4 \times 3 = 12$

So, 92 students from Stewart School were at the museum.

C

Another Way

Another strategy is to use an algorithm.

$$\begin{array}{r} \overset{1}{2}3 \\ \times\ 4 \\ \hline 92 \end{array}$$

Multiply the ones. Regroup if necessary.

Multiply the tens. Add any regrouped ones.

Convince Me! **Construct Arguments** When you multiply by 23, why would you use 20 and 3?

Name ____________________

Practice Buddy Tools Assessment

Guided Practice

Do You Understand?

1. Use the model below to find 3 × 26.

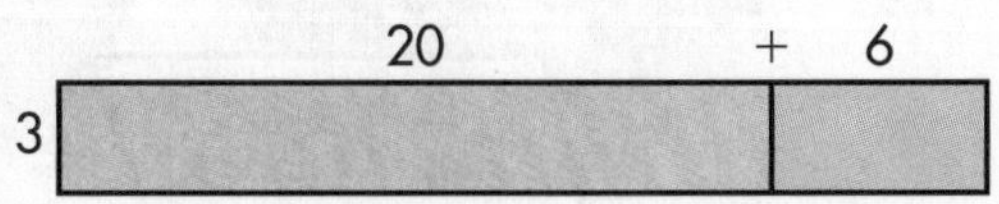

2. How could you break apart 18 to find 3 × 18? Explain.

Do You Know How?

In **3–8**, choose a strategy to multiply.

3. 6 × 16 = ____

4. 4 × 10 = ____

5. 12 × 8

6. 11 × 9

7. 24 × 3 = ____

8. 2 × 18 = ____

Independent Practice

In **9–25**, choose a strategy to multiply.

9. 5 × 14 = ____

10. 13 × 7 = ____

11. 6 × 15 = ____

12. 9 × 9 = ____

13. 2 × 48 = ____

14. 24 × 4 = ____

15. 6 × 8 = ____

16. 19 × 0 = ____

17. 31 × 3 = ____

18. 6 × 7

19. 10 × 8

20. 15 × 5

21. 57 × 1

22. 22 × 4

23. 13 × 4

24. 46 × 2

25. 9 × 8

Problem Solving

26. Mason picked a basket of apples every day for a week. How many apples did he pick in 7 days?

Each basket holds 14 apples.

27. **Make Sense and Persevere** Amelia picked 5 baskets of apples and Carlos picked 2 baskets. How many more apples did Amelia pick than Carlos? Explain.

28. **Look for Relationships** What pattern can you use to find any product with 5? Explain how to use the pattern to find 5×13.

29. Marni wrote a report on lions. Her assignment had 11,211 words. Benji wrote a report on emus. His assignment had 12,111 words. Which student's report had more words?

30. **Construct Arguments** Explain how to use a strategy to find 8×8.

31. **Higher Order Thinking** Carrie said she can find 4×19 by subtracting 4 from the product of 4×20. Is Carrie correct? Explain.

Assessment
ISTEP+ Ready

32. Use two different strategies to find 3×25.

One way	Another way

Name ______________________

Help Practice Buddy Tools Games

Homework & Practice IN 1
Multiply Within 100

Another Look!

There are 12 weeks until Anthony's vacation. How many days is that?

Find 7 × 12. Choose a strategy to multiply.

There are 7 days in a week. To find the number of days in 12 weeks, multiply 12 times 7.

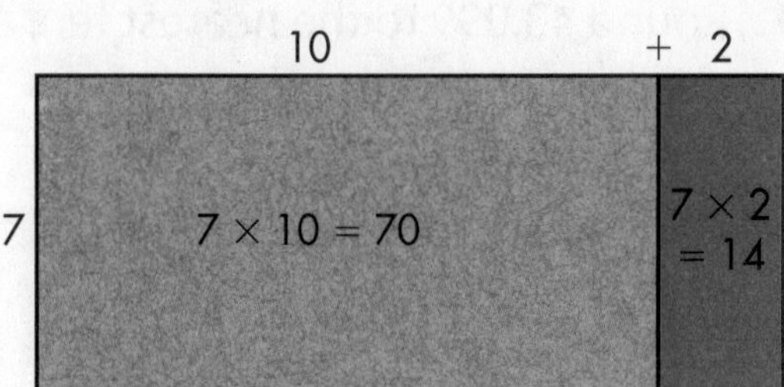

Use Mental Math

$7 \times 12 = (7 \times 10) + (7 \times 2)$
$= 70 + 14$
$= 84$

Use Partial Products

$$\begin{array}{r} 12 \\ \times\ 7 \\ \hline 14 \\ +\ 70 \\ \hline 84 \end{array}$$

Use an Algorithm

$$\begin{array}{r} \overset{1}{1}2 \\ \times\ 7 \\ \hline 84 \end{array}$$

There are 84 days until Anthony's vacation.

In **1–17**, choose a strategy to multiply.

1. 46 × 2 = ____ **2.** 20 × 4 = ____ **3.** 28 × 3 = ____

4. 11 × 7 = ____ **5.** 6 × 10 = ____ **6.** 17 × 4 = ____

7. 9 × 6 = ____ **8.** 16 × 3 = ____ **9.** 8 × 8 = ____

10. $\begin{array}{r} 13 \\ \times\ 3 \\ \hline \end{array}$ **11.** $\begin{array}{r} 17 \\ \times\ 5 \\ \hline \end{array}$ **12.** $\begin{array}{r} 19 \\ \times\ 5 \\ \hline \end{array}$ **13.** $\begin{array}{r} 89 \\ \times\ 1 \\ \hline \end{array}$

14. $\begin{array}{r} 16 \\ \times\ 5 \\ \hline \end{array}$ **15.** $\begin{array}{r} 38 \\ \times\ 2 \\ \hline \end{array}$ **16.** $\begin{array}{r} 25 \\ \times\ 3 \\ \hline \end{array}$ **17.** $\begin{array}{r} 4 \\ \times\ 9 \\ \hline \end{array}$

18. How many legs would 7 crabs, like the one shown on the right, have?

19. **Make Sense and Persevere** Ari caught 8 crabs and Cody caught 5 crabs. How many more legs were on Ari's crabs than Cody's crabs? Explain.

20. **Look for Relationships** What strategy or pattern could you use to find any fact with 4? Explain how to use the pattern to find 4×21.

21. Round 43,099 to the nearest ten, and nearest ten thousand.

22. **Construct Arguments** Explain how to use a strategy to find 8×7.

23. **Higher Order Thinking** Kevin said 6 times a number is always 5 times that number plus the number. Is Kevin correct? Explain.

24. **Model with Math** What multiplication problem does the picture at the right model? Find the product. .

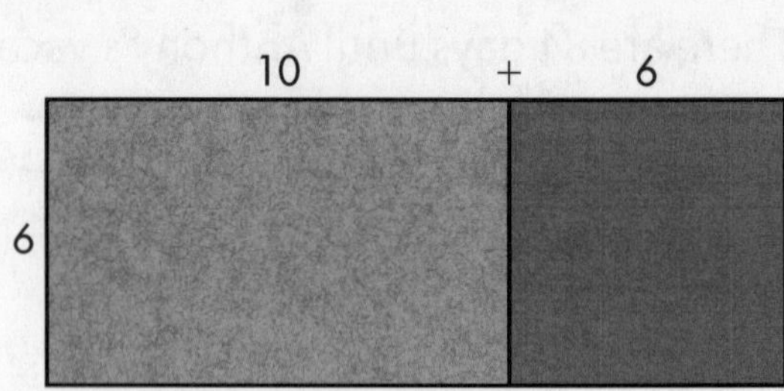

ISTEP+ Ready

25. Use two different strategies to find 3×17.

One way	Another way

Name ______________________________

TOPIC 3

Assessment

ISTEP+ Ready

1. Marissa placed 3 rose buds in 28 bud vases. How many buds did Marissa place in the vases?

Ⓐ 28 buds

Ⓑ 60 buds

Ⓒ 84 buds

Ⓓ 94 buds

2. Find 3 × 33. Explain the strategy you used to find the product.

3. A store owner ordered 5 boxes of ink cartridges. There are 19 ink cartridges in each box. How many ink cartridges did the store owner purchase?

4. Find the product of 4 × 23 using two different strategies.